Dr Brian Iddon

SCIENCE & POLITICS:
AN UNLIKELY MIXTURE

AUTOBIOGRAPHY, 1940-2010 (VOLUME 2)

Dr Brian Iddon

SCIENCE & POLITICS:
AN UNLIKELY MIXTURE

AUTOBIOGRAPHY, 1940-2010 (VOLUME 2)

MEMOIRS
Cirencester

OTHER BOOKS AND SELECTED CONTRIBUTIONS IN JOURNALS AND BOOKS BY THE SAME AUTHOR

A Timeline Of Political And Related Events That Affected the People Of Bolton – 1970-2010, published in 6 volumes which can be accessed in the Bolton History Centre in Bolton Central Library.

Science & Politics: An Unlikely Mixture, an autobiography, Memoirs Publishing, Cirencester, Volume 1, 2015.

James Lawrence Isherwood (1917-1989), a biography, Memoirs Publishing, Cirencester, 2013.

"Science in Parliament", *Memoirs and Proceedings of the Manchester Literary & Philosophical Society*, 2012, **149**, pp. 24-37.

"Government Seeks More Impact from Its Research Investment", *Future Medicinal Chemistry*, 2009, **1**(3), pp. 427-430.

Alfred Gill, Chapter 6 in *Men Who Made Labour: The PLP of 1906 – the personalities and the politics*, (A. Howarth and D. Hayter, eds.), Routledge, Oxford, 2006, pp. 60-65.

Fizz, bang, whizz – behind the magic show, B. Iddon, R. Lancaster and C. Stirling, *Chemistry in Britain*, 1993, **29**, pp. 656-657.

Bromine Compounds: Chemistry and Applications, (D. Price, B. Iddon and B. J. Wakefield, eds.), Elsevier, Amsterdam, 1988, pp. 181-251.

The Magic of Chemistry, published by B.D.H., Poole, Dorset, 1985 (a booklet based on a 90 minute demonstration lecture) (out of print, but copies can be found for sale on the internet).

"Polychloroheterocyclic Compounds", B. Iddon and H. Suschitzky, in *Polychloroaromatic Compounds* (H. Suschitzky, ed.), Plenum Press, 1974, pp. 197-364.

Mereo Books

1A The Wool Market Dyer Street Cirencester Gloucestershire GL7 2PR
An imprint of Memoirs Publishing www.mereobooks.com

Science and Politics: An unlikely mixture (VOLUME 2)
ISBN 978-1-86151-730-2

First published in Great Britain in 2017
by Mereo Books, an imprint of Memoirs Publishing

Copyright ©2017

Dr Brian Iddon has asserted his right under the Copyright Designs and Patents Act 1988 to be identified as the author of this work.

A CIP catalogue record for this book is available from the British Library.

This book is sold subject to the condition that it shall not by way of trade or otherwise be lent, resold, hired out or otherwise circulated without the publisher's prior consent in any form of binding or cover, other than that in which it is published and without a similar condition, including this condition being imposed on the subsequent purchaser.

Although the author has made every effort to ensure that the information in this book was correct when going to press, he does not assume and hereby disclaims any liability to any party for any loss, damage or disruption caused by errors or omissions, whether such errors or omissions result from negligence, accident, or any other cause. The views expressed in this book are purely the author's.

The address for Memoirs Publishing Group Limited can be found at
www.memoirspublishing.com

The Memoirs Publishing Group Ltd Reg. No. 7834348

The Memoirs Publishing Group supports both The Forest Stewardship Council® (FSC®) and the PEFC® leading international forest-certification organisations. Our books carrying both the FSC label and the PEFC® and are printed on FSC®-certified paper. FSC® is the only forest-certification scheme supported by the leading environmental organisations including Greenpeace. Our paper procurement policy can be found at www.memoirspublishing.com/environment

Typeset in 11/16pt Plantin
by Wiltshire Associates Publisher Services Ltd. Printed and bound in Great Britain by Printondemand-Worldwide, Peterborough PE2 6XD

CONTENTS

ACKNOWLEDGEMENTS
DEDICATION
ABOUT THE AUTHOR
PROLOGUE

PART 3: POLITICS IN BOLTON*

CHAPTER 1 - Engagement with politics in Bolton (1972-1980)	P.1
CHAPTER 2 - Labour in power in Bolton (1980-1997)	P.60

PART 4: POLITICS IN WESTMINSTER

CHAPTER 3 - Preparing to change the world	P.121
CHAPTER 4 - Business of the House: The 1997-2001 Parliament	P.159
CHAPTER 5 - Business of the House: The 2001-2005 Parliament	P.195
CHAPTER 6 - Business of the House: The 2005-2010 Parliament	P.219
CHAPTER 7 - Private Members' Bills	P.257
CHAPTER 8 - Adjournment Debates	P.272
CHAPTER 9 - Locally-based Campaigns	P.289

  - University of Bolton
  - Bolton Magistrates' Court
  - Fort Stirling
  - Bolton Wanderers Football Club
  - Fred Dibnah
  - Road Safety
  - Violent and Sex Offender Register (ViSOR)
  - Other Campaigns

CHAPTER 10 - Nationally Based Campaigns	P.314
- Women's Land Army	
- Ground Rent Grazing	
- Health Food Industry	
- Euthanasia	
CHAPTER 11 - Internationally-based Campaigns	P.333
- Palestine and the Middle East	
- Kashmir	
CHAPTER 12 - Science and Technology Select Committee	P.359
CHAPTER 13 - Other work for the STEM subjects	P.380
CHAPTER 14 - All-Party Parliamentary Groups	P.394
CHAPTER 15 - Openings, visits, receptions and lobbies	P.421
CHAPTER 16 - More about life in Bolton	P.446
CHAPTER 17 - Last days as a Member of Parliament	P.458
APPENDIX 1 LIST OF PARLIAMENTARY SPEECHES	P.470
APPENDIX 2 PHOTOGRAPHS AND OTHER ILLUSTRATIONS	P.482
INDEX	P.486

*Parts 1 and 2 are in Volume 1.

ACKNOWLEDGEMENTS

I want to thank all those who have shared my life with me, whether they are mentioned in this book or not, especially my close family and those who have inspired me in any way. I thank my wife Eileen, my daughters Sally and Sheena, my brother Graham, Merrilyn Guest,* my good friends John and Elaine Hartshorne, Dr Tom McC. Paterson, Dr Michael Rodgers, George Caswell and Cllrs Noel Spencer and Frank White for reading the manuscript and for spotting factual errors and suggesting improvements to the original manuscript. Any remaining errors of fact are entirely mine. I also thank Karen Lawrinson for her help in preparing the manuscript.

This book would not have been possible without the excellent professional help I received from Chris Newton, Tony Tingle and designer Ray Lipscombe at Memoirs Publishing, and I thank them also.

*Merrilyn, my first wife, sadly died at the age of 69 on 20 May 2014 in Ireland. Eileen, my second wife, and I attended her funeral at the Hop Kiln, Risbury Court, near Leominster, on 12 June 2014.

THIS BOOK IS DEDICATED TO THE FUTURE
GENERATION, OUR GRANDCHILDREN

Calvin Rhys Harrison (born 30 July 1994)
Abigail Jayne Howard (born 10 June 1997)
Matthew Peter Joseph Howard (born 15 September 1999)
Cameron James Harrison (born 29 March 2004)
Noah Harrison-Machin (born 2 September 2010)

ABOUT THE AUTHOR

Dr Brian Iddon was born on the West Lancashire Plain in Tarleton and was educated at Tarleton Holy Trinity C. of E. Primary School, Christ Church Boys' Secondary Modern School and the Technical College in Southport, and at the University of Hull from which he graduated in 1961 with a BSc in Honours Chemistry. Hull awarded him a PhD in 1964 and a DSc in 1981.

He was employed teaching and researching chemistry at the Universities of Durham (1964-1966) and Salford (1966-1997) and became well-known for presenting a demonstration lecture – The Magic of Chemistry – throughout Britain and elsewhere in Europe.

Brian was elected to Bolton MB Council in 1977 and held various positions and served several committees of the Council until 1997 when he was elected to Parliament in the safe Labour seat of Bolton South East from which he retired in 2010. He was chairman of Bolton's Housing Committee from 1986 to 1996.

Brian's interests in Parliament covered a multitude of topics in the education, health and social services, housing, home affairs and science and technology policy areas. He grasped some controversial subjects such as the policy on illicit drugs, euthanasia, legislation surrounding health food products, the Middle East Peace Process and Kashmir. He helped to steer through three Acts of Parliament and was a Member of the Science and Technology Select Committee.

Since his retirement in 2010, apart from his various writing projects, Brian has held a number of voluntary posts in the science policy area, in education and with a community charity.

PROLOGUE

In January 2014 I decided that, because my autobiography might be of interest to two separate groups of readers, I should divide it into two volumes; the first volume, now published, is about my early life, education and career in chemistry (1964-1997) and this volume is about politics, both in Bolton and Westminster (1972-2010). I did not hold any positions in the three Labour Governments of 1997 to 2010, so I have tried to describe in Part 4 what life was like for a backbencher at that time.

Why did I decide to write the story of my life? They say that there is a book in everyone; the problem is that the story has to be recorded in some way to be of any benefit to others. Many fascinating stories have passed away with the people who knew them best. In any case, I have a passion for writing and I have always been interested in local history.

I believe I have had an interesting life that reflects the social and political history of my time, and I hope that future generations will gain something from me telling 'My Story', but I write it mainly for my children and grandchildren and their children and grandchildren to read. I have always regretted that I didn't find out more about my family from those who knew the facts before they passed away. Sadly, genealogical searches only reveal the bare facts of a life and not its intimate details. Here then is the story of 70 years (1940-2010) of my life.

'My Story' is divided into four parts. In Part 1 (Volume 1) I describe my early years on the West Lancashire Plain, my primary and secondary school education and my decision to be a chemist, ending up with three degrees from Hull University (BSc in 1961, PhD in 1964 and DSc in 1981).

In Part 2 (Volume 1) of 'My Story' I write about my academic life, beginning at the University of Durham in 1964 and ending at the

University of Salford in 1997. There are separate chapters on my role as the Safety Officer in what was at the time the largest department of chemistry in Britain and on presenting The Magic of Chemistry.

In Part 3 (Volume 2), I discuss my involvement in politics in Bolton.

I always said that I had three careers before my election to Parliament in 1997. I was a Reader in Organic Chemistry at the University of Salford, where I also ran a research group; I presented a stage show entitled The Magic of Chemistry, which became quite famous; and I served on Bolton Council for 21 years (ten as chairman of the Housing Committee). As a result, in 1998 Bolton made me an Honorary Alderman for my services to the town.

I was privileged to be elected to Parliament in the Blair landslide General Election of 1 May 1997, with a huge majority, 25,211, and a significant turn-out of 65.2% for a safe seat, which was an indication of how fed up the electorate were with the Tories under John Major's leadership. People had had enough of 'Thatcherism' and it was time for a change (a powerful political slogan). It was the first time that Bolton had returned three Labour Members of Parliament, the others being David Crausby (in the Bolton North East Constituency), previously a lathe operator and shop steward in the engineering industry, and Ruth Kelly (Bolton West), an economist and journalist. She was the Head of the Bank of England's Inflation Report Division when she was selected. Being elected to Parliament was the high point in my political career. Life in Westminster is discussed in Part 4 (Volume 2) of 'My Story'.

*Paragraph 2 to the end repeated from Volume 1.

Volume 1 published in April 2015
Volume 2 published in May 2017

∽

Dr Brian Iddon

DR BRIAN IDDON

SCIENCE AND POLITICS
AN UNLIKELY MIXTURE

PART 3

POLITICS IN BOLTON

CHAPTER ONE

ENGAGEMENT WITH POLITICS IN BOLTON (1972-1980)

∽

Merrilyn, my first wife, Sally, Sheena and I moved to 19 Woburn Avenue, in a cul-de-sac in Tonge Moor, Bolton from Boothstown, Worsley in the spring of 1972 as only the second occupants on a small estate of new homes. Bikku Patel was our only neighbour for several months, and we put up with the mud and the inconvenience of living on a new housing estate for a further 12 months.

Demolition contractors cleared away Firwood Hall in 1969. Built in 1815 by the Starkie family, it was once the home of Frank Hardcastle, Member of Parliament for the Westhoughton Division of Lancashire from 1885 to 1892. His grandfather established Thomas Hardcastle and Son, bleachers and dyers at Firwood in 1803, which Frank inherited. Frank Hardcastle also owned the Breighttrust Colliery. From 1886 he was President of the United Bleachers Association of Lancashire and Cheshire, and he was High Sheriff for the County of Lancashire from 1895 to 1896. Soon after the war Firwood Hall was converted into a hotel. Its last owners, Mr and Mrs Ernest Sutton, sold it in 1968.

Joe Morley (part of the M.W. Falkner Group), the builder of our new house on the Firwood estate, provided us with a few problems that we had to resolve. We discovered that the rear garden fence between us and our next door neighbours at number 17 was in the wrong position. Our neighbours could not back their car out of their garage either, because the house was built at such an angle to the drive that they ended up with their car on our front lawn, which was a short drop below the level of the drive. In the end we gave up some of our front lawn

19, Woburn Avenue, Bolton as it is today.

to help solve this problem. These problems gave us a bad start with our new neighbours, but the couple didn't stay long in Woburn Avenue.

Then we discovered that the builder had sold us 100 square yards of land that the occupants of the 'old school house' in Firwood Fold had made into their garden. We agreed to sell them the land for a small sum. After that I was able to consider what to do with a back garden that sloped steeply down to Firwood Fold. I decided to terrace it by building dry stone walls and lay stepped paths running down the middle and across the bottom of the garden, which gave us access to Firwood Fold. Fortunately, the builder had knocked down some dry stone walls on the former Firwood Hall estate, so I bought the stone, transported it to our garden in a wheelbarrow and learned the art of dry stone walling.

But I was still short of stone. On our trips to Leeds to visit Merrilyn's parents I noticed some road works near Rochdale where a small stone bridge was being demolished. On one of these trips I stopped and bought the bridge. A Bolton haulage company was hired and, one Saturday morning, a lorryload of dressed stone arrived and was duly tipped at the end of our long drive. I was surprised at how little clay and soil there was in the stone compared with the pile I had seen on the Littleborough road out of Rochdale. The driver told me that he had separated the good stone from most of the rubbish that he had left behind before a JCB loaded the clean stone into his lorry. He got a good tip.

It took me the best part of a year to terrace the garden at Woburn Avenue, but it was a satisfying job, and it made me quite fit. In the process of the work I discovered that the

Sheena (left) and Sally Iddon in the garden of our Woburn Avenue home – Crompton's cottage can be seen to the left in Firwood Fold.

builders had buried a small tree in our garden and that had to be dug out. My young children adopted a bent tree at the bottom of the garden, where I planted sackloads of daffodil bulbs given to me by my father; they called it their 'giraffe tree'. My final act was to repair a dry stone wall in Firwood Fold that had collapsed and build some steps down into the Fold, which didn't please all our new neighbours.

Late one afternoon, when I was terracing our garden, I heard a loud bang on the light industrial estate below Firwood Fold (the former bleach works), and I saw a man emerge from a shed that looked as if it was on fire, with smoke rising from its roof. After making sure that Merrilyn was calling the emergency services, I ran as quickly as I could down to the scene of this explosion. By this time several residents of the Fold were running with me.

A man was standing there in a state of shock, with only shreds of his clothing hanging from him. His skin was hanging off him in strips too in places. It was a most distressing sight; something I had never witnessed before. We managed to sit the man down on a chair, by which time the emergency services were arriving.

The factory units had been broken into several times and one company, Holden Vale Manufacturing Company, employed older men as security guards. This poor man, 63-year-old Frank Unsworth, had entered his office inside the factory and attempted to light a gas stove. The office had filled with propane gas that had leaked from a cylinder, and tragically, Frank died a few days later from over 70% burns to his body (see *Bolton Evening News* dated 12 September 1974 for the inquest details).

The Starkie family, the original owners of Firwood Hall, which had been demolished so that our small estate could be built, planted an arboretum on their estate. Bolton Council protected the trees with a Tree Preservation Order. Sadly, one or two of our neighbours demolished some lovely mature trees in their gardens without seeking permission.

Sally started to attend Castle Hill Primary School, where she made friends and did well academically. She was seven years old when we moved and Sheena was four. At the age of five, Sheena was enrolled at the same school as Sally and she too flourished. At the age of 11 each of them was required to take the 11-plus examination, which was still in place in Bolton under a Conservative-controlled council. They proceeded to Smithills Moor Grammar School, Sally in 1976 and Sheena in 1979.

At that time Bolton Council operated a 'base system' of education, with three schools built on each of several sites on the outskirts of the town, one base at Smithills, one at Ladybridge, Deane, and one at Great Lever (the Hayward schools), with another base planned for Heaton. On each of the 'bases' was a grammar school for the 'academically gifted' children, a secondary modern school and a technical school for the 'more vocationally inclined pupils'. In theory, as children's abilities were measured against time, it was possible to transfer between the three schools on the base, but in reality, this was not a regular occurrence.

Merrilyn's mum and dad, Evelyn and Cyril Muncaster, who moved from Leeds to Spofforth Hill on the Harrogate Road out of Wetherby, were keen members of the Caravan Club and were often away caravanning at the weekends and when Cyril took his annual holidays. He was a technical representative for a paint company, and much of his business involved troubleshooting, mainly for the large caravan-building industry which was based in Hull.

One advantage that their interest brought to my family is that Sally and Sheena were often away with them and saw quite a lot of Britain. The Muncasters became even more adventurous and started to take longer caravan trips abroad, often taking Sally and Sheena with them, to places as far away as Italy and Austria.

Cyril Muncaster always had an eye for a bargain. On one of our visits to see them he produced a suit length of grey flannel and recommended a tailor in Bradford who would make it up for me. I made a couple of trips to Bradford to be measured up and fitted out with the suit. On the second trip I put my hands in the trouser pockets but I couldn't feel their bottoms. I remarked on this to the tailor who told me "Them's Yorkshire pockets lad. Tha'll not get thi money out o'them in a hurry".

We had family holidays too. We particularly enjoyed a holiday in the Irish Republic where we stayed at Salthill in County Galway and in Killarney, which we used as a base to explore the Dingle Peninsula, the Burren limestone landscape and the Atlantic coast of the Irish Republic. I had been moved by David Lean's 1970 film *Ryan's Daughter*, which was filmed at Slea Head and other places on the Dingle Peninsula, and which also featured the magnificent Cliffs of Moher, five miles long and rising to 702 feet on the Atlantic coast. We visited all these places.

In the summer of 1980 we visited Vienna, where Professor Fritz Sauter and his wife lent us their summer chalet at Die Hinterbrühl in the Vienna Woods. The young Sheena was inspired by the wildlife there, and developed a passion for collecting snails. Sally had a 'pen pal' in Heidenheim on the River Brenz, not far from Stuttgart, who we visited after our stay in the Vienna Woods. We returned home *via* the Romantische Strasse, visiting medieval towns such as Nordlingen, Rothenburg and Dinkelsbuhl.

We spent Christmas 1983 through to the beginning of 1984 on our first-ever package holiday (Thomsons) in Sousse, Tunisia, where we stayed in a large beachside hotel. The girls remember me and another guy entertaining people in the lounge by dressing up as a camel. While we were in Tunisia President Habib Bourguiba, founder and first President of the Republic of Tunisia, announced that he was doubling the price of bread in the New Year, which precipitated a strike and riots in some places. A curfew was called in the holiday area of Sousse, which prevented us travelling into the Sahara Desert or visiting Tunis. It wasn't safe to travel, we were told.

Not long after we moved to Woburn Avenue I came home one evening to find Sally unable to move herself off the toilet seat. I noticed that there were red lumps appearing on her body, mainly around her joints. It looked like blood to me, and I realised that Merrilyn and I had to get her straight to the

A&E Department at Bolton General Hospital (Townleys) in Farnworth. Sally was in quite a state by this stage. The first doctor who examined her thought it was rheumatic fever – Sally was unable to move her arms or legs properly – but we could see that he wasn't sure.

I encouraged him to seek a second opinion. The second doctor thought that it might be scarlet fever, but he wasn't sure either. Meanwhile, more of the red lumps were appearing and Merrilyn and I became quite desperate. An older, very experienced paediatrician was sent for (the children's wards were at the opposite end of the hospital down a very long corridor). As luck would have it the more experienced doctor had seen this relatively rare condition – Henoch-Schoenlein purpura – before. Nevertheless, more tests were needed and, just in case it was scarlet fever, Sally was transferred to the isolation unit at Hulton Lane Hospital, where we could visit her only by looking through a window until she had been correctly diagnosed.

It wasn't scarlet fever and the older doctor had been right with his initial diagnosis. Sally became a curiosity, and other doctors came to see this relatively rare condition, caused by inflammation of the small blood vessels, which enables blood to leak from them into surrounding tissue. The exact cause of this purpura is unknown, even today. It is more prevalent in boys than girls (by 2:1) and appears mainly during the winter months.

My father's generation (five brothers and two sisters and their spouses) began to pass away in the 1960s. The first of my seven aunts to die was Aunt Jane Ellen (who married Robert Iddon); she died aged 68 on 24 October 1963 during my postgraduate years in Hull. When I lived in Durham, Uncle

Harry (16 August 1964) and his wife Bessie (6 February 1966) died, both aged 62. Uncle Bob died on 30 November 1966, aged 70. Aunt Beatrice died in January 1967 and her husband, Uncle Bill, died on 8 March 1968, both aged 73. My Aunt Ellen Johnson (one of the two surviving Iddon sisters of my dad's generation) died on 21 June 1971, aged 78; she had been ill for some time.

My father died on 10 January 1973, aged only 68. I had been visiting him in Southport Infirmary for a few days after another stroke had struck him down (see Volume 1). But this time I could tell that there was no fight in him. He had suffered from diverticulitis for several years, as well as 'dry eye', both of which had worn him out. On the last evening that I saw him alive in hospital he asked me to put his false teeth in and call for an ice cream. He was so weak that I couldn't get the false teeth in, and I had to call for the assistance of a nurse. He got his ice cream though. The call came early next morning from the Ward Sister to say that he had passed away in the night.

My brother inherited the market gardening business and the house, as I had agreed with dad, and I was left the sum of £1,000 (the total sum in his bank account), which I couldn't find it in me to spend. Instead, I invested it on the advice of my bank in an insurance company that went into liquidation. Eventually, I got 95% of the money back and decided not to invest it again.

The last of the five Iddon brothers of my father's generation, my Uncle Dick (Richard Iddon), died on 12 March 1975, aged 73. On the day of his funeral a few days later I felt very low, and I suggested to Merrilyn that we go to Southport and try to walk that feeling off. Professor Hans Suschitzky was interested in art and had collected some nice paintings, which I had seen in his home in Hale Barns, near Altrincham. During one of our conversations about art and artists he had mentioned a living impressionist artist who had obviously impressed him. I hadn't heard of James Lawrence Isherwood until that point in my life. However, on that day in Southport, whilst walking down Lord Street, close to its junction with Neville Street, I noticed three paintings in the window of a building society. They were Isherwood's and were there to advertise an exhibition of his paintings, then showing at the Scarisbrick Hotel a few hundred yards further down Lord Street. We decided to go along and visit the exhibition, and there was the artist himself, who became one of my personal friends. I have written separately about my memories of Lawrence.[1]

The second of the surviving Iddon sisters, my Aunt Alice, died on 29 June 1977, aged 68; her husband, my Uncle John Thomas Thompson, survived until 30 April 1995. He was 88 years old when he died. The last of my aunts on the Iddon side of my family, Aunt Ada (who was married to Richard Iddon), died on 20 February 1997, aged 92. That was the end of my father's generation of Iddons and their spouses.

My mother's sister, my Aunt Maggie (Stazicker), who then lived retired in a bungalow at The Grove, Rufford, died at the age of 70 on 17 April 1978 in Ormskirk General Hospital. She never married and is, hopefully, buried with her mother and father in front of Holmeswood with Rufford St Mary the Virgin Church; I say hopefully because the church had lost its graveyard records at that time and the Stazicker grave is not marked by a headstone.

My brother Graham and I were shown the spot where our grandma and granddad Stazicker were buried, but this was some time before Aunt Maggie died, and our undertaker Bill Hull spent some time with us 'mapping out' the graves in that area of the graveyard with a long iron spike, which he shoved into the ground. He found a brick-lined grave containing two coffins in the area where we believed our grandparents were buried and had to assume that that was the grave we were looking for. Fortunately, we had an old undertaker's receipt that told us a brick-lined grave had been provided for the burial of my maternal grandparents.

After my brother Graham inherited the family business he realised that it was too small to ensure a good future for himself and his wife Pam. Competition from the Dutch growers had always been a problem for British growers because the government of The Netherlands subsidised their businesses. As the air-freighting of fresh fruit, vegetables and flowers began, initially from Spain but then from further afield, encouraged by the development of supermarkets, it became even harder for British growers to stay in business. Many of the growers in Tarleton were offered money by house building companies for their land and sold out.

My cousin Frank had run the adjacent market gardening business that my Uncle Dick had started up, and he had died too, so I suggested that Graham approach my Aunt Ada with a proposal that he buy their market garden, which had been dormant for a few years. I also proposed that he mortgage his home to enable him to do so. Across Hesketh Lane from my brother's business was a plot of land with greenhouses on it that came up for sale later. I encouraged my brother to make a bid for that land also, and he expanded his business again.

Eventually, the house building companies set their eyes on my brother's business, and several began to make offers to buy him out. By this time the adjacent Melling's corn mill had closed, and when it was demolished it provided access from Hesketh Lane to the rear of 72-78 Hesketh Lane. My brother decided to sell his business to the company which made the best offer, Fairclough Homes. He also sold our family home, 74 Hesketh Lane, knocked down the greenhouses on the piece of land on the opposite side of Hesketh Lane and built his family a new house there, where they live today.

Nos. 74 and 76 Hesketh Lane (see Volume 1) have no longer any connections with the Iddon family and 78 Hesketh Lane, the last home of my Aunt Ada and Uncle Dick is now a children's nursery. On the field adjacent to number 78, where I played as a young boy with my mates, stands Tarleton High School. Its playing fields are partly the land that my father rented from the Lilford estate to grow his outdoor crops.

Tarleton is served by a 'retained' fire brigade. The new fire station was built on the site where the health clinic I visited as a baby once stood and where the 'Green Goddess' was kept during the war years. Along with a number of other market gardeners and farmers, Graham enrolled on 1 February 1968 to serve the local Lancashire County Fire Service as a volunteer. These men are on call 24 hours a day, unless they telephone in to say that they are taking time off. They receive an annual 'retention fee' and are paid whenever the brigade is on call. They are expected to report in once a week for maintenance work and any training that might be necessary. In his early years of engagement with the fire service the main call was for grass fires and fires in the local community. Fires in Dutch barns on farms were quite common.

The Tarleton fire brigade also 'stands in' when other fire brigades have all their vehicles out on emergencies, in places like Southport and Leyland. Road traffic accidents became the bulk of their work as time passed and the roads got busier. My brother was the Station Commander of the Tarleton Fire Brigade when he retired from the service on 12 June 2004. For many years he was the driver of the fire engine when they were on call. Altogether, he gave 36 years of service to the Tarleton Fire Brigade.

1972, the year of our move to Bolton, started with a miners' strike, which ended in February, and Ted Heath signed the 'Brussels Treaty' to take Britain into the European Economic Community (EEC) on 22 January 1972.

In the same year the Conservative Government passed The Housing Finance Act, which forced council house rents to rise significantly. This resulted in a mutiny across the land of Labour-led councils, but the threat of a surcharge on their councillors forced most of them to comply with the Act. One notable exception was Clay Cross Council in Derbyshire, where Labour councillors were surcharged by the Conservative Government.

1972 was also the year when, in January, Little Lever Labour Club announced that it was going to hold striptease sessions in order to solve its financial problems. There was uproar in the village and local papers. Nevertheless, it went ahead and the first show was held at the club on 24 January 1972.

Whenever Little Lever is mentioned I am reminded of the names of some of the Conservative candidates who have stood in local elections in the village – D. Dziubas, S. Windle, G. Twist, E. Crook and S. Jinks. You couldn't make it up!

After Sheena started to attend Castle Hill Primary School in 1973 Merrilyn started to work part-time. Her mother passed some needlecraft skills on to her and she was good at embroidery and dress-making, as well as crafts in general. She was also a good cook.

We became friendly with the people in Firwood Fold, in particular with George and Lavina Robinson, who lived in a beautiful little cruck cottage at the bottom of our garden, which overlooked a lodge that had formerly been used by the nearby bleach works (bleaching cotton for the local cotton mills). The cottages in Firwood Fold were occupied by workers at the bleach works in former years.

Merrilyn and Lavina became good friends because they had similar interests. Both George and Lavina enjoyed visitors, and George in particular liked to show his lovely old cottage to visitors to Firwood Fold and tell them something about the history of the Fold. George, who had been a warehouse transport manager and transport consultant, was 'good with his hands', and he completely refurbished their Firwood Fold home internally. George claimed to 'know a thing or two about restoration' and had a secret recipe for a restorative wood treatment. He was keen too on building models of ships.

Lavina designed tapestries for the well-known Bolton firm of William Briggs, who, in the 1970s, were in the Eagley Mill complex in Bolton. J. & P. Coats UK Ltd. announced closure of the 170-year-old Eagley Mills, with the loss of 600 jobs, in January 1972. William Briggs moved to the Halliwell Industrial Estate, next door to the small housing estate where I now live. The firm which was established in 1874 became part of Coats Crafts.

After Lavina designed a tapestry Briggs made up kits for sale. Before these were launched on the market, they had to be 'tested' by a likely customer, so, Lavina enrolled Merrilyn to test Briggs's new tapestry kits before they hit the shops. One in particular I remember well. Lavina designed it when the first Tutankhamun exhibition caused a sensation in London in 1972; it was attended by 1.7 million visitors. When Merrilyn completed the Tutankhamun tapestry it looked stunning. These completed tapestries were used by Briggs to advertise their kits in the shops which sold them.

Lavina was also an accomplished artist but, although she had several paintings to her credit, including some of Firwood Fold, she was not known for her paintings locally.

We made some good friends too on our estate. Our daughters became good friends with Ray and Barbara Mort (and Duncan and Lindsey, their children) next door to us at 21 Woburn Avenue, and with the Stone family (Ron and Vanessa Stone and their daughters Claire and Kath) who lived at 1 Woburn Avenue. We also got to know the Peacocks very well; they lived in Ashdown Drive. Norman was the founding chairman of Bolton-Le-Moors Round Table (No. 1154) in 1974-1975, and I attended a number of their dinners with him. Diana Dors was the guest speaker at their Fifth Charter Anniversary Dinner at the Pack Horse Hotel on 7 March 1980. When Ray Mort gave up his job through illness and the Mort family moved to Staton Avenue, Margaret and Dave Price moved into their house at 21 Woburn Avenue. Cllr Frank and Eileen White also moved onto our estate to live in Ashdown Drive.

One of the liveliest couples on our estate was Richard and Athena Juan-Thomas; Athena was born in Greece. Richard always claimed that he was from a circus family, although he was involved in engineering when we knew him. In the autumn of 1973 they attended a function at Belle Vue in Manchester and, as they returned home in their car, they hit a very bad storm of hailstones. As they approached the bridge at the bottom of the Farnworth slip road onto the A666 (St Peter's Way) the car skidded and hit the bridge, and Athena was flung out of the car and broke her back. She spent months in the spinal injury unit at Southport Promenade Hospital but eventually returned home to Ashdown Drive to live as a paraplegic, still with a great zest for life. Not long after the *Bolton Evening News* interviewed her in 1985 (see *Bolton Evening News* dated 6 March 1985) she died of a cancer which had been diagnosed five years earlier.

Merrilyn started to teach crafts to elderly people in community centres and to people with learning difficulties, who either lived in Smithills Hall or attended the day classes there. She also taught part-time at the Clarence Street

George and Lavina Robinson's 'cruck' cottage (No. 8) in Firwood Fold, Bolton.

A view of numbers 9 and 10 (Crompton's cottage) in Firwood Fold, Bolton.

The 'old school house' in Firwood Fold (opposite Crompton's cottage); 19, Woburn Avenue lies behind this house.

Women's College, which specialised in handicrafts and vocational subjects (it was demolished in 2009 after a long battle to save it). Merrilyn was a popular art and crafts teacher.

Bolton had a teachers' training college in Chadwick Street which specialised in training mature students. I was very pleased in view of the fact that I had interrupted Merrilyn's earlier teachers' training in Darlington when she enrolled to take a degree course at this college that would qualify her as a teacher. It was a proud moment for me when she received her

Bachelor of Education Degree at the University of Manchester in the autumn of 1981. For a few years after that she taught at the Withins School in Breightmet, specialising in mathematics.

A former champion horse jumper, Arnold Barnes, managed stables in Firwood Fold. His main business was to stable ponies and horses there for other people, but he also taught children to ride ponies and horses that he owned himself with the help of his assistant, Ann Kirkpatrick. Firwood Fold was an excellent place to own stables because it is on the edge of the Bradshaw Valley, which leads to Four Acres, and there was plenty of space, in addition to a small paddock attached to the stables, for local people to enjoy riding. My young daughters became enthusiasts and spent a lot of time at the stables in Firwood Fold. It was a convenient and safe place for them to spend their early years.

Arnold's sister, Gladys Barnes, lived in a small cottage in Firwood Fold. We befriended her and remained her friends until she passed away. Gladys was a lonely woman who was difficult to get to know. She never seemed to fit in with the rest of the inhabitants of Firwood Fold.

I decided to gain support for the formation of a Tonge Moor Residents' Association in 1973, initially to monitor Copperfields nightclub, which opened in late 1972 next to the Castle public house (footballer Nat Lofthouse was one of its landlords; it is now the Bolton Castle) at the junction of Tonge Moor Road and Crompton Way. Formerly the building was the Casino Club and, before that, the Crompton Cinema. This was the beginning of my 'political' career in Bolton. At our first public meeting on 29 May 1974 residents were invited to put questions to the three Tonge Ward councillors, Cllrs Jim Rigby, Kevin Knowles and Susannah Harrison, all Conservative, and to Greater Manchester County Labour Cllr Frank White. About 100 people turned up to what proved to be a lively meeting.

Firwood Fold was a designated conservation area when we arrived to live there in 1972; it was declared as such in February 1969. All the cottages and land were purchased from the owners of the bleach works, when it closed, for the sum of £5,750. In the spring of 1972, Bolton County Borough Council agreed to sell any cottages in Firwood Fold to the sitting tenants with a condition that the owners agreed to keep them in good condition, after improvements had been carried out first (which affected their valuation, of course).

The Council of Europe designated 1975 as European Architectural Heritage Year, and Bolton County Borough Council was offered a grant in the autumn of 1973 to refurbish all the cottages in Firwood Fold and to reset the cobbles of the road that ran through it, originally a main route into Bolton for horse-drawn carriages. The total cost of the work was estimated at £55,000, for which a grant of £10,000 was received from Europe. The work got under way in 1973 and was to be completed towards the end of 1974. The original cobbles were actually replaced by stone sets.

Thatcher John Burke, who learned his skills in the West of Ireland, made a superb job of reroofing Samuel Crompton's cottage in 1972. He reroofed it previously in 1947 with straw, but claimed that the new reed roof should last 70 to 80 years. To my knowledge it hasn't been reroofed since 1972.

Prior to the restoration of Firwood Fold a barn stood adjacent to the 'old school house' and the 'village green'. It was demolished as part of the conservation scheme. Firwood Fold had a large ash tree on its village green, estimated to be about 110 years old, which became diseased and hollow over many years. To prevent local children from lighting fires inside it residents of the Fold bricked up the hole. In 1980, the tree was declared dangerous and was felled and removed.

In September 1974, a notice appeared in the *Bolton Evening News* to announce that Ashdown Drive, the other cul-de-sac on our small enclosed estate, was to be extended through to Firwood Fold and that the main access point to the Fold, off Crompton Way, would be closed to traffic. In my opinion this proposal would destroy the paddock of Firwood Stables and jeopardise Arnold Barnes's business. Of course, I had a vested interest and decided to object to this proposal. There was an alternative route into Firwood Fold from Thicketford Road, which would also have prevented through traffic in Firwood Fold, thought to be destabilising the ancient buildings.

I decided to enlist the help of our Member of Parliament, David Young, who was elected in the first General Election of 1974, and Cllr David Dingwall, and they met a group of about 30 residents on 10 September 1974.

On the first day of the second General Election campaign of 1974, Monday 23 September, we held a meeting about the proposed road extension in Firwood Special School. Conservative Cllr James Rigby, chairman of the Planning Committee, attended along with the Director of the Planning Department, Robert Ogden, and other officials. At that meeting the restoration costs for Firwood Fold were reported to stand at £72,000; another grant of £10,000 was secured from the Greater Manchester County Council. In December 1974, the *Bolton Evening News* reported a figure of £81,167. The costs of the road extension were put at £5,500. I suggested that figure was wrong and that the true cost was likely to be closer to £12,000 (see also *Bolton Evening News* dated 22 November 1974).

In January 1975, the Director of Planning reported that the costs of refurbishing Firwood Fold stables would be double the original estimate of £3,387, which did not include a replacement roof. Even worse, we heard that there was a possibility of converting the riding stables into homes.

The Observer newspaper, on 20 December 1974, questioned the use of public money to improve the Firwood Fold cottages, when Bolton Metropolitan Borough Council (as it became through implementation of the reorganisation of local government in 1974) was planning to sell them all off.

The proposed extension of Ashdown Drive was approved at a meeting of the Planning Committee on 11 December 1975. However, the councillors present were not aware of all the objections that had been submitted, so I decided to step up a campaign by calling a meeting in my home with the Bolton and District Civic Trust, who had been in favour of all Bolton's plans for Firwood Fold, and representatives of the Sports Council and Bolton Riding Club. My campaign came to the notice of local radio stations and I took advantage of their offers of interviews.

Construction of the road extension began during the first week of March, 1975, an event which sealed the fate of Firwood Stables. Plans were submitted in April 1985 for a change of use to 'mews cottages', and that's what they became after the Council sold them in 1987.

Firwood Fold is as pretty today as it has ever been. It has probably been painted and photographed as often as any other place in Bolton, and is often a scene on Christmas cards that are sold locally. Before its restoration I commissioned Sale artist Wynn Hyde to paint several views of Firwood Fold for me. She sat on the steps that I had created from my garden into the Fold, and I treasure that particular view of the Fold, which I have hung in my lounge at home.

In 1976, the restoration of Firwood Fold won national recognition, when it came second in a competition organised jointly by *The Times* newspaper and the Royal Institution of Chartered Surveyors. Cllr James Rigby, Mr Robert Ogden and the leader of Bolton's Conservative-controlled Council, Cllr John Hanscomb, collected the award from Environment Secretary Peter Shore in London on 13 July 1976.

The Casino nightclub, which went into liquidation in February 1972, was purchased by The First House Group, who also owned the very popular Blighty's nightclub in Farnworth, and it became Copperfields nightclub. The problem was that it had no car park, which limited attendance. When the new management acquired a pair of post-war semi-detached houses next door to the club and started digging up the back garden in the spring of 1973, local residents became concerned about the future intentions of the managers of the club. The vacant land became a car park without planning permission.

The secretary of Tonge Moor Residents' Association, Alice Simpkins, lived in the next house that the club had obviously identified for demolition. Through our pressure a 'stop notice' was served on the club, who were made to apply retrospectively for a 'change of use permission' to use the vacant land as a car park. Under threat of an appeal being made to the Secretary of State, planning permission for the car park was granted by Bolton Council's Planning

Committee. In January 1976 Copperfields nightclub became the Bees Knees disco-dining club.

The club management proceeded in their attempts to buy the second pair of semi-detached houses, succeeded, and unsuccessfully applied for planning permission to demolish them in March 1976. Despite a pledge from local councillor Kevin Knowles to oppose any 'change of use' application that the club management might make, the club got its way again and the second pair of semi-detached houses was demolished in the autumn of 1977.

Alice Simpkins, secretary of our residents' association, who lived in one of these houses, moved to the Bury end of Crompton Way and Tonge Moor Residents' Association was disbanded. We had fought and lost two battles, but I was now wound up enough to fight my way onto Bolton Metropolitan Borough Council. I had seen how its Planning Department worked under a Conservative administration.

In April 1981 the first planning application to convert the former Bees Knees nightclub into a supermarket was rejected. The Council accepted a second application (see *Bolton Evening News* dated 31 July 1982) and the building became a Kwik Save supermarket.

Bolton's Planning Committee made several mistakes in the 1970s; they were minded, for example, to accept a proposal to build homes for 9,000 people around the Rumworth Lodge wildlife sanctuary. After a bitter campaign of opposition, the Council decided not to proceed with this development and, on 6 September 1974, the Editorial in the *Bolton Evening News* reported: "During the Rumworth confrontation, some councillors and officials were distressed to discover that local residents had a poor opinion of the Council". Surprise

surprise! It seemed to me that it was time for a change.

In the summer of 1976, I joined residents on the Eldon Street estate in their campaign for a children's playground. Children were crossing the Blackburn to Bolton railway line to play on fields on the opposite side of the line. A tunnel under the line was closed. This campaign was the beginning of the formation of the Eldon Street Residents' Association which flourishes today. Joe Swinton was the guiding light for me on the Eldon Street estate; he died at the age of 86 at the end of February 2011. His funeral was on Monday 7 March 2011.

As a Labour Party member I was keen to engage with the Bolton Labour Party. I discovered that there was a Labour Club in Tonge Moor so, one night in 1972, I decided to make inquiries at the club with an intention to join Tonge Ward Branch of the Party. As luck would have it I was standing next to one of the local Party members, Andrew Grimes, Political Correspondent of the *Manchester Evening News*. It wasn't long before I started to attend the local branch meetings which were held in the club.

The chairman was Gordon Power and those who regularly attended these meetings, apart from me, were Gordon's wife Jean, Andrew Grimes, Bert Trainor, Kevin Meagher, Florence Flitcroft, Peter Lowe, Frank and Eileen White and Eileen's mother Lilian Crook, Barbara Lomax, Billy Smith and his son Graham, Peter and Betty Burke, Renee Cavanaugh, Mr and Mrs David Scowcroft, Wilf Stirling, May Brown, Wyn Molyneaux, Paul Perry, Sam Taylor, Don Eastwood and his daughter Tracy, and Vince Simpson.

Frank White was selected to fight the Bury and Radcliffe Parliamentary seat and was elected to Parliament on 10 October 1974, defeating Conservative Michael Fidler. He won the seat again in 1979 after several recounts but lost the new Bury North seat (boundary changes took effect from 1980) to Conservative Alistair Burt in 1983.

Frank White served in the Government Whips' Office at a time when every vote counted. He was allocated the job of 'lower bog trotter' by the Deputy Chief Whip. As an ex-footballer and football referee Frank could run fast which, he believes, was why he was allocated this position. During a division his job was to ensure that all Labour Members came out of the toilets and other hiding holes to vote.

The Trainor family (Bert and Tommy) are a legend in Tonge Branch (now Tonge with The Haulgh Branch) of the Labour Party. Committee member Tommy Trainor was instrumental in purchasing a house in Horsa Street, which allowed the original club house – gifted to the Labour Party by an older member – to be extended. As I write Bert Trainor, now well into his eighties, is still attending Tonge with The Haulgh Branch meetings as well as meetings of the Bolton North East Constituency Labour Party General Management Committee and the Local Government Committee.

The 'new' purpose-built Tonge Ward Labour Club on Ainsworth Lane had a big cabaret room, a committee room, a sports room and a lounge, where we held our meetings. After 33 years in cramped conditions at Horsa Street the new club, which cost £30,000 to build, was opened on 23 May 1962. Merrilyn and I became frequent visitors at the club on Saturday nights, where we enjoyed the excellent cabarets that were prevalent in all clubs at that time.

Another founder member of Tonge Ward Labour Club that I came to know well was Harry Howarth, who was a Trustee of the club. When Harry became housebound I often visited him at his home in Glenbrook Close in North Ward. Occasionally I would persuade him to visit the club with me on one of his rare nights out.

On Monday evenings Tonge Branch ran the bingo evening at the Labour Club and kept any profits for branch funds, which were used to provide leaflets for our local election campaigns. Gordon Power 'called' bingo and Eileen White and her mother Lilian sold the tickets near the door to the concert room. They were very keen to get me involved.

It wasn't long before I was 'calling' the second half of the bingo evening. I stuck it out altogether for three years, and did almost every Monday night. I learned all the calls: "two fat ladies, all the eights, 88", "two little ducks, all the two's, 22", "the Brighton line, five and nine, 59", "top of the shop, blind 90", "key to the door, two and one, 21", "Maggie's den, number 10" (which brought cries of "get her out"), and so on.

One night there was a dispute about a full house. The caller of a bingo game is always right in the minds of the players, even if s/he isn't. A member of the club committee, Joyce Marsh, intervened and tried to tell me I was wrong, and I was, and all hell let loose. I should, of course, have stuck to my original decision and the punters would have just carried on, grumbling but without complaining. I decided that was the end of bingo for me; I had done my bit. In any case there was another contender for the job.

I always offered my services to deliver leaflets when the local elections came round in May. Jack Knight, a stalwart of the Bolton Labour Party, had been a Tonge Ward councillor and he, Gordon Power and I could deliver the whole of Tonge Ward in a weekend, and we often did, accompanied by Jack's dog. Unfortunately, Jack had been a steward in Bolton Town

Hall on 28 January 1972, when Bernadette Devlin came over from Northern Ireland to raise funds for their civil rights campaign, which was not popular in England. 700 people attended the meeting and £102 was collected. After that Jack was considered to be unelectable as a member of the 'green armband brigade'.

To raise money for Tonge Branch, I organised a number of dances, Valentine's Dances and Christmas Dances, at Tonge Ward Labour Club, dancing to a five-piece band (the Roy Francis Sound or the Johnny Dennis Sound) and with a bar extension to midnight. The Bolton Labour Party organised the New Year's Eve Dances in Bolton Town Hall every year, and I volunteered to help Cllr David Dingwall organise those as well. When David died I took over the organisation of these dances, until disco took over from ballroom dancing and they lost their popularity. The New Year's Eve dances raised about £1,000, which was distributed between the Bolton Constituency Labour Parties (CLPs).

Tonge Ward Labour Club was famous for its Tuesday and Friday sessions of rock and roll, with blue suede shoes and Teddy Boy suits for the 'boys' and layers of flared skirts for the 'girls'. B Bopper played the same records at the same time every week. Sadly, the club was forced into receivership on 10 September 2009, which became the end of an era. A few years before it finally closed on 23 September 2009 it had been completely rebuilt. For a few more years it traded as a social club.

There were two General Elections in 1974, on 28 February and 10 October, which kept us extremely busy that year. Bolton had two Parliamentary constituencies, Bolton East and Bolton West, prior to the boundary changes of 1980, when three Parliamentary constituencies were created, Bolton North East, Bolton South East and Bolton West.

When Bolton had two Parliamentary constituencies it received a lot of media attention. It was considered that if both Bolton constituencies were won by Labour candidates, here would be a Labour Government, and *vice versa*; if a Labour candidate won one of the seats and a Conservative candidate won the other, then it was likely to be a hung Parliament. We were considered a barometer or weather vane town for the rest of the country, and it was an exciting place to be during a General Election campaign.

It is very difficult to get political activists to turn out to fight elections in winter. Nevertheless, David Young, who was selected as the Prospective Parliamentary Candidate (PPC) for the Bolton East seat before I moved to Bolton, was elected to Parliament on 28 February 1974 (my first attendance at an election count) as a Labour Member of Parliament. He defeated Conservative Laurance Reed with an overall majority of 1,613.

Our candidate in Bolton West, Ann Taylor (admitted to the House of Lords as Baroness Taylor of Bolton on 13 June 2005), failed to defeat Conservative Robert Redmond (his majority was 603) and, true to form, Prime Minister Harold Wilson was the head of a minority Government. It was clear to us all that the Government couldn't last, and another General Election was called for 10 October 1974. On that occasion both David Young and Ann Taylor won their seats, with overall majorities of 4,065 and 906 respectively. We were jubilant and we celebrated. Ann Taylor was born and bred in Bolton. She attended Johnson Fold Primary School and the independent Bolton School.

David Young, son of a Clydeside shipyard worker, was born in Greenock on 12 October 1928. He was educated at Greenock Academy and Glasgow University, where he studied Latin and History. He trained as an insurance executive in Coventry before enrolling at St Paul's Teachers Training College, Cheltenham. David taught history at a school in Coventry and rose to become Head of the History Department. He joined the Labour Party in 1955 and married Grace McCowat, also a teacher, in 1960. David Young was chairman of the Coventry East CLP, MP Richard Crossman's constituency, from 1964 to 1968, was appointed as an Alderman in 1972 on Nuneaton Borough Council, then elected as a councillor on the Shadow Nuneaton and Bedworth Borough Council, which he served from 1974 until 1976, and fought the unwinnable Parliamentary seats of South Worcestershire in 1959, Banbury in 1966, and Bath in 1970.

In the early 1970s, Terry Whalebone (his predecessor was Wally Edwards) was our full-time election agent in Bolton, but agents spent as much time raising money to pay their own salaries as fighting elections or raising money for the party, and it was clear that these positions couldn't last; sadly, since Terry was forced to retire in 1976, the Bolton Labour Party has not had another full-time agent. Today the NW Regional Office of the Labour Party is in Warrington but then it was in Frederick Road, Salford, with Paul Carmody as the Regional Officer. I worked closely with his able assistants Frank Aveyard and Peter Killeen.

Elections are hard work. A place has to be found where the election campaign can be co-ordinated by the election agent and his or her helpers. In the 1970s the National Union of Miners (NUM) offered use of the headquarters of the

Lancashire Miners, the Miners' Hall in Bridgeman Place. I remember staying up until the early hours of the morning stuffing envelopes with election material and preparing leaflets for distribution by hand, at the railway station, on Ashburner Street Market, in Victoria Square and outside Burnden Park football ground. Years later, my friend Martin Donaghy said, "And we stuffed envelopes with old people"! Our older members certainly enjoyed coming together in a large hall putting the election manifesto in brown envelopes which were addressed by hand for a free delivery by the Post Office. Today, they are printed using computer technology, with the addresses already on them.

David Young MP

Those were the days of the big political rallies in our large towns and cities. Later, election campaigns were conducted through the medium of television and whistle-stop tours of leading politicians. Harold Wilson attended a rally in Bolton's Albert Hall in the Town Hall on 1 October 1974, and I was a steward at the meeting. The Albert Hall was packed and I was told to let in only people who could produce a ticket for the meeting. I refused to let in the senior political correspondent of the *Manchester Evening News*, which didn't go down well with the organisers. At that time I didn't know him from Adam. Harold Wilson arrived very late, and the warm-up speakers kept the meeting alive until he arrived. David Young was a brilliant orator and by the time Harold Wilson arrived, the atmosphere in the Albert Hall was electric.

The Bolton East and West Conservative Organisations, in conjunction with the North West Area, held a similar rally in Bolton's Albert Hall on 4 October 1974, at which Ted Heath was the guest speaker. We heard that it was to be broadcast on national television, so Norma Perry and I acquired tickets and attended to heckle Ted Heath as he spoke in the glare of the spotlights. Ted Heath was quite taken aback by the heckling; he couldn't handle it like Harold Wilson could.

I suggested to Norma that we leave quickly as Ted was receiving a standing ovation, because we had not made ourselves very popular with his faithful supporters. We got out as fast as we could; even so, legs appeared across the gangway in an attempt to trip us up, and one or two people actually spat at us. We were undeterred; job done!

In the General Elections of 1974 Harold Wilson promised a referendum on Britain's membership of the European Economic Community (the EEC – the Common Market); Labour's policy at the time was to withdraw from membership. However, when the referendum was held on 5 June 1975 the verdict of those who voted was to retain our membership. I campaigned against membership in 1975 and am still a 'Euro sceptic', although today I support reform rather than withdrawal.[2]

Despite my failure to learn to play a musical instrument, both Merrilyn and I were very keen that both Sally and Sheena would be given an opportunity. Sally learned to play the flute and Sheena was provided with a poor-quality clarinet at Castle

Hill Primary School which, later, we replaced with another of better quality.

Bolton had a few peripatetic music teachers in the early 1970s; most were older men who played in brass bands. They taught part-time and most had not been trained as teachers. Ian Campbell, a full-time peripatetic woodwind tutor, visited Castle Hill Primary School and taught our two daughters. He was highly critical of Bolton Metropolitan Borough Council, who spent very little on music tuition. Ian pointed out to me that Bolton no longer, unlike in earlier times, had an active Youth Orchestra and that different musical instruments lay in cupboards in schools in various stages of disrepair because there wasn't even a procedure to get them repaired. Halle Orchestra leader Martin Milner had played in the Bolton Youth Orchestra, so matters had obviously deteriorated rapidly. The Bolton Youth Orchestra was formed in 1943 and celebrated its 21st Anniversary in March 1964 with a concert in the Albert Hall conducted by Frank Milner.

Fired up by Ian Campbell, I decided to embarrass Bolton Metropolitan Borough Council by starting up a privately-funded venture. On a cold and damp Saturday morning in October 1975 the Music Centre Concert Band was formed at SS Simon and Jude's Church House in Rishton Lane, Bolton. I agreed to set up a parents' support group and became its first chairman. Ian became our first Musical Director. My daughter Sally was a founding member of the band; Sheena joined later. It became a popular venture and, as word spread, we were forced to move to St Paul's Parochial Hall in Astley Bridge, a larger venue, in January 1976. By this time 60-70 children were attending our sessions.

The parents' support group organised various social events

for the children too. In the summer of 1977, for example, we organised a summer camp at the Staithes Youth Camp, near Whitby on the Yorkshire coast. The children gave two concerts in Staithes, appreciated by local residents (see *Bolton Evening News* dated 9 September 1977).

I encouraged my two daughters to engage with music in other ways too. Sally was enrolled, for example, at Gawthorpe Hall in a master class with Atarah Ben-Tovim, a flautist with the Liverpool Philharmonic Orchestra. This encounter enabled me to persuade Ms Ben-Tovim to take an interest in our Music Centre in Bolton, which she visited on more than one occasion. For several years both our girls visited a woman musician in Bromwich Street, who taught them to play the piano.

A Junior Band and a Stage Band were formed from the growing number of performers, and both bands featured in a Christmas Concert in 1978. Ian Campbell was ambitious for his children and entered them into their first competition at Solihull in 1979, where they won two major awards. In 1980, a joint concert was held with the Wingates Temperance Band in the Victoria Hall, Bolton.

In the meantime I was trying to persuade our education spokesman on Bolton Metropolitan Borough Council, Cllr David Dingwall, that music was not taken seriously in Bolton by the Conservative-controlled Council. Of course, we invited local councillors from across the political divide to attend our concerts. We had established a very active parents' support group, which also began to campaign for better music provision in Bolton. As a result, the Local Education Authority's officers felt they had to take some action.

I have in my possession a report that the Director of

Education, Philip Waddington (his Chief Adviser was Mr D. W. T. Watson) submitted to the Further Education Sub-Committee of Bolton Metropolitan Borough Council on 13 July 1977, which painted a rosy picture of music provision for children in Bolton. It gave the impression that our private venture, then at St Paul's Parochial Hall, Astley Bridge, was local authority inspired. Nothing could have been further from the truth. For the next three years not much changed either. There was a total lack of political will at that time.

Cllr David Dingwall set me a challenge. Should Labour take control of Bolton Metropolitan Borough Council, what would be our policy? Consequently, I consulted Ian Campbell and others on this question and spent a considerable amount of time putting together a music policy for Bolton. It was my opinion that we needed more full-time teachers and that a 'school structure' should be introduced, with a Head of a Bolton Music Centre. More instruments were needed and a permanent building was required to house the Music Centre. I still have copies of the original documents.

When the Labour Party won control of Bolton Metropolitan Borough Council in the May local elections of 1980 (based on an all-out election, precipitated by boundary changes) and Cllr David Dingwall became chairman of the Education Committee, my policy was introduced, and the Bolton Music Centre has gone from strength to strength ever since.

The Local Education Authority provided St George's Church on St George's Road, Bolton for the Music Centre and, eventually, my position as chairman of the parents' support group was handed over to others as I became an active local councillor. Ted Watton, a musician who played in local dance bands, was the secretary. His son Gary played drums in our bands and later became a teacher at the Bolton Music Centre.

The parents' support group committee members in 1977-1978 were: me as chairman; Ted Watton (secretary); Norma and Derek Wardlow (joint treasurers); Enid Watson; Barbara Woods; Betty Syed; Don Fleming; Eric Phipps; John Drakely; and Ted Donnelly. The auditors were Tom Sloane and Mrs E. Welsby.

In May 1981, the Youth Concert Band travelled abroad for the first time, to Paderborn in Germany, our twin town. 1982 was a year of change for the Music Centre. Ian Duckworth was appointed in April as Conductor of the Junior Band (which became the Schools Concert Band) and as tutor to the brass section of the Youth Concert Band. In May 1982, the Music Centre moved again, to Derby Street School, where it stayed for several years. The local authority felt that it had to advertise the post of Head of the Music Centre, which annoyed Ian Campbell. He felt that because he had got this venture off the ground that he should automatically become Head of the Music Centre, then under local authority control.

The post was advertised and I persuaded Ian Campbell to apply for it, but the local authority appointed Nigel Taylor, who took the Music Centre to new heights. Sadly, Ian Campbell, always a volatile character but very passionate about music, quit the Music Centre in April 1982 and formally resigned from teaching in Bolton in October 1982 and owned an off-licence in Astley Bridge for five years. That was the end of one era and the beginning of another for Bolton's Music Centre.

Ian Campbell died on 10 March 2015 after spending

another period teaching music to primary school children in Salford and Bury; he retired from Tottington Primary School in 1995.

Sally lost interest in playing her flute but Sheena continued to play her clarinet, and she was a member of the Youth Concert Band and Youth Orchestra. She became their Principal Clarinettist. She left school in 1987 to go to Bretton Hall College near Wakefield to pursue a career as a music teacher.

Under Music Director Nigel Taylor several ensembles were formed at the Music Centre – a jazz band and a dance band included – and these bands travelled. They entered and won competitions, they appeared at the Albert Hall in London and, in my opinion, they helped to put Bolton on the map. I am proud of their achievements, but people have long since forgotten how it all started (or restarted).

Bolton has always welcomed immigrants. The Irish arrived first in modern times. They were followed by Polish, Ukrainian, Afro-Caribbean, Pakistani and Indian people. In 2011, 20.6% of Bolton's 276,800 citizens were members of British Ethnic Minority (BEM) communities, with people practising the Muslim faith outnumbering those who practise the Hindu faith by two to one. In the early 1970s tensions between the indigenous communities and those from the Indian sub-continent began to rise as temples and mosques began to appear in various parts of the town. Bolton Racial Equality Council (BREC) made strenuous efforts to build bridges between the different communities and fight racial prejudice.

In February 1977, Independent Cllr Raymond Halliwell, a former compositor with the *Bolton Evening News* who represented Church, East and North Ward on Bolton Council, was appointed as the Bolton Community Relations Officer. He succeeded Tom Tootell. Raymond had been a Conservative councillor but had fallen out with his branch of the Conservative Party. His two Conservative Ward colleagues at the time were Cllrs Albert (Bert) O'Neill and Ernie Crook, who lived in a house on Crompton Way that overlooked the Firwood estate where we lived. When I put Labour posters in our front windows, they put up large Conservative posters in their back garden, which faced us.

In the 10 October 1974 General Election a trade unionist, Geoffrey Booth, received 1,106 votes in the Bolton East Parliamentary Constituency as a National Front (NF) candidate. Both he and John Hamilton were candidates for the NF party in the 1979 General Election in Bolton East and West Parliamentary constituencies, respectively. Between the October 1974 and the 1979 General Elections the NF were very active in Bolton, and their efforts became increasingly opposed by the Anti-Fascist League, which I joined.

Wood Street Socialist Club, Bolton, birthplace of William Hesketh Lever – later Lord Leverhulme, who founded Port Sunlight.

Soon after I joined Tonge Branch of Bolton East Constituency Labour Party, I became its secretary. I was reminded recently that the minute books from those days have been kept. I wrote minutes that were far too long – blow by blow accounts of the meetings – but at least they reflect in detail our concerns in the early 1970s. In 1976 I served as vice-chairman of our Branch and became a vice-chairman of the Bolton East Constituency Labour Party, which met at that time in Wood Street Socialist Club in the town centre.

While some Labour party members are also members of Wood Street Socialist Club it is not a Labour club. Most of those who have attended it down its century of existence have been far to the left of most Labour Party members. It has sponsored many heated debates and, today, runs a 'Red Fridays' programme of debates, lectures, films, poetry readings, etc. I have made presentations there on the oppression of Palestinians and on the 'War on Drugs'. The club always struggles financially but it has survived. Its worst time in recent years in my opinion was when some anarchists infiltrated the club and drove many other members away, including me. I rejoined later.

Wood Street Socialist Club is the birthplace of William Hesketh Lever (later Lord Leverhulme), who started up the soap empire at Port Sunlight which has become the Unilever of today. He is one of Bolton's most famous sons. When his wealth had accumulated he bought Hall-i'th-Wood, where Samuel Crompton built his spinning mule, refurbished and furnished it and presented it to the town, and presented Leverhulme Park to Bolton. Later, the Leverhulme Trust endowed Bolton School (a successful independent school in the town). Lord Leverhulme built a bungalow on the slopes of

Winter Hill which was set on fire by a suffragette. It was never rebuilt. His locally famous Japanese Gardens are kept in average condition today so that those who climb Winter Hill can enjoy their lay-out. The Lever family also built a dovecote on the top of Rivington Pike, which has become a local landmark.

My first local election as a Labour Party candidate was on 6 May 1976, when I failed to gain a place on Bolton Metropolitan Borough Council against a sitting Conservative candidate in Tonge Ward, where I lived. I was 35 years old.

In 1977 Guy Harkin was selected to fight the Bolton No. 4 (North, Tonge and West Ward) seat in the Greater Manchester County Council Elections. The Labour-controlled Greater Manchester County Council was created by a reorganisation of Local Government in 1974, with Sir Robert Thomas, former Leader of Manchester City Council, as its Leader and with the following councillors representing Bolton: Sam Cohen (Conservative); David Dingwall (Labour); John (known as Jack) Foster (Labour); Frank White (Labour); and Walter Walsh (Conservative).

The 1974 reorganisation of Local Government brought part of Turton, Blackrod, Horwich, Westhoughton, Bromley Cross, Farnworth, Kearsley and Little Lever into the new Bolton Metropolitan Borough, with Cllr Doris Berry (Conservative) as its first Mayor. She followed Labour Cllr Harry Devenish as the last Mayor of the former County Borough of Bolton; Cllr John Hanscomb was the transitional Mayor and chairman but only for one day. The composition of the new 69-member Council was: 45 Conservative; 23 Labour; and 1 Liberal. Aldermen could no longer attend Council meetings and vote.

One night the Labour Party Chief Whip, Cllr David Dingwall, turned up at my home and explained that, despite the fact that we had already delivered thousands of leaflets in Guy Harkin's name, he had gone off to France with his family without signing his nomination papers, which had to be submitted at the Town Hall within a few days. "Will you stand in his place?" was the question, and I agreed. At the election on 5 May 1977 I was unsuccessful; the sitting Tory County Councillor, Frank Telford, was returned, albeit with a substantially reduced majority of 548 votes.

I was chairman of Bolton East Constituency Labour Party (CLP) General Management Committee (GMC) at the time, elected in March 1977.[3] The previous chairman, John Perry, served for four years. Our secretary was Cllr Cliff Scull, who also served as David Young's local secretary, the treasurer was Tony Moon and our vice-chairmen were Tommy Reagan and Morrell Atkinson. In my first term as chairman of the CLP General Management Committee I spent a considerable amount of time rebuilding some of the inactive branches.

Raymond Halliwell had been appointed as Bolton's Community Relations Officer and was still a sitting Conservative councillor, which I felt was wrong and said so in letters to the *Bolton Evening News*. Raymond was a very good chairman of the Social Services Committee. On 13 June 1977 he decided to retire and a by-election was called for 25 August 1977.

Cllr David Dingwall appeared on my doorstep again, late one night, and suggested that I let my name go forward as the Labour Party candidate to fight this seat. Again, I submitted to his charm, especially in view of the fact that he explained that this was a safe Conservative seat and had never been won by a Labour candidate.

Election manifesto (p.1) for the by-election in August 1977 in Church, East and North Ward when I was elected to Bolton Metropolitan Borough Council.

Election manifesto (p.2) for the by-election in August 1977 in Church, East and North Ward when I was elected to Bolton Metropolitan Borough Council.

I won with 955 votes, a majority of 142 votes over the Conservative candidate Mary Kershaw (813 votes), which surprised everybody, including me. David Dingwall had calculated that demographic changes in the Ward had given us a fighting chance, which turned out to be the case. One of my opposition candidates was John Hamilton of the National Front, who received 101 votes; the Liberal candidate, James Walton, came last with only 72 votes.

I made Bolton's failure to adopt comprehensive education one of the key election challenges in the 1977 by-election campaign. However, one of the difficult issues that we had to face was the changing face of the so-called 'Lake District' area of Bolton, off Blackburn Road (the North Ward area). The first problem facing that area was the on-off proposal of Greater Manchester County Council to build a Blackburn Road by-pass, from the end of the recently constructed St Peter's Way (the A666) through to the north side of Astley Bridge. Eventually the Conservative-controlled Bolton Metropolitan Borough Council was forced to drop this proposal through a lack of Government funding, despite the fact that they had cleared hundreds of houses in an area with an expanding ethnic minority population.

The second problem in the area was the conversion of a former Co-operative grocery store at the junction of Ulleswater Street and Lena Street into a madrassa/mosque for the Muslim population, who were increasingly purchasing properties in the 'Lake District'. This was an issue that the National Front exploited throughout the 1970s. Their objections to this development had resonance with the local white population, and the issue became the subject of a wider debate that was covered by NW and national television.

The third issue in the area at that time was 'white flight' away from the local primary school. Chalfont Street Primary

School became a wholly Muslim attended school, which was not thought to be conducive to good community relations at that time. There was even talk of bussing some children out of the area and white children into the school. Some Muslim parents started to send their children to predominantly 'white' schools further up Blackburn Road in Astley Bridge, because they wanted them to speak English at school rather than Gujarati.

Bolton Town Hall

The 1977 by-election campaign was a memorable election campaign in another way. One of the busiest polling stations was in a Methodist chapel hall (now demolished) in Castle Street. During the day I gave lifts to a lot of people, mainly elderly, to this particular polling station, only to find that I was obstructed badly by a large steam roller bedecked with Conservative posters. It was driven by a fellow in a cloth cap with a broad smile on his face, a man whom I didn't recognise.

After we moved to Woburn Avenue I rented an allotment behind Tonge cricket club, which I also joined. Richard Heyes was our secretary. About two weeks after my election to Bolton MB Council I was working on my allotment early one Sunday morning when I saw a battered old Land Rover coming along one of the access roads on top of which were two very long wooden beams, which I learned came from a demolished mill. They were intended to help a neighbouring allotment holder to build raised growing beds. Hanging out of the driver's window was the same fellow wearing his cloth cap. "By heck" he cried, "I caused thee a lot o'bother tuther Thorsdy when thi wor standin for election." The name on the side of the Land Rover was 'Fred Dibnah, Steeplejack'. That was my first meeting with Fred, who I discovered later was one of my constituents and a Conservative supporter.

My first case as a councillor was to clear pigeons from the area of the East Ward flats (off Turton Street), where their deposits on window sills and windows were not welcome. I dutifully put in a report to the Environmental Health Department and, a few weeks later, there was no sign of the pigeons. I shouldn't have asked the question but I did. I was curious to know why the pigeons disappeared so suddenly. To my horror I discovered that poisoned corn had been put down in a disused building near to the flats, where the pigeons roosted at night. I heard from residents that some were shot too in the early hours of the morning.

In the same area the residents of Charles House complained to me that an alcoholic gentleman who lived in a ground floor flat threw empty bottles through his lounge window on a regular basis and his windows were perpetually either broken or boarded up. Even worse, when they could, the local yobs threw the bottles back into his lounge. I decided to solve the problem. The Housing Direct Labour Organisation dutifully fitted Perspex windows. Then I got a complaint from the mother of one of the yobs. Her son had attempted to throw a bottle through one of these windows and it had bounced back and hit him in the face. That was justice as far as I was concerned, and I told her so. Two of my main supporters in East Ward were Eddie and May Holt.

I joined the Arts and Housing Committees of the Council (1977-1978). I spoke at my first full Council meeting, can't remember what about, but I do remember Tonge Ward Cllr Kevin Knowles suggest that I wouldn't last long on the Council. In fact, I outlasted Cllr Knowles, who was the steward at Tonge Ward Conservative Club. After his election defeat he put a lot of effort into supporting his son Tony, who became a successful professional snooker player. In 1978-1979 I also served the Policy Review Sub-committee. In 1979-1980 my committees were the Housing, Social Services and Management and Finance Committees

Another Tonge councillor, Cllr Susannah Harrison, didn't take too kindly to a speech I made at my first meeting of the Social Services Committee. "This isn't a political committee" she told me. She didn't last long either. The Conservative victory in the 1979 General Election and the sweeping changes that Margaret Thatcher and her Government started to make made the Conservatives very unpopular in local elections, and they lost a lot of council seats in the 1980s.

Because Raymond Halliwell had less than a year of his four-year term to serve, I also fought my seat on 4 May 1978, and won again. In 1979, we succeeded in getting John Farmer elected as a Labour councillor in the same Ward.

On the 10 February 1978 the National Front held a rally in Bolton Town Hall. 2,000 police were required to control a huge demonstration in Victoria Square and outside the north entrance of the Town Hall, where all hell broke loose as the

NF members entered our Town Hall. There was uproar when the NF supporters gave Nazi salutes from its windows.

I moved at a Labour Group meeting held in December 1977 that the NF should not be allowed to hold this rally in our Town Hall. The Deputy Leader of the Labour Group at that time, Cllr Lawrence Cunliffe – later Member of Parliament for Leigh – seconded my motion, and both of us gave passionate speeches to the Group. Judging by the body language of our colleagues, we were winning the argument. Cllr Cliff Scull, Cllr Tommy McEwen, Cllr Raymond Cornthwaite and other older members of the Group were nodding in agreement with our arguments. Some of them had fought fascism in their youth.

Sensing that we were going to win, Cllr David Dingwall, who was imprisoned during World War II as a conscientious objector, rose to his feet and gave an equally passionate speech about the value of free speech in our country, and opposed our motion, thumping the bench in front of him as he spoke with a hint of anger in his voice. The body language of those older members who had appeared to support Lawrence and I changed, and it was clear that David was winning the debate. We lost, and Lawrence Cunliffe resigned as Deputy Leader of the Labour Group, a decision that made the front page of the *Bolton Evening News* on Friday 16 December 1977, the day after the Council meeting that confirmed the Labour Group decision.

The Bolton Council for Community Relations (BCCR), under the chairmanship of Vincent Simpson, backed our call to ban the NF from using Council facilities.

1980 was a crucial year for the Bolton District Labour Party; there was a chance of taking control of Bolton

Metropolitan Borough Council on the formation of its new boundaries. It was an 'all-out' election; all 60 seats (a reduction of nine seats) were to be contested. The old Church, East and North Ward disappeared and most of it became the new Central Ward.

The Council Chamber in Bolton Town Hall.

John Farmer decided not to stand again in 1980, which left four of us to contest selection in the new Central Ward: Cllr Bob Howarth, who was Leader of the Labour Group, Cllr Donald Clarke, Cllr Mrs Gladys Hart (all three had represented West Ward previously) and me. The selection conference was held on 21 December 1979 in the small hall at the Spinners Hall on St George's Road. Those who had been through the mill before knew how to do it. Donald had brought a couple of carloads of his supporters into the well-attended conference. Even so, he paced up and down all evening in the belief that there was a move to deselect him. I think he suspected that I was behind it.

Gladys Hart was not popular amongst members of the ethnic minority communities who lived in the new Ward, especially around the Blackburn Road area of Bolton. It was my guess that she might be the one to be deselected, and that turned out to be the case. Following her deselection she proceeded to resign her seat on Bolton MB Council and her membership of the Labour Party and attack us in the local media. In the May 1980 local election she stood as an Independent candidate and gathered almost 1,000 votes, but was not elected.

Elected councillors in the new Central Ward (left to right); Cllr Dr Brian Iddon, Cllr Donald Clarke and Cllr Bob Howarth.

On Thursday 1 May 1980, Cllrs Donald Clarke, Bob Howarth and Dr Brian Iddon were elected as the first councillors to represent the people of Central Ward. Because I obtained the lowest number of votes of the three of us, I was the first to stand for re-election in 1982. It had been a busy few years for me. I served continuously as a representative of Central Ward, winning successive local elections in 1986, 1990, and 1994, until I resigned in 1998 after 21 years as a Bolton councillor. I was elected to Parliament on 1 May 1997 (see Chapter 2).

Cllr Donald Clarke, who served as Mayor of Bolton in 1977-1978, was one of the directors of a well-known catering company in Bolton. His triplet brother Alan and sister Barbara were also directors of the company. The Lamplighter Restaurant in the basement of the Market Hall in Knowsley Street was part of the company, as was the outside catering firm Percivals. Alan Clarke was one of the key influences in Bolton becoming twinned with Paderborn in Germany and with Le Mans in France.

Donald retired from Bolton Council at the May local elections in 1983 and was succeeded in Central Ward by David Dingwall, who lost his seat in Kearsley Ward twelve months earlier. Donald and I both believed that Bolton should attract people to live in the town centre again, a passion that I pursued when I became chairman of the Housing Committee later.

In September 1978, Cllr David Dingwall organised a delegation of Bolton Labour Party members to travel to Paderborn to establish a town-twinning link with the SPD there, a link that has lasted until the present day. I was very pleased to be able to return to Paderborn with my wife Eileen and other Labour Party members to take part in the 30th anniversary celebrations of this town-twinning venture, held during a visit from 9 to 17 September 2008.

Paderborn holds a Libori Festival in July every year. The town hosts a very large funfair and holds a parade. One of the highlights of the week-long celebrations is the annual Libori Dinner (Libori-Mahl) in the Town Hall. Those who are privileged to attend sit down with a specially decorated Libori stein in front of them, which they can keep. I attended Libori-Mahls with my fellow Paderborn SPD councillors or with the town's solicitor Dr Rudi Salmen and I collected four of the prized steins, in 1976, 1981, 1983, and 1987. These are valuable collector's items in Paderborn. Merrilyn and I took our two children to Paderborn several times; the children particularly enjoyed visiting the large funfair that assembles in Paderborn on these occasions and watching the parades.

The Bolton Labour Group meets on the Friday evening following a Thursday election to decide who should hold the key positions on the new Council. We called it the 'night of the long knives'. Cllr Bob Howarth, who served as the Member of Parliament for Bolton East from 1964 to 1970, became Leader of Bolton Metropolitan Borough Council, taking over from Conservative Councillor John Hanscomb in 1980. I became vice-chairman of the Housing Committee, with Cllr Peter Johnston as its chairman. Bob Howarth became Leader of Bolton MB Council Labour Group after Cllr Ellis Dobson lost his Horwich Ward seat on 5 May 1975.

In 1977, when I joined the Housing Committee, Roland Carr was its Conservative chairman; he was succeeded, on 28 June 1979, by Cllr Kevan Hornby who, on 2 March 1978, launched Bolton's first Housing Action Areas which were in the Castle Street part of my Ward and in the Goldsmith Street area. The residents were told that their houses would be given an extra 30 year's life. They are still there over 30 years later and are likely to stand for a long time yet.

Early in the morning of 16 February 1978 Ann Taylor, the Member of Parliament for Bolton West, alerted me to the fact that there had been a massive gas explosion in Castle Street in my ward. When I reached Castle Street it was a scene of devastation; the emergency services were there in force. At the Bury New Road end of Castle Street two men turned up to open up their Dart Radio Service Company basement radio

Founders of the link between Bolton Labour Party and the SPD in Paderborn (left to right): me, Hans Thone (SPD Chief Whip), Cllr Peter Johnston, Graham Gough, Cllr David Dingwall, Gunter Bitterberg, Karl Nolden, and Rudi Salmen (see *Bolton Evening News* dated 11 September 1978 for the names of other delegates).

repair business without realising that the premises were filled with gas and an explosion occurred. Sitting in a chair in her house above was 78-year-old Mary Brown; amazingly she survived the blast, which broke nearly every window along both sides of Castle Street, from Bury New Road to Bradford Street. The site of the explosion is still derelict today.

The most likely cause of the explosion was an overnight leakage of gas into the basement of the building from a cracked cast iron gas main below the pavement outside. Two days later a similar explosion occurred in Cecelia Street, off Nelson Street. As a result, numbers 11-17 Cecelia Street were demolished. It was explosions such as these in Bolton and other towns and cities that prompted a major programme to replace cast iron gas mains with the now familiar yellow polypropylene mains. The parking of heavy vehicles on footpaths was thought to cause the cracking of the old cast iron gas mains.

I was a local authority representative on the Castle Hill Youth Club Management Committee before my election to the Council, and I continued to serve in this capacity through to 1998 (I was its vice-chairman for most of this time). In 1980, I took over chairmanship of the Governing Body of Sharples School from Cllr Mrs Barbara Hurst (former chairman of the Education Committee), a secondary school, and served for six years when Frank Kenyon was the Head Teacher. Cllr Mrs Hurst was the first chairman of Governors at Sharples School; she too served in that position for six years. For a time I was a governor on the Boards of Governors of Birtenshaw Hall Special School and Canon Slade C. of E. School and I also chaired the Joint Governing Body for Oldhams Lane, Chalfont Street and Wolfenden Street Primary Schools.

After becoming chairman of the Governing Body at Sharples School and vice-chairman of the Housing Committee in 1980 I decided to concentrate from the 1982-1983 Council cycle of meetings on the Housing and Management and Finance Committees.

Undoubtedly, one of the most colourful characters in Bolton politics in the 1970s and 1980s was Cllr David Dingwall, who lived in Bramhall Avenue, Harwood. He was born in Gateshead on 18 September 1918. David cut his teeth in politics on Turton Urban District Council, of which he was chairman in 1965. He represented Eagley Ward and was also a Lancashire County Councillor. Later he was elected to the Greater Manchester County Council which was abolished under the Thatcher Government elected in 1979.

David hadn't been involved too long in Bolton politics when I arrived in the town in 1972. From 1973 until 1981 he represented Breightmet Ward on Bolton Council. Later, he represented Kearsley Ward and Central Ward. David worked for a short period in the chemical industry but for most of his life he was a greengrocer, with a stall on the market at Ramsbottom, where he also sold fish. He never locked his old cars but, if ever you were offered a ride, it was obvious why nobody would want to steal them; they stank strongly of fish. He wasn't the most careful of drivers either; he was always too busy talking to his passengers to take much notice of the direction in which his car was travelling.

David Dingwall was influential in my political career; I learned my politics from him. His passion was education and, when we took control of the Council in 1980, he became chairman of the Education Committee after Cllr Mrs Barbara Hurst. Prior to that, they had been 'sparring partners' in the Council Chamber.

The big issue of the day was comprehensive education. Under the Labour Government, which lost power at the 1979 General Election, Conservative-controlled Bolton Metropolitan Borough Council refused to end 11-plus selection. At a Special Council Meeting, held on 1 August 1978, I had the audacity to move a vote of no confidence in the chairman of the Education Committee, Cllr Mrs Barbara Hurst, over her failure to meet the Labour Government's repeated requests to reorganise its secondary education system.

David Dingwall was passionate in debate, and he held the attention of his audiences better than most, but he hardly ever finished a sentence before rushing on to the next one. Later, when I saw John Prescott (Member of Parliament for Hull East) in action in the House of Commons, he reminded me of David, both self-made men with a passion for their individual version of politics but with flaws in their entertaining manner of speaking.

When David wasn't working on his market stall he was organising something, often with people like the likeable Party member Harry Entwistle or Morrell Atkinson (who served as a County Councillor and as a Bolton councillor for Great Lever) at his side. He was chairman of the Bolton County Borough (later District) Labour Party (1973 to 1984) which was responsible for recruiting candidates for the list that would lead to the nomination of our 20 candidates (after 1980) representing the Labour Party in Bolton when local elections were called. It seemed to me that David often made up his own Labour Party rules when a meeting got bogged down with protocol, but few people challenged him. He was much loved and respected by all who knew him.

For many years he organised visits to successive Local Government Conferences, which were held all over the country. I often attended those with him and several other colleagues. David married again during the time that I knew him, and his teacher wife Vera always accompanied us. I enjoyed most of these weekend events. A visit to Leicester was the most memorable, but for the wrong reasons. David was late booking us into our accommodation. We arrived in Leicester late on a Friday evening and eventually found our so-called 'accommodation'. When we knocked on the door, which was locked, a window slid back, rather like those in the doors of some nightclubs at that time. After a conversation between David and somebody inside, we were admitted and shown to our bedrooms. In mine the damp wallpaper had rolled down the wet wall until it had come to rest on the bed head. It was too late at night to go looking for alternative accommodation.

We often shared bedrooms (though not beds) to save on costs but I was horrified to find that I was expected to share a double bed with an older colleague, Cllr Cliff Scull. The breakfast was none too impressive either; we could have played football with the boiled eggs. David was reminded of our trip to Leicester for years after that experience. We christened our so-called 'hotel' in Leicester the 'Bombay Hilton'.

Anyone who has ever been canvassing at election time will have stories to tell. Dogs are the worst danger; ask any postman. Often they lie silent behind the front door until somebody starts to push something through the letter box, then they pounce. Whilst delivering an election leaflet for my colleague Bob Howarth on Halliwell Road in Central Ward, a dog gripped my right index finger so tightly that I couldn't remove my hand from the letterbox. In the end I had to have a tug-of-war competition with the dog. I won, but my finger was badly damaged by the incident. I also learned not to deliver leaflets to houses with ferocious dogs barking in the garden.

On one occasion, when I had been elected to the Church, East and North Ward in Bolton, I was canvassing in Bromwich Street (I think it was for the May 1978 local elections) with my wife Merrilyn, who was calling out those on the electoral register at each property and marking our canvass cards with voter intentions.

I had just knocked on the door of one of the large Victorian terraced houses and the door was beginning to open, when I heard a voice behind me shout "There are no voters there!" It was too late. I was facing an enormous West Indian man who filled the entire door frame (I later learned that he was a well-known former wrestler). While I gave him the standard words and asked him for his vote, I could see half-clad young women appearing behind him at the back of the hall. They had come out to see what was going on. After I had finished, the West Indian guy asked "Which party man?" And I repeated "It's the Labour Party." He replied "Oh, there's plenty of labour going on here man!" That is the only time I have knowingly canvassed a brothel.

On 7 February 1979, Greater Manchester County Council approved an extension of the A656 (St Peter's Way) from its junction with Turton Street to the Blackburn Road-Halliwell Road junction to the north, and a double carriageway town centre northern by-pass from the A666-Turton Street junction to St Georges Road. The northern limb of the inner ring road was named Topp Way after Benjamin Topp. Ben was a Justice of the Peace and a staunch member of the Labour Party. He never married and spent much of his time collecting 'pennies for politics' for the Labour Party in all the Labour clubs of the town.

On the same day, 7 February 1979, Eccles artist Colin Johnson was appointed as Director of the first Bolton Festival, which was held the following August to commemorate the bicentenary of Samuel Crompton's invention of the spinning mule. Colin fell out with Cllr Dennis Priestley, who was chairman of the Festival Committee as well as chairman of the Council's Arts Committee, and the second of these biennial festivals was organised by a consultant, Tom Wolfe, until he resigned. It celebrated the life and work of Lord Leverhulme

(1851-1925). Much of the groundwork for the second festival was put in place by Colin.

The late 1970s were years of growing strength for the 'Militant Tendency', seen by many Labour Party members to be a party within the Labour Party. This was accompanied by a growing conflict between the Labour Government and the unions which culminated in the 'Winter of Discontent' and the Labour Government's downfall in 1979. Tonge Branch member Andrew Grimes, Political Correspondent for the *Manchester Evening News*, resigned from the Labour Party, backed the Conservative Party to win the imminent General Election, and started to attack us in the media.

In the run-up to the 1979 General Election, held on 3 May, Bolton saw a significant number of political heavyweights visiting the town. Harold Wilson visited seven Labour clubs with the two Bolton MPs on 28 April and Prime Minister Jim Callaghan spoke from the Town Hall steps to 1,000 people assembled in Victoria Square on 20 April.

The Bolton 'weather vane' broke down; whilst both David Young and Ann Taylor were returned to Parliament, albeit with reduced majorities of 1,852 and 600, respectively, Britain woke up to a Tory Government on 5 May 1979, with Margaret Thatcher as the new Prime Minister. Labour wouldn't take power again in Westminster for the next 18 years.

The House of Commons held a debate on capital punishment in July 1979; Mrs Thatcher voted in favour. However, the House rejected the call to bring back hanging by 363 votes against the motion and 243 votes for the motion.

Income tax reductions were introduced by the new Tory Government, which proceeded also to cut local authority budgets. Bolton lost £3 million of its Housing Allocation in

1979 and there was a threat to withdraw its Assisted Area Status (this threat was reversed on 22 January 1982 by Industry Secretary Patrick Jenkin). A 12% council house rent rise was announced and the mortgage rate increased to 15%. A period of severe austerity had begun.

NOTES

1. *James Lawrence Isherwood (1917-1989): A Biography* by Dr Brian Iddon, Memoirs Publishing, Chichester, 2013.

2. On 23 June 2016 I voted against Brexit.

3. I served until 1980 when I was succeeded by Morrell Atkinson. In 1984 I succeeded Morrell Atkinson to become chairman of Bolton NE CLP and served until 1988 when Dave Rutter succeeded me. After my retirement from Parliament in 2010 I served again as chairman of the Bolton NE CLP from 2011-2013 (I succeeded Sue Whittle and was succeeded by Sue Haworth).

CHAPTER TWO

LABOUR IN POWER IN BOLTON (1980-1997)

～

Throughout the 1970s Bolton haemorrhaged jobs, mainly in the textile industry, but also in engineering. Among the job losses announced in the *Bolton Evening News* were: Hick Hargreaves Ltd. at their town centre factory (160 jobs, 5 Jan 1972); Hawker Siddeley Dynamics at Lostock (263, 5 Jan 1972); J. & P. Coats UK Ltd. at Eagley Mills (600, 21 Jan 1972); Littlewoods Mail Order at Croal Mill (300, 21 Jan 1972); Montague Burton Ltd. in Halliwell (240, 11 Feb 1972); Walker's Tannery in Nelson Street (350, 2 March 1978); Tootals at Sunnyside Mills (536, 5 April 1978); and Montague Burton Ltd. (600, 24 Aug 1978). The people employed at Back-o'th-Bank power station (110 on 1 Oct 1976) were promised other jobs when it closed.

This situation continued throughout the 1980s with the following job losses reported in the *Bolton Evening News*: Tootals at Sunnyside Mills (280 jobs, 27 Feb 1980); Edbro in Nelson Street (500, 25 Feb 1981); Metal Box Co. Ltd. at Westhoughton (190, 25 Feb 1981); Robert Fletcher's paper mill in Kearsley (230, 12 Dec 1981); and Beloit Walmsley on Crompton Way (57, 6 Dec 1982). Platt Saco Lowell at Bradley Fold and Mather and Platt in Farnworth shed jobs too, and British Rail's Horwich Locomotive Works closed in this decade, with the loss of 1,700 jobs (see also *Bolton Evening News*, 15 September 1982).

In the first six months of 1980 34 firms announced 1,500 engineering job losses, and unemployment in Bolton rose to 10%. By 25 June 1981 it was 15.6%, compared with a NW figure of 13.5% and a national figure of 10.9%. In March 1986 the unemployment level in Central Ward reached 32%, with a 50% youth unemployment rate.

In November 1980, the National Front (NF) marched in Bolton to protest against Bolton Council's funding of community centres at Vishwad Hindu Parishad (Hindu) on Chorley Old Road and at the Unity Centre in Johnson Street (mainly West Indians). 600 Anti-Nazi League and SWP opponents were held back by the police at Bolton Institute of Higher Education. This demonstration was reported to have cost almost £50,000. After that the NF were relatively inactive in Bolton. Later the British National Party (BNP) emerged as the predominant party of the far right.

The Conservative-controlled Bolton Council refused to reorganise secondary education along comprehensive lines but, ironically, on 26 June 1981, Conservative Education Secretary Mark Carlisle announced that Bolton's Labour-controlled Council's scheme for reorganisation of secondary education was acceptable. We wanted to avoid another 11-plus selection process, so the Local Education Authority, led by Cllr David Dingwall as chairman of the Education Committee, proceeded as quickly as reasonably possible to reorganise Bolton's secondary education system.

Those already at grammar schools were able to proceed to age 16 or 18 with their existing curriculum, while pupils entering all Bolton's secondary schools in September 1982 followed a comprehensive curriculum. My daughter Sally was 17 in 1982 and involved with her A-Level GCE subjects. Sheena, who was 14 in the same year, was caught up in the turmoil of reorganisation.

I was attending a function on the evening of Saturday 14 November 1981 when my youngest daughter Sheena rang me to say that Bolton Town Hall was on fire. I didn't believe her and stayed at the function. However, when I returned home, it was clear that she had not been having me on. We went into town and sure enough, flames were pouring out of the roof of a part of the Town Hall. I have never seen as many fire engines in one place as I saw in Bolton town centre that evening. A large crowd stood in shock watching the proceedings. There was a chrysanthemum show in the elegant Albert Hall that afternoon during which flames burst through the stage from a room below where rubbish was stored.

The debate about rebuilding the Albert Hall complex – fortunately the administrative part of the Town Hall was not affected – went on for months and split the Council and the town. There were traditionalists who wanted to rebuild the hall as it had been, despite the fact that concerts could not be held there because the acoustics were so bad. There were others, like me, who wanted to see the disaster as an opportunity to provide the town with two halls, which is what happened.

Downstairs today we have a modern Festival Hall and, upstairs, the Albert Hall is rebuilt, with its mighty new organ and the Four Seasons Statues which were salvaged from the fire and restored, in the four corners of the ceiling of the new Albert Hall. Merrilyn and I attended the Albert Halls Gala Opening, which was held on 12 April 1985. The event was followed by a week of events in the Albert Hall and its new sister hall, the Festival Hall.

When the local elections were held in May 1982, I had served as vice-chairman of the Housing Committee for two years with our chairman Cllr Peter Johnston, who had a sharp style of chairmanship, often not tolerating the views of his Labour Party colleagues too kindly in committee meetings. The Bolton District Labour Party set up working parties for councillors and ordinary party members to attend. John Hartshorne chaired the Housing Working Party for a number of years, which was one of the more active of these. We formulated an annual policy, which was submitted to the Bolton District Labour Party's Annual Policy Conference for approval.

I learned that Peter's style and the policies that he was (or was not) pursuing were not popular, either with Labour Housing Committee councillors or with ordinary members of the Party, and I was under pressure to challenge his position, which I did at the 1982 Annual Group Meeting. I failed to remove him and resigned as Peter's vice-chairman on 14 May 1982. The grumbles continued and grew louder with time, and

I knew that there would have to be another challenge in the future.

When Peter became chairman and I became vice-chairman of the Housing Committee in 1980 our first duty was to put something right that we had all complained about for some time, namely that tenants with complaints could only take them to a tiny office in Paderborn House which we had called the 'black hole of Calcutta'. In there, packed as it often was, with noisy children getting more and more frustrated as their parents waited for attention, long queues developed, which led to arguments at the small counter, with its metal grill between customer and officer. Nobody had any idea of the name of the officer who they were talking too.

There were press reports of bottles of cockroaches being brought in and of dead rats being slapped down in front of officers (see *Bolton Evening News*, 30 April 1976, 13 December 1979, 22 August 1986 and 5 September 1987). We provided a much bigger room, with magazines to read and seats to wait on, and a bigger counter without the metal grille, with more officers to attend to customers, but I knew that we had to do more for our customers.

Under Peter's chairmanship the Housing Committee decided on 25 September 1980 to cease to publish lists of the names of people who were in rent arrears in the local newspapers. We had complained about publishing these lists to successive Tory chairmen of the Housing Committee, but they felt that publication of the lists was a stick to beat tenants with into paying up.

Peter wasn't the best dressed man in the Council Chamber. At a Council meeting held on a hot summer's evening he turned up dressed extremely casually (see picture in *Bolton*

Evening News dated 23 August 1984), wearing shorts and, it soon became obvious, no underpants. Conservative Cllr Mrs Hurst, who was sitting on the benches opposite to him, protested about the view she had of him.

In 1982, I acquired the nickname 'Biggles'.[1] Cllr Terry Lewis, who always took the credit for inventing this name, said in explanation, "Brian really gets stuck into an issue and takes a high moral stance, like a knight in shining armour. But sometimes he is guilty of getting his head stuck in the clouds". However, in a letter to Gary Miller, Editor of the *Bolton Chronicle* (2 September 1982), Cllr Peter Johnston wrote "I protest – it wasn't Terry Lewis who thought up 'Biggles' for Cllr Brian Iddon, it was me. I don't mind Lewis pinching my best lines, and anyway he does it regularly. But I'm f.......d if he's claiming credit for writing them as well. One of these days I'll think one up for him."

They must have got very confused one evening in the Moss Rose public house in Kearsley, where they were boozing partners in those days. Colleagues who met there were nicknamed 'the Moss Rose tendency' in the Bolton District Labour Party. We already called Terry 'Nobby Stiles', after the MUFC footballer, Norbert Peter Stiles, who he was the spitting image of. Others called him 'the Sweeney'.

Cllr David Dingwall had earned the name 'The Godfather', Cllr Don Eastwood, who was always seen with David, was 'the Minder', Cllr Jack Foster, who had a passion for water policy, was 'Hydraulic Jack', and Cllr Eric Johnston, who was well-known for quoting from *Daily Mirror* news items at Council meetings, was 'Buzby'.

Gary Miller dared me to appear in the Council Chamber dressed as 'Biggles'. He was surprised when I took him up on

SCIENCE AND POLITICS: AN UNLIKELY MIXTURE

Left: 'Biggles'; picture taken at Barton Aerodrome (see *Bolton Chronicle* dated 19 August 1982).

Below: With Cllr Terry Lewis raising money for charity in Victoria Square, Bolton (pictures of this event, though not this one, appeared in the *Bolton Evening News* on 27 November 1982).

his offer. A flying helmet and suit and the obligatory white silk scarf were 'borrowed' from the Army Surplus Store on Bradshawgate, and Biggles appeared in the Council Chamber (see *Bolton Evening News* dated 12 August 1982). I was expecting the Mayor, Cllr John Hanscomb, to throw me out but he didn't. Most people thought I livened up the proceedings.

Part of the 'deal' with Gary Miller was to accompany him to Barton Aerodrome to pose for a photograph in front of an appropriate light aeroplane, which I did, and the photograph appeared in the *Bolton Chronicle* to accompany the story. I was offered a free flight for my troubles. I asked Gary if he had ever flown and he hadn't, so I offered him the chance to take a flight in the two-seat aeroplane instead of me. When he came down with a green face I understood why he had never flown before. That's what I call justice!

On 8 March 1983 during a debate in Bolton MB Council Chamber, which led to a ban on hunting mammals with dogs on land in council ownership, Cllr Martin Donaghy produced a stuffed fox, borrowed from Bolton Museum. The Conservative opposition accused Labour Party members of receiving a bribe in the form of a donation of £80,000 to our central funds from the League Against Cruel Sports. The same argument was deployed more than ten years later when Michael Foster's Bill to ban hunting mammals with dogs was presented to Parliament (see Chapter 7).

Martin Donaghy, a deeply religious Roman Catholic, has been known to visit his councillor colleagues in hospital wearing the dress of a Bishop – last rites and all that. It's when he takes out his tape measure that the sick colleagues get really worried!

In 1983, Parliamentary boundary changes gave Bolton three Parliamentary constituencies, and selection procedures were put in place to choose the three Prospective

Parliamentary Candidates (PPCs). The safest of these seats by far was the new Bolton South East (SE) constituency, and the front runners in the contest were David Young (Member of Parliament for Bolton East), Ann Taylor (Member of Parliament for Bolton West), and Cllr Terry Lewis (Deputy Leader of Bolton MB Council), who was also the PPC for the disappearing Farnworth Parliamentary constituency (Labour-Co-operative Member of Parliament John Roper defected to the SDP on 2 March 1981).

Hours before the selection conference, which was held in the Co-operative Hall in Bow Street on 12 April 1983, Terry Lewis announced that he was withdrawing his candidacy for the Bolton South East seat. He heard that John Evans, who was a contender for the new Worsley seat, had been selected as the PPC for St Helens North, which made Terry a front runner for the Worsley seat, and he became the Worsley Labour PPC.

It was a difficult selection process in the Bolton SE constituency but David Young, who had successfully courted the trade unions (he was a member of the Transport and General Workers Union, the TGWU), beat Ann Taylor. One of Ann Taylor's supporters, a NUPE member, hung on as long as he could but had to leave to play in a darts match before the final ballot. In the first ballot the vote was evenly split – 42 votes for David Young and 42 votes for Ann Taylor. In the second ballot David Young secured the nomination by three votes – 43 to 40.

Michael Foot attended a rally in Bolton on 27 May 1983 as Leader of the Labour Party. He had visited Bolton previously, on 11 December 1981. Gerald Kaufman (Member of Parliament for Manchester Gorton) described the 1983 election manifesto as "the longest suicide note in history". The Labour Party suffered one of its worst-ever defeats.

Following David's re-election to Parliament, Ann Taylor sought another seat, and became the Member of Parliament for Dewsbury at the 1987 General Election. She served until 2005 when she was given a peerage. Some local activists would not support Ann because she had won a scholarship to Bolton School, today an independent school endowed by the Leverhulme Trust. Then it was a Direct Grant Grammar School. On 7 April 1983 the *Bolton Chronicle* reported: "The 'middle class' socialism of the former Bolton School girl isn't going down well with down-to-earth voters".

David Young's wife, Grace, was his tower of strength. She was well loved by all who knew her. Unlike David, who could be rather gruff with people, Grace had a very pleasant manner. She was well known, both in Bolton and in Westminster, for wearing knitted woollen 'tea-cosy' hats. Tragically, she suffered a serious stroke in 1989 and was confined to the Bolton General Hospital (Townleys) until 25 June 1992, when she died after a long illness.

In the late 1970s and early 1980s, student unions at universities throughout the country were naming buildings and rooms within buildings after Nelson Mandela, leader of the African National Congress (ANC) Party who was incarcerated on Robben Island, off Capetown, South Africa. In Britain members of the Labour Party campaigned strongly against apartheid, whilst many members of the Conservative Party saw ANC members as terrorists, and would not support their freedom struggle.

I decided that it would be a good idea if the Bolton Council for Community Relations (BCCR) had a cricket trophy to

With Ann Taylor MP at Rumworth Labour Club, Bolton (May 1996).

Vince Simpson presents the Nelson Mandela Cricket Trophy to Little Lever Secondary School (Margaret Watt is holding the trophy).

present in honour of Nelson Mandela. I provided the money anonymously and Margaret Watt, a silversmith and jewellery designer who lived in Heaton, made a magnificent trophy. It was in the form of an arm, black on one side and white on the other (ebony and silver), delivering a cricket ball.

Vince Simpson, chairman of BCCR, presented it to Little Lever School, when they won the first cricket tournament organised by BCCR, in October 1983. I was very disappointed by BCCR, who thereafter kept the trophy in a drawer for many years. I don't know where it ended up after I complained to them that it wasn't being used for the purpose intended and an attempt to recover it in 2015 failed.

I was a local authority-appointed member of BCCR at the time (serving from 1981 to 1984). At one meeting Vince Simpson announced that the anonymous donor had suggested that the trophy should be named after Nelson Mandela, which brought loud objections from Conservative Cllrs Ernie Crook and Bert O'Neill. That was typical of what the right thought of Mandela at that time. Mandela was released from prison on 11 February 1990.

Vincent Louis Constantine Simpson came to Britain in 1944 as a graduate electrical engineer to enrol in the RAF, in which he rose to the rank of sergeant. He spent most of his working life in industry, where he took a keen interest in the work of the engineering unions. I first met him in 1972 at a Tonge Branch Labour Party meeting at Tonge Ward Labour Club.

Vince joined the Bolton Commonwealth Friendship Council, which held its inaugural meeting on 13 December 1965 during the UN's International Co-operation Year; Labour Home Office Minister Maurice Foley (Member of

Parliament for West Bromwich) attended its first meeting. Bolton was the second town in Britain to establish such an organisation. Cllr Frank White and Campbell Benjamin, who later became Bolton's first black Mayor, were founder members. In 1968, it became the Bolton Council for Community Relations (BCCR), established to improve community relations in Bolton. Vince was chairmen of BCCR from 1976 until August 1986, and retired from this organisation in 1992 (it became the Bolton Racial Equality Council – BREC at its AGM on 18 June 1990).

Vince also served as a Justice of the Peace – appointed in 1979 as Bolton's first black magistrate – and was a member of several school governing bodies. His wife Phyllis died in 1980. They had three girls, Sylvia, Maria, and Cynthia (she tragically died of cancer on 23 June 1994 at a very young age), who I thought was a spitting image of Motown singer Diana Ross, and one boy. Young 'Vinny' Simpson was a fireman who rose through the ranks to become Station Commander of the Greater Manchester Fire and Rescue Service in Bolton at Moor Lane Fire Station, a job from which he retired a few years ago.

In the early 1980s, the Conservative Government introduced Compulsory Competitive Tendering (CCT) for Direct Labour Organisations (DLOs), such as the Bolton Housing DLO (HDLO). In April 1984, the Housing Committee prepared a detailed questionnaire which was sent out to companies who were considering tendering for council house repair and maintenance contracts. Our Conservative opposition objected to the wording of this document, which was a sign of things to come.

The longest running miners' strike in my lifetime was

underway from 1984 to 1985. At the height of the strike, the SPD in Paderborn sent a delegation, led by German TUC colleague Cllr Bernard Hollenbeck and Cllr Gunter Bitterberg, a key figure in the Bolton-SPD Paderborn town-twinning link, to bring a vanload of parcels sent by Paderborn families to the families of striking miners who lived in Bolton. Sid Vincent, the NW miners' leader, and representatives of the Bolton District Labour Party, including me, received this delegation at the Miners' Hall in Bridgeman Place (see *Bolton Evening News* dated 12 December 1984). I believe that Jim Sherrington still possesses the video recording that was made of that visit.

After his defeat in 1983 in the Bury North seat, Frank White served as an 'agony uncle' on the BBCs *Breakfast Time* show in 1985. He was shortlisted for the safe Labour seat of Eccles, where Joan Lestor was selected on 29 April 1985; she won the seat in 1987. On 27 July 1985, he was selected as the PPC for the Bolton North East seat from a shortlist of Ann Taylor, Frank and Cllr Lindsay Sutton, Leader of the Labour Group on Blackpool Council. He failed to unseat Conservative Member of Parliament Peter Thurnham at the 1987 General Election.

Frank White has always been one of the most reliable elected members that Bolton has ever seen. He was appointed a JP in 1968 at the age of 28 (Bolton's youngest ever magistrate) and, when he retired at the age of 70 in November 2009, he was the longest-serving magistrate in the country, with 41 years' service. Frank was first elected to Bolton County Borough Council for Tonge Ward in 1963 and served until 1974, when he was defeated by a Conservative candidate. Eileen and I (and, previously, my first wife Merrilyn) and

Frank and his wife, also called Eileen, have been friends since I came to Bolton in 1972.

When I became chairman of the Housing Committee in May 1986 I was given access to a file containing the complaints that the department received from elected members. Frank, who had been re-elected to the Council in 1986, wrote in to complain about a goat causing a problem on one of his housing estates. He received a letter from a Principal Housing Assistant that contained the following paragraph:

"My Area Manager has now visited the tenant concerned and elicited an assurance that the animal will be removed responsibly. I should add perhaps that the tenant was aware of one incident only when the goat strayed into Mrs T's garden, and we have received no complaints from any other tenants. Indeed, it appears that several tenants in Tintern Avenue welcomed a controlled visit from the goat as a means of keeping the grass down!"

The letter was signed by Gareth Evans, who became the Manager of Age Concern in Bolton.

After the 1986 May local elections I decided that the time was right to challenge Peter Johnston's chairmanship of the Housing Committee again. Bolton's Housing Direct Labour Organisation (HDLO) lost £500,000 in its first year (1984-1985) under Compulsory Competitive Tendering (CCT) rules, and rents were raised for a second time in July 1985 to meet this loss. Many loss-making HDLOs were forced to close at that time, so the Conservative Group called for Peter's resignation in January 1986. On 14 May 1986 the Labour Group elected me as chairman of the committee and Cllr

Laurie Williamson as its vice-chairman. Peter had failed to get to grips with the HDLO losses and there were fears that another loss would be announced later in 1986, which turned out to be the case when the results were announced in November 1986. I was determined to save the HDLO.

I have to give a lot of credit to Peter, who was one of Bolton's most able local politicians. After I succeeded him he bore no grudges, at least none that he made obvious. We remained good friends and he moved on to other political interests within the Council. He was active in the Labour Party in Bolton almost until the day he died.[2]

Peter believed in low council house rents – that was the way to win elections, he thought – but it was clear to me that more money would have to be raised for their repair and maintenance. Most of our council houses were extremely cold and damp, with single-glazed windows and poor heating systems. Our estates were an environmental disaster; the Conservative administration made tenants responsible for their own fencing repairs and replacement. Peter wasn't too keen either on the proposal that we should consult tenants more about their needs.

In the private sector it was clear that we could not continue to clear properties and that we had to turn our attention to the refurbishment of those that could be saved as a priority. We had discussed all this at successive Housing Working Parties, but Peter had taken little notice.

The day after my appointment as chairman of the Housing Committee I agreed to have a long conversation with the Director of Housing, John Roe.[3] "I don't suppose there are going to be major changes in policy, are there?" asked John. How wrong he was! After each Annual Policy Conference I prepared a list of our 20 priority policies, and I gave my first list to John Roe. He looked startled.

I placed homelessness at the top of our agenda, but another high priority was to save the HDLO. It was training about 42 apprentices at that time, in all the construction trades. In fact, we were probably the only organisation in Bolton with anywhere near that number of apprentices. John Roe suggested that they were a burden on the HDLO; I disagreed. I had had many conversations with the men and women who worked for the HDLO, both in offices and 'on the tools'. We met in pubs all over Bolton. By the time I took over as chairman of the Housing Committee I believed that I knew what the main problems were.

My first suggestion was that the HDLO was poorly managed, which surprised John Roe because the Building Services Manager had only been in post for three years. I suggested what John should do and, in November 1986, we were looking for another Building Services Manager.

(Left to right) Cllr Peter Johnston, John Roe (Director of Housing), Cllr Kevan Hornby, and me.

The HDLO showed a loss of £328,000 in its second year (1985-1986) under CCT rules. When we asked other council departments to allow the HDLO to tender for work the Conservative opposition accused us of featherbedding them. In actual fact it would have cost a lot more than the reported losses to make the whole HDLO workforce redundant and, in any case, the HDLO was saving council house tenants £1 million per annum by comparison with the next lowest tender.

In February and March 1987, the opposition parties blasted the Labour Group for allowing a tender to refurbish outhouses on the Breightmet Hall estate to be given to the HDLO which was not the lowest tender (a difference of only £82). Both Tory Members of Parliament for Bolton, Peter Thurnham and Tom Sackville, were by this time engaged in a direct assault on the HDLO. A high-level meeting was held in the Chief Executive's (Peter Bounds') office with the Leader of the Council, Cllr Bob Howarth, present along with me, several senior Council colleagues and John Roe and his Assistant Director of Housing, George Caswell, who had joined the Housing Department from Dundee City Council in the autumn of 1983.

Bob's initial position was that I had put the Council deeper in an already deep hole. I disagreed. He asked me what I proposed should happen next and I recommended that our new Assistant Director, George Caswell, be seconded for at least six months to the HDLO, and that he and I should work closely together to resolve our difficulties. That was one of the best decisions I ever made. George was brilliant; with his help the HDLO was taken back into profit so that we could compete on the unlevel playing field of CCT.

The next question we had to resolve was how Bolton could

attract another Building Services Manager in view of our severe difficulties. I recommended that some carrots be attached to the advertisement for the post, such as a reasonable salary and use of a car provided by the 'firm'. Initially, there was a hostile reaction to my proposal, especially from the officers present – they thought that was setting a 'dangerous precedent' – but all was agreed and we proceeded to apppoint Ian Brown as the new HDLO Operations Manager.

As I saw it, there were two serious problems to sort out. First, there was little or no stock control at the HDLO main depot in Thynne Street. As a result, I discovered, it was only too easy for men to drop materials off that got 'lost'. Deliveries too far in advance of a job being done meant that the delivered materials were often stolen or spoiled by the weather. I was assured too by some of the HDLO workmen that a small number of men were doing 'foreigners' at the weekend. A computerised stock control system was essential, and one was introduced.

The second problem was that the HDLO main depot in Thynne Street was completely inadequate for a modern business. Wagons went into the loading bay but the only way out was backwards, which meant other delivery wagons waited in the yard until the one, or two at the most, in the bay had been loaded. Our logistics were hopeless. George had the macro-view, as I saw it. I left it to him to micromanage the situation; obviously some reorganisation was inevitable. George reduced the white collar workforce by 20 jobs.

George Caswell agreed with me that we would try to keep as many apprentices in training as possible. Some of the smaller depots dotted around the town inevitably closed. One trade where profitability had been a problem for some time was the painting trade; we agreed that we would run down our painting workforce.

On 19 November 1986 a Management Committee was set up for the HDLO under the chairmanship of Cllr Ken MacIvor, which reported directly to the Management and Finance Committee and indirectly to the Housing Committee. Ken had been a leading union official with the GMB and we knew that his views and political leadership would be respected by the workforce. The culture at the HDLO had to change from one of a job for life to a more business-like attitude. Ken MacIvor was succeeded in this post by Cllr Donald Grime, who worked in the construction trade. He also did an excellent job for us.

Throughout our difficulties with the HDLO we kept the unions completely informed; I have nothing but praise for the shop stewards at Thynne Street, Ken Coward and his successor John Story; they were a bridge between us and the workforce. They were fair, but tough when they needed to be in favour of their workforce.

John Roe retired as Director of Housing on 31 September 1988[3] and was replaced by George Caswell. Some months later George asked me to meet him privately with the newly-appointed Building Services Manager, Tom Quayle. I believe we met in the Cattle Market public house on Thynne Street. George did a lot of his 'business' out of hours in pubs, either the Howcroft public house, off Vernon Street or the Ainsworth Arms on Halliwell Road. He proposed that we should buy a speculative office development on Adelaide Street that Lantor had built on their land but were unable to sell.

I knew that this office block had been on sale for about

eighteen months, with an initial asking price of £1.5 million. I was stunned, until George said he thought we could buy it for about £750,000. An added attraction was an adjacent piece of land which would be ideal to build a new HDLO headquarters. To cut a long story short, the deal was sealed, underpinned, of course, by a capital income from the sale of all our land and property at Thynne Street. By 1995 the HDLO had moved into their new premises in Adelaide Street, which cost an additional £800,000.

When I was elected chairman of the Housing Committee one of our top priorities was to make all our 23,000 plus council homes warm and draughtproof. In 1986, a lot of council houses only had a solid fuel-burning fireplace, often with a back-boiler to provide hot water. Condensation collected on the single-glazed windows and ran down onto the window sills continuously in damp weather, and especially in the winter months. Therefore, we decided in November 1991 to begin a major programme to fit uPVC double glazed window frames and modular gas-fired heaters in as many rooms of our houses as possible (some tenants could not afford to run full central heating systems).

I had been in consultation with the small number of organisations that represented tenants as well as with individual tenants. Providing warmth was their top priority. They also wanted to improve the look of their estates (fencing – the 'f' word as it became known – was a major headache) and improve the quality of the repair and maintenance (R&M) service. This needed money which was not going to be forthcoming from the Conservative Government. I pointed out to them that Bolton's rents were some of the lowest in Greater Manchester, and I proposed that we add another £1 a week to them at the next opportunity. In addition, I promised that if they agreed, this money would be ring-fenced to improve the R&M service and to improve their homes. That was one of the best decisions we ever made.

I was very keen too to improve the quality of the work that contractors were delivering on our estates. I knew that some painting contractors were painting wood that had not been treated for years without applying an undercoat first. They even painted over rotten woodwork without following the specification to replace it. I put enormous pressure on our inspectors to get tough with contractors like that. "It's only a council house" was an attitude that didn't belong in our Housing Department. If I wouldn't put up with it, why should our tenants suffer? That was my attitude. Some companies in the private sector adopted a very poor attitude towards the work they did for the public sector.

I spent hours at the weekends 'inspecting' a lot of the work being carried out on our estates myself, and I asked my political colleagues to keep an eye on work being executed on estates in their wards. Some of the contractors who won the tenders to fit uPVC window frames were excellent; others caused us real problems. External beading on some of the frames allowed the windows to be removed easily by burglars (see *Bolton Evening News*, 3 July 1987), using spades for example. We decided in November 1991 that it would be a lot cheaper and give the customer a much better product if we started to manufacture our own uPVC window frames to a high specification. Twenty-five jobs were created at the HDLO headquarters at Adelaide Street and for an investment of £860,000, which was quickly returned, we set up our own manufacturing unit which was officially opened in April 1995.

We were not popular with the 'trade'.

On 17 April 1986, Cllr David Dingwall died in Bolton General Hospital (Townleys) after a short illness, aged 67. For those of us who knew him this came as no surprise. He had had trouble with his stomach for several months and refused to slow his pace of work down. The respect in which he was held, across the political divides, was demonstrated when 700 people attended his funeral on 24 April 1986 in Victoria Hall, Bolton. We had lost one of our best politicians, and I lost a friend as well. Cllr Don Eastwood succeeded him as chairman of the Education Committee, Jim Sherrington succeeded him as a councillor in Central Ward on 8 August 1986; John Hartshorne had succeeded him as chairman of Bolton District Labour Party on 27 July 1984.

In June 1987, we announced that we would build the last Government-subsidised council homes, in Westhoughton; Tony Berry of the Houghton Weavers officially opened this development in May 1988, a sheltered scheme of 13 bungalows. In addition, 34 of our HDLO apprentices built four bungalows in Violet Avenue, Farnworth with the aid of the Council's Youth Training Scheme Managing Agency. These were handed over for occupation in March 1990.

George Caswell wanted to introduce a customer care policy in the Housing Department, but I agreed with the Leader of the Council that it would be better for the whole Council to go down this route. After a delay of about 12 months, we decided that the Housing Committee would go it alone. We recommended that our staff wear identification badges and that they be trained in customer care policies. At first the staff unions were resistant to the idea, which, looking back today, does seem strange. I held several meetings with our staff at which I explained how councillors worked. Staff wore name badges from 19 September 1987.

By the end of 1987 we were discussing the impending introduction of the Thatcher 'Poll Tax' (Community Charge), which eventually led to some of the worst demonstrations that the UK has seen in modern times.

The Conservative Member of Parliament for Bolton West, Tom Sackville, jumped on a popular bandwagon of the day and accused young women of getting pregnant in order to be allocated a council house.

Bolton MB Council invited me to attend a Buckingham Palace Garden Party on 23 July 1987; I took Sally with me. I had attended my first Buckingham Palace Garden Party, with my first wife Merrilyn as a guest, from the University of Salford a few years earlier.

In February 1988 Bolton NE Constituency Labour Party presented Keith and Helene Partington with a carriage clock to thank them for hosting our meetings at the Spread Eagle (off Folds Road) and Falcon (at the junction of Kay Street and Turton Street) public houses. Both pubs were demolished, the latter to make way for extension of the A666 (St Peter's Way) through Kay Street to the junction of Blackburn Road and Halliwell Road. Keith and Helene moved for the second time to the Bowling Green public house on Blackburn Road and their regulars, me included, stayed with them.

In March 1988, Gary Titley was selected to succeed Barbara Castle MEP in the Greater Manchester West European constituency, and was subsequently elected. Former Bury Housing Committee chairman David Crausby was nominated for this position by the Bolton NE Constituency Labour Party.

On 11 October 1988, Bolton celebrated the 150th Anniversary of its Chartered Borough Status, when Cllr Brian Allanson was the Mayor.

Together with the chairmen of the Housing Committee's sub-committees I held weekly briefing meetings with John Roe and his senior officers, and I continued these with George Caswell on Monday afternoons. We sorted out a lot of delegated matters without the need for a committee agenda item, and agreed the committee agendas at these meetings. We also discussed our policy ideas with the officers. George told me later that one of his dislikes about my chairmanship was receiving another list of 20 policy priorities after each of our Annual Policy Conferences.

Some of these sessions were robust, to say the least; we often agreed to disagree. On at least two occasions my best friend and colleague Cllr Jim Alker walked out on us. He always came back after he had calmed down. Jim had worked down pits most of his life and his language could be ripe at times – I called it 'pit talk'. It wasn't always easy chairing the Housing Committee; each member of the committee naturally pursued the interests of their own constituents.

One of the most memorable occasions was when Cllr Betty McCracken, one of my sub-committee chairs at the time, who came from Glasgow, intervened at one of these sessions and asked me to ask George, who came from Dundee, to slow down his speech so that she could understand him. What chance did we mere English mortals have of understanding him if one Scot could not understand another?

The Housing Act 1988 gave council house tenants the right to choose an alternative landlord to the Council. In 1989 we organised 14 public meetings across the Borough to seek tenants' views on this proposal, beginning on 4 January 1989. I spoke at all these meetings, Cllr John Walsh spoke at all but one (Cllr John Hanscomb stood in for him) and Albert Nicholls, chairman of the Bolton Affiliation of Tenants' Associations (BATA) spoke at all of them. All these meetings were packed with tenants wanting to voice their opinions. There was no support for the idea of stock transfer at that time.

Sadly, the chain-smoking Albert Nicholls, who was appointed on 6 July 1985 as the first chairman of the Bolton Association of Tenants' Associations (BATA) (later it became BATRA – the 'R' for residents), died in October 1993, aged 74. He was succeeded by Joe Sydall, then Richard Smallman, who has been the longest-serving chairman of BATRA to date. I was always very keen to foster the formation of tenants' and residents' associations. My view was that they could add weight to my arguments for improvements in the service that was delivered to them, and they did and still perform the same function today. I think there were only five of these organisations when I was elected as chairman of the Housing Committee; when I resigned there were over 40. We even set up a network of Tenant Liaison Officers to oversee their work and to bring other associations into existence.

My Labour colleagues were not too keen on developing what they initially saw as organisations that could be used for political purposes. I believed that the tenants had the common sense to prevent that happening. When I proposed that we set up five area forums as umbrella organisations for the individual tenants' associations in their area, I met with considerable opposition within the Labour Group. This idea had come originally from the officers, and George Caswell was extremely frustrated when I told him that I could not deliver the policy there and then. I worked hard over the course of a year to persuade Labour Party members that this was a step worth taking.

I was relieved when, in September 1988, it was announced that the HDLO had made a profit of £600,000. Three successive losses would have meant its closure. We finally closed the painting department, with the loss of 30 jobs. We won all five of the annual tenders that the HDLO tendered for under CCT rules. We calculated that each CCT exercise cost £500,000, or an additional 50p per week on every council house rent.

On 22 January 1988, pressure from the Conservative opposition and Bolton's two Tory Members of Parliament forced Bolton's HDLO to explain its tendering procedures for the housing repair and maintenance contracts to the Secretary of State for the Environment, Michael Howard. Rather than let one large contract, which ruled out a lot of smaller firms from engaging in the tendering process, they wanted the HDLO to tender several smaller contracts, an exercise which would have been even more costly. On 1 July 1988 Michael Howard ruled that Bolton's HDLO had tendered its contracts correctly.

In October 1989, Cllr Frank White announced that he would stand down at the next May local elections. In January 1990, it became clear that he was making a serious attempt to return to Parliament, when he was shortlisted for the Bury South seat along with David Bookbinder, the Leader of Derbyshire County Council, Ivan Lewis and Helen Jones who later became the Member of Parliament for Warrington North. Ivan Lewis was selected and won the seat for Labour at the

1997 General Election. Frank returned to the Council in the May local elections of 1994.

By 15 December 1987, the figure for homeless people in Bolton was recorded as 1,299. Abolition of fair rents in the private sector had not helped. The Housing Act 1988 resulted in private sector rent levels no longer being set by Rent Officers and in the introduction of shorthold tenancies and Mrs Thatcher's popular Right-to-Buy policy. We were forced to sell council homes at a discounted valuation and the money was not made available to rebuild them (Bolton's Conservative-controlled Council started to sell council houses in 1974).

Single homeless men were in the worst position; the only major provision for them in Bolton was a new Salvation Army Hostel in Duke Street which opened in December 1987. In the early 1980s the Government proposed to close the 82-bed resettlement unit for single men in Sharpe Street, Walkden, to which many single homeless men from Bolton and Wigan were referred. To replace this accommodation the Peterloo Housing Association opened accommodation for 14 single homeless men on Chorley Old Road and another home on Manchester Road, Bolton. Later, they got into financial difficulties, but the properties were transferred to another Housing Association.

In 1990 we held a seminar on homelessness and, arising from that, it was proposed that a charity be set up, the Bolton Accommodation Project (BAP), to secure accommodation for homeless single people. The project was launched on 25 March 1992 by actress Carmen Silvera (café owner René's wife Edith in the memorable TV comedy series *'Allo 'Allo!*).

Despite initial opposition beginning in 1988, 24 Albert Road, a large house that the Council used during World War II to rehouse people whose houses had been destroyed by bombing, was opened in 1989 as accommodation for lonely people by Richard Carr-Gomm. It took a public meeting and a visit by Richard Carr-Gomm to persuade the residents of Albert Road in Heaton to accept our plan.

The idea of Bolton Bond Board was given to me in a chance conversation that I had with a surgeon who knew of similar schemes in Australia. Homeless people could not access private sector accommodation because they were unable to supply landlords with rent up-front or the 'bond' required to cover any damage to the property or its contents. On 1 October 1992, the Bolton Accommodation Project (BAP) convened a meeting at which we agreed to launch the Bolton Bond Board as a charity. It was launched on 15 April 1993 with start-up money provided by Bolton MB Council. Both BAP and the Bond Board have survived.

In addition, we strongly supported Fortalice (then based in Castle Street), a charity formed in Bolton to help women who were the victims of domestic violence, and helped Housing Associations to provide accommodation for young mums and their babies in Eldon Street, Tonge Moor, and in Argyle House, off Brownlow Way. We also supported a similar venture by the Catholic Children's Rescue Society, which opened accommodation for single pregnant and homeless young women on Radcliffe Road.[4]

One venture that failed to get off the ground, however, was a proposal to open a half-way house for recovering drug addicts in Darley Street, Farnworth. This resulted in a public meeting in Farnworth Town Hall in January 1995. The hall was packed with very angry people and I thought I might have to make a quick escape *via* the back door. In the end we were forced by public opinion to drop this proposal. There was little sympathy for those addicted to illegal drugs at that time.

I presented George Caswell, the Director of Housing, with the idea of introducing a telephone service for vulnerable people. After consultation with the Social Services Committee and the discovery by George that the Engineering Department had £1 million of unspent capital funds, George did a deal and bought so many telephones that their storage became a real problem. He assured me that they were all used.

On 22 February 1990, we announced the concept of Careline, telephones for vulnerable people, mainly the elderly. Careline was launched during National Housing Week in June 1990 and became active on 27 October 1990. It was launched officially on 6 June 1991 by the Mayor, Cllr Gerry Riley, at Skagen Court, and is still going strong today.

During National Housing Week we organised a 'Sleep Out' on the Town Hall steps. I was joined by the Directors of Social Services and Housing, Marion Canvin and George Caswell, as well as by broadcaster Alan Beswick, *Bolton Metro News* reporter Karen Morley, and my wife Eileen among others. We collected over £1,000 for homeless people. The photograph of me sleeping in a cardboard box that night haunted me for several years after that event.

One month later we launched the Johnson Fold Credit Union, the first in Bolton. Today, Bolton has a borough-wide credit union called 'Hoot' (previously Quids In).

I had been quite keen to decentralise housing management to the estates throughout Bolton, and this got under way in the 1990s (see *Bolton Evening News* dated 6 June 1991). We stopped door-to-door collections of rents in 1993; several attacks had occurred on our rent collectors. This was a service that I knew tenants missed, and an estate office gave tenants back a facility to pay their rent locally again. In addition, tenants were able to report and chase up repairs and get housing advice from our officers on site.

With the Right-to-Buy policy of Margaret Thatcher resulting in the sale of thousands of our council properties (between 1979 and 1997 Bolton lost over 3,000 homes), often the best quality ones on the more desirable estates, and the absence of further council house building to replace those lost, as well as an expanding population and demographic changes (more people choosing to live alone and a growing elderly population) the Housing Waiting List started to rise significantly. I knew we needed to take some action to relieve the pressure.

In a magazine article I noticed that Leeds City Council had introduced an innovative partnership with some of the Housing Associations with which they were working at the time, and I showed this article to George Caswell at one of our weekly briefing sessions in 1991. Within a matter of weeks George's Deputy Hilary Eastham had consulted with the leading Housing Associations that Bolton's Housing Committee were working with, and had come up with a much better scheme. In April 1992, Bolton Community Homes was launched. It involved Bolton Council providing 50 acres of land to five Housing Associations at nil cost to them (actually valued at £8 million) in return for the Housing Associations providing 1,400 low-cost homes for rent along with another 200 houses for sale, at a total cost of £60 million.

The Housing Associations shared resources, such as architects, and homes were delivered £10,000 cheaper than anywhere else in the region, which meant that 1,700 homes were delivered rather than the 1,400 initially planned. We had persuaded all the Housing Associations working with us in Bolton to allocate tenancies from a joint Housing Waiting List. Prior to this agreement those looking to rent a house in the public sector had to make several independent applications.

The Housing Waiting List had risen from 5,000 applicants in 1986 to 8,500 before these houses were ready for occupation. This scheme, which exists today, brought the Housing Waiting List down again to a manageable figure.

Under my chairmanship and the directorship of George Caswell the Housing Committee redeveloped the Wilkinson Gardens, School Hill, East Ward and Rose Hill areas of Bolton in partnership with private sector companies. We also ceased clearing thousands of properties a year and developed instead zoned area refurbishment schemes in the private sector by declaring several major Housing Action Areas.

Until the 1990s one of the major complaints to officers and councillors alike in Bolton was about various problems with neighbours. On council estates this got worse when the Right-to-Buy policy was introduced and the management of many former council homes passed out of local authority control. In 1991 I had a conversation about this over lunch with John Percy, one of our librarians at the University of Salford. Quite by chance I learned that John's brother was involved in a privately-run mediation service in the south of England.

This gave me the idea of setting up Britain's first local authority mediation service to deal with disputes between neighbours, whether living in a council property or a privately-owned property. Plans to launch the Bolton Neighbour Dispute Service were announced in January 1992, and we appointed a very committed woman, Sue Parry, to start up the service for us. Sue remained dedicated to this service for many years. We chose to trial the idea in an area of Deane/Daubhill, with 5,000 properties.

The first 12 voluntary mediators were trained, and the pilot scheme proved to be a success, so we started to roll out the project across the Borough. The number of complaints that officers and councillors received dropped as the general public became more aware of the scheme. It became a model for the rest of the country and I became very proud of our achievement.

Out of the Bolton Neighbour Dispute Service spun out the idea of dealing with bullying in schools through mediation, and the Bully Free Zone concept was born in 1995. I take no credit for that idea.

In my capacity as chairman of the Housing Committee I felt the burden of responsibility heavy on my shoulders, particularly when we made serious errors or when somebody died. In the winter of 1991-1992 a contractor was refurbishing properties at Rostherne Gardens when 58-year-old Derek Lomax died of carbon monoxide poisoning following renovation of his property.

Contractors were fitting uPVC double glazed window frames and insulation materials, as well as ensuring that the heating systems were adequate in each property. In these properties, which had traditional chimneys, a chimney sweep cleaned all the chimneys. An investigation concluded that a combination of a reduced air flow through the property due to the refurbishment work and dislodged brickwork in the chimney had caused carbon monoxide to leak into Derek's lounge from a gas appliance newly fitted in his fireplace. We launched a major gas safety programme as a result of this tragedy.

The main contractor, who faced prosecution on 5 October 1992, went into liquidation; there was no prosecution and no recovery of our losses. In May 1993, Bolton Council was fined £20,000, with over £5,000 costs awarded against it, as a result of this tragedy. We carried the can for the serious mistake of a private contractor, who had escaped responsibility for the incident, despite the fact that the firm had carried out £1 million of work in Bolton alone.

In July 1992, Ian Foster, a security guard, was collecting the day's takings, mainly rent payments, from our housing office in Farnworth Town Hall, when he was shot dead on the steps at the front of the Town Hall. Tragically, Ian recognised one of the two men involved in the incident; they had been at school together. Ian was the son of my friend and colleague Cllr Jack Foster and his wife Joyce. Jack was chairman of the Planning Committee. Several days later the police received a report that the gun used in the shooting had been placed down a grid at our accommodation for homeless people at Clare Court. Its recovery and other evidence led to the arrest of the two men responsible for this murder.

When I was elected to Parliament in 1997 Jack and Joyce Foster asked me to campaign for stricter legislation to be introduced on the sale and ownership of handguns, and I did so. However, the Dunblane shootings caused the whole nation to make this same demand, and the Labour Government brought in new legislation as a result.

The Bolton City Challenge Action Plan was signed on 24 March 1993 by Heritage Minister Robert Key MP, Leader of the Council Cllr Bob Howarth, also chairman of the City Challenge Company Board, vice-chairman of the Company

Board Ros Warburton, Lois Patel, a Community Director on the Company Board, and Gerry Fitzhenry, Chief Executive of the Company. This five-year programme provided £37.5 million to regenerate Bolton's chosen City Challenge Area, which included large parts of Halliwell and Central Wards to the north of the Borough. As chairman of the Housing Committee I served as a director on the City Challenge Board because a considerable amount of the City Challenge investment was in housing. Gerry Fitzhenry helped Bolton MB Council make its bid for City Challenge money then he was appointed in December 1992 as Chief Executive of the Board.

Towards the end of 1994 we had considered the possibility of reducing crime on the Mancroft Avenue estate by installing CCTV cameras across the estate, at an estimated cost of £250,000. As chairman of the Housing Committee I was opposed to this proposal, but I found myself in a minority. I was supported by a petition from some residents as well as by David Young (Member of Parliament for Bolton SE). On 28 February 1995, it was announced that, of 192 of the 229 residents who were entitled to vote, only 12% had voted against, so the scheme proceeded. I was concerned that a code of practice be introduced that ensured the privacy of tenants in their own homes and gardens (see *Bolton Evening News* dated 11 January 1995).

The above is not an exhaustive list of our achievements between 1986 and 1996. Amongst our many other achievements were being awarded the Crystal Mark Award by the Plain English Society in July 1995 for our new Tenancy Agreement and the introduction (in April 1995) of a contents insurance scheme for our tenants, which saved money for those willing to participate. Under continuous fire from the

Conservative Little Lever councillors we refurbished and extended the number of 'pitches' at the Hall Lane travellers' site at a cost of over half a million pounds. We also refurbished homeless accommodation in Farnworth and agreed on 7 February 1989 to name the site Clare Court in memory of the late Cllr Derek Clare, who was a member of the Housing Committee. He also worked for the HDLO.

I have always considered that the period 1986-1996, when I was chairman of Bolton MB Council's Housing Committee, was the most productive of my political career. I had the strong support of some excellent political colleagues as well as some outstanding officers. Whilst George Caswell and I disagreed quite often on how to take housing policy forward, the chemistry between us worked. He was an outstanding officer who could motivate his staff to give their best. He 'flattened' the management structure in the Housing Department, which resulted in better communications from top to bottom of the structure. It also saved money by taking out layers of management.

All of us together built one of the best housing departments in Britain. The Government recognised this fact by awarding us the maximum of four stars for the service that we delivered to our customers, and that position was maintained until the houses were transferred into the ownership of Bolton at Home, a Registered Social Landlord. Our success allowed us to attract some excellent young officers when we advertised for staff, and success bred more success.

Other Housing Departments recognised our success and recruited our best officers. Neil Litherland became Housing Director in Camden in June 1991, Hilary Eastham became Director of Housing in Rochdale in 1995, Hugh Broadbent became Director of Housing in Oldham, also in 1995, Gordon Perry became Director of Housing in Kensington and Chelsea, and others achieved senior posts elsewhere.

During most of my ten years as chairman of the Housing Committee, and even before that, I had long debates, both in committees and at council meetings, with the Conservative spokesman on housing, Cllr John Walsh, who always defended his corner, even against the plain facts.

When I was first elected to Bolton MB Borough Council there were stories of long Council meetings, often filibustered by characters such as Brian O'Hara, who was a legend in the Bolton District Labour Party. The longest council meeting I ever attended was on Wednesday 28 January 1986, which lasted from 7.00 p.m. until 2.15 a.m. the following morning. No prizes for guessing the subject – housing! After that the Council passed a resolution that no council meetings could proceed beyond 10.00 p.m. without a change in Standing Orders being approved for one night only.

There were some good debates in Bolton's Council Chamber. Guy Harkin, a former President of the Oxford Union, was a fluent speaker. In one debate he called a motion from the Liberal Democrats to allow members of the public to ask questions at Council meetings 'a nutter's charter', which prompted a member of the Nutter family of Pendle (Alice Nutter, accused of being a witch, made their family name famous) to write to him to ask him not to use the Nutter family name in that way again.

Whenever any councillor asked Cllr Jack Foster, chairman of the Planning and Engineering Committee, a question, his response was eagerly awaited by all present. Jack had a unique sense of humour. When Cllr Cliff Scull complained that new

SCIENCE AND POLITICS: AN UNLIKELY MIXTURE

Visiting new developments at School Hill (left to right): Nick Moule, Cllr Campbell Benjamin, Mo Mangera, Nick Raynsford MP, me, Cllr Noel Spencer, Cllr Martin Donaghy and Cllr Anthony Connell – 2 June 1995.

Nick Raynsford MP at the HDLO with Ruth Kelly, David Crausby and me, before the 1997 General Election.

lamp posts had been installed in his ward and the old ones left standing in their place for several weeks Jack told him that this was a clear case of double standards and promised to investigate.

Despite our successes in Bolton under a Conservative Government, the facts were plain for all to see. The Government forced council house rents up to unaffordable levels, and all councils suffered massive rate (later 'Poll Tax', then Council Tax) rises, with huge rises in Housing Benefit and Council Tax bills that would have serious consequences for later Governments.

From council house rent arrears of a modest £170,000 in 1980 the figure had risen to over £1.25 million by the end of the decade. We broke through the £1 million barrier in February 1989, when 8,300 tenants were reported to be in arrears, almost double the figure of 4,200 that had been reported a year earlier. Controls on private sector rents were removed in addition.

Council house building was stopped by the Tories, and councils were forced to sell off the stock they had, which exacerbated the problem of homelessness. Mortgage interest rates hit 15.4% in February 1990 and repossessions of owner-occupied properties doubled in 12 months.

In Bolton we lost almost 80% of the Housing Investment Programme (HIP) allocation that we had received under the previous Labour Government, which also meant that we were unable to regenerate the private sector housing in the town. These houses were falling into a state of disrepair faster than we could improve them. Clearance of pre-1919 owner occupied properties more or less stopped too. In March 1992, we sent what the *Bolton Evening News* described as our

'Dossier of Shame' to show Environment Secretary Michael Heseltine just how bad the state of private sector housing was in some parts of our town.

We persuaded successive Government Housing Ministers to visit Bolton so that we could try to persuade them of our needs. Of all of them I had the greatest respect for Sir George Young; he was the longest-serving Conservative Housing Minister between 1979 and 1997. I remember George being taken, in June 1991, to a two-up, two-down mid-

Photographs from the 'Dossier of Shame' sent to Michael Heseltine.

John Hartshorne

terraced house in Sutcliffe Street that was undergoing refurbishment in a Housing Action Area. George is tall and he had to stoop to enter the property and, as he proceeded from the front room to the back downstairs room and into the back yard, I watched his face and concluded that he had never been in a house like that before. He was seriously amazed at how small the property was and by the condition that it was in prior to refurbishment.

If anything persuaded me to become a Prospective Parliamentary Candidate (PPC) it was a sense of feeling badly bruised by over a decade of a Tory Government. I wanted to go to Westminster to tell the Conservatives how much they had damaged our town. In particular I wanted to fight for more resources for housing.

During the time I was on the Housing Committee, and especially during the years 1986 to 1996, I worked very closely with John Hartshorne and his wife Elaine, both on housing policy and on health and social services policy. The three of us also served on the Community Health Council (CHC) in Bolton. Its first secretary, June Corner, was previously a journalist with the *Bolton Evening News*. She did a remarkable job for the CHC. The drop-in centre for mentally ill patients on St Georges Road stands as one of her memorials today.

In late 1993 and most of 1994 John and Elaine, and others, were trying to persuade me to stand as the PPC in the Bolton South East Parliamentary constituency. There was one problem; it already had a sitting Labour Member of Parliament – David Wright Young. I had worked with him since I came to Bolton in 1972 and had helped to get him elected in all his Parliamentary elections in the Bolton East seat before he won the Bolton South East seat in 1983, with the help of boundary changes. I had been chairman of the Bolton East Constituency Labour Party several times during that time.

From 1977 to 1979 David served as Parliamentary Private Secretary to Fred Mulley, Secretary of State for Defence. David campaigned for comprehensive education to be introduced in Bolton, and regularly pressed Ministers of both the Labour and Conservative Governments for better facilities to be provided at Bolton General Hospital (Townleys, which became the Royal Bolton Hospital on 21 October 1996), and he constantly pressed the Government about the high unemployment rates and factory closures that Bolton saw in the 1970s and 1980s, as the town was forced to reinvent itself.

But his main policy interest areas were defence and foreign affairs, for David Young was a constant traveller. He visited the Falkland Islands twice after the 1982 war, in the November of that year and again in November 1984, and was a passionate supporter for the continued British ownership of Gibraltar. David often visited countries in the Middle East. He opposed the introduction of television cameras in the House of Commons chamber. He served on the Employment Select Committee (1982-1997) and was chairman of the House of Commons Motoring Club.

There had been growing dissatisfaction with David in the constituency of Bolton East before he became the Member of Parliament for Bolton South East. He never opened an office in Bolton and it wasn't easy to contact him. Advice surgeries were run on a regular basis when he was first elected but irregularly towards the end of his career, and he relied on an older but loyal and likeable local councillor, Cllr Cliff Scull, to provide his constituents with a contact point for him. With growing minority populations in the town, particularly those families that had arrived from SE Asia (India and Pakistan in particular) to work in the textile industry, there was more demand to see a Member of Parliament.

Cllr Frank White mounted the first major challenge against him in 1989 in the selection of a candidate for the 1992 General Election but withdrew his challenge. There was still a lot of sympathy for David Young at that time because his wife Grace was seriously ill in hospital. She died on 25 June 1992. David Young survived until the General Election of 1997. Activists in Bolton were surprised that Frank didn't fight the new Bury North seat in 1987; he was loved and respected when he was the Member of Parliament for Bury North and Radcliffe. Frank made a bid too in October 1992 for the St Helens South seat, where Gerry Bermingham's popularity had taken a dip, but he survived.

The next selection of a PPC began in the Bolton South East seat in mid-1994 (the safest Labour seats are always dealt with first). The Labour Party annual conference in September 1987 decided that votes at selections and party conferences would be conducted on a 'one member, one vote' (OMOV) principal in future, which reduced the strength of the trade unions in determining the outcomes of party elections. Bolton South East Constituency Labour Party decided again to move to a shortlist rather than reselect its sitting Member of Parliament.

I decided to let my name go forward for this selection

process. Cllr Frank White and Cllr Jim Siddelley, a Labour and Co-operative candidate, who lived in Stockport and served on Stockport Council, were seen as the other main contenders.

The freeze date on Labour Party membership for this selection process was 20 June 1994, invitations to nominate were sent out by the Bolton South East Constituency Labour Party Executive Committee on 19 August, and the closing date for nominations was 20 October 1994, which was also the date of the shortlisting meeting.

The selection process was long and hard fought, both in the seven Labour Party branches and in the Labour clubs, of which there were also seven at that time – Great Lever, Little Lever, Derby Ward, Rumworth, Dixon Green, Farnworth and Kearsley, and Bradford Ward Labour Clubs. Today only Farnworth and Kearsley has survived as a Labour club.[5]

According to the minutes of the Special General Management Committee of the constituency, held on 20 October 1994, those nominated were me (nominated by Daubhill, Derby, Harper Green and Little Lever Branches and by Derby Ward Labour Club), Jean Gabrielle Johnson, a union official who lived in Accrington [nominated by UNISON (COHSE) Bolton Branch], Caroline Pinder (nominated by MSF Bolton 0891 and CIS 458 Branches), James Edwin Siddelley (nominated by Bolton District Labour Party Women's Council), Cllr Eve Rae Walker, who served as a Bolton councillor (nominated by Bolton South East CLP Women's Section), Cllr Frank Richard White (nominated by Burnden and Kearsley Branches and by GMB 19 Bolton Branch) and David Wright Young (nominated by Farnworth Branch, AEEU Bolton 7 Branch, GMB 223 Bolton Branch, GPMU Merseyside and Central Lancs Branch, TGWU 6/215 and 6/351 Branches, Bolton Socialist Club, Bolton Unemployed Workers' Advice Centre, and Farnworth and Kearsley and Rumworth Labour Clubs).

On the day of the shortlisting meeting Jim Siddelley withdrew his nomination. In a letter written to me the same day he wrote:

"I wish you the best of luck with the rest of the selection process. My reason for withdrawal is very straightforward: I don't think I can possibly win; I do think you can win, and that you are the only candidate available who is at all likely to win who isn't called Young. I don't think Young is finished by a long chalk yet; I do think that for me to continue on a shortlist knowing I can't win is foolish in that it will merely split the anti-Young vote and might leave the selection process open to Young to win. I have therefore withdrawn".

I first met Jim Siddelley when I presented The Magic of Chemistry (see Volume 1) at Stockport Grammar School, where he was a teacher until he was forced to retire through ill health. After the Bolton South East selection contest we became great friends. He died on 4 May 2010, leaving his body to medical science, and Eileen and I attended a packed gathering at the Alma Lodge Hotel in Stockport on 26 June 2010 to commemorate his life. He was loved and respected by a lot of people in the Labour movement.

The final Bolton South East CLP selection conference was held on 10 November 1994 in Bradford Ward Labour Club. There were several ballots; I received the majority of the transferred votes and beat David Young by receiving 62.5% of the 123 votes cast in the final ballot.

This was the first deselection of a sitting Labour Member of Parliament under the new OMOV rules. TV cameras were at the club, and the news was out on TV that evening, and covered by the majority of the national newspapers the following day. I was grateful for the number of cards and letters of support which I received following my selection, from colleagues at the University of Salford and other professional colleagues, as well as from a wide cross-section of Bolton society.

I was informed 'officially' in a letter, dated 8 February 1995, written by Gregg Cook, the Legal and Constitutional Officer of the Labour Party at John Smith House, Walworth Road, that the National Executive Committee had endorsed my selection at its meeting on 14 December 1994, although Peter Coleman, Labour's Director of Development and Organisation had already written to me on 1 February 1995 to give me this information.

David Young was understandably extremely bitter about his deselection, and he began to attack me and the Labour Party in general in the local media. In the end I was forced to seek the help of the Chief Whip of the Parliamentary Labour Party, then Derek Foster (Member of Parliament for Bishop Auckland). In my safe seat I could afford to take the flak, but I was concerned about surrounding marginal constituencies that we also needed to win. The Whips' Office handled the situation by encouraging David to travel more abroad.

Paul Flynn (Member of Parliament for Newport West) wrote in his book *The Unusual Suspect*:

"One Labour MP, David Young, was deselected by his local party in Bolton because they did not see enough of him. He protested to *The Guardian* that this was unjust. *The Guardian* could not resist pointing out that, when they contacted him, he returned the call from his hotel room in Kathmandu."

On 11 April 1996, I announced that I would stand down as chairman of the Housing Committee to concentrate on my role as the PPC for the Bolton South East Parliamentary constituency, which I did in August 1996. Up to that date I was the longest-serving chairman of the committee. I was succeeded by Cllr Noel Spencer, who was one of my vice-chairmen and, by 2010, he had exceeded the length of my term of office. At my retirement party we raised money for homeless charities.

I continued to serve as a Bolton councillor until I was due for re-election in 1998, when I resigned. John Noble succeeded me as a councillor for Central Ward in May 1998. On the 12 August 1998 Bolton Council conferred on me the title of Honorary Alderman in recognition of 'eminent services rendered to the Council'. Cllr Campbell Benjamin, who served as Bolton's first black Mayor from 1993 through to 1994, received the same recognition on the same day.

The wedding of David Young to Vera Dingwall, the widow of David Dingwall, was reported in the *Bolton Evening News* on 30 July 1996.

Pat Entwisle, chairman of the Bolton SE CLP, volunteered to be my first election agent. She had had previous experience in this capacity, so she was well-aware of election law and procedures in general. I now needed to raise some money to conduct my General Election campaign. The constituency's General Election Fund account balance was just over £2,000 and Pat estimated that we would need about £7,000 altogether.

Fund-raising is a constant problem in any branch of any political party. If a member wins a raffle or tombola prize at one of our social gatherings it is frequently given back to the organisers for the next fund-raising event. I have seen the same prizes circulate for months on end in the Labour Party. Some of our social occasions became fixed events, such as the Annual Barbecue of the Astley Bridge Branch of Bolton North East (previously Bolton East) CLP, which was held in July every year.

Apart from the inevitable speeches, entertainment as well as food and drink were provided at this event. In the days when I was chairman of the Bolton East CLP the 'Bee Gees' (three trade unionists: Tony Phillips, Dave Rutter and Brian Northey) and 'Shirley Bassey' (me) provided the entertainment. On another of these occasions I was one of the 'Three Degrees'. We got into trouble for 'dressing up' from the feminists, who were very active at that time. Frank White 'blacked up' and sang the songs of Al Jolson, which wasn't politically correct either in its day, and Dave Bolton and Mark Wrigley (Shirley's son) performed sketches based on *It Ain't Half Hot Mum*. Shirley's daughter Carolyn Wrigley performed as a very racy Madonna, singing *Like a Virgin*.

None of these occasions would have been complete without Shirley Marsland singing *Bird in a Guilded Cage* and Cllr Noel Spencer performing as 'Frank Sinatra'. I am constantly reminded by Shirley that she has captured some of these performances on videotape.

Fortunately, my earlier political activities in Bolton had already given me a high local profile in the media. On Friday 29 March 1995, Dennis Skinner, the 'Beast of Bolsover', spoke to a packed audience at Rumworth Labour Club in my

SCIENCE AND POLITICS: AN UNLIKELY MIXTURE

Campbell Benjamin with his family and me and Eileen, holding our Honorary Alderman certificates.

Retirement of Cllrs Jim Alker and myself from the Housing Committee (left to right) Cllr Linda Thomas, Cllr Betty McCracken (arm in a sling), Cllr Margaret Clare, Cllr Jim Alker (with present), Cllr Donald Grime, Cllr Tom Anderton, Cllr Martin McLoughlin, Leader of the Council Cllr Bob Howarth, Cllr Raymond Stones with Cllr Campbell Benjamin standing behind, Cllr John Byrne, me, Cllr Anthony Connell, Eileen (my wife) and Cllr Noel Spencer.

support, and we raised almost £1,000. That was a good start. I presented The Magic of Chemistry to families on the afternoon of Saturday 7 December 1996 at Rumworth Labour club, which raised more money. My council friend and colleague Cllr Peter Birch raised £300 at a social that he organised at Club Mistry (the former Bantry Club) on Derby Street, and Derby Ward Labour Club and Farnworth and Kearsley Labour Club made substantial donations to our General Election Fund through the Labour Party branches who held their meetings in those clubs.

Dennis Skinner returned to Rumworth Labour Club on 14 November 1998 and helped us to raise more money. He still travels the country giving speeches and must have raised hundreds of thousands of pounds for the Labour Party in his long political career. I first heard Dennis in Bolton at Great Lever Labour Club on 16 November 1989.

I sent hand-written letters to all the national trade unions, both to their national headquarters, with a request for the letters to be forwarded to local representatives, and to any local contacts that I knew. Some of the larger unions channelled their political funds into Regional Offices, who decided where to deploy the money so that it would be most effective, usually to marginal seats ('key seats') and not to those seats considered safe like mine.

The Merseyside, Central Lancashire and North Wales Branch of the Graphical, Paper and Media Union (GPMU), the Union of Shop, Distributive and Allied Workers Union (USDAW), the Clerical, Managerial, Sales and Technical Staff Branch of the GMU, Region 5 of the Fire Brigades Union (FBU, £400), the Bolton and Bury Branch of the Communication Workers Union (CWU, £250), United

Norwest Co-operatives Ltd., and the Transport Salaried Staff Association Manchester North Branch 80 all donated various sums of money.

Together with a number of other Labour Party branch donations, a collection raised at my adoption meeting and personal donations, we started the campaign with adequate funds. Altogether we raised £5095.14p. Our campaign headquarters was established at Bradford Ward Labour Club in Bridgeman Street, now demolished. A block of flats stands on the site of this former Labour club.

I was very pleased when Cllr Bob Howarth, Leader of Bolton Council, was made a Freeman of the Metropolitan Borough of Bolton on 16 June 2001 and that Eileen and I were able to attend the ceremony. This is a rare honour that has been bestowed on only a few Boltonians.

David Young died at the age of 74 of pneumonia on 1 January 2003 in the Royal Bolton Hospital where he had been an in-patient since the previous October after suffering a series of strokes. He was buried on 17 January 2003 with his first wife Grace in a remote cemetery at Tighnabruaich by the Kyles of Bute on 17 January 2003. "But what made him laugh was that the cemetery was built on the site of an old gunpowder factory", said his second wife Vera in an interview with the *Bolton Evening News*, "He always was a fiery character. David liked that idea". In fact David's father was born near Tighnabruaich.[6]

Tam Dalyell (Member of Parliament for Linlithgow), in his obituary in *The Independent* newspaper, published part of a letter that David had published in *The Daily Mail* on 14 March 2002, less than a year before he died. Here it is in full:

"As the longest serving MP Labour has ever had in Bolton, I got the go-ahead for what is now the Royal Bolton Hospital. But New Labour has effectively destroyed all I worked for over 23 years. The hospital is deep in debt, bottom of the league of North-West hospitals and 80-year-old patients are kept on trolleys in corridors for up to ten hours without meals. Parking is a nightmare. Patients, including pensioners, have to pay £1 for any visit, no matter how short and have to arrive half an hour before an appointment to try to get a parking place. Yet, despite the charge, there is no security for cars.

As a pensioner, I find New Labour at national and local level as ineffective as I find the management of this hospital. I know this from the experience of the sharp end.

I've challenged our three New Labour MPs to tell us if they are members of private health schemes – without response.

I saw my wife die slowly after a stroke while New Labour is impervious to the costs involved.

New Labour has been as ineffective in dealing with crime prevention and drugs as it has been in supporting the elderly. At 73, I'm interested in my quality of life and that of my family, and I feel cheated by New Labour, locally and nationally.

If there is no radical change before the next election, I'm no longer prepared to support Tony Blair and the arrogance of New Labour. I will have to consider whether I can support the party of the very rich and Tony's cronies that New Labour has become. I hope pensioners and old Labour will remember that they still have a vote."

"I am sad that Young, who for so many years was a loyal Labour Parliamentary henchman, should have been reduced to bitterness", wrote Tam Dalyell. "Truth to tell, Young was never the success in the House of Commons which was predicted of him in earlier years. It was a classic case of being elected too late."

The obituary published in *The Scotsman* on 22 January 2003 was a more sympathetic one. Jean Corston (Member of Parliament for Bristol East), who read David's obituary to a meeting of the Parliamentary Labour Party as its chair, said, "When the occasion demanded it, David Young was a very powerful orator indeed, but this secret weapon was infrequently deployed." And so he was, as I have written above.

My eldest daughter Sally was offered a place in 1984 to study Business Studies at Sheffield Polytechnic (which became Hallam University), and she graduated with a Second Class (Division II) Degree in Business Studies in 1988. My youngest daughter Sheena decided that she wanted to teach music and in 1987 was offered a place at Bretton Hall College next to the Yorkshire Sculpture Park outside Wakefield. She graduated on 24 July 1990 with a Second Class (Division II) Bachelor of Arts Degree in Music from the University of Leeds, which was awarded in the Great Hall at the University of Leeds.

Sally cut her teeth in Human Relations, working during her undergraduate years for Richard Ellis, a property company, and William Sindall, a construction company. Her first full-time job was with BT in London, with whom she won a Junior Travel Award which allowed her to work in Tokyo for a month. While out in the Far East she backpacked from Bangkok to Bali for another month.

After that she decided to back-pack round the world and booked all her tickets for a one-year round trip. Sally and a friend crossed Europe, visited the Indian subcontinent and several countries in Asia before ending up in New Zealand and Australia, where she met her future husband Andrew who played trombone in a big band in Melbourne. They married on Saturday 29 March 1997, during my General Election campaign, at Mere Hall in Bolton; the reception was at Smithills Coaching House.

Wedding of Sally Iddon and Andrew Chambers (left to right) Graham and Pam Iddon, Andrew and Sally Chambers, me and Eileen, and nephew John Iddon.

With Sheena on her wedding day.

SCIENCE AND POLITICS: AN UNLIKELY MIXTURE

The Howard Family (left to right): Darren, Matthew, me, Sheena and Abigail Howard with Jazz.

When Sally announced that she was undertaking her backpacking trip we were, of course, worried, but we didn't stand in her way. In any case she was determined to undertake what was probably, for her, the trip of a lifetime. The worry intensified when she parted company with the friend who she had set out with, but she seemed to fall in with various groups of like-minded people.

Sheena's first teaching post was in Worcestershire before she moved to teach at a school in Oswaldtwisle. She lived first in Clayton-le-Moors, then in Burnley. On 10 August 1996, she married Darren Howard at All Saints' Church in Clayton-le-Moors, close to where she lived in Burnley, and the wedding reception was held at Burnley Rugby Club. Later, the family moved to Worcester, where they have lived ever since with their children Abigail (born 10 June 1997) and Matthew (born 15 September 1999). Darren, a former engineer, now teaches science.

Merrilyn and I had provided lots of books and activities for our children and we believed that if we purchased a television it would distract them too much from their studies. As I had done in my youth, they sloped off to watch it at their friends' houses.

Before I met Merrilyn she had been an outdoor girl, keen on rambling and climbing in the mountains. As our children passed through secondary school and she acquired her qualifications for teaching, slowly she returned to these activities. I was out most weekdays at meetings or presenting The Magic of Chemistry at some venue or other and home quite a lot at the weekends. Merrilyn was home most weekdays and away a lot at the weekends, so there came a period in our lives when we were not seeing an awful lot of each other. At the weekends I either stayed at home alone or accepted the various invitations that I received to attend events. I became very unhappy, despite my busy life outside our home, and slowly it dawned on me that our marriage was on the rocks and probably irrecoverable.

Eileen and me at Bolton Town Hall – May 1989.

Up to this point Merrilyn and I had led quite an active life together. We attended a lot of parties and other functions and threw quite a few parties of our own. Merrilyn was supportive of the Labour Party, although not as keen as I was to be an activist. Nevertheless, we raised a lot of money for the Party by holding barbecues in our back garden in the summers. I employed Tommy Hobbs (his father was Mayor of Salford from 1986 to 1987), a chef at the University of Salford, to help us with the food and Bob Gilnow, the landlord of the Lamb public house (which became a restaurant), near the Jumbles Reservoir at Bradshaw, to run a bar (he had a special licence that enabled him to do this).

I regularly attended Tonge Branch Labour Party meetings and was struck by a new recruit called Eileen Harrison. She had striking red hair and was confident in her political views. Eileen's husband Roger was a steel erector, and his work often took him away from home. They had two children. Lee was an apprentice joiner with the Housing Direct Labour Organisation and Ian was in his early years at Sharples Secondary School. Occasionally, I saw Roger and Eileen together and I formed the opinion that they were not a happy couple. Eileen left home on 13 October 1986 and rented an unfurnished upstairs flat on Bury New Road. Frank and Eileen White and Elaine Sherrington were extremely generous in helping her to furnish it.

Eileen regularly attended the Tuesday rock and roll sessions at Tonge Ward Labour Club with her best friend Pat Entwistle and other mates. I often called in on my way home from my evening meetings. She continued to attend the sessions with Pat Entwistle and Karen Tomlinson, who lived below Eileen in her Bury New Road flat, after she left home. Eileen and Karen became good mates too. At that time there was a lot of music in Bolton's pubs and Eileen, and Pat and Karen could often be found at the 'bottom Bull' on Bury Road, Breightmet. They enjoyed a good night out together.

By 1986 my marriage was clearly unsustainable, and I asked my Labour Party colleague Vince Simpson if I could move into his home on a temporary basis until I could collect my thoughts and arrange more permanent accommodation. Vince and I got on so well that I actually stayed at 8 Stanley Park Walk for about 15 months before Eileen and I decided to live together in an upstairs furnished flat on Chorley Old Road in Smithills which I had rented when Vince had formed a close relationship with Dolores Morley, who moved in to live with him.

Eileen moved in to live with me on 3 February 1989. We moved into a new house in Avoncliff Close, Halliwell on 30 October 1989, where we live today. Built by Bellway, it cost £57,000 and stands on the site of the former sports ground of a Burtons factory.

A Decree Nisi of divorce was issued against me by Merrilyn on 17 May 1988, and it became absolute on 9 January 1989. We parted amicably and remained in contact. At Eileen's suggestion Merrilyn attended my 60th birthday party in July 2000, and they met on several other occasions. Merrilyn remarried but, sadly, parted from her second husband, although they too remained good friends.

Eileen and I were married at the Gretna Green Register Office at 12.30 p.m. on 16 September 1995, with a reception afterwards at the Queensbury Arms Hotel in Annan nearby. Some of our guests stayed there and others at the Golf Hotel at Powfoot on the Solway shore, a few miles away. Eileen gave Barrie Entwistle, her best friend Pat's husband who was my chauffeur for the day, the following note:

"Barrie – please make sure Brian cleans his nails, does not plaster his hair down too much, puts aftershave on, and does not forget the ring. Make sure that he does not put his coat on

My marriage to Eileen at Gretna Green.

until he gets there [the Register Office]. Eat this on completion."

Following the official ceremony we all proceeded to the Gretna Green smithy, where Eileen and I had more photographs taken to remind us of our important day. Eileen's eldest son Lee, who now lives in Gran Canaria with his Spanish partner Lilian, has one son, Noah, whilst her youngest son Ian has two children, Calvin and Cameron.

On Friday 4 July 1997, I organised a leaving party in the Department of Chemistry and Applied Chemistry at the University of Salford. Dr Tim Wallace gave me a colour print of the Houses of Parliament (I hung it in my office at 60 St George's Road), which was in the same frame that had hung in the foyer of the Department in the Cockcroft Building to display all the photographs of my old colleagues. "When you look at this framed print in future, please remember that all your colleagues are behind you", said Tim.[7]

NOTES

1. Captain James Bigglesworth ('Biggles') was the name of a fictitious aviator created by author Captain W. E. Johns (pen name for a former pilot, William Earl Johns) as the hero of a series of popular children's stories published in the 1930s and 1940s; he was accompanied in his adventures by Algy Lacey and Ginger Hebblethwaite.

2. Peter Johnston died on 14 March 2013; I presented a eulogy at a commemoration of his life at the Friends Meeting House in Bolton and he was buried in his home town of Carlisle.

3. John Roe died on 17 October 2013.

4. The closure of this home was announced in 2012 but later it secured new funding and managed to remain open.

5. Dixon Green Labour Club became a social club.

6. Some biographies and obituaries of David Wright Young quote his date of birth as 1930 and age when he died as 72 but his date of birth is registered in the Greenock West register of births as 12 October 1928.

7. When I retired from Parliament I returned this record of past members of the Department of Chemistry and Applied Chemistry to the University of Salford for its archives.

SCIENCE AND POLITICS:
AN UNLIKELY MIXTURE

PART 4

∽

POLITICS IN WESTMINSTER

CHAPTER THREE

PREPARING TO CHANGE THE WORLD

∽

The 1997 General Election was announced on Monday 17 March 1997, my Adoption Meeting was held on 25 March and I was elected to Parliament as the Member of Parliament for Bolton South East on 1 May 1997, with a majority of 21,311 and a 68.9% share of the vote on a turnout of 65.2%, figures that are unlikely to be repeated. This was the Blair landslide which gave the New Labour Government its massive majority. My daughter Sally, Sally's husband Andrew and Eileen were present at the count in the Lancaster Suite at Bolton Town Hall. Labour's 'anthem' for the duration of the 1997 election campaign was D-Ream's *Things Can Only Get Better*.

Bolton elected three Labour Members of Parliament that evening, the others being Ruth Kelly in Bolton West and David Crausby in Bolton North East. We served until the General Election of 2010. David Crausby was re-elected in 2010 but Ruth and I retired from Parliament; Ruth found employment with the HSBC Bank in the City.

My opponents in 1997 were Paul Carter for the Conservatives (with 19.7% share of the vote), Frank Harasiwka for the Liberal Democrats (with 8.8% share of the vote), Billy Pickering for the Referendum Party (with 2.2% share of the vote) and Lewis Walch of the Natural Law Party (with 0.4% share of the vote). Frank Harasiwka stood against me in all three of my General Election campaigns, increasing his share of the vote on each occasion, to 11.5% in 2001, then to 19.0% in 2005 with the 'Iraq factor'. He was always a candidate who played by the rules. Paul Carter, the Conservative candidate, was an odd sort of fellow. He had spent some time in Japan and was obsessed with transferring Japanese ideas to British culture. The Natural Law Party candidate really believed that they could cure all the country's ills by combining the mental power produced by 'yogic flying' during their meditation sessions.

In the 1997 General Election campaign I was very enthusiastic about the possibility of the first Labour Government for 18 years. Several times I went out on the 'blower' in my car. At the end of one long day, when I was feeling very tired, I parked in a cul-de-sac in Farnworth. I was extolling the virtues of Labour's policy on the NHS,

My manifesto for the 1997 General Election (p. 1).

A new start for Britain

Brian Iddon
working for all of us

Crime has doubled under the Tories and the 1,000 extra police promised by them in the 1992 election have not materialised. Instead statistics show that we are 1,000 police down. Same old Tories, same old lies! **Labour will be tough on crime and tough on the causes of crime.**

A new Labour government will:

◆ cut class sizes to 30 or under for 5, 6 and 7 year-olds

◆ introduce fast-track punishment for persistent young offenders

◆ cut NHS waiting lists by treating an extra 100,000 patients by cutting bureaucracy

◆ get 250,000 under-25 year olds off benefit and into work

◆ get tough on government spending and borrowing to ensure low inflation and strengthen the economy

Labour believes in strong partnerships with the voluntary sector, schemes like Bolton shopmobility.

There are 20,000 more managers and 50,000 fewer nurses in the NHS now than in 1989. Labour will cut back this bureaucracy by £100 million and treat 100,000 extra patients.

Patients now wait to get on NHS waiting lists. In this way the Tories can fiddle the published waiting list figures. More than one million people were waiting for hospital admission in the UK in 1991. Three years later the figure was 1,063,302 for England alone, yet the Tories claimed they had cut waiting lists.

Two million fewer people are on NHS dentists' lists than two years ago. NHS acute beds have been cut by a third in the last fifteen years but private hospital beds are up by two thirds. **Labour will reverse privatisation of the National Health Service.**

How you will have a stake in a new Britain

More than four million people are denied the opportunity to work in Britain today. To run our "high-tech" industries the Tories have created a low-paid (often part-time), low-skilled workforce. They pay out £3 billion in benefits to low-paid workers. **Labour will tackle unemployment, provide better training for our workers and introduce a minimum wage.**

Brian Iddon lives in Halliwell and works at Salford University. With an International reputation for his research activities he is well-known also as a presenter of science to the general public.

Brian has served Bolton Council for almost 20 years and was its Chair of Housing from 1986 to 1996.

new Labour new Britain — **Make the difference**

My manifesto for the 1997 General Election (p. 2).

Announcement of the 1997 General Election result in the Lancaster Suite of Bolton Town Hall (me and Eileen with Andrew and Sally).

particularly our policy to reduce waiting lists, when I ended my statement with "...and Labour will put more people in hospital." Oh dear! This was the age of John Prescott's pledge cards; one of our pledges was to reduce waiting times in the NHS. We made five pledges on the card in 1997 and fulfilled them all, as well as a lot more. Things really did get better.

On Friday 2 May 1997, along with millions of other people, I watched Tony Blair and his family enter Downing Street on television. There were scenes of jubilation as he did so; people expected so much of him and his Government. Monday 5 May was the May Day Bank Holiday, so I travelled down to London on the Tuesday for a meeting of the Parliamentary Labour Party (PLP) on Wednesday 7 May in the Great Hall of the Institution of Civil Engineers on Great

George Street. As I arrived, Mo Mowlam (Member of Parliament for Redcar) was dashing out and announced that the meeting had been moved to Church House, in the grounds of Westminster Abbey. Our 1997 majority was so big that we couldn't all fit into the hall originally hired for our first meeting of the PLP.

After the meeting the 101 women of the Parliamentary Labour Party were photographed in a group with Tony Blair on the steps of Church House, an image that has been seen in the media many times since it was first recorded. They were christened 'Blair's babes' by the media. The Labour Party had positively discriminated in favour of women being selected as candidates through all-women shortlists, and this was the largest group of women ever elected to the British Parliament.

Meetings of the PLP were held after that in the largest committee room of the Palace of Westminster, committee room 14 on the main committee corridor. In our first Parliamentary session (1997-1998) the PLP met on Wednesday mornings at 11.30 a.m. and on Thursday evenings at 7.00 p.m., until 19 February 1998 when the Thursday evening meetings were discontinued. Later it was decided to open Wednesday sittings of Parliament at 11.30 a.m. and PLP meetings were moved forward to 10.00 a.m., on 8 January 2003. From 19 April 2004, meetings of the PLP were held every Monday evening when Parliament was sitting, at 6.00 p.m.

I regularly attended these meetings during my 13 years at Westminster and kept all the minutes. Journalists lined up in the main committee corridor to interrogate Members as they left committee room 14. Most of the accounts that appeared in the press were accurate, despite the fact that these were supposed to be private meetings. There was always a feeling that we were being preached at by the Executive and not listened to. The introduction of 'Soley Days', when backbench Members could choose a topic for discussion, helped to dilute this feeling. My last PLP meeting was held on 29 March 2010.

The chairperson of the PLP is elected annually. Clive Soley (Member of Parliament for Ealing, Acton and Shepherd's Bush, now Lord Soley) was our chairman from 1997 to 2001. He was followed by Jean Corston (Member of Parliament for Bristol East, now a peer) (2001-2005), Ann Clywd (Member of Parliament for Cynon Valley) (2005-2006) and Tony Lloyd (Member of Parliament for Manchester Central) (2006-2010). Labour Party staff member Alan Howarth (now a peer) was secretary to the PLP from 1997 to 2004. He was succeeded by Fiona Gordon (the first woman secretary, 2004-2007) – she joined the Political Office at 10 Downing Street – and Martin O'Donovan (2007-2010).

In 1997, the General Secretary of the Labour Party was Tom Sawyer (now a peer), who served until 1998. He was succeeded by Margaret McDonagh (the first woman General Secretary) (1998-2001), David Triesman, previously the General Secretary of my union – the Association of University Teachers (now a peer) (2001-2003), Matt Carter (the youngest General Secretary to date) (2003-2005), Peter Watt (2006-2007) and Ray Collins (2008-2010).

The first few days of a new Government are the most hectic for a Prime Minister. As well as moving his family into 10 Downing Street, Tony Blair also had to think about appointing his Ministers and discuss with them the Bills that were to be included in the first Queen's Speech, as well as the Budget requirements of his new Chancellor of the Exchequer, Gordon Brown. It has been reported by journalist Andrew

Rawnsley and others that Gordon did not discuss the contents of his Budgets with Tony Blair.

On Wednesday 28 March 2001, David Blunkett (Member of Parliament for Sheffield Brightside) invited me to a 'thank-you' party for his senior Department for Education and Employment (DfEE) staff. He obviously sensed a General Election approaching and knew that he would not be Secretary of State at the DfEE after the election (which in the event was put back from 3 May to 7 June 2001). He wanted to thank all the staff, and some Members, like me, for all the work we had done since the election of 1997. Also present was his Permanent Secretary, Michael Bichard, who was to leave as the election was called to go to pastures new.

In his leaving speech Michael Bichard explained that the period immediately prior to the May 1997 General Election had posed an interesting problem for his staff. They knew David had been our education spokesman in opposition but they could not be sure that he would be the new Secretary of State. However, they prepared for that eventuality by searching the world for a machine that would turn typescript into Braille and *vice versa*. Eventually one was located in Sweden.

When David arrived at the DfEE a briefing was prepared for him to attend his first meeting with the Prime Minister, so that proposed Bills and policies could be discussed for Labour's first session in Government. When David took out the briefing, which he hadn't had time to read in advance, to his horror it had been printed out in Swedish. The civil servants forgot that their new machine needed to be switched over from Swedish to English!

Our first summer in Government was punctuated by the death of Diana, Princess of Wales, in a road traffic accident in the Alma tunnel in Paris on 31 August 1997. In his tribute to her on 6 September Tony Blair uttered the immortal words, "She was the people's princess".

I was sworn in as a Member of Parliament on Tuesday 13 May and the Queen's Speech was on 14 May 1997. New Members are always sworn in last. My first Advice Surgery as a Member of Parliament was held on Friday 16 May at 4.30 p.m. in Bolton Town Hall.

All Members of Parliament get 'regulars' at their Advice Surgeries, people who come time and time again, often to spend the time of day or to report fairly trivial events. We had our fair share of those. A woman came to several of Margaret Beckett's surgeries to complain about 'waves'. It took a long time for this woman to get over to Margaret that these 'waves' were being emitted by her television set and that they were ruining her enjoyment of programmes, such as *Coronation Street* and *East Enders*. Margaret became so frustrated at trying to deal with this apparently mad woman that she said: "Mrs Jones [not her real name], have you ever tried wearing green Wellingtons when you watch TV?" It must have worked because the woman never went to see Margaret again, probably thinking she was mad.

In one of my finest hours I listened to a man go on and on about his mental health problems at one of my Advice Surgeries. I gleaned that he had tried to commit suicide on at least one occasion. I was very patient and helpful, but my unfortunate parting shot was "Well, look, if you ever feel suicidal again, don't hang around, please contact us or anybody else you believe can help". Oh dear! Karen, my Office Manager, kicked me under the table.

Members of Parliament see, or receive correspondence

from, quite a few constituents who are mentally ill, and sometimes their complaints seem quite plausible. 'Being followed' or 'having a house that is bugged' are the usual kinds of complaints. Several times we saw an Iranian university student who was convinced, and nearly convinced me, that he was under observation by MI5. He claimed that his brother was a nuclear scientist in Iran, which lent credibility to his story. After several meetings with him, I decided to ask him "How many people follow you and where?" When he alleged that several MI5 officers had followed him in Sainsbury's supermarket in Bolton I am afraid that his story fell to pieces. Even MI5 haven't got resources on that scale.

Members of Parliament are advised to organise their Advice Surgeries very carefully. Although attacks on Members and their staff are rare, they do happen. In 2009 Stephen Timms (Member of Parliament for East Ham) was stabbed in the stomach by an Asian woman attending one of his Advice Surgeries and, on 28 January 2000, Andrew Pennington (assistant to Nigel Jones, Member of Parliament for Cheltenham) was killed at an Advice Surgery by a man brandishing a Samurai sword.[1]

A Member of Parliament can expect their office windows to be broken and all kinds of undesirable materials may be put through their office letter boxes or left on doorsteps. We received threatening correspondence at home, which the police investigated, and one of my constituents regularly sent letters to me in Westminster that clearly suggested that he needed psychiatric help, one of which contained broken glass. Westminster Security Officers screen all incoming packages, and they fortunately detected the glass and removed it.

Inspired by my performance as Guy Fawkes (see Volume

1, Chapter 8 on The Magic of Chemistry) I received a present from Vanessa Stone, one of my former neighbours in Woburn Avenue, Bolton in the form of a round, black old-fashioned bomb, complete with a fuse to light it. When I had opened it I took it back to the Security Officers on the gate where it had been handed in for me in a package. Like me, they had a laugh. Vanessa had bought a rather strong Lancashire cheese on Todmorden market as an appropriate present for me.

When the debate was raging in the first session of the Labour Government about restricting the use of handguns, Ian Stewart (Member of Parliament for Eccles) was visited by a man who took a handgun out. Within seconds Ian had turned the table over on him and pinned him to the ground, so that the handgun could be removed. It turned out that his constituent had no malicious intentions; he had come to discuss a Bill before the House with Ian and talk to him about his interest in shooting.

I had sought advice from Terry Lewis (Member of Parliament for Worsley), one of my constituents, about what to expect when I entered the Houses of Parliament. First, I knew that I had to take with me a copy of my election manifesto so that the policemen and doorkeepers would know who I was. On arrival, they all had copies of our photographs available to make their checks and, within a period of days, they and Madam Speaker, Betty Boothroyd, were expected to be able to put a name to our face from memory.

I was advised too to collect my mail on arrival on a daily basis. I remember seeing Helen Southworth, the newly elected Member for Warrington South, in the Post Office just off Members Lobby in the House of Commons, collecting her mail for the first time several days into the new Parliament.

The counter assistant asked whether she had anybody with her to help her to carry it, which seemed to surprise her.

Dari Taylor (Member of Parliament for Stockton South; her father, Dan Jones, was a former member of Parliament for Burnley) was on one of the North East radio channels one morning shortly after she was elected in 1997, and was describing the difficulties of the new job to her interviewer when she said, "One of the most difficult features of the job is that I get six inches of mail every morning"!

I was advised too that I would have to wait patiently for an office. The Serjeant-at-Arms has very little time to ensure that the rooms of departing Members of Parliament (a lot of them departed unexpectedly in 1997) are given a deep clean before being decorated and refitted with furniture so that a new Member can take the room over.

When I arrived in Parliament, Portcullis House had not been constructed; there was a big hole where it stands today, in which Westminster Underground station was being rebuilt, with access to the new Jubilee Line. In 1997, most Members were expected to share a room. We worked in the House of Commons Library until Janet Anderson (Member of Parliament for Darwen and Rossendale), the Whip responsible for room allocations to Labour Members, could allocate us a room.

The first room I was allocated was in the Palace. It was very small and there were no windows, so I was reluctant to accept it. A doorman kindly pointed out another room on the same corridor, which had been occupied previously by Conservative Member David Mellor. It was slightly larger and with windows, but Janet Anderson would not or could not allocate it to me. I discovered later that there was a pecking order for room allocations. As well as rooms being allocated to new Members, re-elected colleagues are given an opportunity to move to better rooms after a General Election.

Eventually, I was offered Room 2/28 in the Northern Shaw North Building, along with Alan Hurst (Member of Parliament for Braintree), who was a chain smoker. When he found out that I didn't smoke he decided to seek another room and ended up in the Palace. I was allowed to keep Room 2/28, which was equipped with two sets of furniture and, eventually, all my Westminster researchers shared the room with me, which was an advantage for them and also for me. The cramped accommodation for Parliamentary assistants was provided in basement rooms or in rooms without windows until Portcullis House opened.

The Norman Shaw North and South Buildings are connected by a covered bridge; they were better known as Old Scotland Yard, with Canon Row Police Station attached (now the Canon Row Pass Office). They can be approached from Parliament Street, where the Red Lion public house stands, or from the Embankment. At either end of the yard which lies between them are impressive pairs of wrought iron gates. In my youth I had seen those at the Embankment end swing open to allow police cars to speed out with flashing blue lights on their way to an emergency in a cops and robber series of programmes on television.

I was allocated a locker, conveniently situated close to the Members' Tea Room and the Library's main entrance, and a place to hang my 'cloak' in the Members' Cloak Room, where each hanger was newly fitted with a loop of pink ribbon, traditionally provided for Members to hang their swords on. In the first few days Members are required to acquire an official pass, with their photograph on it, and a pass to the car parks should one be required.

Below New Palace Yard, outside the House of Commons Members Entrance, there is a large underground garage, which I used for several months until I decided that it was more convenient to park in the yard of the Norman Shaw Buildings. During my 13 years in Parliament I almost always travelled by car to London. Eileen travelled down with me once or twice a month, especially in the early years. I tried travelling by train and flying from Manchester Airport but the total travel times were the same as by road. The journey time from Manchester Piccadilly Station to London Euston was significantly reduced after improvements to the west coast main railway line. That journey now takes just over two hours compared with over three hours in 1997.

For several weeks I lived out of a suitcase in hotels. In 1995, I had asked Dolphin Square to put me down on their waiting list (I found out later that they didn't operate one), and Eileen and I moved into a one-bedroom flat on the sixth floor of Hood House, on the east side of Dolphin Square, at the end of May 1997. We lived there for 13 years and did not even consider 'staircasing' into better properties as the second home allowance increased.

It never seemed right to me that Members of Parliament used public money for their own advantage. Most Members saw the capital gains that they could make on buying properties in London and selling them on again on their departure from the House of Commons as part of their 'pension', or as compensation for the relatively low salaries that Members of Parliament are paid for their duties, compared with those in similarly responsible positions (not a view held by the general public).

When I was selected as a Prospective Parliamentary Candidate in 1994 I was earning £34-35,000, about the same as Members of Parliament were earning at that time. Before I was elected to Parliament in 1997 there was a review of Members' pay (voted on by MPs in July 1996), which meant that my starting salary was just over £44,000.

The blame for keeping the pay of Members of Parliament down was placed on the shoulders of Margaret Thatcher who, it was always rumoured, encouraged Members to take advantage of the allowance system that had developed. On 8 May 2009, *The Daily Telegraph* started to publish details of numerous abuses of the allowance system; they published a supplement on 20 June 2009 which listed all the expenses claimed by MPs over a four-year period. The Fees Office was replaced by the Independent Parliamentary Standards Authority (IPSA), an unwieldy independent body that controls the payment of Members' allowances today. Ironically, senior staff of IPSA are paid more than Members.

When I left Dolphin Square I was claiming just over half of what I could have claimed from the second home allowance. I decided to rent a flat in Dolphin Square because I had discovered from Neil Litherland, one of the officers in Bolton's Housing Department when I was chairman of the Housing Committee (he was the son of Bob Litherland, Member of Parliament for Manchester Central until he retired), that rents were reasonable – at least I thought so when I heard what Bob was paying. However, my initial rent was almost double that figure when I was allocated a flat in Hood House. My final rent was just over £11,000 a year, but that figure included the cost of the district central heating system and the provision of central heating and hot water from it.

Dolphin Square, which is on the River Thames embankment in Pimlico, was built by a not-for-profit housing trust (today's term would be a registered social landlord) in the 1930s. It survived several direct hits by bombs during World War II. There are approximately 700 flats in four blocks built on the sides of a square containing a large garden which I never had the time to enjoy. In 1997 about 70 of the flats were occupied by Members of the House of Lords or the House of Commons. For most of the time I lived there the north side of Dolphin Square was the Dolphin Square Hotel. Its restaurant was managed for a while by chef Gary Rhodes as Rhodes on the Square. The 'Square' has a small shopping mall and a health club with a swimming pool (residents pay extra for these facilities).

Princess Anne lived in Dolphin Square, as did the fascist Oswald Mosley of 'Black Shirt' fame, Christine Keeler, who brought Tory Minister John Profumo down, Charles de Gaulle (during World War II), Harold Wilson, and C. P. Snow. Jack Cunningham, whom I had known at Durham University, had a flat above me and William Hague, before he married Ffion, lived in our block. Eileen liked the place because she felt safe there. When we arrived, Dolphin Square was monitored by CCTV cameras, with night vision. These were installed by the Government when Roy Mason was Secretary of State for Northern Ireland, at the height of the IRA Troubles. He was probably the most threatened of the Ministers who worked in Northern Ireland.

I now had an office and accommodation in London, but I hadn't appointed any staff. I was advised to do the job first for a few months until I decided where I wanted to establish my offices and employ my staff. I calculated that I could afford two and a half staff. Initially, I kept up with my case work by handwriting my responses but, towards the 1997 summer recess, this became increasingly difficult as the number of cases began to pile up.

I always held regular fortnightly surgeries, one in Bolton Town Hall at 4.30 p.m. on the third Friday of every month and one in Farnworth Town Hall, on the first Saturday of every month. Cllr Noel Spencer, a Farnworth councillor, helped at the Farnworth surgeries.

Before the summer recess of 1997 I decided to employ Sadia Choudhry, a young and very charismatic Pakistani woman, as my first Parliamentary assistant in my Westminster office; she started work for me on Monday 18 August 1997. Sadia had worked for three other Members of Parliament and knew her way around Westminster.

During the summer recess I attended a Labour Party function in Bolton and was engaged in conversation by Karen Lawrinson. I discovered that Karen was working for a haulage company in their office and had the secretarial skills I was looking for. Furthermore, she was quite keen to change her job and suggested that she would like to work for me. I decided to advertise the job, but Karen was the best candidate who applied and I employed her in my Bolton office from Monday 24 November 1997; she stayed with me, eventually as my Office Manager, until 5 July 2010.

When I appointed Karen she lived in my constituency and was my eyes and ears in Bolton, as well as an excellent Office Manager. She was treasurer to the Bolton South East CLP for several years before she moved house into the Bolton West constituency. Her greatest expertise is in ICT (Information Communication Technology) and, while working for me, she gained a degree in this subject area from the Open University. After my first appointment I always advertised and interviewed candidates for vacant posts. There were always far more applicants for jobs in the Westminster office than for those in the Bolton office.

When I had been selected by the Bolton South East CLP I had given an undertaking that I would open an office in the Labour Party building at 60 St George's Road, Bolton, and employ staff to work there. I fulfilled that undertaking. We employed a professional surveyor to determine the rent that should be paid.

Sadia left my Westminster office on 30 November 1998 to work with Minister of Sport, Tony Banks (Member of Parliament for West Ham), in his Ministerial office. Then I appointed Rob Tattersall, who stayed with me for a number of years. When Rob decided to undertake a law degree at the University of Manchester, I employed him in the Bolton office on a part-time basis and replaced him in London with Kathryn Sutcliffe, on 8 January 2001.

After Rob graduated and moved on we appointed Joanne Whittaker, who worked in the Bolton office for a short period. Joanne, who lived in Burnley, left on 8 June 2007 to work with Kitty Usher (Member of Parliament for Burnley). She was elected in 2005 and decided not to stand at the 2010 General Election when Labour lost the seat to the Liberal Democrats. The big issue in Burnley at the time was closure of the A&E Unit at the local hospital.

When Joanne left, we appointed Chris Peacock, who was my Principal Case Worker until I retired. Chris was also an excellent member of staff. A Member of Parliament's casework grows exponentially. More cases are opened as the years go by

SCIENCE AND POLITICS: AN UNLIKELY MIXTURE

(Left to right) Maureen Barlow, me, Chris Peacock, Gemma Reay and Karen Lawrinson.

than are closed. Some problems can be dealt with quite quickly while others take years to sort out.

I inherited about 12 dusty and out-of-date files from my predecessor, David Young, but I left hundreds of open files for my successor, Yasmin Qureshi. The Data Protection Act caused a lot of extra work for Members of Parliament, who now have to contact all their constituents for whom files exist to ask them how they wish their files to be treated when the sitting Member retires.

I had my fair share of prolific letter writers, including a GP who wrote to me regularly complaining about bureaucracy in the NHS. After several run-ins with the Bolton Primary Care Trust (PCT) he put up a notice in his surgery:

Question: What is the difference between the PCT and the Mafia?

Answer: One of them is organised.

Kathryn Sutcliffe was exceptional as both a case worker and a researcher in my London office. Her partner was an architect who decided to lead a quieter life in Bournemouth, and it was a sad day when Kathryn handed in her resignation, both for her and for me. Kathryn was followed in the Westminster office by Gemma Reay. Even though my last vacancy was advertised with an announcement that I would retire at the next General Election, we had 103 applications for the post. Gemma, who had worked previously in public relations, was head and shoulders above the majority of applicants and was also an outstanding member of my staff.

I have always maintained that a Member of Parliament's reputation is reflected by the abilities and loyalty of their members of staff, and I was blessed with some excellent employees. In my opinion it is essential for a Member to keep control of their diary appointments. Turning up late for meetings or not turning up at all is a quick route to a bad reputation. I believe also that a Member should look through all their correspondence after staff have opened it and sorted it out into categories.

I received some strange requests for help when I was a Member of Parliament. One evening Cllr Rosa Kay approached me in Derby Ward Labour Club and asked me if I would write a letter of condolence to a friend and Labour Party member, Joan Dearden.[2] I immediately thought she [Joan] had lost her husband, Richard, but it turned out to be her parrot, Toby. Joan, who was an animal lover, was genuinely grieving over the loss of Toby, who swore like a trooper. Richard and Joan often argued as to which of them had taught the parrot such dreadful language. When Joan left for the Labour club the parrot called out phrases that it had picked up from Richard such as "She's off to that f.........g Labour club again; she's got a fella down there".

One day Joan was cooking some fish for tea and gave some to Toby. After a while she saw Toby lying at the bottom of his cage but still breathing, so she rushed him off to the vet., who suspected that Toby might be choking on a seed, or something Joan had given him, so he cut a nick in Toby's neck to see if his airways were blocked, but sadly Toby died.

The loss of Toby was so great to Joan that a post-mortem was carried out on him, at a cost of £100, which revealed that he had been poisoned by a gas, probably by perfluoroisobutane, which is given off in trace quantities when Teflon is heated to a very high temperature. The fish was fried in a Teflon-coated frying pan.

I was reminded of the classic Dead Parrot Sketch (it can be watched on the internet), first broadcast on 7 December 1969 in an episode of *Monty Python's Flying Circus*, which featured a pet shop allegedly in Bolton (pronounced Notlob). Mr Praline (played by John Cleese) tries to return a dead parrot to a pet shop whose owner is played by Michael Palin.

Probably one of the most remarkable of all the cases we dealt with was when a woman came to seek our help to release her husband's body from a sunken vessel in Scapa Flow, where German battle ships were scuppered during World War I. Her husband had been a very experienced amateur diver, and his diving club had been exploring these vessels when he had got stuck in a confined space. Tragically, he had died when his air tank ran out and his colleagues and others were unable to release his trapped body.

I suggested to my Office Manager Karen that she seek some advice from the Ministry of Defence in the first place.

After two days of negotiations a submarine rescue team was dispatched on an exercise to Scapa Flow and, with the help of specialist equipment, they were able to release the man's body for burial. The lady wrote a very nice letter to the *Bolton Evening News* to thank us for our efforts on her behalf.

Members of Parliament are usually approached by many very desperate constituents and they deal with some very interesting cases. I could write a whole book on the cases that we dealt with, but confidentiality prevents me from doing so. With the permission of a few of my constituents I have archived a number of the most interesting cases that we dealt with in my 13 years in Parliament.

After Ruth Kelly, David Crausby and I were elected on 1 May 1997, we each occupied a small office at 60 St George's Road. As we began to appoint staff, and the number of callers increased, it became apparent that we couldn't all operate from 60 St George's Road. Ruth Kelly decided in any case that she was too far from her constituency and moved to Horwich, which relieved the pressure for a while. Next to go was David Crausby, who moved to Astley Bridge.

Relations between David and I were never good. He always objected to me having an office at 60 St George's Road because the building is in his constituency, by a few hundred yards. However, I reminded him of the undertaking that I had given at my selection conference, and I was determined to stick to it. I am one of several party members who worked hard to earn the money in order to purchase our headquarters in Bolton, for just over £11,000 in the 1970s. For several years we organised fund-raising events and collected waste paper, which we sold to a local firm.

Owen Oyston, an estate agent who had provided a property

for the Labour Party in Lancaster, came to Bolton to give us advice on the purchase of a property in Bolton town centre. A small group of us met in the Lamplighter Restaurant on Knowsley Street, including Cllr David Dingwall, Cliff Morris and me. Owen arranged to have the property surveyed for us and gave us a cheque to cover the deposit, which we paid back later.

David Crausby suggested that I shouldn't even be living in his constituency, despite the fact that I had lived in Halliwell since 1989. He believed that Members of Parliament should live in the constituencies they represent. David lived in Breightmet when he moved to Bolton from Bury. Later, he moved to a detached house at the corner of Moss Bank Way and Smithills Deane Road. When boundaries changed for the 2010 General Election he found himself in the Bolton West Parliamentary Constituency, but he didn't move back into his own constituency.

What irritated David the most when we were elected was that I was both a Bolton councillor (1997-1998) and a Member of Parliament for Bolton South East. I was well known in Central Ward (in the Bolton North East constituency), so my constituents were still asking me to deal with their local problems, and I did until I retired from the Council, although I did refer many of them to my two Ward colleagues. My last meeting of the full Council was on 11 March 1998.

Inevitably, as a former Bolton councillor and a former chairman of the Council's Housing Committee, I received invitations to attend occasional functions in both the Bolton West and Bolton North East constituencies. Ruth Kelly and I developed an understanding that this was acceptable. Indeed

Ruth, especially when she was a Minister, quite often attended events in my constituency. We kept each other informed. However, David jealously guarded the boundaries of the Bolton North East Parliamentary constituency, and both Ruth and I got into trouble if we crossed those boundaries, even if we told him in advance.

There is no Parliamentary rule which states that a Member should not visit another Member's constituency. The Parliamentary advice is that it is advisable for the visiting Member to inform the other Member of their intentions.

I was responsible for launching the Bolton Neighbour Dispute Service and was invited to attend its tenth anniversary celebration, which was held at Mere Hall in David's constituency on 29 March 2004. He heard about this and, even before I had had a chance to inform him of my intentions, he went ballistic with those responsible for the invitation. They were shocked by his behaviour.

When the political correspondent of the *Bolton Evening News*, Andrew Greaves, telephoned me in London to ask what I thought about the emerging news items on the MPs 'expenses scandal' in *The Daily Telegraph* newspaper (publication began on 8 May), I told him that I felt embarrassed to be a Member of Parliament, although I was not directly embroiled in these stories. After the resulting story appeared on the front page of the newspaper, it was suggested that I should resign from Parliament immediately if that was what I thought. This incident also typified the tensions that existed between Members of Parliament at the time over the 'expenses scandal'.

There were many examples in the House of Commons of Members from the same towns or cities representing the same political party who were well-known not to get on with each other. I often envied those Members who were the only Member of Parliament representing their town.

Selection procedures for Labour candidates to fight seats at the next General Election start with the Party's 'safe seats'. For me the first reselection process began in the summer of 1999 for the 2001 General Election. It was agreed by the Bolton South East CLP that I would fight the seat without the need for them to draw up a shortlist of potential candidates and go through the whole selection procedure I had been through for the 1997 General Election. This 'trigger vote' decision was repeated for the 2005 General Election. I was always grateful for the support I received from my constituency members. The majority of them would have been happy for me to fight the 2010 election as well.

For the 2001 reselection process, I reminded my members in a statement that was sent to them that in the 1994 selection process, I had promised "to fight for a higher spot for housing on the political agenda, Regional Government for the North West, abolition of QUANGOS, reform of the House of Lords (with an elected second chamber), modernisation of procedures in the House of Commons, separation of public from private health care, retention of a hospital for the elderly at Hulton Lane, reform of the judicial system, bringing back the utilities and transport under public control, greater democracy in the work place, restoration of trade unions rights (I mentioned GCHQ at Cheltenham in particular), reform of the Child Support Agency, and a Freedom of Information Bill." The three successive Labour Governments between 1997 and 2010 did not do too badly on these issues. My biggest disappointments are that we did not achieve full House of

Lords reform (although I changed my mind about 100% election of its Members) or renationalisation of the utilities and public transport systems, which the Tories placed in the hands of private companies, many of them with their headquarters abroad.

For the 2001 General Election our constituency secretary, Bob Evans, agreed to be my Election Agent, and we ran my second campaign from Bradford Ward Labour Club. USDAW generously donated £500 to that campaign as well as a lot of election materials, both Kearsley and Farnworth Branches donated £250 of funds that they raise every Tuesday evening at a 'sing-along' night at Farnworth and Kearsley Labour Club, and a number of other contributions were made as well. Along with the balance left over from my 1997 campaign and the monthly £100 donations from me to the General Election Fund, we had enough money to fight my second campaign.

My opponents at the 2001 General Election were Frank Harasiwka for the Liberal Democrats (see above), Haroon Rashid for the Conservatives and William Kelly, who lived in Farnworth, for the Socialist Labour Party. I received a 61.9% share of the vote, which gave me a majority of 12,871 on a 50.1% turnout. Haroon Rashid, of Kashmiri heritage, was a very difficult opponent. A few months before the General Election he dined a significant number of my constituents at considerable cost in a restaurant, presumably in an attempt to gain their support.

A series of letters started to appear in the *Bolton Evening News* painting me as a Member of Parliament who worked more for my constituents with Asian heritage than others, clearly intended to work up a white backlash against me. When we checked the addresses we could not find any of the people whose names were at the bottoms of these letters in the electoral register. On receipt of about the fifth of them a journalist from the *Bolton Evening News* telephoned me to ask whether I was suspicious of these letters or not. I asked him how they were received and, when he said they had been faxed, I asked him to look at the top of the faxes to see whether the sender could be identified. They all came from Haroon Rashid's home fax machine in London; he worked at Heathrow Airport. I gave the story to *The Guardian* newspaper after it was published by the *Bolton Evening News* in March 2001.

At a meeting held at the Emmanuel Church Hall in Deane on 31 May Haroon Rashid attacked my wife Eileen for 'jumping the queue' to get into hospital. Whilst I was down in Westminster she had been almost paralysed in bed on the night of 8 May by a herniated disc and had had to call an ambulance. It was a genuine emergency; there was nobody at home to help her. He failed to attend an important meeting in Farnworth on 4 June 2001 which the Council of Churches organised to question all the Prospective Parliamentary Candidates.

On 7 June 2001, the day of the election, Haroon Rashid and his collaborators broke every rule in the book. My Election Agent, Bob Evans, reported them several times during the day to the Returning Officer, also Bolton's Chief Executive, for alleged infringement of election rules, but little or nothing was done about our complaints. I was so incensed that I spoke about these infringements in an Adjournment Debate on 'Electoral Law' that was led by Mike Gapes (Member of Parliament for Ilford South) on 4 July 2001.

When I heard that Haroon Rashid had been chosen by the Conservative Party to oppose my colleague Marsha Singh in

Bradford West at the 2005 General Election, I gave Marsha the file I had compiled on Rashid's antics in Bolton.[3] Later, in 2009, he was one of several people charged with electoral offences in Bradford, but he was acquitted, unlike some of his supporters.

By 2005 Bradford Ward Labour Club was closed and we ran my third and last General Election campaign from the former Cannon Street Health Centre. On that occasion our constituency chairman, Kevin Meagher, was my Election Agent. By 2005 there had been many mergers of unions, and those unions then in existence were concentrating their funding, as they had done in 2001, on 'target seats' in marginal constituencies. Fortunately, Bolton South East CLP had built up adequate funds to fight the 2005 campaign. I continued donating £100 a month to their General Election Fund until my successor was selected to fight the 2010 campaign.

The 2005 General Election campaign was much quieter than the 2001 one had been. My Conservative opponent was Deborah Dunleavy, who fought David Crausby in the Bolton North East seat in the 2010 General Election campaign. She lost both times. Frank Harasiwka fought the seat again for the Liberal Democrats, Florence Bates was a candidate for the UK Independence Party, and David Jones fought the seat for the Veritas Party. The invasion of Iraq shifted a lot of my votes to increase the Liberal Democrat vote, but I received a 56.9% share of the vote, with a majority of 11,638 on a 50.0% turnout.

The Labour Government of 1997-1998 set up a Modernisation Committee to modernise the procedures of Parliament. In the early years of the 1997-2001 Government there were few guillotines on debates and we often continued business well into the early hours of the next day. I remember one or two occasions when the House of Commons sat almost until the next day's scheduled business had to be abandoned. Members slept in the Library, in their offices and in the Members' Tea Room. People in the country often asked how on earth we could function efficiently with business hours like those we inherited in 1997. With more women elected in 1997, many with young children, it became essential to reform the sitting hours, and they were reformed, thank goodness. After the 2010 General Election crèche facilities were provided for Members of Parliament with young children.

When I was first elected to Parliament we finished Government business on Thursday evenings at 10.00 p.m. (excluding time for any votes). The only way to get home at that time of the night was to drive, which meant arriving home in the early hours of the next morning. I was relieved when it was announced at the PLP meeting on 15 July 1998 that proceedings on a Thursday in the chamber would be brought forward by three hours, with a 10.30 a.m. start and a 7.00 p.m. finish, which allowed us to get home at a reasonable hour.

Later, it was decided to start Government business on a Wednesday at 11.30 a.m. and to conclude at 7.00 p.m., and start on Thursdays at 10.30 a.m. and finish at 6.00 p.m. (excluding time for votes). Instead of Prime Minister's Questions being two 15 minute slots on Tuesdays and Thursdays before 1997, the Government allocated a 30-minute slot on Wednesdays. This change of business on Wednesdays had the advantage of being ahead of the 1.00 p.m. news bulletins and one slot a week allowed more time for the Prime Minister to travel abroad or within Britain.

The Labour Government introduced Programme

Motions, which set out the order in which a Bill's clauses are debated, either in the chamber or in committee, and 'knives' are inserted in the Bills, which effectively end discussion of those clauses that haven't been debated up to that point in the debate. Although this procedural change means that Members of Parliament can get to bed at a reasonable hour, it also means that a lot of business is not debated adequately on the floor of the House of Commons or in its committee rooms.

The Labour Government agreed to publish Draft Bills in the Queen's Speech, which are usually referred to Select Committees for consideration before bringing them before either House. It also passed legislation that enables uncompleted Bills to be carried over from one session of Parliament to the next, but not from one Parliament to the next. Constituency weeks were introduced to coincide with school half-terms, which means parents can spend more time with their children. The Labour Government also insisted that the Explanatory Notes that accompany all Bills are printed in as plain English as possible.

The Palace of Westminster needs completely rewiring, costs a fortune to maintain and has more than its fair share of mice, especially in the Members' Tea Room. One invaded the chamber during my time in Parliament and got captured by the cameras on television.

John Barrett (Member of Parliament for Edinburgh West) tabled Early Day Motion 1393 on 10 June 2002 on 'The House of Commons Cat':

"That this House is concerned at the large number of mice which currently reside in the Palace of Westminster including the dining rooms; believes that it would be fiscally prudent for the Serjeant-at-Arm's Department to invest in a House of Commons cat to try to tackle the problem; and calls upon the House of Commons Administration Committee to investigate this matter."

Once I had the audacity to write to Robin Cook, when he was Leader of the House and chairman of the Modernisation Committee, to suggest that the Palace of Westminster was a totally unsuitable building for modern times, that we should build a new Parliament building close to Birmingham, and that we should convert the present building into a tourist attraction. I pointed out to him too that most Parliaments have enough seats for all their Members to sit in a semi-circular arrangement rather than in the confrontational arrangement of our Parliament. He wrote back to say that although I had made a valid point, it was "a bridge too far at the moment".

In 1997 newly-elected Members of Parliament received no induction in the procedures of the Houses of Parliament. That has been changed too. The increased number of women Members objected to there being only toilets for men in the 'Ayes' and 'Noes' lobbies and to the fact that there wasn't a tights machine anywhere in the Palace. These matters were put right. Accommodation for Members and their staff is much better today than it was in 1997. I mention other changes later.

The Palace of Westminster receives a lot of visitors, who follow the 'Line of Route' when neither House is sitting. The visitors used to arrive at the Sovereign's Entrance at the Victoria Tower end of the Palace, where they were collected by a guide who showed them round the Palace, free of charge. Following the 'Line of Route' takes about one and a half hours. The starting point is the Queen's Robing Room and visitors are then shown the Royal Gallery, the Prince's Chamber, the House of Lords, Central Lobby, the 'Noes' lobby in the House of Commons, the chamber of the House of Commons, St Stephen's Hall and the Great Hall of Westminster.

A modern entrance to the north of Cromwell Green was provided for visitors, which also improved security for the Palace. Whereas there are no public toilets at the Victoria Tower end of the Palace, a new Visitors' Centre is now available adjacent to the new entrance, with a cafe and toilets.

Visitors to the Palace of Westminster can also book in advance, through approaching their Members of Parliament, for a guided tour of the clock tower[4] where they are able to ascend 334 steps and inspect the prison, go behind the clock faces and look down on Big Ben and the other bells as they strike the hours and quarters. The best tour sets off at 11.30 a.m. from the Embankment entrance to Portcullis House and arrives above the bells just in time for them to strike twelve at noon. I accompanied my brother, his wife and some of their friends on this tour on 10 June 2003 and found it very interesting.

For my 1997 General Election campaign Gary Titley MEP lent me a 'mobile telephone'. It was as big and heavy as a brick but it allowed me to keep in contact with my Committee Room and Election Agent, Pat Entwisle, throughout the campaign. When I retired, the mobile 'phone I had then slipped easily into the top pocket of my shirt, and I could silence it when I was in the chamber of the House of Commons. Now, that's progress, and all in less than 13 years.

Just before I retired, Members were given permission to take 'electronic devices' into the chamber, providing that they remain silent. It does annoy me to see Members today, allegedly listening to business in the chamber, head down receiving and sending e-mails, texts, or tweets on their electronic devices, watched by all the viewers of the Parliamentary Channel, millions worldwide during Prime Minister's Questions.

In 1997, Labour Members of Parliament received messages from the Whips' Office on pagers, but these were received on our mobile telephones after the autumn of 2004. The Speaker reprimands any Member who allows a pager or mobile 'phone to ring during a sitting of the House.

In 1997, the computers that were issued to us were large clumsy machines. By 2010, they were faster, had much larger memories, and took up far less space, with their flat screens. Members of Parliament now buy laptop computers too, which allow them to transport information and work on the train. Most of us could give PowerPoint presentations. But the growth in electronic communications between 1997 and 2010 has not helped Members. The serious constituency inquiry has to be sorted from the spam and the rest of the correspondence. Many constituents expect instant responses to their electronic correspondence, and some get annoyed when they don't receive one.

When computers were first introduced for Members to use we received all the 'spam' too, including pornography. This was highly offensive, especially to our female members of staff. Karen, my Office Manager, helped to sort this problem out with the IT staff appointed to run the system in the Palace. Initially, it was suggested that all documents with the word 'sex' in them should be filtered out by the Parliamentary servers until it was realised that documents with words like Middlesex and Essex would be removed too.

Between 1997 and 2010 the increasing influence on politics of the 24-hour news channels was very noticeable. It is very easy too today to track the work of all Members of Parliament by putting their name into an internet search engine. The most useful websites are www.theyworkforyou.com and www.publicwhip.org.uk

The first of these can be used to alert a constituent when their Member of Parliament has spoken or received a response to a written question in the House of Commons. All Members of Parliament, past and present, have entries in Wikipedia, while most run their own websites (on which their speeches or links to them are posted) and have Twitter accounts. Twitter seems to have outpaced blogging, although Members such as Tom Harris (Labour Member of Parliament for Glasgow South) and Nadine Dorries (Conservative Member of Parliament for Mid-Bedfordshire) established blogging reputations, for better or worse; they now tweet as well. Some Members of Parliament also run Facebook or other social networking sites.

There is no doubt in my mind that all this electronic traffic has occupied a great amount of the valuable time that Members of Parliament could be spending on more important matters. Members are often criticised by the general public for not spending enough time in the chamber listening to debates. However, they can watch the debates from their own offices in Westminster on television screens that keep Members up-to-date with proceedings of the House and also call Members to the lobbies to vote.

Parliament improved the allowances system between 1997 and 2010, which meant, for example, that we could employ an extra full-time member of staff and equip our offices with better photocopiers and other equipment. Unfortunately, the system was never audited, which resulted in its abuse. All Members were abused for weeks on end by *The Daily Telegraph* newspaper, beginning on 8 May 2009; we were all tainted by their accusations and, undoubtedly, a small number of Members have caused a lot of trouble for the rest. The Independent Parliamentary Standards Authority (IPSA) that has replaced the old Fees Office is, in my opinion and in the opinion of the majority of Members who deal with it, not fit for purpose and is causing the present Members of Parliament financial loss and a lot more work.

When I was elected to Parliament it was possible to furnish an unfurnished rented flat in London by receiving a Parliamentary allowance. It was also possible to enter into a selection process without spending a lot of money. Today, those seeking to become a Prospective Parliamentary Candidate (PPC) issue more than one glossy leaflet to woo constituency members and some give up their jobs for a short period to win the candidature and, when they are elected, they are expected to furnish properties in London at their own expense. A Member of Parliament can no longer afford to rent a flat in Dolphin

With the Political Correspondent of the Daily Mirror, Paul Routledge.

Square. I am afraid we are now excluding a lot of people from becoming Members of Parliament.

Labour Members donate 1% of their salary to the National Labour Party and another 1% to their Regional Party. They also pay a higher membership fee to the Party than the rest of the members. I agreed also to donate £100 monthly to my CLP, £12,000 in my 13 years in Parliament. My constituents and friends and relatives believed that the Labour Party paid for us to attend our annual conferences, either the national or regional conferences, which is not the case. It cost Eileen and me in the region of £500-600 to attend the national conference. I am not complaining, but there are considerable expenses associated with the job that have to be met personally.

The big event of every annual Labour Party conference is the Leader's Speech, which takes place on the Tuesday afternoon of conference week. Although delegates to conference and Members of Parliament are allocated seats in a defined area for the rest of the conference, for the Leader's Speech the stewards fit us in wherever they can. One year I found myself sitting next to an attractive women dressed in red. We had a long wait before Tony Blair appeared, so I tried to engage her in conversation. She was very friendly and I asked her if she was a delegate and where she came from, just to open up a conversation. No, she wasn't a delegate but she was a Labour Party supporter, obviously from Wales. Further on in the conversation I was told that she was a professional opera singer, and she gave me the impression that I should know who she was. Well, I'm not a follower of opera, so I didn't. To cut a long story short I had found myself sitting next to Katherine Jenkins, who was there to close the conference later in the week. She is much better known today than she was then.

I lost count of the numbers of signed bottles of House of Commons whisky and other Parliamentary souvenirs that I willingly donated to raise money for charities and other organisations. When Billy Joe Dean was killed (see Chapter 9) and an auction was held at the Hare and Hounds pub in Stoneclough, the couple who won the bottle of whisky, already signed by Tony Blair, asked me if I would agree to get it signed too by Cherie Blair. In 13 years that was the only bottle I brought to my constituency with both those signatures on it.

I classify politicians by my 'four Ps of politics'- the passengers, the posers, the professionals and the passionate. We need fewer of the professionals and more of the passionate in Parliament. More and more Labour politicians now possess university degrees and very few come from what used to be regarded as the working class. Of course, politicians need a brain but they also need a heart, as well as gut feelings that something is right or wrong for the country or their constituents. Being a Member of Parliament is not just a job, it's a commitment.

People sometimes ask me why I was never promoted to a Government post. The truth is that I don't really know. Certainly there were many of my colleagues who were not up to it at the Despatch Box, and I often thought that I could have done a better job. I was a 57-year-old when I was elected, and I expect that was one reason that I was never given a position of responsibility. A lot of new blood was elected in 1997 and there were some very ambitious individuals among us. Indeed, we had a lot of talent in the Labour team. I also voted against the Government several times (see Chapters 4-6) and was not afraid to speak my mind.

Ministerial positions are distributed on a regional basis by the Prime Minister, and Ruth Kelly, the Bolton West Member of Parliament, was chosen as a 'rising star' of the Parliamentary Labour Party to be the Economic Secretary at the Treasury following the 2001 General Election. Later, she was Secretary of State at the Departments of Education and Skills, Transport, and Communities and Local Government. I was very pleased that we had a Minister amongst our ranks in Bolton. Greater Manchester had its fair share of Members who held Ministerial posts between 1997 and 2010.

My criticism of the establishment's position on the misuse of drugs probably had something to do with it as well. I was probably seen as an unsafe pair of hands after my high profile in the national media on this issue following the murder of Dillon Hull (see Chapter 4), although I always spoke against the misuse of any drugs, legal or illegal.

NOTES

1. Tragically, Jo Cox (MP for Batley and Spen) was killed after an Advice Surgery in Birstall by Thomas Mair on 16 June 2016.

2. Joan Dearden died on 7 January 2014. I presented a eulogy at her funeral on Friday 17 January; Cllr Rosa Kay died on 26 July 2016.

3. Marsha Singh MP died on 17 July 2012.

4. Renamed the Elizabeth Tower in 2013.

CHAPTER FOUR

BUSINESS OF THE HOUSE: THE 1997-2001 PARLIAMENT

∽

One of the annoying customs of the House of Commons is the 'pecking order' that exists for Members who wish to make speeches in important debates. Privy Counsellors (they are called Right Honourable Members) are always taken first, after opening speeches by Ministers and Shadow Ministers, as are chairmen of Select Committees and other senior Members of the House. These people need not sit in the chamber all day; they are taken soon after they arrive and often leave within a few minutes of delivering their speech. Recently-elected Members are taken last; who speaks when is determined by length of service to Parliament. I have sat in the chamber for up to six hours without being called and often, when I have been called towards the end of a debate, I have been allocated just a few minutes to get my points across.

Another custom that I found annoying is the 'green card' system used to reserve a seat in the chamber for the day. Some Members reserve their seat every day but others only on special occasions, such as Budget Day. There are not enough seats to accommodate every Member in the chamber. Some Members stand behind the Speaker's Chair or below the bar of the chamber; others sit in a Special Gallery observing proceedings from above. However, only Members who have taken a seat in the chamber within the bar can take part in the proceedings.

A green card with a Member's name on it is placed on the seat where the Member intends to sit after Prayers, usually when the Member arrives in Parliament on the morning of that day. Providing that the Member actually attends Prayers, the card can then be placed in a card holder at the back of the seat. Dennis Skinner breaks this tradition (it might even be a rule) every day that he is in the chamber. He 'green cards' but never attends Prayers. Some Members who are not religious attend Prayers and sit through the proceedings in order to be able to reserve a seat for the day.

At my first reception in Speaker's House, Madam Speaker (Betty Boothroyd) recommended that new Members should sit in the same seat so that she could learn to recognise us. "Men should wear a distinctive tie", she told us. In 13 years I only saw one male Member excluded from the chamber by the Speaker for not wearing a tie. When I saw what some of the women wore in the chamber I wondered how bad their appearance would have to be before they were excluded. Betty

Boothroyd also advised us that it would be usual for a backbencher to be called to speak in a major debate about twice in a full session of Parliament.

One or two traditions were dispatched to the history books after 1997. For example, when a Member wanted to raise a point of order during a division they collected a collapsible opera hat from the Clerks of the House and wore it. These hats were so tall that they looked like a chimney pot on top of a Member's head. Now they are in a museum somewhere. Visitors to the Palace were referred to as 'strangers'. That practice has also been consigned to the history books, although the 'Strangers' Gallery', the 'Strangers' Bar' and the 'Strangers' Dining Room' are terms that have survived, and the policeman in Central Lobby still shout 'Hats off strangers' when the Speaker's procession passes through and they remove their helmets.

Members have eight minutes to get into the division lobbies before the doors are locked after a division bell rings. Division bells can be heard throughout the Parliamentary estate and within a one-mile radius of the Principal Doorkeeper's seat at the entrance to the House of Commons chamber, where the lever is pulled, even in bars and restaurants. In 1997 and for a few years after, when policemen on duty saw Members running towards Parliament to vote, they stopped the traffic for them to cross the roads. When Portcullis House opened and the tunnel under Bridge Street was reopened, this tradition ceased, although my understanding is that Members can, if they wish, stop the traffic themselves. Who dare try in London?

It is still possible for Members and Officers of the House of Commons to acquire snuff from the Principal Doorkeeper.

The snuff is kept in a box made of wood recovered when the chamber was destroyed by bombing in 1941. Stonework on the arch between the Members Lobby and the chamber, adjacent to the statue of Sir Winston Churchill and the Principal Doorkeeper's seat, has been deliberately left in the condition in which it was found after the bombing.

In my 13 years in Parliament only one Member of Parliament was elected as an Independent Member, the 'man in the white suit' and former BBC journalist Martin Bell, who was elected for Tatton in 1997 in place of Conservative Neil Hamilton. Quite a few Members on both sides of the House became Independent Members of Parliament, either by resigning their Whip or by having their Whip removed from them.

Four Conservative Members crossed the floor of the House in these 13 years and joined the Labour Party – Peter Temple-Morris (on 21.06.98, who later became a peer), Shaun Woodward (on 18.12.99, who later became a Labour Minister), Robert Jackson (on 15.01.05, briefly before he retired at the 2005 General Election), and Quentin Davies (on 26.06.07, who also became a Labour Minister).

Labour Members Tommy Graham (on 9.09.98 for misconduct), Dennis Canavan (on 26.03.99 for standing against a Labour candidate in an election), Ken Livingstone (on 6.03.2000 also for standing against a Labour candidate), and George Galloway (on 23.10.03, who formed the Respect Party on 25.01.04) were expelled from the Labour Party.

David Chaytor, Elliot Morley, Margaret Moran (all three on 2 June 2009) and, later, Jim Devine were barred from standing as Labour candidates during the 'expenses scandal' (see page 249), while Margaret Moran, along with Patricia

Hewitt, Geoff Hoon and Stephen Byers, was suspended from the Labour Party on 22 March 2010 for her involvement in the 'cash for influence' scandal (see page 248). Ian Gibson was also barred from standing as a Labour Party candidate, on 2 June 2009 (see page 249).

Paul Marsden crossed the floor of the House to become the first Labour Member to join the Liberal Democrat Party, on 10 December 2001; on 6 April 2005 he became an Independent Labour Member but was defeated at the 2005 General Election. Clare Short resigned the Labour Whip on 12 May 2003 and sat with the Opposition; after 20 October 2006 she became Independent. Bob Wareing was deselected on 16 September 2007 (Liverpool West Derby CLP chose Stephen Twigg to fight the 2010 General Election) but stayed on the Labour benches, resigning the Labour Whip on 17 September 2007. On 25 April 2010 during the run-up to the 2010 General Election Brian Sedgemore defected to the Liberal Democrats.

A 'maiden speech' should not exceed 10-15 minutes, but they can be shorter. During a session when Lady Astor was banging her drum against the demon drink a Labour Member who represented a mining constituency got up and made the shortest ever maiden speech – just six words long. He said, "No bloody beer, no bloody coal". In a maiden speech a Member is expected to extol the virtues of their constituency, say something about the successes of their predecessor, and give an indication of their future interests in Parliament, in my case a campaign to raise housing policy up the political agenda.

There is a traditional superstition that a maiden speech goes better if a Member touches a foot of the statue of Winston

Churchill at the entrance to the chamber. I am not superstitious.

Many new Members plan their maiden speeches carefully and ponder over their contents for days. After the 1997 General Election there was a long queue of us waiting to make one. We were not allowed to make any other speeches or put down any oral or written Parliamentary Questions until our maiden speech was made. I made mine on 21 May 1997 during the Whitsuntide Adjournment Debate, when there were few names of Members down to speak on the 'Speaker's list'.

There are no votes on such days, and many Members leave Parliament for home the day before. Ann Taylor, as Leader of the House, was sitting on the Treasury Bench listening to all the speeches, which she responded to at the end of the debate. I asked her whether it would be appropriate for me to make my maiden speech during the Adjournment Debate. When she replied positively, I approached the Deputy Speaker to request him to add my name to his list of speakers, dashed out to the nearby Library, wrote some bullet points down, and returned to the House of Commons chamber to await my turn. The Government Stationery Office sent me the customary bound copy of my speech a few days later, which I kept.

Conservative Leaders during the 1997-2010 Labour Governments were William Hague (1997-2001), Iain Duncan Smith (2001-2003), Michael Howard (2003-2005) and David Cameron (2005-2010), who became Prime Minister in 2010. The Liberal Democrats were led by Paddy Ashdown (1997-1999), Charles Kennedy (1999-2006), Menzies Campbell (2006-2007) and Nick Clegg (2007-2010), who became Deputy Prime Minister in the 2010 Coalition Government.

Attending Parliamentary Question Times at the beginning

of business on Mondays to Thursdays is the best way to learn about the main political issues of current concern in the House of Commons.

My first written question, on small and medium-sized enterprises in Northern Ireland, was answered on 11 June 1997, I intervened during a debate on the Second Reading of the Local Government Finance (Supplementary Credit Approvals) Bill on 17 June, and my first oral question was to the Attorney General on the treatment of the victims of crime by the Crown Prosecution Service, on 19 June 1997.

Two events occupied a considerable amount of my time in the summer of 1997. On Monday 7 July, a hired Mercedes coach carrying 16 pupils from St James's Church of England Secondary School in Farnworth plunged 60 feet down a ravine in the Savoie Region of the French Alps, between the villages of Notre-Dame-des-Près and Longefoy. Two pupils, Nicole Moore, aged 15, and Keith Riddings, aged 14, died at the scene of the accident and Robert Boardman, aged 14, died later in hospital. Two teachers, 13 other pupils (aged 11-16), four instructors and the driver of the coach Jim Shaw were taken to hospital in Chambrey. The French coach was not fitted with seatbelts. Altogether 41 pupils and five staff had undertaken the journey to France to take part in various outdoor activities.

It was necessary for me to liaise with civil servants in the Foreign and Commonwealth Office, with David Bowes, Head Teacher at the school and with the Local Education Authority to ensure that everything that could be done to assist was being done. The school closed for a week and reopened with a special assembly on Monday 14 July.

I called for all coaches to be fitted with seatbelts and a

campaign began in the European Parliament. I have never understood why coaches are fitted with seatbelts today but not trains.

This tragedy gave fuel to the arguments of those who believed that schools should not be involved in any outdoor activities with their pupils. On the day of the tragedy David Blunkett, Secretary of State for Education and Employment, was making a statement at the Dispatch Box on a White Paper, when he interrupted his speech to send his and our condolences to the families who had lost their loved ones, and to the others whose children or partners were injured in the disaster.

At 5.00 p.m. on Wednesday 5 August, a beautiful summer day, 28-year-old John Bates was taking Dillon Hull, aged five, to the shop from their home in Jauncey Street, Deane, when they were confronted by 26-year-old gunman Paul William Seddon, who shot Bates twice in his abdomen. A third bullet hit Dillon's head and he died in the middle of Bankfield Street. Later, it was revealed that Bates had refused to work as a drug dealer for the notorious Bolton gang leader Billy Webb, who controlled most of Bolton's illegal drugs trade at that time. The following day I visited the 'shrine' that had been established for Dillon at the end of St Saviour's Terrace in Bankfield Street and laid some flowers.

On 9 August 1997 neighbours presented a petition for the removal of John Bates and 29-year-old Jane Hull (Dillon's mother) from the area, and they were rehoused on 13 August. On 12 August Jane Hull was due in court in Preston to answer a charge of supplying heroin but the case was adjourned. She was on probation following an appearance at Burnley Crown Court in 1996. Three weeks previously she had given birth to Codie, a heroin-addicted baby.

At 7.16 p.m. on the evening of the 13 August three men were arrested in Brandwood Street, Daubhill in connection with Dillon's murder. Paul Seddon was charged with the murder on 15 August and the two other men were released on police bail on 14 August. Several months later Seddon was gaoled for the murder along with two other men, who were gaoled for conspiracy to commit murder. Seddon did not confess to the murder until 13 years later, when I was about to retire from Parliament. The handgun has never been found, despite a search of a lodge after the confession. The people of Deane raised money for a plaque to be placed on the wall of the house in Jauncey Street where Dillon lived, and I attended its unveiling on Saturday 1 November 1997.

This murder touched the hearts of people not only in Bolton but throughout the world. Dillon's photograph appeared on news bulletins for weeks after his tragic murder. John Bates and Dillon's mum Jane Hull, who was later charged with supplying heroin, had to be taken to a secret location, such was the press interest in this case.

As the Member of Parliament for the constituency in which Dillon was shot, I was involved in interviews with the local and national media. A public meeting was held on 19 August in Emmanuel Church Hall in Deane to discuss what could be done about the supply and use of illegal drugs. Dillon's murder precipitated a country-wide debate on this issue. The 'War on Drugs' did not seem to be working, and the new Government was under pressure to change the strategy for tackling the supply and use of illicit drugs. Apart from cannabis, heroin was the major problem in the north at that time; the widespread availability and use of cocaine, then considered to be the 'champagne drug' (it was expensive), came in the early years of the new century in the north.

The turning point for me in this debate came when the BBCs *The World This Weekend* programme interviewed me on the Sunday following Dillon's murder. I gave my honest opinion, namely that the 'War on Drugs' was not working, could not work and that a different strategy was needed. I called for a Royal Commission to be set up. This did not go down well with the new Government. My views were splashed across the front page of *The Guardian* newspaper and covered by its editorial the following morning, and the country was split in its views as to what should be done about this problem. I was precipitated into a round of television and radio appearances which lasted for months afterwards.

I have a professional background in medicinal chemistry and my research students at the University of Salford spent 12 years trying to separate the addictive and pain-killing properties of the opiate drugs, so it was inevitable that I joined the All-Party Parliamentary Group (APPG) on Drug Misuse, which I served for the next 13 years (see Chapters 12 and 14). I was chairman of this APPG for ten years and the debate continued for the rest of my Parliamentary career.

I made my first speech, on Oxford and Cambridge college fees, on 19 November 1997 and my second speech, made on the same day during an Adjournment Debate, was about illegal drugs.

In December 1997, Quadir Hussain was forced to stop his taxi on the A666 St Peter's Way, to flee from his customers, who had started to attack him, and in doing so, he was hit and killed by a passing car. On 22 December, I raised the safety of taxi drivers with the Home Secretary at Question Time. This incident resulted in a march through Bolton in January 1998, which I addressed before it set off from Burnden Park.

In the first session of the 1997-2001 Parliament I remember being present at a debate on 1 November 1999 about printing Acts of Parliament on acid-free paper for their storage in the Victoria Tower (Parliament's archives are housed there). I voted to maintain the tradition of using parchment, which is made by a small company in Milton Keynes, and received a thank you note from them, appropriately printed on a piece of parchment, which I kept.

My first question at Prime Minister's Questions (PMQs) was actually answered by his Deputy, John Prescott, on 25 March 1998; it was on the wastage of water by the privatised water companies.

In my first session in Parliament I put down only two Early Day Motions (EDMs), on the 'European Sustainable City Award' (13 January 1998) and 'Bolton Institute's Bid for University Status' (27 April 1998). I put down more EDMs as time went by, as did most other Members. These motions are rarely, if ever, discussed on the floor of the House but are a useful way for a Member to flag up important issues. Tony Banks (Member of Parliament for West Ham, later Lord Stratford, now deceased), who was a strong advocate of animal welfare, put down several amusing EDMs; below are two examples.

Early Day Motion 648 in the 2000-2001 session of Parliament:

"That this House congratulates the now deceased bull who was able to gore the matador Jose Thomas at the Maestranza bull ring in Seville; wishes a future bull greater success; and calls upon the European Parliament and Commission to effect a total ban throughout the European Community of the cruel, barbarous and anachronistic slaughter of bulls in the name of sport."

Early Day Motion 1255 in the 2003-2004 session of Parliament:

"That this House is appalled, but barely surprised, at the revelations in MI5 files regarding the bizarre and inhumane proposals to use pigeons as flying bombs; recognises the important and life-saving role of carrier pigeons in two world wars and wonders at the lack of gratitude towards these gentle creatures; and believes that humans represent the most obscene, perverted, cruel, uncivilised and lethal species ever to inhabit the planet and looks forward to the day when the inevitable asteroid slams into the earth and wipes them out, thus giving nature the opportunity to start again."

At the Department of Environment, Transport and the Regions (DETR) Question Time on Tuesday 24th April 2001 Hazel Blears (Member of Parliament for Salford) announced that she was chairman of the All-Party Parliamentary Motorcycling Group and proceeded to ask a question on road congestion. Keith Hill, Parliamentary Under-Secretary of State at the DETR, started off his answer by saying: "I am grateful for that characteristic intervention from my Hon. Friend Blears the Bike", at which the whole House degenerated into laughter. All the sketch columns were full of this the following day. The most vitriolic coverage came from Quentin Letts in *The Daily Mail*, who reported:

"Up popped Hazel Blears (Lab, Salford) a tidy little woman

SCIENCE AND POLITICS: AN UNLIKELY MIXTURE

who comes across as a frightful goody two-shoes. She is as spick and span as a spring clean. Should Mr Blair fail to promote her in the future there will be no one more surprised than Ms Blears herself."

The matter she wanted to raise was Government policy on motor bikes. "As chairman of the All-Party Commons Motorcycling Group," she began, teeth sparkling like rhinestones.

Mr Hill listened patiently to her point, then, inclining his head towards her and giving her a full, ghastly, gargoyle smile, told her what a pleasure, a joy, it always was to be offered advice by 'Blears the Bike'.

It took a second or two for the House to realise quite what his remark could mean.

Ms Blears, slow to catch up on the horrid (though possibly unintended) sexual nature of the slur, initially stretched her face into a look of delight at the Minister's answer.

Then, as the ramification of 'Blears the Bike' sank in, there was a Tom and Jerry tinkling as her grin disintegrated.

A near-packed House reacted with violent mirth. Ben Bradshaw (Lab, Exeter) near wept with laughter. John Heppell (Lab, Nottingham East) chortled so long that his face went a Leander Club pink. The greater the hoots of delight, the faster did Blears the Bike's eyes blink with fury.

The nickname may be undeserved but it is almost certain to stick."

We all suffered at the hands of Mr Letts, who was well known for his caustic comments. In the same article he referred to my good friend David Taylor (Member of Parliament for North West Leicestershire) as "a nonentity", and he once referred to me as "a deflated little balloon". David Taylor was one of our best backbenchers; he was a wordsmith and had a brilliant sense of humour. Tragically, he died on Boxing Day 2009. David had already announced his intention not to stand at the 2010 General Election.[1]

Keith Hill, the last Parliamentary Private Secretary to Tony Blair, who retired at the 2010 General Election as the Member of Parliament for Streatham, told me that he will be remembered for three things. The first was his reference to Hazel Blears as 'Blears the Bike', and the second was a 30-minute Adjournment Debate in Westminster Hall during which he had to repeat 'short sea shipping' 18 times in his 15-minute response, as the Minister responding to a Member. In trying to get these words out so many times Keith fell about laughing, all televised (Paul Flynn thought that this was one of the funniest moments in politics and placed an edited version of these 15 minutes on his website). The third thing was rapping in Trafalgar Square. A television camera caught Keith rapping with a baseball hat on. It became part of a competition of the ten worst moments in politics on BBCs *Newsnight* programme. Viewers were asked to vote for one of these 'moments' night after night. Keith didn't win.

In responding to a question from Europhobe Tory Bill Cash (Member of Parliament for Stone) on 6 November 2001, the Parliamentary Secretary of State representing the Lord Chancellor's Department in the House of Commons, Rosie Winterton (Member of Parliament for Doncaster Central) said, "The Hon. Gentleman and I have been together upstairs all morning but now I have him on the floor of the House". If the reader looks this up in the *Official Record* (*Hansard*) they will not find it recorded as it happened. Those who produce

Hansard often change the spoken word in recording the day's proceedings, usually for the better, although they try to preserve the meaning.

In this and the next two chapters I give summaries of some of the highlights of the three Labour Governments of 1997-2010. The journalist Andrew Rawnsley has given full accounts of the highs and lows of 13 years of the three Labour Governments in his two books *Servants of the People* (published by Penguin Books in 2001) and *The End of the Party* (published by Penguin Books in 2010).

Our early debates, in the first long session of the 1997-1998 Labour Government, were on the Child Support Agency (good in principal but bad in practice), devolution of government, student fees, assisted places in public schools, nursery vouchers, the control of handguns, landmines, the future of the proposed Millennium Dome at Greenwich, freedom of information, a national minimum wage, food safety, underfunding of the NHS, Northern Ireland, the misuse of fireworks, the Middle East Peace Process, Sierra Leone, break-up of the former Yugoslavia, the previous Government's policy on drug misuse and the thorny issue of welfare reform. A New Deal Task Force was established and Britain signed up to the European Social Chapter, providing better employment rights for British workers.

The concept of prelegislative scrutiny of Draft Bills was introduced, VAT on fuel was reduced to 5%, people were given free entry to museums and galleries, ISAs replaced TESSAs and PEPs as a means of tax-free saving, the National Endowment for Science, Technology and the Arts (NESTA) was established to support British talent in innovation and creativity, and the National Lottery was reformed to provide money for good causes.

Early legislation based on the belief that local authorities took a long time to make decisions led to the committee style of local government being abandoned and Executive Members being appointed to make faster decisions. Scrutiny Committees were established to ensure that Executive Members would act in the best interests of citizens. Power was given to local residents to hold referendums for the election of all-powerful Mayors, but few local authorities were forced down this route.

Michael Foster's Wild Mammals (Hunting with Dogs) Bill had its Second Reading on 28 November 1997, as a Private Member's Bill, but soon ran into the sand. The legislative programme was so extensive that there was no time to get this Bill through the House of Lords, where the Conservatives had a huge majority, especially when the number of hereditary peers was taken into account.

The money made available by the scrapping of nursery vouchers and the assisted places scheme was used to reduce the size of classes in primary schools to 30 pupils or less. A Competition Bill was passed which prevented predatory pricing, particularly in the newspaper industry. The Government began to sell off its unused assets to provide money for its other projects and reduce the national debt.

Whether to go ahead with the Millennium Dome or not was a debate that divided the House. On balance I was in favour of it being built. I was especially intrigued by architect Richard Rogers's design and by the fact that it would have a Teflon roof. It cost £1 billion to build and was divided up into zones inside – the Faith Zone, the Body Zone, the Talk Zone, the Journey Zone, the Learning Zone and the Mind Zone, for example, each sponsored by a major company. Schoolchildren from each town in Britain were invited in the millennium year to perform in the Millennium Dome, and I was very pleased to be there when children from Bolton's schools travelled down to perform *Bolton – Our Town* on 11 May 2000.

In our first session of Parliament we spent a lot of time in the chamber debating the devolution of government. For Constitutional Bills it is necessary for the Committee Stage to be taken on the floor of the House instead of, as with other Bills, in a committee room. When the chamber is sitting in committee the mace is lowered onto brackets below the table level and the Speaker's Chair is vacated. The chairman of the committee, usually the Deputy Speaker or a Member who has been appointed to the Chairman's Panel by the Speaker (these Members chair Parliamentary committees), sits in one of the Clerk's chairs. Referendums on devolution were held in the 1997 summer recess and resulted in a Scottish Parliament and a Welsh Assembly (the vote for devolution was decisive in Scotland but not so decisive in Wales).

Tony Blair's and the Labour Government's proudest achievement was bringing peace to Northern Ireland. The groundwork was laid by John Major's Conservative Government but, without Mo Mowlam's unorthodox behaviour, Senator George Mitchell's behind-the-scenes work, and the Prime Minister's personal involvement over a long and sustained period of time, the breakthrough of the Belfast Agreement (signed on Good Friday – 10 April 1998) would not have happened.

Tony Blair's Chief of Staff, Jonathan Powell, and the head of the monitoring process, Canadian General John de Chastelain, also played key roles. After Mo Mowlam, four

SCIENCE AND POLITICS: AN UNLIKELY MIXTURE

Prime Minister's Questions in the 1997-2001 Labour Government (I am sitting behind Dennis Skinner, who is wearing a red tie on the front bench – next to him on his right shoulder is Worsley MP Terry Lewis talking to Tottenham MP Bernie Grant).

other Secretaries of State for Northern Ireland – Peter Mandelson, John Reid, Paul Murphy and Peter Hain – carried the process forward.

The Good Friday Agreement was accepted by the people of Northern Ireland in a referendum held on 22 May 1998, when 71% approved the Agreement on an 81% turnout. 90% of voters in the Irish Republic also accepted the Agreement.

Parliament was recalled on 2 September 1997 to discuss the Omagh bomb of the 15 August and its aftermath. In my opinion, this was the tipping point in the Northern Ireland Peace Process; people on both sides of the divide had had enough of the violence by this time. Elections were held for the Northern Ireland Assembly on 25 June 1998 but the Assembly was not to last. After October 2002 the Assembly did not meet for four years despite the fact that its elected members were paid throughout this period. The decommissioning of arms by the IRA was the major problem but this got underway in October 2001.

Chancellor of the Exchequer Gordon Brown handed over control of interest rates to the newly created Monetary Policy Committee (MPC) at the Bank of England and introduced a Comprehensive Spending Review (the first was published in July 1998) and a Pre-Budget Report (announced in the autumn of each year). Our first Budget Day was Wednesday 2 July 1997. A 'windfall tax' was applied on the excess profits of the utility companies to provide money to kick-start the New Deal Programmes. The Chancellor of the Exchequer sold off most of Britain's gold reserves, which Conservative Member Peter Tapsall (Member of Parliament for Louth and Horncastle; I christened him 'Goldfinger') never forgave him for.

Gordon Brown introduced the concept of Public Private Partnerships (PPPs) to provide both public and private capital (mainly private) for major capital projects. A vigorous discussion began when it was suggested that the National Air Traffic Services (NATS) be reformed using private capital. Labour Party members saw PPPs as costly (and they were) and as partial privatisation of public services. However, the plain fact is that there would not have been as many new schools or hospitals without them. Later they were replaced by Private Finance Initiatives (PFIs).

The Government passed an Act of Parliament to set up Regional Development Agencies (the 2010 Conservative Government abolished them and replaced them with LEPs – Local Economic Partnerships), the first Minister for Public Health was appointed, and Deputy Prime Minister John Prescott played a leading role at Kyoto in persuading the attending nations to take climate change seriously.

Tam Dalyell (Member of Parliament for Linlithgow) continuously raised the tragedy at Lockerbie, George Robertson, Secretary of State for Defence, published a Strategic Defence Review, which would settle the future of the armed forces until the Tory Government came to power in 2010, and events in Iraq became the subject of a series of vigorous debates.

When Labour came to power we inherited a ban on the export of British beef, which had been imposed in March 1996 due to an outbreak of bovine spongiform encelopathy (BSE; 'mad-cow disease'). The ban lasted for ten years. Cases of a similar disease, new variant Creutzfeldt-Jacob disease (nvCJD), began to emerge in humans, which was a very worrying development. These neurological diseases are caused by the unfolding of prions (complex folded proteins) in the brain. A man in Kearsley, Bolton, contracted nvCJD and died.

My biggest disappointment with our first session in Government was that the Secretary of State for Work and Pensions, Harriet Harman, brought forward a Social Security Bill to reform welfare benefits, which was almost identical to a Bill that the Conservative Secretary of State before her, Peter Lilley (Member of Parliament for Hitchin and Harpenden), had tried to steer through. On 10 December 1997, after much deliberation, I decided to vote against Clause 70 in the Social Security Bill that would introduce 'a power to reduce lone parent benefit', with the intention of getting lone parents back to work.

I felt physically sick on 10 December 1997 when I did not join my own Government in the 'Aye' lobby. 47 Labour Members of Parliament voted against this measure, so I was not alone. Before the vote I met the Chancellor of the Exchequer, Gordon Brown, on 3 December, Tony Blair on 4 December and Jane Kennedy, my Regional Whip, several times. I wrote to the Minister, Hariet Harman on 8 December about my objections to Clause 70.

On 22 June 1998, I supported Joe Ashton (Member of Parliament for Bassetlaw) in his successful attempt to prevent the Government amending the law to make the age of consent for sex 16 for both hetero- and homosexual activity. This is down on the record as being my second rebellion, but this matter was decided on a free vote.

After the Prime Minister's statement on 2 September 1998 on the Omagh bomb, the House of Commons proceeded to deal with all Stages of the Criminal Justice (Terrorism and Conspiracy) Bill in what became an overnight sitting. Chris Mullin (Member of Parliament for Sunderland South) moved an amendment that would have required the Royal Ulster Constabulary to interview suspected terrorists in the presence of a solicitor and with the interview recorded with audio recording equipment. I supported his amendment to the Bill but it was defeated.

The Government's first session in power wasn't without its troubles. There was more than one rebellion against its policies, a few Members were expelled from the Labour Party (see page 162), and Ron Davies (Member of Parliament for Caerphilly) was forced to resign from the Cabinet as Secretary of State for Wales for 'a moment of madness' (his words) on Clapham Common, a well-known meeting place for gay men. He met a man who later mugged him at knifepoint in 'crack alley', Brixton.

Ron Davies was succeeded as Secretary of State for Wales by

Alun Michael (Member of Parliament for Cardiff South and Penarth). He was unpopular with his Welsh colleagues and was forced to resign. The far more popular Rhodri Morgan (Member of Parliament for Cardiff West) succeeded him and later became the first First Minister for Wales in the Welsh Assembly.

The Government published its first Annual Report in July 1998 but they later abandoned publication of these reports. 22 Major Bills were in the Queen's Speech for the long 1997-1998 session of Parliament and an amazing 52 Acts received Royal Assent.

On 15 June 1998 22 Bills were under way in the second session of the 1997-2001 Parliament. Legislation was passed to set up the Greater London Authority, the Food Standards Agency and the Disability Rights Commission. A 10p tax band was introduced on 6 April 1999 (the basic rate of tax remained at 23p in the pound but was reduced to 20p during the lifetime of the Labour Government), the Working Families Tax Credit was introduced, the literacy and numeracy programmes were launched in primary schools, primary school class sizes were reduced to less than 30 pupils, the internal market in the NHS ('fund holding') was abolished, NHS Direct came online, the National Institute for Clinical Excellence (NICE, to deal with the postcode prescribing of expensive drugs) and Primary Care Trusts (PCTs) were established, the Climate Change Levy was imposed on industry, Anti-Social Behaviour Orders (ASBOs) came into effect on 1 April 1999 as did the National Minimum Wage, all but 92 hereditary peers were removed from the House of Lords, the criminal justice system and legal aid scheme were reformed, and the Government also began to deal with increasing numbers of immigrants.

At this time it was taking several years to determine the

outcome of asylum seekers' applications and the results were often inconsistent. Ports like Dover were overwhelmed with the numbers arriving from across the Channel and the Immigration and Asylum Bill was introduced into Parliament in an attempt to get this problem under control. The National Asylum Seekers Support Scheme (NASS) was established to disperse newly arrived immigrants away from our ports to other towns and cities across Britain.

In 1999, the Labour Government launched one of the largest compensation schemes ever launched by a British Government, which was designed to compensate miners suffering from chronic lung disease or vibration white finger. The Government also compensated former Japanese prisoners of war or their surviving relatives. The President of Bolton United Veterans Association, Captain Bill Harris, who had been a Japanese prisoner of war, persuaded me to join the British Internee and Prisoners of War (Far East Region) All-Party Parliamentary Group, which campaigned for this compensation to be paid. Bill died in November 1999 before we won this battle but his widow benefited.

One good sign was that the number of homeless people sleeping rough on the streets of our major towns and cities was going down.

A cause for concern to Labour Members of Parliament was the work of the Joint Consultative Committee that had been set up in an attempt to work with the Liberal Democrats. At this time their Leader Paddy Ashdown and Tony Blair were thought by people like me to be much too close. Tony Blair set up a Joint Committee of the Cabinet on Constitutional Reform in 1997, with Liberal Democrat membership, and an Independent Commission on Electoral Reform was established under the chairmanship of Lord (Roy) Jenkins. When it reported in October 1998 it recommended the system of 'AV plus' for all UK elections.

The new London Assembly and its Mayor, Ken Livingstone (Member of Parliament for Brent East, who stood in the Mayoral election as an Independent candidate), were elected on 4 May 2000. Those events were preceded by much controversy. The Labour Party's, or should I say Tony Blair's, choice of Mayoral candidate was Frank Dobson (Member of Parliament for Camden). Conservative Leader of the day William Hague suggested that the Prime Minister appoint Frank Dobson as his day Mayor and Ken Livingstone as his nightmare.

Ken Livingstone, who was re-elected on 7 June 2004, was Mayor of London until 2 May 2008, when he was defeated by Boris Johnson (Member of Parliament for Henley), and was the Labour Party's Mayoral candidate for the London Assembly elections in 2012.[2] Boris Johnson was my neighbour in the Norman Shaw North building before he became Mayor of London in 2008. My other neighbour was Anne McIntosh (then Conservative Member of Parliament for the Vale of York).

On the 6 May 1999, elections were held for the Welsh Assembly and the Scottish Parliament using proportional representation and, on 26 May, the Queen opened the National Assembly of Wales and, on 1 July, she opened the Scottish Parliament. Dennis Canavan (Member of Parliament for West Stirlingshire until 1999) stood against a Labour Party candidate to be elected as Member of the Scottish Parliament (MSP) for Falkirk, and was expelled from the Party. This introduction of proportional representation in Scotland resulted later in Labour losing control to the Scottish National Party, with Alex Salmond as their Leader (see later).

The Labour Party did not perform well in the European Elections on 10 June; the turnout was low. A new voting system was in use, based on preferences; Members of the European Parliament represented regions and became detached from constituencies. I am not in favour of different voting systems being used for different British elections. I strongly support the 'first past the post' system for all elections.

On Wednesday 24 February 1999, Peter Brooke (Member of Parliament for the Cities of London and Westminster) launched the Second Reading of the City of London (Ward Elections) Bill, a Private Bill from the City of London Corporation, which was supported by the Government and dealt with in Government time. This Bill was a reform Bill, but I didn't believe that the City of London Corporation should exist or that a Labour Government should support it. I voted against this Bill throughout its various stages, and John McDonnell (Member of Parliament for Hayes and Harlington) tried gallantly, along with a few supporters on the Labour benches, to sink the Bill without trace. Nevertheless, after several days of Government time and three years later, it received its Third Reading in the House of Commons on Monday 15 April 2002.

On 20 May 1999, I supported Roger Berry's (Member of Parliament for Kingwood) amendment to the Government's Welfare Reform and Pensions Bill, which was intended to stop the Government restricting Incapacity Benefit only to those who had made recent National Insurance Contributions. The amendment was defeated in a division of the House.

The Conservative opposition undermined attempts to

implement the Belfast Agreement in Northern Ireland. 'Political prisoners' were released on licence, which was not to their liking.

NATO troops made air strikes on Milosevic's Serbian army, which was ethnically cleansing Kosovan Albanians; their air force was destroyed by bombing.

There were 20 key Bills in the Queen's Speech in 1999. In the 1999-2000 session of Parliament the Learning and Skills Council was established [only to be axed in the final (2009-2010) session of the Labour Government], the Financial Services Authority (which was shown later to lack teeth), the Strategic Rail Authority and an Independent Appointments Commission for the House of Lords were set up. Public Sector Agreements required local authorities to improve their performance, the State Second Pension was introduced, the Freedom of Information Bill was passed, the Human Rights Act came into force in Britain, the Post Office became a Government-owned plc, and legislation was brought in to deal with terrorism and for control of the funding of political parties and their expenditure during a General Election campaign. Money raised from Public Private Partnerships was used to update National Air Traffic Services (NATS) and the London Underground. The Football (Disorder) Bill introduced 'banning orders' to prevent football hooligans from travelling abroad. Community Health Councils were abolished, which I opposed, and vaccine damaged people received better compensation in July 2000.

One of the most popular Acts of Parliament in this session was the Countryside and Rights of Way Act, which gave us all greater access to land in private ownership. The Race Relations (Amendment) Act strengthened the law on racial discrimination, and legislation was introduced to protect vulnerable children and animals.

With Eileen (left) at my 60th birthday party (5 July 2000) at Bolton Town Hall: one cake had a distinctly chemical theme; my first wife Merrilyn (above) made a second cake with a distinctly different theme.

During the Report Stage of the Child Support, Pensions and Social Security Bill I supported an amendment put down by John McDonnell which, if passed, would have linked annual pension increases either to increases in earnings or the Retail Price Index, whichever was the greater, but this amendment was not supported by the Government. Ironically this became Government policy later.

Sittings in the Westminster Hall chamber began on 30 November 1999 with a debate on Palestinian refugees, led by Phyllis Starkey, to which I contributed.

In the election of a new Speaker to replace Betty Boothroyd, which was held on 23 October 2000, I supported Dr David Clark in the first ballot (he was at Salford University before his election to Parliament, so I knew him well), then Michael Martin when the House voted not to elect David.

Ken Livingstone was expelled in the spring of 2000 from the Labour Party for standing against the official Labour Party candidate, Frank Dobson, in the London Mayoral Election. On 6 January 2004 the NEC of the Labour Party voted to readmit him as a member.

I supported a Ten Minute Rule Bill that was proposed by Dr Evan Harris (Member of Parliament for Oxford West and Abingdon) on 31 October 2000, which would have allowed the use of embryonic tissue (containing stem cells) in research on regenerative therapies, but the Bill was defeated when a vote was called. Along with the chairman of the Science and Technology Select Committee, Dr Ian Gibson, I opposed another Ten Minute Rule Bill, presented by the much-respected Alan Simpson (Member of Parliament for Nottingham South), which was very critical of the development of genetically modified (GM) crops. This Bill was illustrative of the opposition to GM materials that existed in Britain in 2000. Other countries have outpaced us in research and, in particular, development in this area of research, which will be crucial in future if we are to provide enough food by 2050 to feed the estimated nine billion people of the world.

Oil prices continued to rise steeply, which led to fuel protests outside refineries in the summer of 2000. These began at Stanlow refinery in Cheshire and almost brought the country to a standstill.

In March 2000, the North West Group of Members of Parliament insisted on a meeting with the Prime Minister about a decision to build the Diamond Synchrotron on the

Rutherford Appleton Laboratory site near Oxford, instead of on the Daresbury site near Runcorn, where all the synchrotron research had been carried out. Although the Diamond Synchrotron was constructed in the south, our meeting with Tony Blair resulted in the award of an extra £25 million to be distributed by the NW Regional Development Agency to further support the NW science base.

A lot was achieved in the truncated fourth session of the 1997-2001 Parliament. Legislation was introduced to ban the advertising of tobacco, to improve the education of children with special educational needs, to provide a Children's Commissioner for Wales, to ban the hunting of mammals such as foxes with dogs (this legislation was delayed again), to set up a Joint Committee (of both Houses) on Human Rights, to simplify tax legislation for businesses, to set up a tribunal to investigate the murders that Dr Harold Shipman had been found guilty of, to tackle homelessness and introduce 'sellers' packs' to speed up the sale of houses (the Homes Bill was reintroduced in the following Parliament before it received Royal Assent), to regulate the private security industry, for example by requiring 'bouncers' on pub and club doors to be licensed, to tackle benefit fraud and to allow those clergy who were disqualified by previous legislation from standing as a Member of Parliament to be able to do so.

The ban on the advertising of tobacco resulted in a major scandal when it was discovered that Bernie Ecclestone had successfully negotiated a delay with respect to advertising tobacco on Formula 1 cars. It was revealed that he had donated £1 million to the Labour Party.

The Political Parties, Elections and Referendums Bill

banned foreign donations to British political parties, limited their expenditure during a General Election campaign, set up the Electoral Commission and required constituency parties and Members of Parliament to register donations.

Britain signed up to the International Criminal Court. The omnibus Criminal Justice and Police Bill allowed the police to issue a number of fixed penalty notices, and it allowed local authorities to ban the consumption of alcohol in designated areas, test-purchase alcohol in shops licensed to sell it with underage children and remove licences from the owners of premises that abuse the law. It also strengthened the law on Anti-Social Behaviour Orders (ASBOs, introduced by the Crime and Disorder Act 1998), which provided the police with more powers to deal with animal rights protesters. It also allowed the police to confiscate passports from those charged for serious criminal offences, such as drug trafficking, and legislated for the police to retain DNA samples.

The Health and Social Care Bill made provision for nursing care in nursing homes to be free at the point of provision. Local Care Trusts were established, which allowed the NHS and local authority provided social services to work together to prevent bed blocking in hospitals. Local Authority Health Scrutiny Committees were established.

The International Development Bill provided legislation to allow the Department for International Development (DfID), the Foreign and Commonwealth Office (FCO) and the Ministry of Defence (MoD) to co-operate in the provision of aid to the developing countries in a more focused way. Britain agreed to provide aid on the basis that the recipient country had to use it on designated health and education programmes. The Government restated its commitment to achieve the target of expenditure on aid at the level of 0.7% of GDP. This Bill was reintroduced in the next Parliament before it received Royal Assent.

In a debate on embryology, held on 19 December 2000 (there had been another debate on embryology on 17 November 2000) my speech was continually interrupted by my Bolton colleague Ruth Kelly, who strongly objected to what the Government was proposing to do on religious grounds; the media revealed that Ruth was a member of Opus Dei. Nevertheless, the Draft Human Fertilisation and Embryology (Research Purposes) Regulation 2000 was approved on 19 December by a substantial majority. This Regulation allowed the UK to become a world leader in stem cell research.

Deferred Divisions and Programme Motions (limited to a 45-minute debate) were used in this session of Parliament for the first time.

At this time the car industry was going through a bad period. Rover announced complete closure of all its plants, and Vauxhall announced closure of its Luton plant. However, Nissan's plant in Sunderland was expanding and the Jaguar plant at Halewood and the Peugeot plant in Coventry were doing well. Manufacturing was declining overall; in 2001 it was 18% of GDP, which represented four million jobs. By 2010 it represented only 12% of GDP (by contrast, the financial services sector had become 18% of GDP by 2010). On 14 March, however, the Chancellor announced that the number of people registered as unemployed in Britain had fallen below one million for the first time in 25 years. Service sector jobs replaced manufacturing jobs.

Until Rover stopped production in this country I always bought their cars, or cars from the companies that became Rover. After that I turned to Vauxhall to supply my cars, although we have bought two Suzuki Swifts for Eileen.

On 20 February 2001, the first case of foot and mouth disease was reported, which led to one of the most serious outbreaks of this disease that Britain has ever seen. The 2000-2001 session of Parliament was dominated by statements (the first was on 26 February 2001) and debates on this issue as the outbreak got out of control. Access to the countryside was restricted and the tourism industry was badly damaged. There were not enough veterinary surgeons to visit all the farms affected and the army had to be brought in to deal with all the carcasses that littered the countryside.

Local Elections were deferred from 3 May until 7 June (also the date of the General Election), which also required legislation. It was the Chief Scientific Adviser to the Prime Minister, David King, who was tasked with bringing this outbreak under control, and he employed computer modellers at the Institute of Animal Health and Veterinary Laboratories Agency to enable him to do so.

Legislation to approve a secret ballot to elect the Speaker was lost by 84 ('Noes') to 82 ('Ayes') on 22 March 2001; I am on record as being a rebel because I was one of the 'Noes'. Joe Ashton received approval to set up a working party to consider 'Provision for Former Members', who had never been given any visiting rights on leaving the Palace.

At the end of a Parliament, when the Prime Minister has

visited Buckingham Palace, Parliament is 'dissolved' (the Dissolution of Parliament). Before that happens Royal Assent for Bills is announced at the Prorogation Ceremony in the House of Lords.

For the first two years of the 1997-2001 Parliament the Labour Government adopted the previous Conservative Government's Budget. Gordon Brown regularly mentioned 'prudence' in his speeches; he was convinced that we had seen an end to 'boom and bust' and adhered to his 'Golden Rule' that 'over the economic cycle, the Government will only borrow to invest, not to fund current spending'. By the end of this Parliament, the significant extra money provided for the NHS, education and the criminal justice system began to make a difference. The first new hospitals were under construction as were new buildings for primary and secondary schools and universities and colleges, old buildings were being refurbished, and the number of police on our streets was increasing, with a consequent reduction in crime.

However, during the 1997-2001 Labour Government the general public became weary of 'spin doctors', who attempted to run the Government by controlling the media, and the mention of targets (6,000 of them at one stage). The growth in the number of specialist advisers (SPADS) was often criticised by the media. There were rumours of two camps in the Government. Tony Blair was closely advised by Alistair Campbell, Jonathan Powell and Peter Mandelson MP (Anji Hunter, Sue Nye, Philip Gould and, later, Matthew Taylor were also part of Blair's 'inner circle') while Gordon Brown was closely advised by Charlie Whelan and MPs Ed Balls and Ed Miliband and later by MPs Douglas Alexander, Tom

Watson and Ian Austin, and by Damian McBride. As time went on the two camps started to 'spin' against each other. One outcome of this tension was that the Government decided in the autumn of 1997 not to adopt the single currency in 1999. Blair was in favour of adopting the euro, but Brown was against.

Not only did Tony Blair get close to the Liberal Democrat Party but his 'Big Tent' policy also resulted in him appointing Ministers from the leaders of industry and commerce, such as Gus MacDonald and Lord (David) Sainsbury, who became the Minister responsible for science, engineering and technology (SET). Later, Lord (Paul) Drayson replaced Lord Sainsbury as the Minister responsible for SET. Lord Sainsbury was a major donor of funds to the Labour Party.

After a period of Tory 'sleaze' (the 'cash for questions' scandal rocked the Tory Government and led to its downfall) Tony Blair promised to clean up the Government. Inevitably the Labour Government was soon embroiled in further scandals. In addition to the Ecclestone affair there were other scandals. Robin Cook dumped his wife Margaret at Heathrow Airport on 2 August 1998 in favour of his assistant Gaynor Regan. Peter Mandelson was forced to resign as Secretary of State at the DTI on 23 December 1998 over his failure to disclose a £373,000 loan from Geoffrey Robinson (Member of Parliament for Coventry North West) to purchase an expensive home and again on 24 January 2001, when he was Secretary of State for Northern Ireland, over his involvement in the Hinduja brothers passport applications.

As Secretary of State for International Development, Clare

Short outraged the evacuated inhabitants of the small island of Montserrat in August 1997 when she said "They'll be wanting golden elephants next", referring to their demands for further assistance following a volcanic eruption on the island. Even the successful return of democracy to Sierra Leone was not without its problems when it was revealed that Tim Spicer's company Sandline International was breaking an arms embargo by exporting arms to help elected President Kabbah to return to power.

The 2001 election campaign was livened up in Rhyl when Deputy Prime Minister John Prescott punched an egg-throwing heckler. His 'Two Jags' title changed to 'Two Jabs'. The campaign was badly launched at a religious assembly at St Saviour's and St Olive's School in London. *Private Eye* had already christened Tony Blair the Vicar of St Albion. There was a rather nasty incident at Birmingham Queen Elizabeth Hospital when postmistress Sharon Storer tackled Blair about the Government's poor record on cancer care. However, the big issue was tax. Conservative Oliver Letwin leaked that their party was considering £20 billion of public expenditure cuts at a time when the general public wanted further improvements in public services. William Hague was unable to pull back Labour's 16-point lead and the Conservatives lost the election badly. The turnout was only 42%: most of the general public saw the result as a foregone conclusion. Labour lost just 12 seats and gained an overall majority of 167.

Tony Benn (Member of Parliament for Chesterfield) and Father of the House Edward Heath (Member of Parliament for Bexley and Old Sidcup) both retired at the end of the 1997-2001 Parliament.

NOTES

1. *Clock Winder Who Wouldn't Say No: The Life of David Taylor MP* by Paul Flynn MP, Biteback Publishing, London, 2012.

2. Ken Livingstone was defeated in this election

CHAPTER FIVE

BUSINESS OF THE HOUSE: THE 2001-2005 PARLIAMENT

∽

Tam Dalyell became Father of the House and supervised the re-election of Michael Martin as Speaker for the 2001-2005 Parliament. Although not a scientist by profession, Tam took a great interest in science and technology in Parliament. For many years he contributed a column to the *New Scientist*.

The Father of the House is not the oldest Member in the House of Commons but the longest-serving Member. If several long-serving Members are elected to Parliament for the first time on the same day, it is the Member who took the oath first who becomes Father of the House.

On 11 September 2001 the world was shaken by al-Qaeda

SCIENCE AND POLITICS: AN UNLIKELY MIXTURE

terrorist attacks in the USA, when four aeroplanes were hijacked in mid-air and three of them flown into each of the twin towers of the World Trade Centre in New York and the Pentagon, near Washington. The fourth aeroplane was brought down by its passengers in a field in Pennsylvania. After 9/11 temporary concrete walls were put in place to protect the Houses of Parliament from vehicular attack and the Government started to protect all its Westminster buildings by walls and iron bollards placed between the street and the buildings.

Jo Moore, spin doctor to Stephen Byers, foolishly emailed "It is now a very good day [9/11] to get anything out that we want to bury" and was forced to resign.

On 7 October 2001, Allied forces entered Afghanistan with the intention of removing the Taliban training camps for al-Qaeda terrorists and providing good governance in a country

Campaigning with Ruth Kelly and Ian McCartney in November 1999.

that had been virtually lawless for decades. I supported the invasion. The issue of the Americans taking prisoners for interrogation to Guantanamo Bay, where they were kept for a long time without trial, became a matter of great concern to many Labour Members of Parliament. Undoubtedly the al-Qaeda leader Osama bin Laden was in Afghanistan when troops entered but the current thinking at that time was that he was probably being sheltered in another country shortly after.[1] Sadly, events in Afghanistan destabilised Pakistan.

The first session of the 2001-2005 Parliament was dominated by further Bills from the Departments for Education and Skills, Health and Home Affairs, bringing further reform to the education services, the NHS, and the criminal justice system.

Legislation was introduced to further control immigration and prevent economic migration, to reform the laws on adoption (to allow, for example, adoption by an unmarried couple), to recover the assets of criminals, on decommissioning of arms in Northern Ireland, on further reform of the House of Lords (little progress was made), to equalise the age (at 60) that men and women receive concessionary fares on public transport, to reform the laws on commonhold and leasehold, to introduce more Sure Start schemes, to write off £1.9 billion of debt that highly indebted countries had accrued, to bring in a rate of maternity payment of £100 per week and increase the period that it could be paid from 18 to 26 weeks, to introduce a landfill tax, and to establish a Disability Rights Commission.

Legislation was also introduced for the Child Tax Credit and Pension Credit (which built on the Minimum Income Guarantee for pensioners on basic state pension) to be paid, to give employment rights to workers and on further reform of the NHS. The Government also introduced the Winter Fuel Allowance and ratified the Kyoto Protocol in this session of Parliament. Ofcom was established to regulate the communications industry, a new police complaints procedure was introduced and legislation was brought in that allowed police to co-operate across county boundaries.

The aims of the omnibus Education Bill were to promote diversity and higher standards in our secondary schools, create opportunities for school sponsorship, provide more options for tackling 'failing schools' and provide greater freedom for head teachers and school governors. This Bill encouraged an increase in the number of 'academies', which many of us were opposed to.

There was great pressure in this session to deal with the question of fox hunting. At the PLP meeting on 24 April 2002 Gordon Prentice (Member of Parliament for Pendle) successfully moved a motion for the Bill that had failed in the last Parliament to be reintroduced in this Parliament and for the Parliament Act to be applied to force it through.

Holding a street surgery in Farnworth shopping precinct (I began these on 30 August 2000).

Some progress was made on the thorny question of House of Lords reform. 750 hereditary peers were removed by earlier legislation but 92 remained. A Royal Commission reported, which resulted in publication of a White Paper for discussion on a way forward. The pre-eminence of the House of Commons was a major concern; the White Paper recommended that only 120 Members of the House of Lords should be elected to take care of this issue. However, the Salisbury-Addison convention, already in place, covered this point.

On 16 July 2001, I voted against the proposed removal of the former chairmen, Donald Anderson and Gwyneth Dunwoody from the Foreign and Commonwealth and Transport, Local Government and the Regions Select Committees respectively. It was this debate that put pressure on Government to reform the way in which the chairman and Members of a Select Committee are appointed, but reform had to wait until the election of a Conservative Government in May 2010. On 14 May 2002, I voted against a Government motion to pay Select Committee Chairmen £12,500 per annum, but the proposal was approved.

Campaigning for Cancer Research UK against smoking.

Merseytravel introduced a Private Bill in the 2001-2002 session of Parliament, which changed the way toll increases are decided for the two Mersey tunnels. Claire Curtis-Thomas (Member of Parliament for Crosby) failed to move the Second Reading of the Bill on the first occasion that the Speaker called her because she was outside the bar of the House with her back to the Speaker, talking to officials of Merseytravel sitting under the gallery. The Second Reading of the Bill was deferred until 9 July 2002. I opposed this Bill because it allowed Merseytravel to use any profits generated by increasing Mersey tunnel tolls to cross-subsidise other transport systems on Merseyside, but I was in a minority. The Bill was carried over into the next session of Parliament and eventually succeeded.

During the 2001-2002 session of Parliament the Modernisation Committee brought several recommendations before the House for approval, which changed procedures of the House. Approval was given, for example, to bring in Draft Bills for prelegislative consideration, to carry Bills over from one session of Parliament to another, for September sittings of the House, for the introduction of an annual calendar, for the provision of Written Statements to be published in *Hansard* by Ministers, and for Parliamentary Questions to be tabled just three days before Ministers were expected to answer them on the floor of the House. There were several motions too on proposed changes to sitting hours some of which were approved, such as completing business on Thursdays at 6.00 p.m. instead of 7.00 p.m., and others which were not, such as sitting earlier than 2.30 p.m. on Tuesdays.

'Business of the House' votes are considered by Party Whips to be 'free votes' (i.e. not whipped). Because I voted against some of the proposals put to the House by the

Modernisation Committee (this is 'Business of the House') and voted several times against both the Mersey Tunnels Bill and the City of London Bill, which the Government supported, I am on record as having opposed the Government more times in the 2001-2002 session of Parliament than during the other sessions that I sat in Parliament.

September sittings of the House were trialled but they were never considered to be successful. The main problem with Parliament returning earlier than October is that the summer recess is the only time when outside contractors can carry out major works inside and outside the Palace.

Changes to the Child Support Agency that had been agreed by previous legislation came into force on 1 April 2002.

Parliament was recalled during the Easter recess of 2002 to mark the death of HM Queen Elizabeth the Queen Mother, who died at the age of 102 on 29 March. She lay in state in Westminster Hall before her funeral service on 9 April 2002 in Westminster Abbey.

On 23 July 2002, the National Executive Committee refused to re-admit the Mayor of London, Ken Livingstone, to membership of the Labour Party (a person who has been expelled from the Labour Party is required to wait five years before they can reapply for membership).

During this session of Parliament media attacks on the Government and its policies intensified and, in some cases, became personal attacks on Ministers. The publication of lists of donors to political parties gave the media more ammunition than usual. It was revealed, for example, that the Labour Party had accepted £100,000 from Richard Desmond before the 2001 General Election. He made his fortune in part from magazine and TV pornography and, later, was given the go-ahead by Trade and Industry Secretary Stephen Byers to purchase Express Newspapers.

Manchester hosted the Commonwealth Games from 25 July to 29 July 2002. I was privileged to be invited to the opening and closing ceremonies and I attended a day of the games in between these events. The main stadium is now Manchester City Football Club's ground.

Parliament was recalled again at 11.30 a.m. on Tuesday 24 September 2002 to debate Iraq on an 'Adjournment of the House' motion (meaning that no vote was scheduled on this Government business). A 50-page dossier on weapons of mass destruction, based on evidence supplied by the Joint Intelligence Committee, was published on the day. Tam Dalyell tried to move a motion that the House should not support a war against Iraq without support from the UN Security Council, but the Speaker was unable to accept it. That week I was in The Netherlands on the Police Service Parliamentary Scheme with other Members. Because one or two of the Members on the delegation were desperate to return to Parliament to take part in the debate, I was one of those who volunteered to complete the programme that the Dutch police had organised for us (see Chapter 15).

The 2002-2003 session of Parliament was dominated by debates on Iraq. The first substantial debate occurred on 26 February 2003, on UN Security Council (UNSC) Resolution 1441. I supported an amendment to the main question, put down by Chris Smith (Member of Parliament for Islington South and Finsbury), which was in opposition to the view that the case for an invasion of Iraq had been proven. I have never believed the case put forward by our Government (in what became to be known as the 'dodgy dossier') that Iraq possessed weapons of mass destruction.

SCIENCE AND POLITICS: AN UNLIKELY MIXTURE

In a personal statement, made at 9.44 p.m. on 17 March 2003, Robin Cook, then Leader of the House, shocked Parliament when he announced his resignation from the Government over his opposition to an invasion of Iraq.

I supported another opposing amendment, again put down by Chris Smith, when the Prime Minister brought a motion before the House on 18 March 2003 for a declaration of war on Iraq. On this occasion I abstained on the main question because the Prime Minister had persuaded the Government to include in its motion words to the effect that a renewed effort would be made to bring peace between the Israeli Government and the Palestinians. I could not vote for war, yet I supported that part of the Government motion. 139 Labour Members of Parliament voted against the invasion of Iraq by allied forces, which began on 20 March 2003. Home Office Minister John Denham resigned from the Government on this day. Before this debate I met John Prescott who tried to persuade me to support the Government.

On 12 January 2003, I wrote to the Prime Minister to tell him that I could not support an invasion of Iraq unless two conditions were met: 1) I was convinced that weapons of mass destruction actually existed; and 2) a further UNSC resolution was secured. The Chilcot inquiry on Iraq completed its work in February 2010.[2]

Clare Short, the highly-respected Secretary of State for International Development from 1997, resigned from the Government on 12 May 2003 over the issue of Iraq. She became an Independent Member of Parliament and sat on the Opposition benches.

After 'shock and awe' it became clear that there had been no post-war planning in Iraq. Even worse, the police service and armed forces in Iraq were totally disbanded, which resulted in chaos. There were some old scores to be settled between the previously minority Sunni ruling Government and the majority Shia population of Iraq. The legality of the war became a main debating point in Parliament and the country, and the failure to achieve a second UNSC resolution to support the invasion also caused problems for the Government.

Iraq was an issue that all Members of Parliament became engaged in in their constituencies too. I was involved in three debates held in Bolton's Central Library lecture theatre which were organised jointly by CND and Stop the War Coalition.

Legislation was brought before the House for further reform of the House of Lords (the House of Lords Bill was blocked in the previous session by the House of Lords), to ban hunting of mammals with dogs, to support enlargement of the European Union, to set up the communications regulator Ofcom, to prepare for referendums to set up Regional Assemblies, to reform the NHS in Wales, to end bed blocking in hospitals, to reform extradition arrangements, especially within the EU (many of our criminals were living on the Costa del Sol at that time), to reform the planning and compulsory purchase legislation, to give NHS hospitals more freedom by setting up NHS Foundation Hospital Trusts (highly controversial in the Labour Party), to establish independent health and social care inspectorates, to set up a Rail Accident Investigation Body, as recommended by the Cullen Report, to set up an Independent Monitoring Commission to monitor implementation of the Belfast Agreement, to reform the sex offender laws, and to deal with international terrorism.

The Licensing Bill proposed a relaxation in the law

managing the sale of alcohol on licensed premises, the Water Bill provided a new impetus for water conservation whilst reducing the regulatory burden on the water companies, and a Bill was introduced that allowed Britain to meet its obligations under the European Landfill Directive.

On 5 June 2003 Gordon Brown announced that Britain would not be adopting the euro despite the Prime Minister's wish to do so. A Bill was passed to deal with the long-running dispute between the Government and firefighters, who were demanding a 40% increase in their salaries to accept reforms that the Government proposed.

There was more legislation on antisocial behaviour, and legislation was passed to bring Magistrates' and Crown Courts under the same management regime. The 'double jeopardy rule' was abolished, which meant that people previously acquitted of serious crime could be retried, providing that compelling new evidence was available. A Local Government Bill brought further reform to local authorities and the highly controversial 'Section 28', which prevented schools from discussing homosexuality, was repealed.

Attempts to remove the remaining 92 hereditary peers from the House of Lords (Phase II of reform) got bogged down again. The House of Commons could not decide between several resolutions, put before the House on 4 February 2003, on whether its Members should be wholly appointed or elected or whether there should be some elected and some appointed and the ratio between the two. The vote on abolition of the second chamber was defeated by 390 votes to 172 (a substantial number of abolitionists). When I was elected to Parliament in 1997 I had been in favour of a wholly-elected House of Lords, but I changed my mind in favour of retaining a percentage (between 20% and 30%) of appointed peers. This issue was not decided before my retirement in 2010. The total removal of hereditary peers from the House of Lords has taken over 100 years so far.

On Thursday 23 January 2002, a trial began of cross-cutting Question Times in the Westminster Hall debating chamber, but was abandoned not long after. 2 August 2003 marked the longest ever period of a Labour Government.

North West Members were told that £3 million per night was being spent modernising the west coast main railway line. When this work was completed it reduced the Manchester to London journey time by about one hour.

Congestion charging was introduced in London on 17 February 2003 in the 'Central Zone'; later it was extended to the west.

The Hunting Bill was carried forward into the 2003-2004 session of Parliament and forced through by Government application of the Parliament Act on 18 November 2004, the date of Prorogation.

When Charles Clarke, Secretary of State for Education and Skills, tried to introduce 'top-up fees' in the Higher Education Bill, I opposed him, both in the chamber and behind the scenes. The Bill applied to England, Wales and Northern Ireland, but not Scotland. Our 2001 manifesto stated clearly that the Government had no intention of carrying out this measure. Labour Members of Parliament were angry when David Blunkett introduced a £1,000 up-front tuition fee in 1998. I constantly lobbied him, as well as his successor, Charles Clarke, not to increase costs for undergraduates.

The Second Reading debate of this Bill was held on 27 January 2004, when I was minded to vote against it. The Whips were well aware from my signature on an Early Day Motion of my opposition and, along with many other Members I was put under a lot of pressure, so much so that *The Guardian* newspaper carried a diary on my hour-by-hour thinking on 26 and 27 January 2004.

I had two face-to-face meetings with Charles Clarke, who was Secretary of State at the time, several meetings with the Minister of State responsible for Higher Education, Alan Johnson, and meetings with the Prime Minister (on 21 January), the Deputy Chief Whip, Bob Ainsworth, Tessa Jowell (26 January), and my Regional Whip, Gillian Merron. On the afternoon of 27 January, the Prime Minister called me on the telephone to try to get me to vote for the Bill's Second Reading. He explained that the Government was going through a difficult time. The Hutton Report on the death of Dr David Kelly (on 17 July 2003) was due to be published the following day. I told Tony Blair that the best that I could do was to abstain, although I do not like abstaining in politics.

At 3.00 p.m., as the Prime Minister admitted to me when I spoke to him, the Government was 30 votes short of a majority. 30 Minutes before the House was due to divide, at 6.30 p.m., the Government was still 27 votes down, according to the Whips, who were in close contact with me. At 6.45 p.m., they told me that they were only eight votes short and, at 6.55 p.m., when the Deputy Chief Whip, Bob Ainsworth, sat on one side of me in the chamber and my Regional Whip, Gillian Merron, sat on the other side of me they admitted that they were still three votes short. I abstained, 71 Labour Members of Parliament voted against the Bill, and it was carried by only five votes (316 'Ayes' and 311 'Noes'). That was a night of great tension in Parliament.

The Bill proceeded into its Standing Committee and returned to the House for its Report Stage and Third Reading on 31 March 2004, with the 'top-up fees' proposal intact. Government Whips packed the Committee with Bill supporters, which didn't go unnoticed by the media. I supported an amendment at Report Stage to abolish 'top-up fees', which failed by a significant number of votes, and then decided to support the Bill's Third Reading. It received Royal Assent on 1 July 2004. I met the Chief Whip before Government business began on 31 March.

The Higher Education Bill also allowed the Arts and Humanities Research Council and an Office for Fair Access (to universities) to be established.

Throughout the passage of this Bill I was placed in a very difficult position. I was also meeting with Charles Clarke and Alan Johnson in an attempt to persuade them to grant university status to Bolton Institute of Higher Education, which they did in May 2004. I thought my opposition to 'top-up fees' would damage that campaign, and I was greatly relieved when I realised that it hadn't. Such are the pressures that Members of Parliament are subjected to from time to time.

Although the Hutton Report on the death of Dr David Kelly, a Minister of Defence specialist on WMD (weapons of mass destruction), published on 17 July 2003, concluded that it was suicide and exonerated Tony Blair, Geoff Hoon, Secretary of State for Defence, and Alistair Campbell of blame, it brought resignations at the BBC. Later, the Prime Minister was forced to set up a second inquiry on Iraq, the Butler inquiry into WMD. On 24 August 2003 Alistair Campbell submitted his resignation to Tony Blair and was replaced by David Hill in September.

From May 1997 to May 2003 the three Bolton Members of Parliament and Gary Titley, Member of the European Parliament, wrote a column each week in rotation for the *Bolton Evening News*, today part of the Newsquest Group. The paper's management ended these columns after I spoke on a platform with their journalists during a strike they held for better pay. The management's explanation for cancelling our columns was that they were 'restructuring the paper'.

When I was elected in 1997 the Political Correspondent for the *Bolton Evening News* was Bill Jacobs, who also worked for other papers in the North West and the North East. In one of their cost-cutting exercises the *Bolton Evening News* axed Bill and thereafter it became more difficult to get the coverage that I thought Bolton's Members of Parliament deserved in the paper.

The 2003-2004 session of our second Parliament also brought in legislation to establish Child Trust Funds (abolished by the Conservatives in 2010), to appoint a Children's Commissioner for England, to protect company pensions when firms become insolvent, to strengthen the law on domestic violence, to improve the rights of disabled people, to improve employment protection, to introduce a National Offenders Management Service (NOMS; a merger of the prison service and the probation service with the aim to prevent reoffending), to improve civil contingency planning, to make the planning process more efficient, and to establish a Nuclear Decommissioning Authority, an Independent Appointments Commission to appoint peers and a Northern Ireland Judicial Appointments Commission. The Housing Act dealt with abuses of the Right-to-Buy legislation.

Housing policy at this time was of great concern to Labour Members. House prices were rising steeply and John Prescott held a competition for the private sector to build a £60,000 house. The market renewal Pathfinder Projects in places like Salford and East Lancashire (Burnley, for example) were beginning to have an impact on private sector renewal. Under the Labour Government the density of housing was increased from 20 to 33 per hectare, which also kept costs down. John Prescott also launched the 'Northern Way' which concentrated on the regeneration of northern towns and cities, from Liverpool through Manchester and across the Pennines to Hull and beyond.

Following revelations that hearts were being removed for research purposes from children at a hospital in Bristol and other organs and tissues were being removed from patients at Alder Hey Hospital, also for research purposes, the use of human tissues was regulated by the Human Tissue Act 2004. This requires the consent of relatives before tissues are removed. Legislation was also passed to allow civil partnerships between same-sex couples and to allow those who undergo operations to change their gender to gain legal recognition of their changed gender.

The Constitutional Reform Bill (this Bill was carried over into the next session) proposed a separation of the highest court in the land (previously the House of Lords) from the political system by establishing a Supreme Court. On 3 July 2007 Jack Straw, Secretary of State for Justice, became the first Lord Chancellor not to sit on the woolsack; a Lord Speaker is appointed to sit on it instead. The Lord Chancellor still delivers the Queen's Speech to the Queen on her throne in the House of Lords at the State Opening of Parliament but doesn't have to be a lawyer any more.

We were lobbied hard to support a complete ban on the smacking of children when The Children Bill came before Parliament. I voted against a complete ban because I didn't see how it could be enforced, and I felt that it would lead to serious problems between neighbours. In any case, other mechanisms are in place to detect serious abuse of children.

In the elections for the Northern Ireland Assembly held on 26 November 2003 there was a significant shift towards the DUP (Ian Paisley's party) from the UUP (David Trimble's party) and away from the SDLP towards Sinn Fein (led by Gerry Adams). Those elected were given six weeks to form a Government. The economic situation in Northern Ireland improved considerably after the Belfast Agreement; tourism went up and unemployment went down, for example.

Decommissioning was still a major barrier to implementing the Belfast Agreement, but the Royal Ulster Constabulary was undergoing reform to become the Police Service of Northern Ireland. Relationships between Dublin and Belfast and between Dublin and London improved. However, a major robbery at the Northern Bank in December 2004, which was attributed to the Provisional IRA (£26 million was stolen), and the murder of Robert McCartney on 30 January 2005 set the peace talks back. The McCartney family campaigned for peace in Northern Ireland in the USA, which was partly responsible for IRA funding from across the pond drying up.

Before the summer of 2004, Tony Blair was at a low point. There was an impasse in Northern Ireland, he was being blamed for an unnecessary war in Iraq that had been based on misleading information, criticism emerged on the treatment of prisoners in Abu Ghraib prison and Guantanamo Bay and of extraordinary rendition, Gordon Brown and his team at

Number 11 were putting pressure on him to hand over the Premiership, public service reform was proving more intractable than he could have imagined, and he was forced to promise a plebiscite on the European Constitution ahead of the Euro Elections in June 2004. On top of everything else he was diagnosed to be suffering from an irregular heartbeat. Cherie Blair negotiated the purchase of a £3.5 million house in Connaught Square "just in case".

The Labour Party launched its 'Big Conversation' with the British people in the 2003-2004 Session of Parliament, which would help form its future policies along with the Warwick Agreement, made with the trade unions. In a referendum held on 5 November 2004, the North East rejected a Regional Assembly, and that was the end of that form of devolution.

The world was shocked at the huge loss of life caused by the 2004 Boxing Day tsunami in the Indian Ocean, which affected several countries. The Disasters Emergency Committee (formed in 1963) proved very effective in providing aid to those countries affected.

On 6 January 2004, the National Executive Committee of the Labour Party voted by 20:2 votes (Michael Cashman MEP and Dennis Skinner MP voted against) to readmit Mayor of London Ken Livingstone to membership of the Labour Party. He was selected as the official Labour Party candidate for the London Elections on 6 June and was returned for a second term as Mayor of London.

In the Easter recess of 2004 a temporary security screen was constructed to separate the Strangers Gallery from the House of Commons chamber, at a cost of £600,000. There were plans to construct a permanent security screen during the following summer recess at an estimated cost of £1.3

million and, in a debate held on 22 April 2004, I voted against the construction of these security screens, which severely restrict the view that visitors have of the House of Commons chamber.

However, I supported the construction of a new visitors' entrance to the north of Cromwell Green, which also improved security. Although an attack on Members of Parliament in the main chamber gets maximum publicity in the media, there are many other places in the Palace of Westminster that are less secure than the main chamber.

At 12.18 p.m. on 19 May 2004, Ron Davies and Guy Harrison, representing 'Fathers4Justice', threw two condoms packed with a 'purple powder' down into the House of Commons chamber from the West Special Gallery during Prime Minister's Questions. One of them hit the shoulder of Tony Blair, who was standing at the Dispatch Box. Before it hit him it hit a microphone cable immediately above my head and shed a lot of the powder over me. I removed most of it by shaking my jacket. When I touched a little of it with a wet finger and applied it to my tongue it was tasteless; it was also odourless. It looked to me like the purple powder used in schools to make paint, and that's what it turned out to be on analysis.

'Fathers4Justice' acquired the two tickets that gained them access to the West Special Gallery (in front of the new security screen) through a charity auction. Baroness (Llin) Golding made them available. Today, a Member of Parliament must identify anyone using the special galleries and take responsibility for their visitors.

When this incident occurred, security procedures were not followed. Members of Parliament rushed out of the chamber when the Speaker interrupted business, and went all over the Palace. If the powder had been contaminated with something like anthrax, Members would have spread it all round the building. They should have been contained in the chamber until an investigation was carried out, or evacuated into another confined area if there was a risk to life.

I was present in the chamber one afternoon when a man threw bundles of 'blood money' down from the Strangers' Gallery. The photocopied five and ten pound notes stained with red ink lay all over the seats and floor of the chamber until the end of business. On 15 September 2004 supporters of fox hunting were able to invade the House of Commons chamber from behind the Speaker's chair during a debate on the Hunting Bill. Other Members remembered a CS gas canister being thrown down from the Strangers' Gallery in July 1970, an incident in November 1976 when demonstrators threw leaflets into the Chamber during a debate on Welsh affairs and another incident in July 1978 when manure was thrown over the balcony by the daughter of the Maltese Prime Minister, Dom Mintoff, while Tam Dalyell was waxing eloquent about the details of Scottish education. In December of the same year a pot of paint was thrown from the Gallery during a debate on pay policy. In January 1983 70 women peace protesters had to be removed from the Strangers' Gallery – some were detained for the rest of the day – and on 1 March 1985 SNP supporters shouted 'English Tories out, give us an Assembly' from the Strangers' Gallery and threw leaflets down into the chamber.

The Local and European Elections on 10 June 2004 were disastrous for the Labour Party. Over 450 of our councillors lost their seats and we gained only 23% of the vote in the

European Elections. The Conservatives didn't make much headway either but the Liberal Democrat Party gained most from the unpopularity of the invasion of Iraq.

In the final session of the 2001-2005 Parliament the Queen's Speech contained a massive number of Bills, 37 in total. Legislation was introduced *inter alia* to improve school inspections, to introduce Education Maintenance Allowances (£30 per week for those 16-19 year-olds in full-time training or education; EMAs were abolished by the Coalition Government in 2011), to establish the Serious Organised Crime Agency (SOCA), to look at the classification of drugs, to strengthen the rights of those who lack mental capacity to make decisions, to integrate the work of the Inland Revenue with the work of the Customs and Excise Service, and to reform the laws on gambling.

The Drugs Bill, which was rushed through Parliament immediately before the 2005 General Election by Home Department Minister Caroline Flint was designed to strengthen the powers of the police to deal with the dealers and users of illicit drugs. However, I vigorously opposed the Minister's attempt to classify magic mushrooms as Class A drugs together with cocaine and heroin.

The Science and Technology Select Committee concluded that the ABC classification of drugs in the Misuse of Drugs Act 1971 was not fit for purpose, and that we should adopt a system of classifying drugs according to the harm they cause to society (see Chapter 12). The evidence shows that cocaine and heroin cause far more harm than magic mushrooms, which I still contend are classified wrongly, even if the ABC classification is accepted. I am not aware of anyone who has died as a result of using magic mushrooms. In my opinion the

Government was trying to halt a rapidly expanding trade in magic mushrooms. This piece of legislation merely displaced users into purchasing other 'legal highs', some of which are more harmful than magic mushrooms. It is not difficult to find magic mushrooms growing in the wild in this country. The active hallucinogenic chemicals they contain, psilocin and psilocybin, are not readily available commercially.

The Mental Capacity Bill was introduced to allow people who could not make decisions themselves to have them made by another person who is granted the Power of Attorney. Whilst most of this Bill was acceptable as far as I was concerned, the fact that it contained clauses on 'living wills' (or 'advance decisions') led me to move amendments to it to delete these clauses. I also supported clauses introduced by other Members, Jim Dobbin, Ann Winterton and Iain Duncan Smith, for example that strengthened the rights of those without the capacity to make decisions themselves. Altogether, I voted against the Government six times during the passage of this Bill.

On 26 January 2005 I supported a return to a 2.30 p.m. start on Tuesdays, against a Modernisation Committee recommendation to retain a morning start that had been agreed by the House previously. Starting in a morning on Tuesdays, Wednesdays and Thursdays severely restricted access to the Line of Route for visitors to the Palace, especially for my constituents who found it difficult to arrive in London before 11.30 a.m. It also prevented Members from attending other meetings and attending to their casework.

The Labour Government continued to make a difference. The Pathfinder projects and the Job Centre Plus policies, along with the continuing New Deal Programmes, were bringing unemployment under control. Britain was making an impact too on the international stage. The Commission for Africa began its work and, together with other developed countries, Britain began to tackle HIV/Aids and malaria in Africa along with other diseases that killed millions on that sub-continent. Public campaigns like Make Poverty History had a major impact on the British Government and the Governments of other countries.

The French closed the camp for 'refugees' at Sangatte and allowed British Customs and Excise officials to operate at French ports. This move was extended to ports in The Netherlands and Belgium. Lorries, particularly those that had travelled through Turkey, were more closely inspected; large X-ray machines and Drager tubes (which detect carbon dioxide) were made available to detect bodies inside them. Security measures were increased on trains travelling through the Channel Tunnel. These and other measures resulted in a significant fall in the number of illegal immigrants gaining access to our shores.

During his second term of office Tony Blair lost four Secretaries of State – Stephen Byers as Transport Secretary in May 2002, Estelle Morris as Education Secretary in the autumn of 2002, Alan Milburn as Health Secretary in June 2003 and David Blunkett (his first resignation) as Home Secretary on 15 December 2004 – and a number of other Ministers as well. One of the problems of the Blair Governments was the rapid game of musical chairs that he played with his Ministers. John Reid had seven different positions in eight years.

Towards the end of 2004 it emerged that David Blunkett had had an affair, resulting in the birth of his son William, with

Kimberly Fortier, American publisher of the Tory *Spectator* magazine and wife of the Managing Director of *Vogue*, the fashion magazine. There was a paternity battle over the boy and David was charged with fast-tracking a visa application for William's nanny. Following an inquiry by Sir Alan Budd there was sufficient evidence for Blunkett's resignation.

NOTES

1. Osama bin Laden was killed in a raid by US forces on a house in Abbottabad, 70 miles north of Islamabad, Pakistan on 2 May 2011; his body was buried at sea.

2. The Chilcot Report was published on 6 July 2016.

CHAPTER SIX

BUSINESS OF THE HOUSE: THE 2005-2010 PARLIAMENT

∽

At the General Election on 5 May 2005 the Labour Government was returned with a reduced overall majority of 66 seats (a loss of 47 seats) over the other parties for an historic third term. Our campaign 'anthem' was U2's *Beautiful Day*. Labour polled four million fewer votes than in 1997 and gathered only 35.2% of the total votes cast. The 'Iraq factor' benefited the Liberal Democrats significantly, both in the General Election and in the local elections. The main issue in the Tory campaign was a cut of £35 billion that they had identified for the public services, which the general public were reluctant to accept. Tory Leader Michael Howard was referred to by his colleague Ann Widdecombe MP as having 'something of the night about him'.

In the reshuffle after the General Election Alan Johnson became Secretary of State for the former Department of Trade and Industry, which was rebranded as the Department of Productivity, Energy and Industry, until Alan pointed out to the Prime Minister that a likely acronym would be PENIS. It reverted to its former name on 13 May. David Blunkett was appointed as Secretary of State for Work and Pensions, former Liberal Democrat Andrew Adonis became a peer and Parliamentary Under-Secretary of State at Education. Allegedly, Tony Blair wanted Adonis to be his Education Secretary of State, but Ruth Kelly refused to give up her position, supported by Gordon Brown. Phil Collins (see Chapter 17) joined 10 Downing Street as a speech writer.

There was joy in London at 1.50 p.m. on Wednesday 6 July 2005, when it was announced by the President of the International Olympic Committee in Singapore, an event shown on huge television screens in Trafalgar Square, that Britain's bid to hold the 2012 30th Olympiad and Paralympics in London had been successful.

The following morning, Thursday July 7, I had a 10.30 a.m. meeting of the Parliamentary Affairs Committee of the Royal Society of Chemistry at their headquarters in Burlington House, next to the Royal Academy on Piccadilly. My researcher Gemma told me before I left the office that there had been a major incident on the Underground and advised me to walk or take a bus. Since all the buses were full, I walked. There was a strange atmosphere in Whitehall; ambulances and police cars were screaming all over the place and I soon realised that something had gone badly wrong. When I arrived at Burlington House for my 10.30 a.m. meeting the first reports of explosions on the Underground were coming in.

Our feelings of joy at winning the Olympics were dashed as we learned of the immense scale of the disasters that had occurred in London that day, which came to be known as 7/7. Three bombs had exploded on the Underground at Kings Cross St Pancras and Edgware Road Underground stations, as well as on the line between Aldgate and Liverpool Street Underground stations, and another had exploded on a bus in Tavistock Square. The first explosion had occurred at 8.56 a.m. By the end of the day 52 people were dead and over 700 more injured.

As I walked back to the House of Commons from Burlington House mid-afternoon, I found central London deserted. There were no buses or taxis and few people around. People left London to go home early. It was eerie. That evening Eileen and I travelled north up the Edgware Road on our way to Bolton. The whole area around Edgware Road Underground station was cordoned off, with police cars and ambulances still attending the scene. Over the weekend the full picture of what had happened began to emerge. An inquiry found that all 52 of the people who lost their lives had been unlawfully killed.

Rescues in the Underground on 7/7 could not proceed until air samples had been analysed, and they were hindered too by difficulties with the blue light communication equipment in the tunnels of the Underground.

The attacks by terrorists on 9/11 in the USA and on 7/7 in London undoubtedly affected the Northern Ireland peace process. These events also led to a more authoritarian approach to security in the UK.

On 22 July 2005 Brazilian electrician Jean Charles de Menezes was shot dead at Stockwell Underground station. An inquiry subsequently proved that he was not involved in terrorist activities. Nevertheless, at least 20 plots to commit terrorist attacks during Tony Blair's term of office were uncovered, including plans to attack Heathrow Airport and the Bluewater Farm shopping complex in Kent.

Tony Blair returned from his successful trip to Singapore – his lobbying made the difference between the 30th Olympiad being held in London instead of in Paris – to land at Gleneagles on 6 July where he was to chair a G8 Summit meeting. On 7 July he travelled to London and back to be briefed on the London bombings. The Make Poverty History campaign campaigned for years to persuade the governments of the world to reduce the high debts of developing countries. The agreement signed at Gleneagles on Friday 8 July 2005 achieved this aim for 15 of those countries and doubled international aid.

On 28 July 2005, the IRA announced an end to terrorism, and decommissioning of its arms dumps was completed on 26 September 2005.

At my invitation Robin Cook (Member of Parliament for Livingstone) visited Bolton on 11 February 2005 to give a speech at the Quebec Hall in Daubhill, Bolton. Tragically, he died on a mountain top in Scotland on 6 August 2005 from heart failure at the age of 59, and Mo Mowlam (Member of Parliament for Redcar from 1987 to 2001), who had suffered from a brain tumour, died on 19 August 2005 aged 55.

The first Bill on Animal Welfare in 100 years was passed during the 2005-2006 session of Parliament, along with legislation to improve road safety, to pave the way for the 2012

Olympic Games, to update consumer credit law, for the management of common land, to establish a Commission for Equality on Human Rights, to set up Natural England, a body to ensure sustainable development, to prevent religious hatred, to reform the laws on charities, for the protection of children and vulnerable adults, to deal with the sale and illegal use of guns and knives, to pave the way for the introduction of ID cards, to improve maternity and adoption pay, to introduce paternity pay and provide workers with rights to more flexible working hours.

The Electoral Administration Bill required local authorities to improve the registration of electors, for example by allowing people to register to vote throughout the year; it also laid down ground rules for party funding and dealt with fraud in the electoral system, particularly regarding the security of postal votes.

An omnibus Health Bill provided legislation to deal with hospital-acquired infections, to allow patients greater choice over their treatment, to ban smoking in public places and for reorganisation of Primary Care Trusts in order to make them more efficient. Although I was in full support of the proposed ban on smoking in public places and had lobbied for it, as a Member of the Non-Profit-Making Private Members' Clubs All-Party Parliamentary Group I supported an amendment to the Health Bill that would have allowed these clubs to set aside a room where their members could smoke. The vote on this amendment was lost, and Secretary of State Patricia Hewitt succeeded in getting a ban on smoking in public places by a majority of 200 on a free vote.

In a debate held on 13 July 2005, I again opposed payment (£12,500 per annum) of the chairmen of Select Committees.

David Blunkett, Secretary of State at Work and Pensions, was forced to resign for a second time on 25 October 2005 when it was discovered that he had broken the Ministerial Code by becoming a director of a DNA testing firm during his six months on the back benches.

The laws on asylum seeking and immigration were strengthened yet again, and the police and security forces were given further powers to deal with terrorism. There was uproar when the Government proposed to detain suspected terrorists in gaol for up to 90 days without trial (14 days was the maximum detention period at the time). The vote on 90 days was lost on Wednesday 9 November 2005 by 323 votes to 290, with 49 Labour Members voting against the proposal. A maximum detention period of 28 days was agreed instead.

My return to London by car on Sunday 11 December 2005 was made difficult by an enormous explosion that occurred at the Buncefield Oil Depot (near Hemel Hempstead); the M1 was shut in both directions for most of the day as a result of the huge volumes of smoke that were blowing across the motorway. At about 10.00 p.m. it reopened and I was able to pass the site shortly after whilst it was still blazing in the distance and lighting up the night sky.

The PLP centenary photograph of Labour Members, taken on 12 February 2006.

The 29 founding fathers who established the Parliamentary Labour Party on 12 February 1906 would have been proud of the fact that Labour was in power a century later on 12 February 2006, as we celebrated its centenary. We gathered in the House of Commons chamber to have an historic photograph taken, and those of us who represented areas that were represented by those 29 founding fathers, me and Ruth Kelly included, were invited to contribute a chapter to a book, *Men Who Made Labour*,[1] to celebrate this centenary event.

I contributed a chapter on the work of Arthur Henry Gill, the first Labour Member to represent Bolton. Ruth contributed a chapter on Tyson Wilson, the first Labour Member to represent Westhoughton. There is a memorial plaque, provided by Bolton Trades Council, in the Labour Party office on St George's Road to celebrate these elections. It was installed originally in the Spinners Hall, also on St George's Road in Bolton.

In a speech he made on 31 January 1913 during the Third Reading of a Bill that restored the rights of trade unions to establish political funds Gill said, "Reference is made to socialism and our Party is spoken of as a Socialist Party. This Party is not a Socialist Party. There are socialists in it and there are those who are not socialists."

On the 24 May 2006, I supported an amendment put down by David Chaytor (Member of Parliament for Bury North) to the Education and Inspections Bill that would have ended 11-plus selection across the country had it been successful. This Bill was steered through by Ruth Kelly and introduced Trust Schools, vocational routes in secondary schools for 14-19-year-old pupils (with 14 vocational diplomas available), a ban on interviews for admissions to secondary schools, powers which enabled teachers to discipline children and powers to set standards for nutritional school meals.

Following the publication, on 25 October 2005, of the White Paper that led to this Bill, there was a lot of opposition to the proposals. 90 Labour Members of Parliament, including myself, put their names to an 'Alternative White Paper'. Tony Blair and his Ministers, Lord Adonis and Ruth Kelly, intended to close bad schools and allow new schools to open in their place outside the control of Local Education Authorities. In the end the proposals were watered down. Nevertheless, at the Second Reading of the Bill on 15 March 2006, 52 Labour Members voted against the Bill and 25 others abstained. I reluctantly voted for the Bill to go into its Committee Stage.

Between 11 and 13 October 2006, representatives of the Irish and British Governments and the Northern Ireland political parties met in St Andrews to reach an agreement which paved the way for Whitehall to hand back power again to the Northern Ireland Assembly. The Northern Ireland (St Andrews Agreement) Act (Royal Assent on 22 November 2006) led to the appointment of Ian Paisley as the First Minister of the Assembly and Martin McGuinness as his Deputy on 24 November 2006. The Agreement required a General Election to be held on 7 March 2007 and restoration of the Executive by 26 March 2007. The Assembly met again on 8 May 2007. In the Assembly elections the DUP won 36 of the 108 seats, Sinn Fein won 28, the UUP won 18, the SDLP won 16 and the Alliance Party won 7 seats.

The Government launched its Energy Review in March 2006, the Stern Report on climate change was published, the first Lord Speaker, Baroness Hayman, was elected in the House of Lords, President Ahmadinejad came to power in Iran in June 2005, MP George Galloway appeared in the *Big Brother* house in January 2006, and work to upgrade the west coast main railway line was completed. Trouble was brewing for the British Government over the European Constitution (agreed by the Lisbon Treaty), which the French people rejected in a referendum.

On 1 November 2006, the House discussed several 'Business of the House' motions. I supported committees considering Draft Bills taking written and oral evidence (this resulted in more pressure on Members' time) but I did not support the principle of a £10,000 'Communications Allowance', nor did I support the Speaker being given the power to limit Members' speeches in popular debates. However, I did support the continuance of September sittings because I thought the summer recesses were too long.

The 2005-2006 session of Parliament was dogged by further scandals breaking out. It was discovered by Jack Dromey, treasurer to the Labour Party and husband of Harriet Harman, that Lord (Michael) Levy had exploited a loophole in the Election and Referendums Act 2000 to cover a shortage of money to fight the 2005 General Election by accepting loans from several rich supporters of the Party. £14 million was donated by 12 wealthy businessmen. Some of these had accepted peerages. Between 1995 and 2005 Michael Levy, a close friend of Tony Blair, raised about £100 million for the Labour Party. The chairman of the Labour Party, Ian McCartney, was also unaware that these loans had been raised.

The 'cash for peerages' scandal first broke in the *Independent on Sunday* newspaper in October 2005. Following a complaint to the Metropolitan Police by a Scottish National Party Member, Angus MacNeil, Deputy Commissioner John

Yates was appointed to investigate the allegations, which resulted in Michael Levy being arrested and charged on 12 July 2006 and Tony Blair being interviewed in December 2006. Sixteen months after the investigation began, the Crown Prosecution Service decided not to prosecute anyone.

On 26 April 2006 the *Daily Mirror* newspaper reported that John Prescott was having an affair with his secretary Tracy Temple. 'Two Jags', having become 'Two Jabs', was now 'Two Shags'.

Not surprisingly, the Labour Party came third, behind the Liberal Democrats, in the Local Elections on 4 May 2006 with only 26% of the vote (the Conservatives gained 40% of the vote).

In the 2006-2007 session of Parliament, Bills were passed to allow the Crossrail project in London to proceed, to introduce a charge of corporate manslaughter, to allow the switchover of analogue to digital broadcasting, to deal with climate change (following publication of the Stern Review), to reduce the increasing number of people on Incapacity Benefit, to provide compensation for those who had contracted mesothelioma, to regulate estate agents, for the merger of the National Consumer Council, Energywatch and Postwatch, for reform of the Further Education sector through restructuring of the Learning and Skills Council, to introduce a Draft Legislative Programme for public debate ahead of the Queen's Speech, for the regulation and efficient delivery of legal services, to reform the tribunal system, for reform of Housing Benefit, to restore devolution to Northern Ireland (see above), to provide for trials without a jury in serious fraud cases, to make the Office of National Statistics independent of Government, and to reform pensions (following publication of the Turner Report). The Child Support Bill was another attempt to reform the controversial Child Support Agency (CSA). The Climate Change Bill was carried over into the next session of Parliament.

I thought publication of the Draft Legislative Programme ahead of the Queen's Speech took the sense of occasion out of the State Opening of Parliament. The first of these documents was published in July 2007.

Trial without jury for very lengthy serious fraud cases became necessary because several lengthy high-profile trials collapsed through loss of jurors, and millions of pounds were lost as a result.

Probably the most popular Bill in this Parliament was the Concessionary Bus Travel Bill, which allowed all those aged 60 or over and disabled people to travel free on local bus services throughout England.

The Pensions Bill provided for the link between average male earnings and the State pension to be restored, albeit not until 2012. The National Offenders' Management Service (NOMS) was established by a Bill in this session of Parliament, with the intention of merging the prison and probation services. It was an attempt to prevent reoffending. By this time the prison population had risen to about 86,000.

I sat on the Standing Committee of the Mental Health Bill, which introduced a new definition of mental disorder and a new 'treatment test' in place of the 'treatability test', which allowed hospitals to deal with a small number of people with 'personality disorders' that had not been treated previously. New Compulsory Treatment Orders were introduced to deal with those with serious mental health problems who had been released back into the community, and the Secretary of State for Health, Alan Johnson, announced separately that more psychologists would be trained to deal with people with mild to moderate mental health problems, such as anxiety and depression, as part of the Government's welfare to work programme.

A major debate was held in December 2006 on the future of the Trident missile system. The Government announced that it would take 17 years to replace the existing delivery submarines, which are due to be decommissioned in 2024. Three new submarines were planned, with a reduction in warheads of a third. The Labour Government believed that its policy was in line with the Non-Proliferation Treaty, and the House agreed to allow the planning stage to begin on the understanding that another Parliament would make the decision whether to build the submarines or not when the costs were more clearly known. In March 2007, 88 Labour Members voted against these proposals proceeding.

Another debate was held on 7 March 2007 in an attempt to resolve Phase II of House of Lords Reform. The House of Commons agreed to retain a bicameral Parliament by 416 votes to 163 but could not decide between a 100% elected second chamber or one that was 80% elected. I voted for the latter but not for the former. The House rejected an Upper House that was either fully appointed or 50% or 60% elected (which I also supported).

When Secretary of State for the Home Department John Reid decided that his Department was "not fit for purpose" a Department of Justice was established, with Lord Falconer as its first Secretary of State. This created another Select Committee.

The House of Commons decided before the summer recess to introduce 15-minute sessions of Topical Questions at departmental Question Times as well as Topical Debates (to be decided by the Leader of the House) on some Thursdays.

The proposal to expand Heathrow Airport, the demands made by the Scottish National Party (SNP) for a referendum on independence for Scotland, the money which Lord Ashcroft, one-time treasurer to the Conservative Party, poured into the 2005 General Election campaign and was pouring again into the run-up to the 2010 General Election, the continuing closure of Post Offices and the losses that Royal Mail was making were all topics for vigorous debate at this time.

I opposed introduction of a Communications Allowance (£10,000 per Member) and Regional Select Committees.

Chancellor Gordon Brown announced a 2p cut in the basic rate of income tax in the 2007 Budget in March, but he also announced a damaging commitment to abolish the 10p tax band. In the local elections in May we lost over 500 councillors and lost control of the Parliament in Scotland to a coalition headed by the Scottish National Party Member Alex Salmond as a result.

During the 2006-2007 session of Parliament there was increasing pressure on Tony Blair to hand over his Premiership to Gordon Brown. In September 2006 17 Labour Members, led by Tom Watson (Member of Parliament for West Bromwich East), Sion Simon (Member of Parliament for Birmingham Erdington) and Chris Bryant (Member of Parliament for Rhondda), sent a letter to the Prime Minister urging him to announce his departure from office. 115 Labour backbench Members published a rival letter of support for the Prime Minister. Tony Blair announced that he no longer intended to serve a full term in office.

On 10 May 2007 Tony Blair announced that he would step down as Prime Minister and held his final Cabinet meeting on 21 June. At his last Prime Minister's Questions on 27 June 2007 he ended by saying, "I wish everyone, friend or foe, well. And that's it. The end." As he sat down the whole House broke out into applause.

Gordon Brown succeeded him unopposed as Leader of the Labour Party at a Special Labour Party Conference, held in Manchester on Sunday 24 June, when Harriet Harman became Deputy Leader. I nominated Alan Johnson for this role but he obtained only 49.6% of the vote to Harriet's 50.4%. John Crudas came in third place with Hazel Blears fourth. As Tony Blair often said, a lot had been achieved but there was a lot more to do.

Gordon Brown succeeded Tony Blair as Prime Minister on Wednesday 27 June 2007. His early months were a baptism of fire. Shortly after he became Prime Minister two car bombs were discovered in London, one outside a nightclub in The Haymarket and another just round the corner in Cockspur Street. Then a blazing Jeep was driven into the main terminal at Glasgow Airport, and there was an outbreak of foot and mouth disease which was traced to a leakage in the drains at a government laboratory.

On 10 August 2007 a credit crisis developed at the Northern Rock Building Society and the Financial Services Authority was alerted. On 13 September the BBC announced that the Bank of England had agreed to save Northern Rock from collapse and its investors started to withdraw their deposits the following day.

Despite all, the Labour Party was ahead in the polls at this point. The shine was coming off David Cameron but the

Labour Government was aware that the full impact of the cut in the 10p tax band would take effect in April 2008.

Gordon's first big mistake was to allow a leak about an autumn General Election to circulate in the media, hopefully so that he could receive a mandate from the country for his Premiership and policies. This was the most talked-about issue at the Party's annual conference in September 2007. I didn't believe this 'leak' until I realised that officers at Bolton Town Hall were actually preparing for a General Election. Gemma, in my London office, was firmly of the opposite opinion and turned out to be right. It is highly likely that we could have won a General Election at that moment in time. In his 2007 conference speech Gordon used the unfortunate phrase "British Jobs for British Workers", which was used against him later.

However, Shadow Chancellor George Osborne's announcement at the Conservative Party annual conference in Blackpool that they would raise the threshold for the payment of inheritance tax resonated in the marginal seats. Brown dithered and announced on the *Andrew Marr Show* on BBC1 that the rumours about an autumn election were untrue. The people never forgave him for 'bottling out'. By this stage the Labour Party had spent a considerable amount of its scarce General Election funds. We were behind in the opinion polls for the next two years.

Arising from the Gambling Act 2005 was an agreement that a super-casino would be built and that its site would be determined through a competition. Manchester and Blackpool entered into a major battle; Blackpool argued that a super-casino would help to regenerate the town, but I supported the Manchester bid because the city is closer to the major transport hubs. In the end the idea of a super-casino was quashed by the new Prime Minister.

Throughout the ten years 1997-2007, the number of Bills on police, crime, the judicial system, terrorism and the immigration and asylum system exceeded the number of Bills on other policy areas. Bills on reforming the NHS and education came close in number. In its first ten years the Labour Government invaded Iraq and Afghanistan and helped to bring peace to Northern Ireland, Sierra Leone and the Balkans. The country saw one of its longest periods of economic stability, with low interest rates, low mortgage rates and low rates of inflation, and there were more people in work than we have ever known since records began. Whereas recorded crime doubled under the 1979-1997 Conservative governments, the Labour governments reduced crime levels by one third.

132 new hospitals were either built or were about to be built. Increased resources were provided for the NHS through a 1% rise in National Insurance Contributions. Obesity and binge drinking became major problems for the Government to confront. An incredible number of new schools were provided and many others had extensions built or major refurbishment work carried out. Whilst the Government was dealing with health inequalities, the pace of change was not fast enough for some of us. The Government was on track to provide a Sure Start scheme or Children's Centre in each ward in the country, beginning with the poorest wards first.

The number of police on our streets increased significantly and each police force appointed significant numbers of Police Community Support Officers. Our judicial system was undergoing a major overall. The Conservative Government left local authorities with a £19 billion backlog of repairs to council homes, which was tackled with money to bring homes up to the Decent Homes Standard. Visitors to our museums and galleries doubled after the 1997-2001 Labour Government abolished entrance charges, and there was a significant investment too in sport.

Mugabe's treatment of his people was a topic that was frequently raised in our Parliament. South Africa was reluctant to put pressure on him to resign because Zimbabwe sheltered members of the African National Congress (ANC) Party during their struggle against apartheid. Problems in the Sudan, especially in Darfur province, the development of nuclear power in Iran, extraordinary rendition and the future of Trident were also high on the political agenda at this time. Throughout the decade Britain tried to negotiate a way forward that would bring peace between Israel and the Palestinians, without much success.

On the positive side, the World Trade Organisation, the World Bank and the International Monetary Fund worked much more closely together than ever before. They were engaged in discussions about poverty in the developing countries and helped the poorest countries by removing their debts and improving their trade with the rest of the world.

Legislation was introduced in the 2007-2008 session of Parliament to enable unclaimed bank deposits to be used to support good causes, to require employers to provide workplace pension schemes, to require young people to remain in full-time education or training until the age of 18, to reform apprenticeship schemes, to introduce a Train to Gain scheme, to establish a Homes and Communities Agency, responsible for the provision and regulation of social housing, and a Tenant

Services Authority, to introduce a Community Infrastructure Levy on construction company planning applications, on radical reform of the planning system so as not to delay major infrastructure projects, to reduce carbon emissions by 80% by 2050 (based on 1990 levels), to require immigrants to be able to speak English and acquire citizenship, and to regulate the income and expenditure of political parties.

The Constitutional Reform Bill empowered Parliament with war-making powers and reformed the Executive's treaty-making powers. The Civil Contingency Act was aimed at dealing with major national emergencies such as flooding. The Climate Change Bill was carried over from the previous session of Parliament and received Royal Assent. This was the session when the controversial Human Fertilisation and Embryology Bill, which I will discuss in detail elsewhere in this book (Chapter 12), entered the Statute Book.

I sat on the Energy Bill Standing Committee, which paved the way for clean energy technologies, such as capture and storage of carbon dioxide. The Government announced that it would provide funds for a competition on post-combustion carbon capture at fossil burning power stations, but I argued in the Bill's Standing Committee that the competition should also include pre-combustion carbon capture technologies. The civil servants were unaware that the Science and Technology Select Committee had published a report on these technologies. Later, the competition was extended to include both carbon capture technologies.

In the Energy Bill Standing Committee we argued for consideration to be given to feed-in tariffs, to encourage microgeneration of electricity, through the use of wind or solar power for example. This requires two-way electricity meters ('smart meters') to be fitted in buildings. Although the Government did not include these measures on the face of the Bill, they changed their mind after the Act of Parliament gained Royal Assent.

In a debate on regional government, held on 12 November 2007, I announced that I could not support Regional Select Committees as distinct from Regional Assemblies. Members of Parliament were already under severe pressure, with more Select Committees for Members to attend than ever before, coupled with the need for them to attend sittings in the Westminster Hall debating chamber and to scrutinise Draft Bills.

The Government went ahead and set up Regional Committees in this session of Parliament but had to 'import' Members into some regions from others in order to provide enough Members to sit on them. Later, the Conservative Government abolished them.

In the 2007-2008 session of Parliament legislation was also introduced for the protection of deposits in banks and building societies and to bring back confidence in the financial services sector, but it was carried over into the next session of Parliament.

In the London Assembly Elections on 2 May 2008 the Conservative Member of Parliament for Henley, Boris Johnson, replaced Ken Livingstone as Mayor of London. The Conservatives secured 44% of the vote against Labour's share of only 24%. We lost Crewe and Nantwich with an 18% swing to the Conservatives in a by-election on 22 May 2008, came behind the Green Party and the British National Party in the Henley by-election on 26 June 2008, and lost Glasgow East with a swing of 23% to the Scottish National Party on 24 July

2008, which demoralised Members, although we won another by-election at Glenrothes on 6 November 2008. It was at this stage that the plotting to remove Gordon Brown as Leader of the Labour Party began.

The NHS was 60 years old on 5 July 2008 (my birthday, also the birthday of my successor Yasmin Qureshi) and the Labour Party celebrated this great achievement. In the 2007-2008 session of Parliament the Next Stage Review on the NHS, which had been put together by surgeon and Health Minister Lord (Ara) Darzi, determined the future direction of our health policy. The Health Reform Act required GPs to open their surgeries at weekends and in the evenings, to allow better access for working people, and provided legislation which resulted in the cost of medicines to the NHS to be negotiated downwards.

Britain prepared to pull out of Iraq, oil and fuel prices began to rise steeply, a long debate about Remploy resulted in the closure of several factories (although the one on Manchester Road, Bolton survived[2]), a vigorous debate on the violence caused by gun and knife crime was under way, the lack of lending by banks to companies became a matter of great concern to Members, and debates on Post Office closures and Post Office card accounts continued.

The Government won a vote in the House of Commons on 11 June 2008 on conditional detention of terrorists up to a maximum of 42 days – to be used under extreme circumstances and with judicial overview – but lost the vote in the House of Lords and decided not to press the matter. In the March 2008 Budget Alistair Darling confirmed abolition of the 10p tax band, which again badly damaged the Government's credibility. Free swimming was introduced for those under the age of 16 or over the age of 60, and Sport England was reformed to provide a greater focus on the local provision of sport.

On 13 February 2007, the Freedom of Information Commissioner, Richard Thomas, ruled at an Information Tribunal that Members of Parliament's allowance claims to the Fees Office should be published in full. The media never distinguished between 'expenses' and 'allowances' in this debate. Speaker Martin and the House of Commons officers delayed their publication until public pressure resulted in the 'John Lewis list' (which I hadn't realised existed) being published, and an agreement was reached to publish highly redacted information.

Then, a leak of all the unredacted information to *The Daily Telegraph* newspaper resulted in a long series of front page

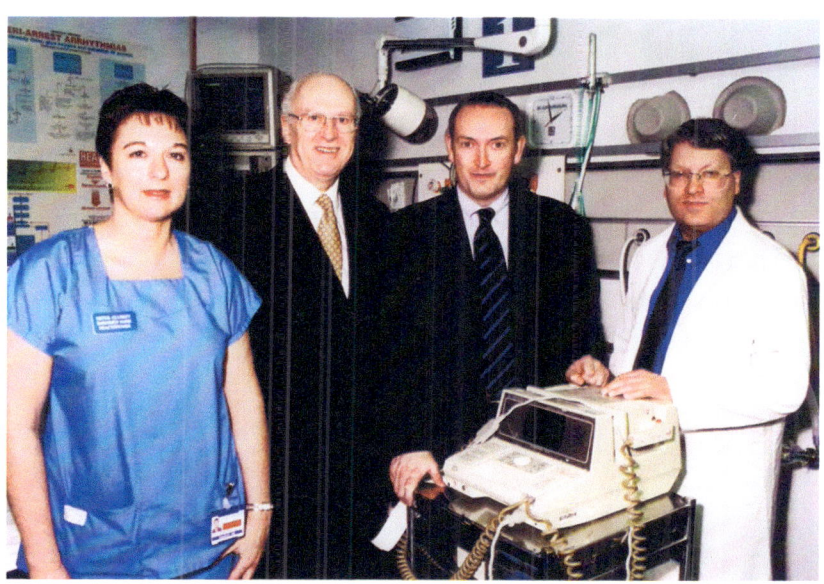

Health Minister John Hutton at the Royal Bolton Hospital
(see *Bolton Evening News* dated 10 and 13 February 1990).

stories appearing from 8 May 2009 that seriously damaged the reputations of all Members of Parliament, whether directly involved in the scandal or not, as well as the reputation of Parliament itself. Speaker Michael Martin was badly damaged by the way in which he handled this affair throughout and was forced to announce his resignation to the House on 19 May

John Bercow was elected to replace him on 22 June 2009 after three ballots. I liked him and voted for him to become the Speaker of the House. When he arrived in the House of Commons John made an instant impact on the Conservative benches. Most people saw him as a Member to the right in the Conservative Party. He married a Labour Party member and moved to the centre ground of politics. However, by the time I retired from the House he had made himself very unpopular with quite a number of Conservative Members. Their dislike for him intensified after the 2010 General Election. Sally Bercow stood as a Labour Party candidate in the 2010 local elections and became a darling of the media. Early in 2011 she posed, dressed only in a bed sheet, for a London *Evening Standard* photographer, which dented her reputation in Parliament and that of her husband. Later, in 2011, she foolishly entered Channel 4s *Big Brother* house. She was the first to be ejected from it.

Another difficulty that was not completely solved at this time was the way donations to political parties were handled. The Government set up a review under Haydn Phillips, which recommended that the cap on General Election expenditure should be £50,000 and that the Electoral Commission be given regulatory powers to oversee these donations.

It was also recommended that legislation should be put in place to prevent donations from 'unincorporated associations' (in an attempt to stop donors such as Lord Ashcroft channelling their money into the Conservative Party). The Conservative Party would not sign up to these principles. They pointed a finger at the donations made to the Labour Party by the trade unions, although these are completely transparent.

For the US Government, which deregulated its financial services under President George Bush following the advice of Alan Greenspan, chairman of the USA Federal Reserve (1987-2006), the financial dominoes began to tumble in the summer of 2007. The US Government was forced to save mortgage lenders Fannie Mae and Freddie Mac (a downturn in the US economy caused an increasing number of mortgage lenders to default on their loans). That was followed by major US financial institutions such as Lehman Brothers (allowed to collapse on 15 September 2008), AIG (saved by the USA Treasury), Bear Stearns (taken over by J. P. Morgan) and Merrill Lynch (absorbed by Bank of America) announcing that they too were in difficulties in July and August 2007. These failures sent shock waves round the world.

The problem wasn't confined to the US. A global financial crisis was precipitated (the 'credit crunch'). In September 2007 people queued to withdraw their deposits from the Northern Rock Building Society and our Government was forced to nationalise it on 22 February 2008. In the same month Lehman Brothers was liquidated in the US. On 29 September 2008, the Bradford and Bingley Building Society was partly nationalised in the UK – the rest was sold to the Spanish bank Santander. That was followed by the Government being forced to invest unimaginable sums of money in the Royal Bank of Scotland (RBS), Lloyds TSB and Halifax Bank of Scotland (HBOS). 6 October 2008 became known as 'Meltdown Monday'. By 8 October Sir Fred Goodwin (later to be known as 'Fred the Shred') and Sir Tom McKillop (who had been a distinguished chemist with AstraZeneca, previously ICI Pharmaceuticals Division) admitted failure at RBS. On 'Black Friday' (10 October) stock markets around the world spiralled downwards. The Government decided to recapitalise the failing banks to the tune of £500 billion; RBS were nationalised on 13 October when the Government also took a 40% share in HBOS and Lloyds. 'Toxic debt' (unrepayable loans) was exchanged for guaranteed Government bonds. Two banks in Iceland also ran out of money in October 2008, as did banks in the Irish Republic and elsewhere in Europe.

Gordon Brown led the world in planning a recovery from the worst financial crisis in my lifetime, but the global financial problems gave the Conservative opposition a chance to attack the Labour Government for what they regarded as profligate public spending, which they blamed for the crisis. Opinion polls plunged against the Labour Party. 'It's time for a change' is a powerful slogan in British politics and the Conservatives adopted it as their slogan.

The Labour Government provided various fiscal stimuli that kept people in jobs, such as a temporary reduction for 13 months in VAT (from 17.5% to 15%, announced on 24 November 2008) at a cost of £12.5 billion and a scheme that allowed the owners of 'old bangers' to trade them in for new cars and save £2,000. Schemes were introduced to save home owners from losing their homes. 'Quantitative easing' put more money into the economy and the Bank of England slashed its base rate from 5% to 2% (later to 1.5%, then to 0.5%), which hit savers badly. The banks were propped up by unimaginably large sums of Government money to prevent their total collapse. They were encouraged to lend money to businesses again to get us out of the 'credit crunch' that was stifling the economy but this didn't happen and the economy ground to a halt. The country headed for recession.

In the fourth session of the 2005-2010, Parliament legislation was introduced to manage our marine resources and provide access for the public to all the British coastline, to introduce a points system for immigration similar to a scheme operating in Australia, to reform the Coroners' Courts in light of recommendations made by Dame Janet Smith following her inquiry into the Shipman murders (especially to reform death certification), to provide guaranteed apprenticeships, to provide a commitment to eradicate child poverty by 2020, to provide financial help for home owners in mortgage arrears, to increase airport security, to improve border controls through the merger of the port customs and immigration services, to equalise pay between men and women, to introduce an independent authority (Independent Parliamentary Standards Authority – IPSA) to manage Members' allowances, to establish Saving Gateway Accounts with the aim of helping people to get on the housing ladder, to move people off benefits and into employment, for the protection of deposits in banks and building societies and to bring back confidence in the financial services sector, and to publish a NHS Constitution that set out the rights of both patients and staff.

I sat on the Standing Committees to consider the Coroner's Courts Bill and the Draft Bribery Bill in this session of Parliament. I tried to introduce a clause on the face of the Coroner's Courts Bill to allow the use of MRI scanning as a means of conducting post-mortems in the Muslim and Jewish communities, with a view to facilitating rapid burial of the deceased. These post-mortems were pioneered in Bolton but I was told that they were allowed in any case in other towns and cities.

On 17 December 2008, I voted against a proposal to appoint the chairman of the Electoral Commission on a salary starting at £100,000 and, on 17 March 2009, I supported an amendment put down by Lynne Jones (Member of Parliament for Birmingham Selly Oak) to pay 18-25 year-olds the same rate of Jobseeker's Allowance (JSA) as those over the age of 25 received. Mr Speaker did not select her amendment to increase the rate of JSA, otherwise I would have supported that amendment too since I had raised this issue several times at different Question Times.

At the Report Stage of the Police and Crime Bill on 19 May 2009 I supported two amendments put down by Dr Evan Harris, one to avoid criminalisation of prostitutes under the age of 18 and the other to prevent criminalisation of men who unknowingly had sex with prostitutes who had been trafficked into Britain. The amendments were lost.

At this stage it was felt that the country was ready for a change of Government, despite the fact that the Party conferences showed that the Labour Party had better policies for the future than the other parties.

Ruth Kelly's Ministerial career came to an abrupt end on 24 September 2008 when she announced during her speech at the Labour Party's annual conference in Manchester that she was standing down as the Transport Secretary. She told Gordon Brown in May that she wanted to spend more time with her four children, all under the age of 12, but she was willing to wait until he had a major reshuffle. Ruth had been forced into the position of resigning early by a leak from an adviser at 10 Downing Street which was circulating at the conference. She was unfairly criticised in the media and by others because her surprise resignation came immediately after Gordon Brown's conference speech, and took the media focus off it. Some commentators believed that she had found it difficult to support the Human Fertilisation and Embryology Bill as a Cabinet Member which, they alleged, was the real reason for her resignation. Ruth was a member of the Roman Catholic group Opus Dei. On 3 October 2008 she announced that she would not seek re-election at the next General Election.

In early 2009 we were officially in a recession, with 1.9 million people out of work. In January 2009 huge losses were announced by the financial institutions in the USA and RBS followed with an announcement of losses of £20 billion. The Government invested even more money in a second recapitalisation of the banks. But at the same time bankers were awarding themselves huge bonuses, even in the failed banks. It was leaked that 'Fred the Shred' would receive a pension of £700,000 per annum at the age of only 50 on top of the lump sum he had received when he resigned from RBS. The general public became very angry; they were suffering because of the apparent greed of bankers in the City of London.

Finally it was admitted that regulation of the banks had been poor. Sir James Crosby, deputy chairman at the FSA, resigned. Gordon Brown set out on a world tour to prepare the ground for a G20 Summit, which was held on 2 April 2009 at the ExCel Centre in London's dockland area. It was regarded as a highly successful summit and set the stage for dealing with the world's economic crisis. President Barack Obama had been elected as the USAs first black President on 4 November 2008 and attended, which was regarded by the media as a coup for Gordon Brown.

In the Budget of 22 April 2009 Chancellor Alistair Darling introduced a 50p tax band for those earning over £150,000 and announced that Government borrowing had reached record levels. National Insurance Contributions (NICS) were increased for all those earning more than £20,000 and employer's NICS contributions were increased too, measures which the Tories called 'a tax on jobs'. After publication of the Budget the Institute of Fiscal Studies announced that there was a £45 billion black hole in it.

Actress Joanne Lumley made a fool of the Government by winning the argument that Gurkhas who had fought for Britain and their families should be allowed to settle in Britain from Nepal. There were 36,000 Gurkha soldiers in this category alone. After the Government lost a vote on this issue in a House of Commons debate, Immigration Minister Phil Woolas tried to resign, but Gordon Brown persuaded him not to and the Government capitulated, despite the cost.

By October 2009, the deaths of 221 soldiers had occurred in Afghanistan, 70 in the preceding six months, and the village of Wootton Bassett marked the homecoming of all those killed in action, which brought these facts home to the British people on television. The Defence Secretary reported at a PLP meeting in July 2009 that 15 members of the armed forces had been lost in 13 days.

Minister Hazel Blears wrote a piece in *The Observer* newspaper on 3 May 2009 which was highly critical of the

Prime Minister. Alluding to a poor YouTube performance by Gordon Brown, she wrote "You YouTube if you want to", an expression that reminded us all of Margaret Thatcher.

In June 2009 there was a spate of Ministerial resignations – Jacqui Smith, Tom Watson and Beverley Hughes on 2 June, Hazel Blears on 3 June, James Purnell on 4 June, Caroline Flint on 5 June and Jane Kennedy on 8 June – which undermined Gordon Brown's position as Prime Minister. He was accused of treating his women Ministers badly. Rumours had circulated for some months about him throwing telephones across offices at 10 Downing Street. It was difficult to separate fact from fiction, so I continued to support him. After the local elections John Hutton quit as Defence Secretary and Geoff Hoon went too. There were 12 resignations altogether in seven days. Gordon began to put a new Cabinet together on 5 June 2009.

Not surprisingly, Labour lost all four of its county councils in the local elections and gained only 16% of the vote in the European Elections, its worst result in a national election since World War I. There was a further plot to remove Gordon Brown, led by Charles Clarke, Stephen Byers and others, but it fizzled out. On Monday 8 June Gordon faced the Parliamentary Labour Party and promised to address his weaknesses. After seeing a vigorous defence of Gordon Brown by Lord (Peter) Mandelson on television the evening before, Geraldine Smith (Member of Parliament for Morecambe and Lunesdale), a Brown loyalist and member of the Communication Workers Union (CWU) who opposed Mandelson over his plans to privatise Royal Mail, said in a speech "I found myself suddenly falling in love with Peter Mandelson". I was stunned by her conversion.

After being banned from standing as a Labour Party candidate by a Special National Executive Committee Endorsements Panel on 2 June 2009, Dr Ian Gibson announced his resignation from Parliament on 8 June. His daughter worked as a civil servant in London and lived with him in his West London flat, allegedly rent free. Ian decided to leave the flat and transfer the mortgage to his daughter and her partner, and move into Dolphin Square. His only sin was that he 'sold' the flat at below market value. Others who committed greater offences in the 'expenses scandal' did not suffer such harsh treatment by the Party. Ian's Norwich North CLP did not want him to resign, and many Members of Parliament, including me, were astonished by the Party's behaviour.[3]

Dr Gibson increasingly voted against the Government: 16 times (1.5% of his total votes) in the 1997-2001 Parliament, 52 times (5.5%) in the 2001-2005 Parliament and 63 times (7.0%) between 2005 and 2009. Commentators believed it was his maverick behaviour that led to his downfall. The Labour Party lost the Norwich North by-election on 23 June 2009 to a Conservative candidate, Chloe Smith, who became the youngest Member of Parliament. She retained the seat at the 2010 General Election when Charles Clarke also lost his seat in Norwich South.

The security of our food and energy supplies became a matter for serious debate. Lord (Peter) Mandelson failed to convince the Labour Party regarding his part privatisation plans for Royal Mail, which continued to lose money. Its main problem was that there was a huge deficit in its pension scheme. Mandelson's proposals were quietly dropped as the 2010 General Election approached.

The Labour Party barred Bury North Member David Chaytor (gaoled on 7 January 2011 on a plea of guilty but released on 26 May 2011 after serving less than a third of his sentence), Elliot Morley (Member of Parliament for Scunthorpe, gaoled on 20 May 2011), and Jim Devine (Member of Parliament for Livingstone) from standing as Labour candidates after they were charged with fraudulent allowances claims. Jim Devine pleaded 'not guilty' but was found guilty on 10 February 2011 for the offences for which he was charged and gaoled on 31 March. Eric Illsley (Member of Parliament for Barnsley Central) was gaoled on 10 February 2011.

A television reporter's sting caught Margaret Moran, Patricia Hewitt, Stephen Byers and Geoff Hoon making fools of themselves and the Labour Party when he tried to recruit them as lobbyists for a fictitious American company, and they were later suspended from the Party on 22 March 2010. Patricia Hewitt and Geoff Hoon circulated a letter asking MPs for help to remove Gordon Brown as Leader of the Labour Party on 7 January 2010.

Thomas Legg's audit of Members of Parliament's allowances (his report was published on 4 February 2010) resulted in hundreds of thousands of pounds being paid back to the Fees Office, whilst Christopher Kelly's proposals for an Independent Parliamentary Standards Authority (IPSA) brought changes to the allowances system after the 2010 General Election.

The Lisbon Treaty (about the European Constitution) was rejected by the Irish people in a referendum (this result was reversed in a second referendum held on 2 October 2009) and the east coast main line railway service, previously run by

National Express, was nationalised in June 2009 after making massive losses.

On the positive side, neighbourhood policing had a major impact on crime levels, the Future Jobs Fund was reducing the number of long-term unemployed young people, plans were agreed to provide a high-speed rail link (HS2) between London and Scotland, and a Labour Member (Willie Bain) was returned in the Glasgow North East by-election, formerly Michael Martin's seat, on 12 November 2009.

Michael Foot and Lord (Jack) Jones attended a Parliamentary Labour Party meeting on 26 January 2009. Unfortunately, I wasn't able to attend this meeting of the PLP. As a 'Birthday Greeting' Neil Kinnock wrote in *Tribune* of a heated debate that had occurred at a summer party thrown by Jill Tweedie to celebrate Michael's 68th birthday:

"In the excitement, Louis Heren – groping for nuts to absorb his whisky – grabbed a handful of pot-pourri, stuck it in his mouth, took another gulp of scotch and munched away without realising that he was chewing scented purple petals and sprigs, not almonds and cashew nuts. When I mentioned the event to him a couple of months later, he said: "I thought it was a bloody strange taste. But when Foot is speaking like that I could chew glass and not notice it.""

It was clear that the Conservatives would abolish the New Deal programmes, the Regional Development Agencies, Education Maintenance Allowances, the Building Schools for the Future Programme and the 18-week target (from seeing a GP to treatment) in the NHS, let the National Minimum Wage drift, reduce the number of undergraduates in our universities, and close Sure Start and Children's Centres should they come to power.

Legislation was introduced in the highly truncated 2009-2010 session of Parliament to introduce a National Care Service for elderly and vulnerable people, to make the 0.7% of GDP target for overseas aid a statutory target, to deal with excessive bankers' bonuses, to require the salaries of top company executives to be published for the benefit of shareholders, to provide a high-speed rail link between London and Scotland, with Phase I to Birmingham, to pave the way for electrification of several important railway lines (Blackpool to Manchester, for example), to create a Future Jobs Fund for NEETS – those not in education, employment or training schemes, to give greater rights to agency workers, to reduce the national deficit by half in four years, to control flooding by improving water management, to provide a stimulus for Britain to lead the world in the age of a digital economy, and to reform the laws on bribery. The Constitutional Reform and Governance Bill was amended to allow for a referendum to be held on the Alternative Vote (AV) system. I support the 'first past the post' system for elections and am not in favour of any of the proportional representation systems.

The year 2009 ended badly, with serious floods in Cumbria, and 2010 started badly with a devastating earthquake in Haiti.

I was drawn out in the ballot for Prime Minister's Questions on 10 February 2010 at number one; Anne Snelgrove (Member of Parliament for Swindon), a Private Parliamentary Secretary to Gordon, was on the telephone to me not long after the draw to see whether I had any suitable questions that I wanted to ask. I sent her several possibilities which she discussed with Gordon's team at 10 Downing Street.

It took us 24 hours to make a decision on which question to pose. Gordon had sent one over to me on social care for the elderly, but I was quite keen to ask one of my own questions. Eventually, Anne and I agreed that I would meet Gordon at 11.30 a.m. in his room behind the Speaker's chair to decide on the most suitable question.

However, when he arrived at 11.40 a.m., he was clearly in no mood to have such a discussion. He thrust a version of the question that Anne had flagged up with me into my hand and said "I want that one", and shot off into his room, leaving me in the anteroom. This was the first time I experienced Gordon Brown at his worst. I had two options, either to wrong-foot him by asking one of my own questions or go along with his wish. In the end, after agonising for a few minutes, I decided to rewrite his question and go with that. I had minutes to spare to take my seat in the chamber and ask the following question, my last at Prime Minister's Questions:

"I am astonished at the orchestrated campaign of opposition to our social care plans that seems to have been mounted in some newspapers this morning, supported by Tory councillors and BUPA, especially as the Conservatives did not oppose those plans when they were before the House. Will my Right Honourable Friend commit to continuing the fight to improve the lot of some of our most vulnerable citizens, the poorest pensioners in the country?"

It was a question about the Social Care Bill that our Party was trying to get onto the Statute Book before the General

Election, with the aim of setting up a National Care Service. Andy Burnham was steering it through as the Health Secretary. Local authorities were expected to meet some of the costs and Tory councillors had begun to make a lot of noise.

Michael Foot and Jack Jones at a meeting of the PLP held on 26 January 2009.

Before Prime Minister's Questions the Prime Minister spends quite a bit of time with his team in 10 Downing Street trying to second-guess what the Leader of the Opposition is going to lead on on that particular day. The Opposition Leader has six questions altogether.

As I asked my question I could feel a wall of sound building up in front of me; the Tories didn't like the question, which is always a good sign for us. As luck would have it Downing Street had hit the nail on the head. We wrong-footed David Cameron; it was the very subject he had been going to lead on.

In May 2010 Labour lost the General Election, but the

Conservatives didn't win it either. They were forced into a coalition with the Liberal Democrats.

All in all, the Labour Government had had a good run. It reformed public services and their delivery beyond imagination. Above all we had stuck to our basic principles of justice and fairness. John Prescott used the expression "traditional Labour Party values, in a modern setting". At times it had been a bumpy ride and I often voted for policies, such as Academy Schools and NHS Foundation Trusts, that I wasn't completely behind. Until Margaret Beckett became the Minister responsible for housing policy and John Healey succeeded her, I had been very disappointed with our housing policies. John Healey announced a major reform of the Housing Revenue Account and a significant house building programme, but it was too late.

Most Labour Members of Parliament became disillusioned by Gordon Brown when he became Prime Minister. Before taking office he appeared to be some distance to the left of Tony Blair in the policies that he pursued, but after taking office, there wasn't much difference between TB and GB. Gordon became very New Labour. He was indecisive and proved to be uncomfortable in policy areas, such as defence, that he had not previously been responsible for. Although he had had a long time to think about the policy changes that he would make when he became Prime Minister there was no noticeable change in direction.

In forming his first Cabinet in 2007 he brought into the House of Lords several people of influence, such as Digby Jones (former Director of the CBI), Professor Ara Darzi (a renowned surgeon), Sir Alan West (the former First Sea Lord), and Sir Mark Malloch-Brown (a former Deputy General of the UN). They all became Ministers. His Government became known as the 'Government of all the Talents' (the peers became known as 'GOATS'). Digby Jones never joined the Labour Party. After I spent an evening with him at a business dinner at the Last Drop Village Hotel in Bolton I concluded that he was more Liberal Democrat than anything else.

Despite absences from Parliament on Select Committee visits I always had a high voting record in divisions – 88.4% (1997-2001), 87.2% (2001-2005) and 89% (2005-2010). In one session of Parliament I had the best voting record in the House, even beating Dennis Skinner. Dennis declined to sit on a Select Committee and I never saw him sitting on a Bill Standing Committee or a Statutory Instrument Committee either. He appeared to confine his Parliamentary activities from 1997 to 2010 to the main chamber or in the media, although he raised a lot of money for Constituency Labour Parties around the country through his public speaking at their events. During the term of the Labour Government he overcame some serious health problems.

I believe I was seen by opposition Members as a Labour Member with an independent mind, which probably didn't play well with the Labour Government – not a safe pair of hands. Although I voted against the Government several times I was not a serial rebel like many of my left-wing colleagues. I realised that serial rebels are not taken seriously in Parliament or even listened to. I called myself a 'barometer rebel', only coming out as a rebel when I felt strongly that the Government was very wrong and was about to experience a storm.

The Public Whip website (www.publicwhip.org.uk) shows that I voted against the Labour Government 24 times out of 1139 votes (2.1%) in the 1997-2001 Parliament, 41 times out of 1087 votes (3.8%) in the 2001-2005 Parliament and 20 times out of 1133 votes (1.8%) in the 2005-2010 Parliament. Many of the votes recorded 'against the Government' on this website were in fact votes on 'free vote issues', votes on Private Members' Business or votes on Business of the House motions, also taken on a free vote basis or on a one-line whip (at least I bothered to attend).

Despite remaining as a back-bench Member for all of my 13 years in Parliament, I think I made a difference. In the next chapters I cover other Parliamentary business that I was closely involved in to support this claim.

NOTES

1. *Men Who Made Labour: The PLP of 1906 – the personalities and the politics*, (A. Howarth and D. Hayter, eds.), Routledge, Oxford, 2006, 60-65.

2. The closure of Remploy, Bolton was announced in March 2012.

3. Ian Gibson also resigned from the Labour Party.

CHAPTER SEVEN

PRIVATE MEMBERS' BILLS

~

There are four kinds of Private Members' Bills, each covered by a Standing Order of the House. They are considered in a priority order by the House of Commons.

At the beginning of each session of Parliament Members are invited to put their names down opposite a number in the Private Members' Bills Ballot Book, which is kept for two days – Tuesday and Wednesday – in the 'Noes' Lobby. On the following Thursday morning, 20 numbers are drawn out at 10.00 a.m. and matched with a Member's name. Ballot Bills are dealt with ahead of all other Private Members' Bills.

Shortly after the draw the 20 selected Members queue up behind the Speaker's chair to present their Bills to the House (the First Reading stage), and the date of the Second Reading debate of the Bill is announced. After passage through the House of Commons, the Member in charge of a Private Member's Bill has to find a peer who is prepared to adopt their Bill in the House of Lords. Only when these Bills pass through all their stages in both Houses of Parliament can they receive Royal Assent and become Acts of Parliament.

Taking second place in the 'pecking order' that exists for Private Members' Bills are Presentation Bills. These Bills are presented to the House (the First Reading) without the need to make a speech and have usually been the subject of a Ten Minute Rule Bill in a previous session of Parliament.

By far the most common type of Private Member's Bill is one taken under the Ten Minute Rule. A Member of Parliament is given up to ten minutes, usually on a Tuesday or Wednesday before Government business, to make a speech to introduce their Bill (the First Reading) and anyone in the House can make an opposition speech, also up to ten minutes. These Bills may be put to a vote, but this happens only with the most contentious Bills – on subjects such as abortion or euthanasia.

The fourth type of Private Member's Bill is one that has started in the House of Lords and comes down to the House of Commons, where a Member is needed to adopt it, if it is to proceed. When a Private Member's Bill proceeds to the House of Lords from the House of Commons, tradition requires that it will not meet with opposition in the upper house. All four types of Private Members' Bills are listed for hearing on the 13 sitting Fridays (in a full session of Parliament) set aside for Private Members' Bills in the priority order that I have described. Few succeed in becoming law.

The first Private Member's Bill I became associated with

was Michael Foster's (Member of Parliament for Worcester; he lost his seat in 2010) Bill to ban hunting of mammals with dogs (Second Reading – 28 November 1997). This Bill failed to become law as a Private Member's Bill. The Government introduced a highly-contentious Hunting Bill later. After many torturous and extremely prolonged debates over several sessions of Parliament it became law but, in my opinion, it has never been properly enforced. Although there are Conservative Members who supported these Bills, most Conservative Members, many of whom represented shire counties, objected to them becoming law. In the General Election campaign of 2010 the Tories promised to repeal the Hunting Act, which didn't happen in the 2010-2015 Parliament.

In November 2002, I was drawn number 17 in the Private Members' Bills Ballot; my interest in cricket persuaded me to put my name opposite number 100 in the Ballot Book.

I wasn't inundated with calls to take Bills forward like those higher up the list of 20 Bills were. Bill Tynan (Member of Parliament for Hamilton South) was drawn number 3 and decided to take a Bill forward to deal with the nuisance caused by fireworks. There had been calls to ban the sale of fireworks to the general public altogether, but I did not support this extreme position. Bill Tynan's Bill seemed the way forward. We were both members of the All-Party Parliamentary Fireworks Group, which had discussed this issue many times. If Bill Tynan had not made this decision I was prepared to deal with fireworks.

When the Government sent out its list of subjects for 'hand me down Bills' (bits of legislation that could not be slotted into Government Bills of the day) I was attracted by the fact that there was a need to improve marine safety. After a consultation with Transport Minister David Jamieson I decided to promote The Marine Safety Bill.

In Brighton with Michael Foster MP (October 1997).

There had been three major oil tanker disasters in the seas around our islands, those involving the *Torrey Canyon* (1967), the *Braer* (1993) and the *Sea Empress* (1996), which caused major environmental damage to long stretches of Britain's 10,000 miles of coastline. Each incident caused outrage amongst the British public. Lord Donaldson (a former Master of the Rolls) was asked to set up two public inquiries, a few years apart, and came forward with several recommendations that the Government implemented.

Following the first inquiry on the *Braer* disaster, four Emergency Towing Vessels (ETVs) were purchased and kept at strategic positions around our coastline, to tow vessels to safety when they got into trouble at sea.

After the second public inquiry on the *Sea Empress* disaster, the post of SOSREP (the Secretary of State's [for Transport] Representative for Maritime Salvage and Intervention) was established, and the first holder of this post, Robin Middleton, was stationed at the Southampton headquarters of the Maritime and Coastguard Agency, although he was independent of them.[1] Robin had complete authority to take charge of any shipping accidents around our coastline and co-ordinate rescue and salvage operations. Although, by this time, Britain had the best marine safety legislation of any country in the world, two loopholes became apparent to Robin, and my Private Member's Bill was intended to deal with them. Both loopholes can be illustrated by real examples.

An oil tanker, bound for an oil refinery in Milford Haven Sound (off the Pembrokeshire coast), developed engine trouble at sea, with a storm brewing. The captain requested permission to anchor his vessel at the oil terminal jetty and unload his cargo of oil while engineers repaired the ship's engines. This request was refused, and the captain had no other option but to take the vessel out to sea again in the eye of a storm. Robin Middleton, who had no powers at that time to commandeer the private facilities (berths, wharfs or jetties) of riparian owners and managers, to aid a vessel in trouble, retained the vessel in Milford Haven Sound with the help of one of the ETVs, which prevented it drifting. One clause of my Marine Safety Bill was intended to give the SOSREP those powers.

In another incident, the *Kukawa*, a role-on, roll-off cargo ferry, suffered an engine room fire 25 miles North West of Guernsey, on 21 December 1997, and the fire spread to the ship's accommodation quarters. The crew were unable to put the fire out and called for help. Many of our coastal fire brigades, such as the Kent Fire and Rescue Service, have specially trained teams that can be air lifted onto vessels when these emergencies occur. On this occasion the Guernsey and Cornwall Fire and Rescue Service extinguished the fire and put in a claim to the ship's insurers. Following the incident, which lasted three days, the insurers refused to pay out, and a judgement was sought in the Admiralty Jurisdiction of the High Court of Session.

The judgement was made in favour of the insurers on grounds that the fire service involved was operating outside its geographical area of responsibility, which was defined by the court as the coastal low water mark. As a result of this judgement coastal fire and rescue services threatened to stop servicing ships in trouble, and some stopped training staff for these operations. The second major clause of my Bill addressed this problem.

The first major obstacle I had in getting this Bill through Parliament was its position on the list of 20 Private Members' Bills. On each of the 13 Fridays when Private Members' Bills Business is taken a Bill from the top third of the list is considered first, then a Bill from the middle order of the list is taken, followed by a Bill from the bottom third of the list. My Bill was scheduled to be heard on Friday 28 February 2003, the third Friday of Private Members' Bills Business, when the Fireworks Bill was also scheduled to be taken. All 20 Bills were presented to the House on Wednesday 11 December 2002 (the First Reading stage), when the Clerk read their titles and asked Members for the Second Reading date.

I liaised very closely with Bill Tynan in particular, but also with Keith Simpson (Member of Parliament for Mid-Norfolk), to ensure that I had enough time to present my Bill at the end of the day's business. Many Members wanted to speak during the Second Reading debate of the Fireworks Bill (I was one of them), but Bill Tynan asked for restraint, in order to give time for the other Bills scheduled to be heard on that day, and Keith Simpson began the Second Reading debate on his National Lottery (Funding of Endowments) Bill at 12.41

p.m. That debate was concluded by 1.47 p.m. The Government agreed not to oppose this Bill, otherwise it would have been talked out and there would have been no time for me to present my Bill to the House. I managed to complete my debate before the 2.30 p.m. deadline (business on Fridays starts at 9.30 a.m.), and the Bill received its Second Reading. It is very unusual for three Private Members' Bills to receive a Second Reading on the same Friday.

One committee room is reserved for Private Members' Bills, and the Bills go into committee in the order that they receive their Second Reading. Bill number 17 would normally have to wait several weeks. The Member in charge of a Private Member's Bill is responsible for making all the arrangements, including persuading fellow Members on each side of the chamber to agree to join the Bill's Standing Committee and arranging the committee date through the 'usual channels' (the Government Whips). The Committee of Selection has to receive a list of Members of the committee for approval.

Through talking to the Government's civil servants in the Government Whips' Office, who are usually extremely helpful to Members on the Government side of the House, and talking to the Government Whip responsible for Private Members' Bills Business, on this occasion Jim Fitzpatrick (Member of Parliament for Poplar and Canning Town), who was also extremely helpful, I discovered that there is a cross-over period for Government Bills coming down to the House of Commons from the House of Lords and those going in the opposite direction, when committee rooms allocated for Government Bills are not required. I sought the permission of our Whips to use one of these rooms to get my Bill through its Committee Stage. Using this little-known procedure I ensured that my Bill reached the House of Lords, where Lord Donaldson steered it through in time for it to receive Royal Assent before the Prorogation of Parliament at the end of the 2002-2003 session. It became The Marine Safety Act 2003 and came into force on 10 September 2003.

The first 'directions' given under the powers provided by The Marine Safety Act 2003 were given in 2004. On 9 February 2004, MV *Altelund* was given a direction to anchor in a safe place and await a contracted tug. On 25 October 2004, when the MV *Nyk Argus* sustained a fire in its hold between the Bay of Biscay and Southampton, a direction was given by the SOSREP that the hold remained sealed until all non-crew persons had been removed from the vessel along with the unaffected cargo, and until fire services were in place to fight any remaining blaze.

In a third use of the Act, on 19 November 2004, the master of the MV *Fione*, which ran aground on rocks at Margate with the possibility of pollution of the sea surrounding the vessel, was given a direction to await an Emergency Towing Vessel to enable the ship to be towed to a place of safety for inspection. The ship's master was attempting to free the ship from the rocks without assistance. Up to the end of 2010 the SOSREP had given 13 'directions' under the Marine Safety Act 2003.

Before the General Election of 1997, Joyce Quin (Member of Parliament for Gateshead East and Washington West) was Patron of the Society of Registration Officers (SoRO) in England and Wales. She became the Minister responsible for prisons in the Home Department after the election, and I was chosen to succeed her as SoROs Patron.

This came about as a result of SoROs General Secretary Karen Knapton taking advice from Registration Officers around the country as to which Members of Parliament would be likely candidates to succeed Joyce. The Principal Registration Officer at the Bolton Register Office, Oliver Barton, recommended me to her. We had worked together on the City Challenge Board, which managed Mere Hall, where the Register Office had been moved from Paderborn House in the town centre. Mere Hall, which was completely refurbished with City Challenge money, is set in a small park close to Bolton town centre. My daughter Sally chose to be married there during my 1997 General Election campaign.

I saw wedding parties coming out of the former Register Office in Paderborn House many times. The office itself was very plain and unsuitable for weddings in my opinion, and wedding parties stepped out into the street to face a taxi rank. The only decent place for wedding photographs nearby was in front of Bolton's magnificent Town Hall. I suggested to Cllr Bob Howarth, Leader of the Council and a Ward colleague, that Mere Hall would be an excellent venue for weddings.

I first met Karen Knapton on 21 October 1997, when I learned that I would be required to keep SoRO informed of anything that was happening in Parliament that might affect the Registration Service, whose headquarters are in Southport, and address their Annual Conference, which moved round the country. I prepared annual addresses for Wolverhampton in 1998, Sheffield, Southampton, Epping Forest (actually presented by Karen Knapton because I was involved in the 2001 General Election campaign), Scarborough, Llangybi in the Vale of Usk, Runcorn, Grange-Over-Sands (Karen also presented this speech for me because the date clashed with the 2005 General Election campaign), Bryn Meadows Golf Club and County Hotel, Ystrad Mynach (Caerphilly), and Leicester.

I also learned of a major difficulty which I was asked to address, namely that Registration Officers were Statutory Officers, which meant that they had no formal employer and, consequently, that employment legislation was not applicable to them, about 1,700 of them in total. Members of police forces, the armed services and members of the clergy were also Statutory Officers at that time. Rent officers had been Statutory Officers but their situation had been addressed.

If a Registration Officer was unfairly dismissed, they could not apply for their case to be heard by an Employment Tribunal; only the Registrar General, whose office is in the Office of National Statistics in Pimlico, could hear their case, and only if new evidence could be provided that had not been available when he had dismissed them in the first place. This seemed a very unfair situation to me. At that time the Economic Secretary in the Treasury was responsible for this service. I decided to take on this campaign for SoRO.

I started by lobbying successive Economic Secretaries at the Treasury, including my Bolton colleague Ruth Kelly, and successive Employment Ministers at the Department of Trade and Industry, either by means of written or oral Parliamentary Questions, as well as by letter, or by seeing them personally. I highlighted the plight of Registration Officers also in an Adjournment Debate on 3 June 2003. The Government promised the first major reform of the Registration Service since 1837, when the service was established to officially record all births, marriages and deaths. Prior to that churches had had this responsibility.

Ruth Kelly chose to introduce reform by presenting two Regulatory Reform Orders to the Regulatory Reform Committee (set up by the Labour Government, with Peter

Pike, Member of Parliament for Burnley, as its first chairman). It was my opinion that these reforms required consideration by the whole House, so I was not surprised when the committee refused to deal with the first of these Orders.

I decided to proceed with a Private Member's Bill under the Ten Minute Rule, on 23 November 2005. Local authorities appoint, accommodate, pay and provide pensions for Registration Officers, so it made sense to require local authorities to be also their legal employers, which would bring Registration Officers under the employment legislation. My Bill also included a TUPE [Transfer of Undertakings (Protection of Employment)] clause that would protect their existing terms and conditions of employment when this transfer of responsibility occurred.

Although Eric Forth (Member of Parliament for Bromley and Chislehurst) objected to my Bill at its First Reading, he did not put it to a vote. However, when I turned up on successive Fridays, he objected to the Bill receiving a formal Second Reading (i.e. without debate), and it never proceeded into its Committee Stage. Eric Forth regularly attended on Fridays, and he would object to all Bills proceeding that had not been debated on the floor of the House. He died suddenly of cancer on 17 May 2006, but it was too late for me to resurrect my Bill.

When the Queen's Speech was made on 15 November 2006 I noticed that a Statistics Bill was announced that would make the collection and compilation of statistics independent of Government. I approached the then Financial Secretary at the Treasury, John Healey (Member of Parliament for Wentworth and Dearne), who was made aware of my work for SoRO when he was Economic Secretary at the Treasury, and proposed that he adopt my Ten Minute Rule Bill. He did, and Royal Assent to the Statistics and Registration Service Act 2007 (Second Reading on 8 January 2007), on 26 July 2007, ended my long campaign. I sat on the Standing Committee of this Bill.

My tenth and final Annual Address was made to SoRO at Leicester Town Hall on 9 May 2007, when I announced that I would be standing down as their Patron. I had completed what they had asked of me. They made me their first and, as far as I know, their only Honorary Member. On 12 March 2009, SoRO passed a winding-up resolution, and the Registrar of Trade Unions concurred that they should be wound up in January 2010. Most of their members became members of UNISON.

In November 2009, I entered my name in the Private Members' Bills Ballot Book opposite the number 200. On 26 November, when I was on the way to a Royal Society of Chemistry Public Affairs Committee meeting in Burlington House, Gemma rang me from my Westminster office to say that she was being inundated with telephone calls and emails because I had been drawn out at 10.00 a.m. that morning with the number 1 Ballot Bill. Even with the short Parliamentary session ahead of us, six available Fridays instead of the usual 13, it was surprising how many people took a sudden interest in me. We estimated that we received over 3,000 emails, not to mention the letters and telephone calls that also arrived. I explain elsewhere in this book Lord (Alf) Morris's interest in me taking forward his Bill on contaminated blood and my reasons for not doing so (see Chapter 14).

John Healey, then Minister of State for Housing and Planning, brought my attention to an issue that he was keen to resolve, if possible before the General Election. Since it concerned homelessness I felt that it was worth using my Private Member's Bill to resolve this problem. It seemed likely that my proposed legislation would get cross-party support.

During the term of the Labour Government house prices had risen to such a degree that few young people could afford a mortgage. The stock of council houses declined, as more and more houses were sold under the Right-to-Buy legislation, and fewer new and affordable houses were built. As a consequence the buy-to-let market exploded. A landlord entering this market pays a higher fee to set up a commercial mortgage and an interest rate higher than the domestic interest rate. These landlords rent their properties out on assured shorthold tenancies, which require two months notice to be given for the tenant to quit.

Some landlords borrowed money from building societies or other lenders by giving the impression that they were going to live in the property when they were not. These Residential-Turned-Let (RTL) tenancies were unauthorised and were not covered by housing legislation at the time. If these landlords defaulted on their mortgages, action was taken against the landlord and not the tenant. In about 2-3,000 cases a year RTL tenants found themselves homeless, often without knowing that their landlord had defaulted until the bailiffs turned up to evict them. Some tenants came home from work or from a visit to find their furniture dumped on the pavement outside their home. Crisis, Shelter, Citizens Advice and the Chartered Institute of Housing received an increasing number of complaints and pressed the Government to correct this 'loophole' in housing legislation. I met representatives of these four charities and decided to help them change the legislation so that RTL tenants would be protected in future.

The First Reading of the Mortgage Repossessions (Protection of Tenants etc) Bill was on 16 December 2009. The Second Reading debate was held on 29 January 2010. I had the full backing of John Healey's civil servants at the Department of Communities and Local Government, and the Bill proceeded into its Committee Stage with full cross-party support. The Committee Stage of the Bill was held on 10 February and the Third Reading of the Bill was completed without debate on 26 February 2010.

Lord (Richard) Best, a cross-bencher, agreed to take the Bill through the House of Lords on an extremely tight timetable. Both of us lobbied hard for this Bill to succeed. Together we met the Labour Chief Whip in the House of Lords, Lord (Steve) Bassam, who was responsible for arranging the Government's business in 'the other place'. Finally, we got the Government to agree to deal with our Bill in the 'wash-up' period of the Parliament. This is when the 'usual channels' (Whips) agree which Bills or parts of a Bill are non-contentious and can proceed to Royal Assent. The First, Second and Final Stages of the Mortgage Repossessions (Tenants Protection etc) Bill were held in the House of Lords on 1 March, 30 March and 8 April (the last day for business), respectively, and Royal Assent was also granted on 8 April.

This Bill, which protects those whose tenancies are not binding on mortgages and requires mortgagees to give notice to tenants of the proposed execution of possession orders when a landlord defaults on a mortgage, came into force on 1 October 2010. For our efforts Lord Best and I jointly shared the Citizens Advice Parliamentarian of the Year Award 2010.

I also made strenuous efforts to update the 1871 and 1881

Pedlars Acts, which have been the subject of abuse in modern times, but I describe these efforts in Chapter 14 of this book.

David Taylor (Member of Parliament for North West Leicestershire) presented a Ten Minute Rule Bill to the House on 24th April 2001, which I agreed to sponsor. After his speech, he went through the usual performance. He bowed at the Bar of the House, walked to the middle of the floor, bowed again, walked to the Table, bowed again, and handed the dummy Bill to the Clerk of the House, just below the Speaker's chair. The Clerk read out the Bill's title – Protection from Smoking (Employees and Young Persons) Bill. The Speaker asked the usual question – "Second Reading, what day?" With a smile on his face, David replied "Friday June the eighth, Sir." The Prime Minister was expected to announce the date of the General Election as Thursday 7 June the following week!

NOTES

1. A second SOSREP, Hugh Shaw, was appointed on 1 January 2008.

CHAPTER EIGHT

ADJOURNMENT DEBATES

There is a 30-minute Adjournment Debate at the end of each day's business in the chamber of the House of Commons. A Member speaks for up to 15 minutes and a Minister responds to the points made. In 1997 other Adjournment Debates were held on certain sitting mornings, which restricted visitors from following the 'Line of Route'.

The Modernisation Committee of the House of Commons decided to trial Adjournment Debates in the Grand Committee Room, which is just off the Great Hall of Westminster. The first debate was held in the Westminster Hall chamber on 30 November 1999. Today, these debates have become a fixture of House of Commons business.

30-minute-long and 90-minute-long Adjournment Debates are held on Tuesdays and Wednesdays (apart from during Question Times) and a longer debate is held in the Westminster Hall chamber on Thursday afternoons, when the House is sitting. The longer debates are usually on Select Committee reports.

I was so keen to spread the idea of local authorities starting up mediation services to settle disputes between neighbours that I decided that my first Adjournment Debate, on 17 December 1997, would be on 'Mediation Services' (see Appendix 1 in which I list all the Adjournment Debates that I have either initiated or taken part in). My second Adjournment Debate in the first session of the new Labour Government (which ran from the May 1997 General Election through to November 1998) was on 23 July 1998, when I raised 'Procedures in the Case of Sudden Death; the Case of David Cunliffe'.

David Cunliffe, who was known by other names too, died of a heroin overdose, and was buried in an unmarked grave in Manchester's Southern Cemetery. It was some months before his family, who lived in my constituency, became aware of his death. Initially, they wanted to exhume his body for reburial in Bolton. A second body was buried by Manchester Social Services above David's body in the same grave. My office found a Bolton undertaker who was willing to open the grave and exhume the two bodies at cost – i.e. no profit – to the family, and Karen Lawrinson in my Bolton office spent a considerable amount of time negotiating with the Home Office for permission for David's re-interment to go ahead. In the end the family decided that they could not afford to proceed.

My Adjournment Debate persuaded Greater Manchester

Police to change its procedures for announcing the deaths of people like David, so that improved attempts could be made in future to track relatives. At that time they did not check whether all the local newspapers published their press releases. Nothing appeared in the *Bolton Evening News* about the death of David Cunliffe.

My third Adjournment Debate in the second session of the Labour Government, on 7 December 1999, was on 'Methadone and Other Heroin Substitutes'. The only heroin substitute prescribed in the UK by the NHS at that time was methadone, which, for most individuals, is as addictive as heroin. The green liquid medicinal formulation also rots teeth. France was mainly prescribing buprenorphine (the generic name) and I was quite keen that the Government should also treat our heroin addicts with this drug. Buprenorphine is more expensive than methadone but its use has advantages for the addict. As Temagesic, a trade name, it had been available in the UK and become a drug of abuse in earlier years, especially in the Strathclyde District of Scotland. Other heroin substitutes are available too, and I tried to persuade our Government at least to carry out trials with them.

Methadone is actually a mixture of two molecules of identical chemical composition which are the mirror images of each other. It has a narrow window of safety and it is easy to overdose when using it, which is one of the reasons that pharmacists prefer it to be taken under supervision. A former University of Salford colleague, Dr Feodore Scheinmann, developed a process for separation of the two types of methadone, and he wanted the Department of Health to clinically trial the active L-methadone, which is safer to use in the absence of its inactive mirror image. Consultants at

Prestwich Hospital were prepared to conduct these clinical trials. As far as I know, such trials have still not been carried out in Britain despite my lobbying of the Home Office and the Department of Health on this issue.

As chairman of the Drug Misuse APPG I also held Adjournment Debates on 'Hepatitis C' (14 November 2001), 'Workplace and Roadside Drug Testing' (14 January 2004), 'Liver Disease' (21 May 2008), and 'Addiction to Prescription and Over-the-Counter Medicines' (16 June 2009).

When I became chairman of the Drug Misuse APPG, a former Dumfriesshire policeman, David Grieve, who had started up a charity called OverCount, approached me about addiction to legally available codeine-containing products. He had become addicted to cough mixture, and drank litres of the stuff at the height of his addiction, which rotted his teeth. He lost his job as a result, which ruined his life.

David and I started up a joint campaign and appeared on television and various radio stations together and separately, but nobody would take us seriously at that time (1997-2000). We wanted the boxes of products containing codeine to carry a warning that this opiate was also addictive (morphine and heroin are opiates; the former is in the latex of the opium poppy and becomes the latter through a reaction with acetic anhydride, which produces diacetylmorphine or diamorphine, also known as heroin).

Addiction to the benzodiazepine tranquillizers (Valium and Librium were the first marketed), readily available prescription drugs, was highlighted by Esther Rantzen in her popular consumer programme *That's Life* in the 1980s, and she published a book on this problem in 1984, but very little happened as a result. An APPG on Tranquillizer Addiction has campaigned in Parliament for several years on this issue.

When the United Nations flagged up the fact that addiction to over-the-counter and prescription drugs was becoming a greater problem worldwide than the trafficking and misuse of illegal substances, I decided that the time had come for the Drug Misuse APPG to carry out an inquiry. Gemma Reay, my Westminster researcher, set up the inquiry on Select Committee lines, and the report she wrote was published in early 2009, in partnership with the charity DrugScope who administered the APPG. It became the subject of articles published in most of the national newspapers, including the Sundays, and many magazines, was an item on the BBCs *One Show*, and addiction to codeine-containing products became a storyline on *Coronation Street*.

As a result of all this activity, the Department of Health decided to take action and set up a small team to carry out some research. I lobbied successive Public Health Ministers, but Dawn Primarolo (Member of Parliament for Bristol South; she became a Deputy Speaker) was the one who really listened. At the time of writing I am not sure whether the new Conservative Government has taken any action as a result; a report was due to be published in 2010.[1] In addition, over-the-counter drug producers were persuaded to carry warnings on the boxes of their products about the possibility of addiction to high doses of codeine and some of our other recommendations were dealt with too.

There has always been a very close link between drug addiction and on-street prostitution. In December 1995 the Wigan and Bolton Health Authority commissioned a survey on prostitution which found that most of the on-street prostitutes lived locally, were addicted to heroin and were subjected to more violence than those working off-street in the brothels, saunas and massage parlours. Prostitutes working indoors tend to regard themselves as more professional and see prostitution like any other profession. Many of them travel into Bolton to preserve anonymity, the majority are drug-free, if alcohol and tobacco use is ignored, and are more likely to maintain a relationship with particular clients, which increases their security, although they are less likely to report violent attacks than on-street prostitutes because of their wish to preserve their anonymity. Their services cost more than those of on-street prostitutes because they either need to pay a 'madam' or maintain a property themselves. Some of them work only at certain times of the year to raise money for Christmas presents or special events such as holidays and birthdays.

The traditional red light district in Bolton was in the Bolton South East constituency, in the light industrial and commercial area surrounding Shifnall Street. This area is close to Bolton's entertainment district, is surrounded by car parks, there is no residential accommodation in the area, and it is close to the A666 (St Peter's Way), which connects Bolton to the motorway network.[2]

When the district became an Industrial Improvement Area owners of the new businesses that moved into it complained, not unreasonably, about the activities of prostitutes. The police mounted several operations to clean up this district and displaced the problem into an adjacent residential area, The Haulgh. In these areas of Bolton there were 14 'suspicious deaths' in two years, including those of 17-year-old Carly Bateman and pregnant 21-year-old Danielle Moorcroft, who were murdered on 10 November 2001 and 1 June 2002 respectively. The Haulgh Community Partnership was established and I became its Patron. A vigorous debate began, with some residents demanding a zero tolerance approach to the problem. As the police carried out more patrols in The Haulgh, the problem was displaced over a much wider area, along Manchester Road and throughout parts of Great Lever.

For a while the industrial and commercial area became an unofficial managed prostitution area. A Prostitution Forum was established, with all the agencies involved. Its aim was to get the women off the streets by helping them with their addiction and their associated social problems. Urban Outreach, a Christian charity led by Dave Bagley, set up a drop-in centre in Salop Street. Over a period of several years Bolton reduced the number of on-street prostitutes considerably.

Whilst I don't condone prostitution and I believe that the police should crack down hard on those criminal gangs and pimps who exploit women, especially those who are engaged in trafficking women, I do not believe in the criminalisation of women who are forced into prostitution. When the Government flagged up a change in the law through publication of its consultation paper *Paying the Price* I spoke against further criminalisation of the women involved in the Summer Recess Adjournment Debate on 22 July 2004.

There has been a further change in the law, for the worse in my opinion, and we will now have to await a review of the situation at some point in the future. The internet appears to be playing a greater role in prostitution than it has previously, probably partly due to a hardening of the law, and trafficking of women is now a major problem.

One Sunday, following the murders of five prostitutes in Ipswich, BBC correspondent Mark Simpson tried all day to interview me. Finally, I agreed to meet him outside Bolton's Town Hall north entrance as I set off for London in my car. Because there were no places to park there I asked him to follow me, and I parked up in Salop Street, close to where I was joining the A666. Immediately we got out of our cars two women walked towards us. Mark asked if they were likely to be prostitutes and, when I replied positively, he was quite keen to interview them as well. Mark got several interviews in the end, and I heard his piece on the BBC *Today Programme* the following morning.

Through an introduction from Cllr Frank White, who was on the Greater Manchester Police Committee, I was introduced to Inspectors Ian Seabridge and David Williams. David and his colleagues became concerned that like alcohol misuse, illegal drug misuse had become a significant problem in the workplace. Those in the workforce who operate machinery or who are responsible for driving vehicles are endangering their own lives and the lives of the people with whom they work when they are misusing drugs.

After many consultations, including talks with the trade unions, and a lot of hard work, Inspector David Williams and his colleagues put together a package to deal with this problem. Unfortunately, they were not in a position to roll out their scheme across the workplaces of Britain, and approaches to the Home Department for their help were unsuccessful, so they sought my help. Regrettably, I could not persuade the Home Department either that there was a great need to raise the level of awareness of this problem in Britain and encourage companies to adopt the Greater Manchester Police package to deal with drug misuse in the workplace. This problem is still with us today.

SCIENCE AND POLITICS: AN UNLIKELY MIXTURE

On 21 January 2009, I praised the work of the Bolton Mountain Rescue Team in an Adjournment Debate and pointed out to the Minister present that these teams receive very little help from central Government. The Bolton Mountain Rescue Team is of considerable assistance to the statutory blue light services. I pointed out that even a relief on their VAT payments would be a help to these valuable voluntary rescue services. In February 2011 the Conservative Government announced that it was considering removing this VAT burden from mountain rescue teams.

Flo McBrien, the mother of a daughter with Down's syndrome, brought to my attention the fact that people with Down's syndrome were not treated by the NHS as they should be. A young woman with Down's syndrome, Joanne Harris, who lived in Shrewsbury, was getting a lot of publicity at that time. She required a heart-lung transplant, and most surgeons in this country were refusing to carry out the operation. Joanne's family and Flo McBrien raised money to send Joanne abroad to have the operation. The winner of the first *Big Brother* television show in 2000, Craig Phillips, presented his cheque for £70,000 to Joanne, so that she could undergo this operation abroad. A hospital in Birmingham agreed to help Joanne but, sadly, she died on 10 April 2008.

Flo McBrien believed, and she convinced me, that people with Down's syndrome were being treated as second-class citizens in Britain, so I promised to campaign with them. We appeared on television and radio programmes together. I contacted the Down's Syndrome Association to meet their Chief Executive, Carol Boys, and I became their unofficial Parliamentary adviser. I held two Adjournment Debates on 'Down's Syndrome', one on 4 July 2000 and the other on 14

September 2004. We also lobbied Ministers.

As a result of all this activity the culture in the NHS began to change. We insisted that doctors in training were made aware of the health needs of people with Down's syndrome, and the profession agreed with us that they should be treated like anybody else. That was the subject of my first debate; the second concentrated on the special educational needs of children and adults with Down's syndrome. I believe that the Down's Syndrome Association, the carers of people with Down's syndrome and I changed attitudes towards these people in education too. The plain fact is that these campaigns need reinvigorating from time to time, and I expect that they will be. An APPG on Down's syndrome was set up just before I retired from Parliament.

Sub-prime lending was a real problem when the Labour Government came to power in 1997. This business sector was not regulated at the time through the Financial Services Act. A Little Lever couple came to see me about a second mortgage they had sought with the help of Wilmslow Financial Services. In 1992 the couple, whose husband was self-employed, needed to borrow £5,000 to cover arrears to their mortgage company and other debts. They were persuaded to borrow a further £5,000 to replace their window frames and take out a five-year (although the sub-prime loan was for 15 years) Payment Protection Premium, insurance they thought protected them against defaulting on the sub-prime mortgage, at a cost of £3,526, a total loan of £13,536. The loan was secured from J. & J. Securities but managed by CMR Loans Servicing Ltd. The finance companies negotiating sub-prime loans usually received high commissions for introducing people to the lenders.

The couple told me they were advised that the interest rate would be 13.5%, that a cash payment of £1,000 would be required to terminate the loan early and that the debt payable would be calculated according to the 'Rule of 78', a complicated formula. In June 1993, when they got into financial difficulty through the husband becoming sick, and repossession was sought in the courts, they discovered that the annual rate of interest was actually 31.5%. What they thought was an insurance policy to protect against the eventuality of sickness proved worthless. However, through court action, the annual interest rate was dropped to 21.5%.

One of the complications experienced by solicitors acting on behalf of this couple was that the sub-prime loan cascaded down through a succession of companies, from J. & J. Securities to the City Mortgage Corporation, then to Ocwen Asset Management UK LLC and, finally, to Igroup plc in which the Royal Bank of Scotland had a 49% share.

When the couple sought my help their debt was a massive £44,579.40p, despite the fact that they had already repaid £27,776.88p. Clearly the debt was increasing, even with the reduced annual interest rate, faster than repayment of the loan was possible, and the inevitable consequence was repossession of their property. Fortunately, the courts had not granted a possession order at this stage.

After carrying out some research I discovered that sub-prime lending resulted in thousands of people losing their homes, and I decided that I needed to highlight this problem again in Parliament (another Member had covered the issue a few years earlier). On 25 April 2001, I did so in an Adjournment Debate, 'Secured Lending to Non-Status Borrowers and Igroup plc'.

As a result of this debate I was made aware of a firm of solicitors that was taking a group action against these companies and I introduced the Little Lever couple to them. This group of solicitors was able to save the couple from losing their property. A few years later I was able to recommend that another family approach the same solicitors, which saved them too from losing their property.

The only soldier from Bolton who was shot at dawn during World War I was Private James Smith, who was born in my constituency. Charles Sandbach, a local military historian and film-maker, asked Cllr Frank White to campaign to have Jimmy's name entered into the Bolton Roll of Honour, a book which is kept in Bolton Town Hall, and Frank enlisted my support. Frank was President of Bolton United Veterans Association. On 3 March 2009 the House of Commons completed Government business early, so I was able to present the incredible story of Private James Smith to the House in an extended Adjournment Debate.

The Labour Government pardoned the 306 soldiers who were shot at dawn in World War I through the Armed Forces Act, on 8 November 2006, and Dr John Reid, who was a Secretary of State for Defence involved in these pardons, was present to speak in my debate along with others who had played an important role in fighting for this action, including Andrew MacKinley (Member of Parliament for Thurrock).

Jimmy Smith's story was also told on stage in the autumn of 1998 at the Octagon Theatre in the play *Early One Morning*, written by Bolton playwright Les Smith.[3]

At the age of 18, Jimmy joined the 1st Battalion Lancashire Fusiliers in 1910, trained in Egypt and served in Karachi, India, before landing on W-beach at Gallipoli on 25 April

1915, when half the Battalion was lost and six Victoria Crosses (a record) were won before breakfast. He was transferred to the 15th Battalion Lancashire Fusiliers (the Salford Pals) and dispatched to the Somme, where he won two Good Conduct Medals. Because his Battalion suffered heavy losses on the Somme, he was transferred again, to the 17th Battalion Kings Liverpool Regiment (the 1st Liverpool Pals) as a Lance Corporal.

On the 11 October 1916, he was buried alive on the Transloy Ridge, with bits of his mates buried around him. He was dug out and transferred to the Bolton District General Hospital (Townleys) with serious shrapnel wounds. Jimmy volunteered to give up his stripe after being wounded. Within days Jimmy was back on the Somme, where he deserted his post and was given 90 Days' Field Punishment 1 by a Field General Court Martial, which also stripped him of one of his Good Conduct Medals. Just before the Battle of Passchendaele in the Ypres Salient, Jimmy deserted his post again, which resulted in a further Field General Court Martial. Because they could see that he was unfit to serve, they stripped him of his second Good Conduct Medal and gave him a 90 Days' Field Punishment 1 again. However, before the end of his punishment, he found himself on the Pilckem Ridge, north of Ypres, where he broke down on 30 July 1917 and was found later wandering about in Poperinghe at 11.00 p.m.

At his third Field General Court Martial he did not speak, and was condemned to be shot at dawn. There was no defence. Twelve soldiers from his own Battalion, who knew that Jimmy was very ill, were dispatched to shoot him at Kemmel Château, but the firing squad shot to miss. Jimmy was wounded in the leg but the Officer in charge, who drew his pistol, could not shoot Jimmy dead, and a more senior officer ordered Private Richard Blundell to shoot Jimmy instead with the pistol. This event clearly haunted Blundell, who, 70 years later on his death bed in Southport, uttered the words that led to Jimmy's story being revealed.

I am very pleased to say that Bolton Council added Private James Smith's name to its Roll of Honour, and a short service was held in his honour on the first Armed Forces Day (which succeeded Veterans Day), on 27 June 2009 at Bolton Town Hall. Relatives from the Smith family met relatives of the Blundell family for the first time on that day. It was a very moving occasion for all of us present.

I expressed by concern over our Government's housing policies in an Adjournment Debate on 'The Right-to-Buy Scheme' on 11 January 2006, and in an Adjournment Debate on 'Affordable Housing in the North and Midlands' on 17 January 2007. On the 14 September 1994, the Director of Shelter, Sheila McKechnie, was in Bolton to give a keynote speech on housing, and I was invited to speak as well. Peter Thurnham (Conservative Member of Parliament for Bolton North East) was the subject of national media attention at that time. The press alleged that he had purchased a former council house in London as his second home, so I took the opportunity to be critical of him at the Shelter meeting. I saw him standing at the back of the hall and, of course, my comments provoked a reaction from him.

A memorable occasion for me was when Nicholas Winterton (Conservative Member of Parliament for Macclesfield) invited me and Paul Holmes (Liberal Democrat Member of Parliament for Chesterfield) to speak against stock transfer of Macclesfield's council housing at a public meeting, which he organised at Morton Hall Community Centre on 8 July 2005. Although I sensed that the majority of people present were in favour of the transfer, the Macclesfield Labour Group was in opposition to it. I don't think I ever attended another meeting like that one, at which representatives of the three main political parties spoke on an issue with one voice.

Like the Food Standards Agency, which was set up by the Labour Government, I have always been sceptical about the claims made for 'organic food', and I expressed my concerns in an Adjournment Debate ('Organic Food or Organic Fraud') on 16 October 2007.

My interest in health policy led to two Adjournment Debates, one on 'Biosimilar Medicines' on 1 April 2008, and one on 'Peripheral Arterial Disease' on 2 March 2010.

When the patents run out on synthetically-produced drugs, other companies enter the market and sell copies, called generics, under a different brand name. 40% of the drugs in clinical trial today are complex protein molecules, which are extremely difficult for other companies to manufacture as exact copies when patents run out. Patents on the early biological medicines have been running out of time in the past few years and copies, called 'biosimilars', are now on the market. Several versions of erythropoietins, which are used to treat cancer-induced anaemia, for example, are now available. For several reasons I wanted Parliament to be aware of biosimilars and to debate their regulation by the National Institute of Clinical Excellence (NICE) and the Medicines and Healthcare products Regulatory Agency (MHRA). I was also responsible for hosting two seminars on biosimilars, which led to two reports.

Non-traumatic lower limb amputations have been on the

increase in recent years; 70% arise as a result of people contracting diabetes. Each amputation costs the NHS between £10,000 and £15,000 and causes great difficulties for the people affected. According to some vascular specialists who came to see me, up to 85% of these amputations are avoidable by using various revascularisation techniques. I wanted to make sure that my Ministerial colleagues in the Department of Health were aware of the facts and prepared to act on them.

Every local authority is required to appoint a Public Analyst. However, the Public Analysts Service has been in decline for a number of years, with laboratories closing and a demographic spread that means more Public Analysts are retiring than are entering the profession currently. In 1959 there were 45 Public Analysts Laboratories; in 2009 there were 21. Local authorities are not collecting food samples for analysis in the numbers that they used to do, although adulteration of foodstuffs still occurs today.

In 2008, Britain imported milk products that had been illegally contaminated with melamine in China and, in 2003, 600 products containing a Worcester Sauce manufactured in Rochdale, not to be confused with Lea & Perrins Worcestershire Sauce, that contained imported chilli powder adulterated with Sudan Red I food dye were withdrawn from sale. The adulteration was detected in Italy.

In order to become a Public Analyst it is necessary to acquire a Mastership of Chemical Analysis (MChemA) qualification, which is awarded by the Royal Society of Chemistry (RSC). Before the Labour Government came into power in 1997, the country suffered a number of 'food scares', which resulted in the Food Standards Agency being established. The Conservative Government elected in 2010 announced that this would be one of the QUANGOS that it would abolish, so the current state of the Public Analysts Service is of even greater concern to me now than it was when I raised my concerns in an Adjournment Debate ('Food Safety and the Public Analysts Service') on 2 June 2009.

I refer to other Adjournment Debates that I secured in the following chapters (see also Appendix 1).

NOTES

1. Two reports were published by the National Treatment Agency in May 2011.

2. A Travelodge has been built on the fringe of this area.

3. This play was included in the 2014-2015 season of plays at the Octagon Theatre in Bolton (it ran from 9 October to 1 November 2014) and I was invited to write part of the programme.

CHAPTER NINE

LOCALLY-BASED CAMPAIGNS

University of Bolton

One of my first campaigns was to achieve university status for Bolton Institute of Higher Education (BIHE). The campaign was under way before I was elected to Parliament, but the Principal, Bob Oxtoby (1994-1998), enrolled the help of the three Bolton Members of Parliament, both before and after the 1997 General Election. Tessa Blackstone, a peer in the House of Lords, was our first Minister for Higher Education, and I soon realised that she wasn't going to entertain the idea of a University of Bolton. I lobbied every Secretary of State for Education on this issue, including Ruth Kelly, and every Minister for Higher Education between 1997 and 2005.

Mollie Temple (1999-2005), who followed Bob Oxtoby as

Principal of BIHE and became BIHEs first Vice-Chancellor, was very keen for university status to be bestowed on BIHE before the rules changed to make it easier for further education colleges to become universities, and I agreed with her. BIHE had been awarding its own degrees for several years. There were some weaknesses at BIHE, particularly in the research and scholarship achievements of academics in some departments. However, BIHE had considerable strengths too in other departments, which I played on. The breakthrough came when Charles Clarke was Secretary of State at the Department for Education and Skills and Alan Johnson was Minister for Higher Education. BIHE heard they were to be awarded university status on 26 April 2004.

I attended the Inauguration Ceremony for the new University of Bolton on 24 February 2005 in the Albert Hall, Bolton, when I made a short speech, and I was awarded an Honorary Fellowship at their first Awards Ceremony on 15 July 2005, which was held in the Victoria Hall, Bolton. After Baroness Morris of Bolton (wife of Judge William Morris), a Conservative peer, was installed as the first Chancellor of the University of Bolton on the morning of 16 July 2010,[1] I was awarded an Honorary Doctorate 'in recognition of outstanding contributions to higher education, science and technology and to Bolton and the University of Bolton'. All those who had been awarded Honorary Fellowships previously, including Cllr Frank White, became Honorary Doctorates at the same ceremony.

SCIENCE AND POLITICS: AN UNLIKELY MIXTURE

Lobbying Minister for Higher Education Kim Howells with students and staff from Bolton Institute of Higher Education.

With Mollie Temple, Vice-Chancellor of the University of Bolton, and Bob Oxtoby, celebrating the granting of university status to the former Bolton Institute of Higher Education.

Bolton Magistrates' Court

For more than two decades the future of Bolton Magistrates' Court has been uncertain. After the Labour Government came to power in 1997 the Greater Manchester Courts Committee was asked to review the provision of Magistrates' Courts across the region (the committee announced in May 2002 that Bolton's courthouse could remain open). At that time the Bolton courts were in need of refurbishment. Witnesses and accused were using the same entrance and accommodation inside the building was poor and overcrowded. There was a risk that the courthouse would be closed.

The *Bolton Evening News* mounted a petition, which was signed by over 21,000 of Bolton's citizens. Bolton's solicitors mounted a campaign against closure, and Bolton MB Council and the Chairman of the Bench asked Bolton's three Members of Parliament to prevent the closure by lobbying Ministers and the Greater Manchester Courts Committee, which we did. I argued against closure on the grounds that those without their own transport would find it difficult to get to Manchester or Bury and that it would cost my poorer constituents money that they could ill afford in making these journeys. There was a risk too that the solicitors would transfer their offices and court work elsewhere.

After due consideration it was decided to build a new courthouse in Bolton on the site of the former Water Place, which stood on land between Morrisons supermarket and Hargreaves House, in the town centre. This was a joint scheme to replace both Bolton and Salford Magistrates' Courts; the completion date for the Bolton courthouse was 2006. The plans were in place but the money was not forthcoming.

The Leader of Bolton Council, Cllr Cliff Morris, asked me to arrange a meeting between the officer of the Council responsible for regeneration, Keith Davies, and Bridget Prentice, the Minister responsible for courts in the Department of Justice. We both came away from that meeting on 8 December 2009 feeling that Bolton would get its new courthouse; at this stage two Crown Courts were to be included as well, and Cheadle Square, adjacent to the existing Crown Court building, was being considered as an alternative site.

I arranged another meeting between Cllr Frank White and the Secretary of State for Justice, Jack Straw, for the 7 January 2010, which I also attended, and we received the same assurances. However, it was admitted at that meeting that the Bolton scheme had been disconnected from the Salford scheme and that Salford Magistrates' Court was scheduled for closure.

When the new Government came to power on 6 May 2010, the Conservative Justice Secretary, Kenneth Clarke, announced the closure of the Salford and Rochdale courthouses and indicated that Bolton's scheme was still on course to be completed. However, I have heard rumours that there may be an extension built onto the existing Crown Court in Blackhorse Street.[2] Whatever the outcome, Bolton has waited a long time for a decision to be made.

Fort Stirling

The three Bolton Members of Parliament were approached by the management and unions at Fort Sterling in Horwich (Bolton West constituency), an American-owned paper-making firm then located next to a Tesco store, with a view to helping them relocate Tesco's supermarket onto a neighbouring site. That would allow Fort Sterling also to expand and locate its European Headquarters in Horwich. There was a threat that, if this didn't happen, which it did (John Prescott granted permission for the land swop on 30 June 1999), Fort Sterling's HQ would be located elsewhere in Europe. They were still manufacturing in Horwich when I wrote this chapter.

Bolton Wanderers Football Club (BWFC)

On Friday 25 April 1997 I was invited to attend the last match that Bolton Wanderers Football Club (BWFC) played at Burnden Park, against Charlton Athletic (BWFC 4; Charlton Athletic FC 1); the match was preceded by a reception at the Beaumont Hotel in Beaumont Road, Bolton. I also attended the formal opening of the Reebok Stadium by John Prescott on 10 January 1998.

As soon as the three new Labour Members of Parliament were elected in 1997 we received requests to lobby the Cabinet Office for Nat Lofthouse OBE, 'The Lion of Vienna', to receive a Knighthood. Despite the *Bolton Evening News* launching a very high profile campaign, we were unsuccessful. I have never understood why most other famous footballers of his generation were knighted but not Nat. He died at the age of 85 on 15 January 2011.

In my 13 years in Parliament I lent my name to scores of recommendations for Queen's Awards. Bolton does not seem to do very well when the Cabinet Office is considering these awards. It isn't as though the people whose names are submitted are not the most deserving people either. They are.

With Nat Lofthouse at the Burnden Park Asda store.

The three Bolton Members of Parliament also agreed to sponsor (we provided the player's strip) a BWFC player, which gave us access to home games *via* the Executive Suite and some publicity in their match programmes. We were also invited to travel to Wembley on 31 May 1999 when BWFC was involved in a Football League Division 1 Play-Off Final with Watford FC at Wembley Stadium (Bolton 0; Watford 2) and to the Carling Cup Final at the Millennium Stadium, Cardiff on 29 February 2004 when Bolton also lost (Bolton 1; Middlesbrough 2).

Previously, as a Bolton councillor, I attended the Football League Trophy Final (also known as the Sherpa Van Trophy) at Wembley on 28 May 1989, when BWFC beat Torquay United FC by 4 goals to 1, the Coca-Cola Cup Final at Wembley on 2 April 1995, when Bolton lost to Liverpool by 1 goal to 2, and the Football League Division 1 Play-Off Final at Wembley on 29 May 1995, when BWFC beat Reading by 4 goals to 3.

Dean Holdsworth was our first sponsored player. Unfortunately, he received a lot of bad publicity when it was alleged that he had hit his wife Samantha at Formby Hall Golf Club on 30 August 1999. Ironically, I had just signed an Early Day Motion in Parliament condemning domestic violence, so I wrote to BWFC and asked them if they would transfer our sponsorship to another player, who was Simon Charlton.

Campaigning for Shelter in July 2001 ('Strip for Shelter').

When Simon transferred to Norwich City FC in July 2004 we sponsored Nicky Hunt. After the 2005 General Election, when Ruth Kelly decided not to continue with the sponsorship agreement and David Crausby joined with Lindsay Hoyle (Member of Parliament for Chorley) and his father, Lord Hoyle, in sponsorship of a player, my sponsorship of BWFC players came to an end.

Fred Dibnah

As a councillor, I didn't have a lot of contact with Fred Dibnah, but I was aware that he was not the most popular man at the Town Hall despite his fame through his television appearances. Fred was 'discovered' in 1978 by BBC North West, when their reporter Alistair McDonald covered work that he was carrying out on Bolton Town Hall clock tower. That led to the BBC producer Don Haworth making the award-winning documentary *Fred Dibnah, Steeplejack,* which turned Fred into a television star. Fred was born on 28 April 1938 and lived his early life at 8 Alfred Street in Bolton. He was trained as a joiner but was fascinated by the life of steeplejacks and became one himself.

Fred constructed a steam boiler in his garden to drive all his machinery and burned old wooden window frames to generate the steam. Ironically, these were supplied by the Housing Direct Labour Organisation when they were engaged in replacing wooden single-glazed windows with uPVC double

The home of Fred Dibnah in Radcliffe Road, Bolton.

glazed units. Bolton's Environmental Health Officers sat for hours outside 'Cat Cottage', Fred's home in Radcliffe Road, waiting for him to stoke up his boiler. The minute smoke came out of his chimney, photographs were taken, and a prosecution followed. Altogether, Bolton MB Council successfully prosecuted Fred three times for burning wood in a smokeless zone before he sought my help in November 1998.

After he was fined £100 with £275 costs in September 1997 (he was first fined under the Clean Air Act 1956 in December 1991) we decided to apply to John Prescott, then Secretary of State at the Department for Environment, Transport and the Regions, for a special licence to allow Fred's garden and sheds to be treated as a steam museum. Neighbours were divided on Fred's antics. After a bit of effort on my part he was granted an exclusion licence and, as they say, the rest is history.

Despite our conflicting political opinions I was a friend for life after that. Fred rang me up and invited me to a 'chimney drop' that he was to perform. Tickets were sold – proceeds to charity – and the winner was to sound the alarm before Fred set fire to the wooden props, which were preventing the chimney from falling. He telephoned me to say, "Don't bother coming, the buggers dropped overnight".

Fred got himself into trouble again with Bolton MB Council when he started to dig a model mineshaft complete with winding gear. His house is on a level with Radcliffe Road, but his garden falls steeply down to the banks of the River Tonge below (across the river is Tonge Cemetery, where Fred is now buried). By the time the Council noticed that the mineshaft had not received planning permission it was almost complete. Of course, it wasn't intended to be a working mine, although if he had gone any deeper he would have struck coal, but it added interest to his steam museum. By this time Fred was getting a considerable number of visitors as his fame spread. He invited me to visit him again one Sunday morning "for a chat". "How long will it take?" I asked him. "Oh a'baut ten minutes or so" he responded. I was there almost three hours.

A visit to Fred's garden reminded me very much of one of my favourite television programmes, *Last of the Summer Wine*. Fred had 'groupies', who helped him with all his jobs. I don't believe any of them were under the age of 70. They had a little hut where they all met for a 'brew'. On my arrival we all adjourned to Fred's hut and one of his mates was dispatched uphill to the Cat Cottage to get the 'brews'. I saw this elderly man come to the top step and climb down the steps to the hut, mugs of tea falling over as he advanced. "Don't bother thi'sen", said Fred, "Tha's only lost two". And the conversation turned to how I could help Fred yet again.

Fred lived two doors away from a Hungarian man who had been one of his greatest fans, one of Fred's 'groupies' in fact, but they had fallen out over something. The 'mad Hungarian', as Fred called him, allegedly started to break up concrete flags and throw them over the garden of a young family into Fred's garden as soon as he saw smoke coming out of Fred's steam boiler chimney. Then he would take a photograph and send it to me through the post, without a stamp, addressed to the 'corrupt MP for Bolton, House of Commons'. They all arrived, scores of them over several years. I had received quite a collection of them by the time I retired. I did my job and sent dozens of them on to successive Chief Executives at Bolton Council, but this was a civil matter and the Hungarian gentleman should go to court, I was told. In the end he moved away from Radcliffe Road.

Officers at the Town Hall were trying to rebrand Bolton as a modern go-ahead sort of place, but Fred wanted to stay in an age when Bolton was all mills and chimneys. It was the wrong image of Bolton that he was sending out, in their opinion. After Fred died from cancer on 6 November 2004 at the age of 66, I contributed a sum of money to the statue of him that now stands in Oxford Street in Bolton town centre, appropriately next to a preserved mill engine. Like Fred the statue is larger than life.

Fred's fame lives on; his series of television productions are often rebroadcast, especially on the Yesterday channel. Television producer David Hall and his 'The View from the North' crew (based in Leeds) put together Fred's final television series *Made in Britain* during 2004. It was broadcast after Fred's death in the spring and summer of 2005 on BBC2 TV. The highlight of this tour of Britain was a visit to London where Fred received an MBE from the Queen 'for services to industrial heritage and broadcasting'. One of the stars of this series, Alf Molyneaux, is one of my neighbours in Avoncliff Close.

On Friday 8 April 2011 Eileen and I attended the press night of the play *The Demolition Man*, written by Aelish Michael, at the Octagon Theatre in Bolton, which is about Fred's relationship with his third wife.

Road safety

For the most part the Bolton South East Parliamentary constituency is a densely-populated urban area, highly congested most of the time, with a lot of traffic movements across some extremely hazardous junctions and through narrow streets. I became very concerned by the number of deaths caused by road traffic accidents (RTAs).

Gareth Willis, aged 29, was killed in a head-on crash with a car on the crown of a bridge on 22 May 1999 by a hit-and-run driver whilst riding his motorcycle. Gareth's nine-year-old son Joseph, a pillion passenger, was thrown off the bike and badly injured but survived the crash. Initially, the 31-year-old car driver, Anthony Wynne, was given a 30-month sentence for causing death by dangerous driving and banned from driving for five years. Half the sentence was suspended for community service. Wynne had only had two driving lessons and was driving in excess of 50 mph in a 30 mph area, without insurance or a driving licence. He had previous car crime convictions and admitted to have been drinking alcohol before the collision.

After complaints from Gareth's family about what they considered to be a lenient sentence, the case was referred with my help to the Court of Appeal by Lord Williams of Mostyn QC, then the Attorney General, and Wynne's sentence was increased by one year. The case was heard on 16 November 2000 without the family being informed. This denied them an opportunity to make an 'impact statement' in court on the effect of Gareth's death on their lives, which had been devastating. I raised this lack of communication on the floor of the House of Commons.

Steven Harrison, aged 40, left a public house and was riding his 1,000 cc Suzuki motorcycle on the evening of the 24 August 2002 round a double bend in the village of Stoneclough, on the A667 Bolton to Bury road. Before the bend, he accelerated so that he could perform a 'wheelie'. Harrison lost control of the bike, which glanced off a Porsche travelling in the opposite direction, and the flying bike hit Billy Joe Dean, aged eight, as he was walking home along the footpath, near the Hare and Hounds public house. The bike crushed Billy Joe against a garden wall, and he died on the spot. I attended his funeral in Holy Trinity Church, Prestolee, on 2 September 2002.

Harrison received a six-year prison sentence for causing death by dangerous driving and driving without insurance whilst disqualified from driving, and he was banned from driving for eight years. The Court of Appeal reduced his prison sentence to five years. Harrison was badly injured in this RTA and pleaded guilty in court. As in the Willis case, the Dean family learned about this reduction in sentence through the local newspaper.

Local communities were made very angry by cases such as these and, with the help of other Members of Parliament I requested that the sentences for causing death by dangerous driving, especially when there were aggravating circumstances, as in these two examples, should be reviewed. The Criminal Justice Act 2003 resulted in the maximum sentence for this offence being increased from 10 to 14 years, but courts hardly ever hand down a sentence at the top end of this range.

The BBC made a television documentary about two cases of causing death by dangerous driving, including that which resulted in the death of Billy Joe Dean, which helped our cause. *Britain's Secret Shame* was filmed in Stoneclough on 26 July and broadcast on 1 November 2004.

After Billy Joe Dean was killed in Stoneclough village, there were several more RTAs on the A667 in Stoneclough, one of which resulted in another death. Between December 2002 and November 2005 I established that there had been 17 reported accidents resulting in 26 casualties – four of them serious and 21 regarded as slight. On 5 January 2006, 46-year-old Ellen Newman was waiting at a bus stop at the junction of the A667 with Europa Road, leading into the Europa Industrial Estate, when a car mounted the pavement and killed her. I pressed Bolton Council to take some action and a public meeting was called on 8 August 2006 at which those present impressed on its officers the importance of doing so. I am pleased to say that action was taken, and I am not aware of further deaths or reports of serious accidents on this stretch of road leading up to my 2010 retirement.

I was closely involved in all three of the accidents I have described above, but there was other case of carnage in my constituency as well. In the early hours of the morning on 1 May 2004, a Mazda MX5 car travelling round a bend in Bradford Street, Bolton at 70 mph in a 30 mph area mounted the pavement and hit four 14-year-old girls, then a lamp post. Two passengers, mother of two Lisa Halligan, aged 36, and her boyfriend Michael Jeffries, aged 28, were killed and the four girls were seriously injured. Shaun Connelly, the 22-year-old driver of the Mazda car, drove away from the scene of the accident but reported the accident to the police 12 hours later. He had held a licence for only 18 months. He was convicted of causing death by dangerous driving and gaoled for four years. Judge William Morris told the Court that he could only pass a six-year sentence, which he had to reduce by one third because of a guilty plea in court. Very few prisoners serve their full sentences, and the people I was speaking to were outraged at the lenient sentences handed down to drivers who killed people by their reckless driving.

Steven John Lewis, another hit-and-run driver, killed 13-year-old Carla Bate at the junction of Longcauseway and Worsley Road, Farnworth, on 8 August 2004 and was gaoled for a more significant period of eight years for causing death by dangerous driving and other offences. Ellese Ruth Gore was killed a few hundred yards outside the boundary of my constituency on Kay Street, on 19 October 2005, as she crossed the road with two friends at 9.00 p.m. at night, by another hit-and-run driver travelling at an estimated 55 mph in a 40 mph area, and mother of two children Laura Entwistle, aged 45, was killed on a Pelican crossing at 3.00 a.m. on 21 January 2006 crossing Wigan Road in Daubhill, also by a hit-and-run driver.

According to the charity Road Peace, the proper charge following a road death where someone is culpable should be manslaughter. An indictable offence of manslaughter is available to the Crown Prosecution Service in England and Wales, but it is seldom used to prosecute drivers causing death on our roads.

I came to realise that the police have a very difficult job in achieving a prosecution for causing 'death by dangerous driving' in any case, and that a huge gap existed between that offence and the next possible charge of 'dangerous driving', which is an either way offence with a maximum penalty of only two years in prison.

I was very pleased when the Government included the Road Safety Bill in the Queen's Speech in November 2005. I was fortunate enough to be able to air my views in the Second Reading debate on this Bill, on 8 March 2006, and served on the Bill's Standing Committee. The Bill contained various new driving offences, which I supported, but I was particularly pleased by inclusion in the Bill of a new offence of 'causing death by *careless* driving', which a number of Members of Parliament, including me, had been pressing the Government to bring in. The Bill received Royal Assent on 8 November 2006.

Amicie Onyema Nwokeochar, aged three, was on the footpath outside a chip shop on Highfield Road in my constituency at lunchtime on 15 November 2003 when a car mounted the pavement, hit Amicie and ploughed into the chip shop. Tragically, Amicie died as a result of this accident. The car was driven by a man of almost 90 years old, who had started driving before a driving test became compulsory under the road traffic act of 1934. He claimed that he had pressed the accelerator of his powerful Honda Concerto car instead of the brake whilst parking. He was convicted of 'driving without due care and attention', fined £1,000 and banned from driving for two years. A police officer gave evidence in the Coroner's Court, which recorded a verdict of accidental death, that this accident was probably aggravated by the medical condition of the elderly driver, who surrendered his licence voluntarily to the DVLA. Due to an ongoing heart condition the driver was unable to attend the Coroner's Court, so he could not be questioned by the Coroner.

There is a requirement for all those who reach the age of 70 to be willing to submit themselves for a medical examination every three years. Form D45 is sent out automatically by the DVLA, which contains questions about a driver's health. Any conditions notified to the DVLA may require medical evidence to be provided before a licence is renewed. However, this is not a rigorous test of ability to drive and Amicie's grandmother and the family's solicitors, Carl Chapman & Co., asked me to campaign for compulsory cognitive tests to be brought in for older drivers. They believed that, at the very least, form D45 should be completed and approved by the driver's GP, who has known the driver for at least three years, and that the form should include a section for the GP to give a statement on the driver's ability to drive, including evidence of a recent eyesight test.

Legislating on grounds of age is discriminatory. Therefore, if we are to deal with the dangers that some older drivers present on the road, we need to ascertain their fitness to drive in a more sensible way than we do now.

In late 2004, the DVLA commissioned an independent review to assess the effectiveness of the present medical licensing system. DVLA-commissioned research has shown that the present system is widely abused, with only 10% of drivers with a notifiable medical condition admitting it on the D45 form they return to the DVLA. A draft EU Directive may require drivers over the age of 75 to renew their driving licences every five years instead of every three years as required at present.

I presented my views on older drivers in an Adjournment Debate on 15 March 2006 and appeared on television and radio several times as a result. The day before this debate Granada TV reporter Rishi Battacharya agreed to interview me in a studio at 4 Millbank. However, a change was made and the interview was conducted on the kerbside of College Green – opposite the Sovereign's Entrance to the House of Lords. I had my back to the traffic, so that it was driving constantly past me during the interview. Inevitably, when these interviews are conducted outside there are multiple 'takes' due to a combination of factors – aircraft overhead, members of the general public trying to get in on the 'shot', etc. But, this was an exceptional day. A London open-top sightseeing bus pulled up with its entrance immediately next to the kerbside and the driver opened the door. I could hear him on his intercom telling his mainly foreign tourists that a British Minister was being interviewed by the BBC and that they should have a look. We had instantly become a tourist attraction! He was wrong on both counts – no Minister and ITV, not the BBC. After several minutes of disruption, off went the bus and Granada TV and I got on with the job.

A commercial television company recorded four programmes for ITV under the umbrella title of *Driving Me Crazy*, and I spent an afternoon with them on 8 November 2006 putting a programme on older drivers together, which was 'fronted' by comedienne Jo Brand. Tom Soulby, who had never passed a driving test, refused to give up driving when his GP advised him to do so at the age of 100. This programme, which was broadcast in the spring of 2007, began with comments about older drivers from me while Tom was shown backing out of the long drive at his home. He hit hedges on both sides of the drive, and had to straighten up several times before he shot across the road and hit a neighbour's wall on the opposite side of the road. Some of the comments I was making about older drivers were vividly demonstrated by Tom's antics. Tom, who was a lovely old man, sadly passed away at the age of 101.

I also helped BBC TV Wales put together a 30-minute documentary on the same subject on 21 May 2009.

On 19 November 2008, I highlighted an injustice that I

was unable to correct, when I submitted my Road Traffic (Accident Compensation) Bill to the House of Commons under the Ten Minute Rule. One of my constituents, who lived in Farnworth, was unloading goods from the back of a vehicle in Egerton Street when he was hit by another car, which badly crushed his legs. The seriousness of his injuries forced him to give up his professional career. Because the man in the other car had suffered a heart attack (he later died) before his car had collided with my constituent, neither my constituent's car insurance company nor that of the other driver would pay out compensation.

It is necessary to establish negligence and liability before an insurance company will pay out on an insurance policy. My argument is that people who are injured in this way should receive 'no-fault compensation' from a central fund, funded by all insurance companies. According to the Association of British Insurers, whose help I sought, such cases are rare and the cost to the insurance companies would be negligible. Apparently, some insurance companies do offer compensation without an admission of liability.

I also mounted a campaign to make Heavy Goods Vehicles (HGVs) more visible at night or in bad weather by a mandatory requirement for them to be fitted with conspicuity reflective tape to all their leading edges, at an average cost of about £150 per vehicle. On 5 April 2006 after I spoke in the Standing Committee of the Road Safety Bill on this issue I was travelling home on the M6 when I was held up by an accident which had occurred on the slip road to Stafford Motorway Services. A sports car was wedged under the tail end of a HGV.

However, undoubtedly under pressure from the haulage

industry, the Government announced in September 2009 that it was only going to bring in this measure when an EU Directive required it to be brought in, two years later. In the meantime more people were probably killed through collisions with poorly visible HGVs. The charity Brake recognised my efforts by awarding me their Campaigner of the Month award on 24 November 2009.

Violent and Sex Offender Register (ViSOR)

Ryan Mason, aged seven, was found dead in a wheelie bin on Great Lever Golf Course, on 13 February 2002, after he disappeared from his home on the nearby Orlit Estate. His mother's boyfriend, 22-year-old Ronald Marriner, was charged with murdering him on 11 February 2002, found guilty at his trial and gaoled for life on 24 October 2002. Ryan's grandfather, Syd Pickup, contacted me after Ryan's murder to propose that a Violent Offender Register should be set up similar to the Sex Offender Register, which I thought was an excellent idea. Marriner had committed other violent offences before he had moved to Bolton from another town.

When I started to make enquiries I discovered that a system had been developed by the Lancashire County Police Force and that it was being developed further by the Police Information Technology Organisation (PITO). I visited their headquarters near Tower Bridge in London. Shortly after my visit the Violent and Sex Offender Register was trialled (the pilots were announced on 31 December 2002), then rolled out nationally in November 2004 and completed in April 2005. This enables police forces and other agencies involved in crime prevention to inform those at risk should a violent offender whose name is on ViSOR move from one area to another. It contains very detailed information on each offender, including details of changes of appearance with time and any distinguishing features, such as scars and tattoos.³

Other campaigns

One of my earliest successes as a Member of Parliament was to persuade the Government to allow entry into the UK of five members of the Indian Soni family to decorate the Shree Swaminaryan Gadi – a Hindu Temple in Cannon Street, Bolton. They had been refused entry before I intervened.

Today, this 'Sistine Chapel of the North' has been named a top tourist attraction by Visit England.

Those responsible for Housing Benefit administration in Bolton contacted me when I was elected to Parliament to ask me to campaign to change the rules on 'pension clawback' from pensioners who needed to be in hospital for more than six weeks. I discovered that they lost some of their pension and any

With Mayor Cllr Alan Wilkinson and the five artists who provided paintings at the Shree Swaminaryan Hindu Temple in Cannon Street, Bolton (17 July 2000).

benefits that they were receiving, such as Council Tax Benefit; more was deducted after 52 weeks in hospital.

Those who lived in rented houses, such as council houses, soon got into rent arrears and accumulated other debts when this happened, and some of these people lost their homes as a result. Fortunately, the Government decided that this was wrong and reversed the situation in March 2002; it cost £60 million to relieve 31,500 pensioners of this burden.

Just before I retired, the water companies decided to change the way water rates are collected from non-domestic properties. They decided to collect the rates in proportion to the surface area of the property and any surrounding land. Thus, if the water from a sports field and the car park of a sports club drained into the public sewerage system, those areas were all taken into consideration. Previously it was the rateable value of the property that had decided the water rate payable. This increased the water rate demands for all sports clubs considerably, as well as the water rates of churches and voluntary groups such as scouts and guides.

When I complained to United Utilities, they recommended that some of these premises could provide sumps into which the water could be allowed to drain so that it did not end up in the public sewerage system. This became a major issue in Parliament. We put down Parliamentary Questions, raised the matter in debates and saw the Minister responsible for this policy area. In the end the water companies agreed that the sudden change did challenge the viability of a lot of voluntary organisations and agreed to reconsider their plans.

A company in my constituency brought to my attention the fact that the firewalls on computers in schools, colleges and public libraries that were designed to prevent users getting access to undesirable websites were well nigh useless. The company carried out surveys in a number of schools using a system that was able to tell them which websites children were accessing. The research showed that a considerable number of children were accessing undesirable websites in school, as were some teachers. I decided to draw this issue of internet safety to the attention of Ministers in the Department of Children, Families and Schools and the Home Department, and there were improvements in schools in order to protect children from accessing sites banned to them.

I supported fluoridation of public water supplies, both as a Bolton councillor and as a Member of Parliament. Of my two Parliamentary colleagues, Ruth Kelly was also in favour whilst David Crausby was against.

I took an interest for a while in the controversial debate on Gulf War syndrome. One of my Kearsley constituents believed he was a sufferer following army service during the first Gulf War, after Saddam Hussein invaded Kuwait.

I also campaigned for defective railway bridges in Bolton to be repaired or replaced. The one on Green Lane was closed for several months until, through lobbying the Department of Environment, Transport and the Regions (a delegation from Bolton met John Spellar, Member of Parliament for Warley, who was the responsible Minister, at St Helen's Town Hall on 31 July 2001), it was replaced at a cost of £2 million and reopened on 6 June 2003. When the Conservative Government privatised British Rail the responsibility for repairing railway bridges became unclear.

NOTES

1. The university appointed the Rt. Hon. Lord Justice Ryder to succeed her (see *Bolton News* dated 4 February 2014) for three years.

2. Bolton was back to square one in 2013 when a proposal surfaced again for closure of Bolton Magistrates' Court; later it was decided to move the Magistrates' Court into the Crown Court building on Blackhorse Street when the County Court and Family Court work in the Crown Court building was moved to Manchester (see *Bolton News* dated 17 July 2015).

3. On 1 October 2012, as part of the closure of the National Police Improvement Agency, ViSOR transferred to the Home Department.

CHAPTER TEN

NATIONALLY-BASED CAMPAIGNS

Women's Land Army

Shortly after the General Election in 1997 Alice Sefton, a Farnworth constituent, contacted me with a view to those who worked for the Women's Land Army during World War II being recognised in some way. I began to lobby our Ministers in the Ministry of Agriculture, Fisheries and Food (MAFF) by writing to them and seeking meetings with them. I also began to ask Parliamentary Questions and put down Early Day Motions.

With Alice Sefton at Coventry Cathedral; the inscription on the memorial reads 'In gratitude to God and to command to future generations the self-sacrifice of those who served on the Home Front during the Second World War'

I was delighted when MAFF Minister Elliot Morley (Member of Parliament for Scunthorpe) told me I would be invited to a ceremony on 3 March 2000 at which, in the presence of Prime Minister Tony Blair and other dignitaries, the Queen would unveil a memorial to those who had worked for the 'Home Front', including members of the Women's Land Army. I picked Alice up on that Friday and took her and her brother-in-law Jim by car to Coventry Cathedral, where we sat on the second row in the 'new' Cathedral, immediately behind the Prime Minister, before we followed the Queen into the 'old' Coventry Cathedral next door. There the Queen unveiled a slate memorial. Needless to say, Alice and her brother-in-law were thrilled to have been invited to such an important event. Alice and other members of the Women's Land Army were issued with pin badges in early 2008, and there is a memorial outside the Cabinet Office in Whitehall today that stands as a tribute to all the women who were involved in the 'war effort'.

Ground rent grazing

In the era when long terraces of two-up, two-down houses were constructed in towns that were rapidly expanding, like Bolton, the builders kept ownership of the land and charged the owners of the properties an annual 'ground rent', which is worth between £1 and £5 today. These ground rents became known as 'builder's pensions'. Today they cost more to collect than they are worth, so large tracts of land have been sold off at auction, especially in the northern mill towns on both sides of the Pennines, to companies who extract money from leaseholders in other ways.

A number of my constituents started to receive letters from Estates and Management Ltd. and the Compton Group alleging that ground rents had not been paid for a number of years, and demanding back-payments along with a substantial administration fee (one of my constituents was expected to pay a £45 fee to collect a ground rent of only £2.50p). In some cases a Land Registry search showed that the company claiming to own the ground did not in fact own it. In other cases the leaseholder had continued to pay the ground rent on an annual basis to an agent, often a solicitor, who had not been informed of a change in ownership of the land. These companies could force forfeiture of a home by taking cases to court, so the receipt of these letters was quite a frightening experience for many of my constituents.

Agents of the companies walked the estates to find out

which houses had had extensions or conservatories attached to them without their permission. Householders believed that the only permissions that were required were planning permission and building regulation consent. However, when we looked at some of the Victorian deeds, it was clear that the land owner's permission was required as well. To get such permission retrospectively was another way these companies extracted money out of the leaseholders.

The Leasehold Reform Act 1967 provides a mechanism for leaseholders to buy the freehold of their property but at a cost. These companies also made money out of selling freeholds but it was extremely difficult to contact them.

The companies also had the right to require a leaseholder to insure their buildings through an insurance company nominated by them. This caused most of the complaints, since the amount charged by the nominated companies was almost twice the cost of continuing with the insurance company which the leaseholders were already using.

I decided to highlight all these problems in the Second Reading debate of the Commonhold and Leasehold Reform Bill 2002, which was on 8 January 2002. Taking part in this debate enabled me to become a Member of the Bill's Standing Committee, to which I spoke to an amendment to change the law on nominated insurance. This is now enshrined in the 2002 Act of Parliament.

I also unsuccessfully tried to change the law on forfeiture of a property by a leaseholder, even when they had broken a leasehold agreement.

I continued to receive complaints about Estates and Management Ltd. from my constituents. On 16 June 2005 I put down an Early Day Motion (EDM 342), which was seconded by Barry Sheerman (Member of Parliament for Huddersfield), who was also receiving complaints:

"That this House condemns Estates and Management Ltd. for its exploitation of its leaseholders, especially the elderly and vulnerable; notes that the only way for leaseholders to contact this company by telephone is on an 0906 number, with a charge of 25 pence a minute, and that they can only talk to an answer phone; further notes that leaseholders send cheques for ground rents to this company by recorded delivery which are not banked, yet the company continues to send out penalty notices for late payment, with administrative and late payment charges added on, and without previous written reminders as required by the Commonhold and Leasehold Reform Act 2002; and calls on the Government to take action to enforce the Act and to conduct an inquiry into the conduct of Estates and Management Ltd., which has a complex ownership structure, including companies registered in the Bahamas and the Virgin Islands controlled ultimately by the Tchenguiz Family Trust."

Both of us received a telephone call from Victor Tchenguiz, who wanted to meet us to discuss our problems, and we met him together on 26 March 2006. Mr Tchenguiz brought a number of people with him, including the former Ulster Unionist Member of Parliament for South Antrim, David Burnside, and Walter Goldsmith, the manager of Estates and Management Ltd., who promised to deal with our constituents' complaints, and did. David Burnside, who was also a Northern Ireland Assembly Member (he resigned his seat in 2009 to concentrate on his business interests), had previously worked in public relations with British Airways, where he had been involved in a high-profile court case with Richard Branson. He was a critic of David Trimble's support for the Belfast Agreement.

Victor Tchenguiz and his brother Robert had considerable property interests in the UK. They managed about 600 different companies at that time, organised under the parent company Rotch. In 2003 Rotch was listed 28th in *Estates Gazette*'s 'rich list', with an estimated 'worth' of £330 million, but their 'worth' soared after that. In 2006 they traded as the Consensus Business Group. Their father, Victor, was born in Iraq but left for Persia when the Ba'athists came to power. He was a jeweller and ran the mint for the Shah of Persia until the revolution forced him out of what became Iran, when he settled in London. Victor's and Robert's property businesses were supported by heavy borrowing from Kaupthing, one of the two Icelandic banks that collapsed in the 'credit crunch'.

Health food industry

One of the most difficult and long-lasting campaigns I was involved in during my 13 Parliamentary years involved the sale of vitamins, minerals and herbal products by the health food industry. My campaign began when a family business operating on the Europa Industrial Estate in Kearsley asked for a meeting with me in July 1997. The Food and Diet Company, which employed about 100 people, wanted to draw my attention to the fact that the Government proposed to ban the sale of high-dose dietary supplements of vitamin B_6. The family business in Kearsley was taken over by the Health and Diet Company with whom I continued to work through their Managing Director, Michael Peet.

In 1996, civil servants at the Ministry of Agriculture, Fisheries and Food (MAFF) tried to persuade their Minister, Conservative Angela Browning (Member of Parliament for Tiverton and Honiton), that this was a necessary move, but she refused to proceed with the measure and referred it to the Food Advisory Committee, who referred the matter in turn to the Committee on Toxicity of Chemicals in Food, Consumer Products and the Environment (COT). They recommended that action be taken. After the General Election of 1997 this matter ended up in the in-tray of Labour Minister Jeff Rooker (Member of Parliament for Birmingham, Perry Barr), who decided to proceed with the advice he had received. This announcement disturbed a number of Members of Parliament, including me. When I looked closely into the matter I discovered that the advice given to the Minister was based on work reported in one or two papers in the literature that had not been peer reviewed. The Government proposed to restrict the daily dose to 10 mg, which was way out of line with the high daily doses, 100-200 mg, being taken by some individuals. Reversible peripheral neuropathy, a tingling sensation in the extremities, can be experienced by those who take doses higher than 200 mg of vitamin B_6.

I participated in a debate on 'Vitamin B_6' on 24 June 1998, and the Select Committee on Agriculture considered the proposed ban and rejected it on grounds that there was little or no scientific evidence to support it. Following a meeting which I and a few other Labour Members had with Jeff Rooker, he decided to refer the matter again, this time to an *ad hoc* 'Expert Group on Vitamins and Minerals'.

In 1997 the regulatory regime for vitamins, minerals and herbal products was unsatisfactory. Whilst vitamins and minerals were dealt with under food law, herbal products were dealt with under legislation that applied to medicines. The majority of those using high-dose supplements of vitamin B_6 are women, who use it to ease premenstrual stress (PMS), but some men believe that high doses of vitamin B_6 improves their health. Although vitamins are essential components of food, this could be considered a 'medical use' and the Medicines Control Agency (MCA) suggested the original ban on high dose supplements of vitamin B_6.

Some countries, such as Canada and Australia, developed legislation for 'borderline products', and I proposed that the British Government should also regulate the products sold by the health food industry in a similar way. I called this approach 'the third way'. In the meantime European Directives appeared which caused even more concern in the health food industry, not to mention amongst the consumers of their products. The Health Food Manufacturers' Association (HFMA) and Consumers for Health Choice (CHC) had the ability to mount high-profile campaigns, and Members of Parliament were lobbied hard to oppose these Directives.

There was a suspicion that the pharmaceutical industry was putting pressure on European Commissioners to get the manufacturers of vitamins, minerals and herbal products to conform to the same manufacturing and testing regimes that they were subjected to. Since most of the companies involved in the health food trade were small and medium enterprises, there was concern that they would be driven to the wall by all this increased regulation, and I had a great deal of sympathy with that point of view.

'MLX249' was a proposal by the MCA to amend the EU Medicines for Human Use (Marketing Authorisations etc)

Regulations 1994, to broaden the definition of a medicine, which would capture vitamins and minerals if health claims were being made in the advertising of these products.

Receiving the petition organised jointly by Consumers for Health Choice and the HFMA.

MLX249 generated so much heat that a march was organised from Hyde Park Corner to Trafalgar Square on Saturday 20 June 1999. I was invited by the industry and the consumer groups to lead this march, along with David Tredinnick (Member of Parliament for Bosworth). I still can't believe that my first speech in Trafalgar Square was on MLX249.

Even more heat was generated when the EU Food Supplements Directive was published, in its original draft form in May 2000 and in its final draft form in July 2002. The UK health food industry welcomed attempts to remove barriers to the trade of health products across the European Union, but they strongly opposed attempts to restrict the sale of their products to 'maximum daily permitted levels' (as distinct from the 'upper safe daily limit', established by scientific evidence) of their principal ingredients, such as vitamin B_6 (25 mg was the initially proposed EU limit for this vitamin).

In line with the Napoleonic Law prevalent on the Continent of Europe, a 'Positive List' of permitted sources of nutrients was included in this Directive as well as another listing the permitted vitamins and minerals. The UK industry believed that the list of permitted sources should be a 'Negative List', i.e. of banned sources. 300 nutrients and nutrient sources used by the health food industry were excluded from this 'Positive List'. In order to include these ingredients the industry was required to submit costly dossiers containing evidence of their safety to the European Scientific Committee on the Safety of Food.

At about the same time the EU Traditional Herbal Products Directive was published. Herbal products have been used in Britain since the beginning of time. Even in my youth there were people in my small village with a good knowledge of the use of herbs with curative properties. Some herbal products have 'grandfather rights' under Section 12 of the 1968 Medicines Act; they can be used without the acquisition of a licence for their use. Usually these are substances whose safety has been proved by long-term use. But, the EU Directive required those selling products containing herbal products without 'grandfather rights' (in use for at least 30 years was the requirement) to produce costly dossiers that provided evidence of their safety in use. This European Directive also contained a 'Positive List' of permitted herbal substances.

The industry had had enough of all the regulatory pressure it was being subjected to by what they saw as mainly unnecessary European legislation. The Labour Government established the Food Standards Agency (FSA) which fought the UK corner on the grounds that, providing there was already enough evidence that established products were safe, their continued sale should be allowed. However, unlike the UK and countries like The Netherlands, with liberal regimes for the sale of products containing vitamins, minerals and herbal substances, other countries with less liberal regimes, such as France and Germany, pressed for dietary supplements to receive the same kind of regulation as pharmaceutical products.

Consumers for Health Choice, supported by the Health Food Manufacturers' Association (HFMA) and other trade organisations, collected a petition across the country to oppose the EU proposals. About 20 Members of Parliament presented one million signatures to Parliament, one of the largest petitions presented in modern times. I presented seven boxes of these signatures, containing over 350,000 signatures, in the

House of Commons at the end of the day's business on 19 November 2002. I needed the help of the doormen to carry these boxes into the chamber.

There were regular debates on these EU Directives in which I participated. We saw successive Ministers of Public Health, tabled Early Day Motions and put down hundreds of written and oral Parliamentary Questions. Most Ministers were responsive to our arguments. But, Melanie Johnson (Member of Parliament for Welwyn Hatfield) was not, and Consumers for Health Choice mounted a campaign against her, which partly resulted in her losing her seat in the 2005 General Election.

Although both of these EU Directives have been accepted by Parliament [I spoke against the Statutory Instrument that considered the Draft Food Supplements (England) Regulations 2003 on 21 July 2003, which was passed by only one vote], the debate about the 'maximum daily permitted levels' of vitamins and minerals was still raging when I retired from Parliament in 2010.

This increase in legislation for the UK health food industry resulted in some companies moving offshore, to Guernsey in particular but also to Jersey. Products are marketed in the UK by these companies which contain ingredients that are banned in UK products, such as melatonin, and using medical claims for the products that are also banned in the UK, unless a company can provide evidence for these claims. The Channel Islands are not members of the European Union but, because they are Crown Dependencies, some EU laws are applicable in the Channel Islands, including those that apply in the UK to health foods.

An added problem was that, providing the value of a parcel

sent from the Channel Islands to the UK was less than £18 (2009 values), Low Value Consignment Relief was applicable, which meant that VAT was avoided by the Channel Island companies. By 2010 these Channel Island companies had caused a considerable loss in trade for UK-based health food companies. I campaigned on behalf of the UK industry in an attempt to provide a level playing field for trade between Britain and the Channel Islands by putting down Early Day Motions, written and oral Parliamentary Questions and by highlighting this problem in an Adjournment Debate on 5 May 2009. Before I left Parliament the British Government was making some progress in bringing legislation in the Channel Islands into line with the UK legislation on health foods.

Euthanasia

My interest in euthanasia arose as a result of my interest in the use of opiate drugs in palliative care in the NHS. I was interested in the use of morphine and diamorphine (heroin) to alleviate pain and was aware of rumours that doctors hasten death through the use of high doses of these drugs, the so-called 'double effect'. Titrating exact doses of opiate drugs to alleviate pain is a skill. A small number of doctors have admitted that they have ended the lives of some of their patients in this way. Abuses are possible, of course, as the case of the infamous Dr Shipman illustrated.

Euthanasia is a devolved issue, which means that the law in England and Wales is different from the law in Scotland.

On 10 December 1997, Joe Ashton (Member of Parliament for Bassetlaw, who retired in 2001) moved the Doctor Assisted Dying Bill as a Ten Minute Rule Bill, and

Kevin McNamara (Member of Parliament for Hull North) opposed it and forced a vote. The 'Ayes' were 89 and the 'Noes' 234. Joe gave a moving account of the loss of his mother, who suffered a lingering death from Parkinson's disease, and referred to the death of Annie Lindsall, who had motor neurone disease. His proposition was that the use of diamorphine to hasten death should be legalised, with certain safeguards provided in the Bill.

I voted against Joe Ashton's Bill, which prompted the President of the 'Voluntary Euthanasia Society' (VES), author and broadcaster Sir Ludovic Kennedy, to write to me on 21 June 1999. He referred to the case of Dr David Moor, a Newcastle GP, who had been acquitted on a charge of murdering one of his patients, despite the fact that he admitted to the media that he had hastened the death of his patients "on several occasions". Sir Ludovic suggested that diamorphine was not the best drug to use to hasten death and that doctors often hastened death without consultation. Patients who are heavily sedated over several weeks are likely to die through a lack of food and hydration, a form of death that causes intense pain in any case.

The VES (which became 'Exit' for a short period) was rebranded in 2005 as 'Dignity in Dying' (DiD). It was formed in 1935 and has campaigned ever since for the hastening of death by doctors using barbiturate drugs, along with anti-emetic drugs, to be legalised. In an Adjournment Debate on 'Assisted Dying', held in Westminster Hall on 11 November 2008 (see *Hansard*, 11 November 2008, column 221WH), Crispin Blunt (Conservative Member of Parliament for Reigate) claimed that he had proposed this change of name to the VES.

By 2010 about 150[1] British people had travelled to Zürich to have their lives ended at Dr Ludwig Minelli's Dignitas Clinic (founded in 1998). The term 'physician assisted suicide' (PAS) is preferred by Dignity in Dying because, although the doctor makes the process and the drugs available, they are not present at the death. The Suicide Act 1961 legalised suicide in Britain but made it illegal for a person to assist another person's suicide.

In my opinion, the VES cause was given a boost by the Airedale NHS Trust *versus* Bland judgement of 1993, a landmark case. Tony Bland was a casualty of the Hillsborough football disaster (15 April 1989) and lay in what was then called a 'pre-vegetative state' (the term 'persistent non-responsive state' is preferred today). Although he was capable of breathing without assistance, he was kept alive by providing artificial food and hydration through nasal tubes. The court decided that artificial feeding and hydration could be withdrawn to allow Tony Bland to die. From that moment on the medical profession considered artificial feeding and hydration to be 'medical treatment'.

Between 1993 and 1999 the medical profession began to consult on guidelines they issued to doctors on artificial feeding and hydration, the Government began to consult on proposals that led to the Mental Capacity Act, and the House of Lords Select Committee on Medical Ethics produced a report on euthanasia. It reported that:

"We are concerned that vulnerable people – the elderly, lonely, sick or distressed – would feel pressure, whether real or imagined, to request an early death. We accept that, for the most part, requests from such pressure or from remediable depressive illness would be identified as such by doctors and managed appropriately. Nevertheless, we believe that the message which society sends to vulnerable and disadvantaged people should not, however obliquely, encourage them to seek death, but should assure them of our care and support in life."

On 28 January 2000, I spoke in support of Ann Winterton's (Member of Parliament for Congleton) Medical Treatment (Prevention of Euthanasia) Bill, a Private Member's Bill which attempted to prevent doctors hastening death by omission or commission of medical treatment unless a treatment became too burdensome for the patient. This was an attempt to oppose the conclusion that artificial feeding and hydration was 'medical treatment'. Despite the fact that the Labour Government stated many times that it was opposed to euthanasia, it opposed this Bill and it failed.

In 2000, the Government signed up to the Human Rights Act but, in the Family Division of the High Court of Justice, Dame Butler-Sloss (now a peer) ruled that it did not apply to two cases in which doctors wanted to withdraw artificial feeding and hydration. The Right to Life is a corner stone of the Human Rights Act. She told the General Medical Council on 20 July 2000 that:

"Hospitals may also need to consider the issue of resources, however distasteful that may seem and to consider whether resources should be directed to patients who have no hope of receiving any benefit from that treatment".

Lord Joffe tried to introduce physician-assisted suicide three times in the House of Lords, backed by Dignity in Dying, and failed on all three occasions. On the last occasion, 12 May 2006, he was defeated by 148 votes to 100. On 31 January 2006, a group of people launched Care Not Killing (CNK) Alliance Ltd. to oppose Lord Joffe's third attempt. I became the first chairman of CNK in March 2006 and was a Board member until the summer of 2015, although I handed over chairmanship of the Board briefly to Dr John Wiles, a former palliative care specialist.[2] CNK opposes euthanasia, promotes more and better palliative care and provides educational materials so that people can make decisions on euthanasia with facts at their finger tips. I also support ALERT (Against Legalised Euthanasia – Research and Teaching) and was a Patron of this organisation when I was a Member of Parliament and remained so on retirement.

Dignity in Dying (DiD) has used some very difficult cases to promote their cause – those of Diane Pretty, Kelly Taylor, Daniel James, Dr Ann Taylor and Debbie Purdy are just a few – and will continue to do so until their goal is achieved. The Purdy case, which was taken to the House of Lords, resulted in Director of Public Prosecutions Keir Starmer making available to the general public the grounds on which he makes his decisions on whether to prosecute in cases of so-called 'mercy killings' (see *Bolton Evening News* dated 5 August 2009).

In one of the debates I attended, at the Oxford Union on 15 May 2003, I opposed a motion that 'This House Believes in the Right to Die'. Lord Joffe was one of the proponents of the motion, but we had the formidable debater Ann Widdecombe (Member of Parliament for Maidstone and the Weald) speaking last on our side of the chamber. Everything was going well until she went off at a tangent and started speaking about abortion. I could see the young students switching off, especially the young women in the audience. We lost. I shared a car back to London with her that evening but she was asleep just a few miles out of Oxford.

Debbie Purdy and I debated assisted suicide at the King Street Unitarian Chapel, Macclesfield on 23 September 2012.

Lord Falconer set up a 'commission' on euthanasia which reported in January 2012. Care Not Killing (CNK) refused to give evidence, as did a number of other organisations, because the 'commission' was not independent; it was packed with pro-euthanasia supporters such as Lord Falconer. My main concern was that the law on euthanasia was changing without decisions being made in the House of Commons.[4,5] A 'right to die' may, over time, become a 'duty to die'. In 400 BC Hippocrates said, "I will give no deadly medicine to any one if asked, nor suggest such counsel." How we treat dying patients is a litmus test for our society in my opinion. This debate, which I admit is a moral maze, will continue.

NOTES

1. By 2016 this figure had risen to over 300.

2. I became chairman again in 2012 when John Wiles resigned from the CNK Board.

3. Debbie Purdy died on 23 December 2014, aged 51, in the Marie Curie Hospice, Bradford (where she spent her final year) after refusing food; she suffered for 20 years from primary progressive multiple sclerosis.

4. The first substantive debate since 1970 on euthanasia was held in the House of Commons chamber on Tuesday 27 March 2012.

5. Lord Falconer introduced The Assisted Dying Bill to legalise assisted suicide in the House of Lords in 2013, but it ran out of time. The Bill was re-introduced in 2015 but was superseded when Rob Marris (Member of Parliament for Wolverhampton South West) introduced it as a Private Member's Bill in the House of Commons. It was heavily defeated, by 330 votes to 118, on 11 September 2015.

CHAPTER ELEVEN

INTERNATIONALLY-BASED CAMPAIGNS

∽

Palestine and the Middle East

In October 1999, Eileen and I visited Bahrain at the invitation of Ken Purchase (Member of Parliament for Wolverhampton North East), chairman of the All-Party Parliamentary Group on Bahrain (I was a Member of the APPG). The main points of discussion, apart from Britain's excellent relationships with that country, revolved around human rights (there were a lot of political prisoners in gaol at that time) and the involvement of women in governance at all levels. In Bolton I had dealt with an asylum seeker from Bahrain who had been badly tortured in one of their gaols and I was keen to raise this with the authorities in Bahrain. I got the impression that the rulers of

Bahrain (Sunni Muslims) were preparing for change, and some minor changes did occur a few years after our visit. I was impressed on that visit by the huge new aluminium smelter that Bahrain had built. It was little wonder that the one on Anglesey closed a few years after our visit.

For all of the 13 years I served in Parliament I was secretary to the Britain-Palestine APPG and, for a number of those years, I was also an executive member of the Labour Middle East Council (which collapsed due to a lack of financial support) and a founder member of Labour Friends of Palestine and the Middle East (launched on 13 January 2009).

In the 1960s I was an admirer of the kibbutz movement and sympathised with the Israelis when they came under attack from the Arab nations during the 1967 war. As the Israeli occupation of the Palestinian territories continued and it became obvious to me that the Israeli Government had no intention of ending it, I developed strong sympathies for the oppressed Palestinians, including those who live in Israel today as second class citizens.

When the Peel Commission responded in 1937 to the Arab revolt with a recommendation that Palestine should be partitioned into two States, David Ben-Gurion said "A partial Jewish state is not the end but the beginning, a powerful impetus in our historic effort to redeem the land in its entirety". The facts on the ground today suggest that the Israelis are well advanced in achieving this goal.

Hamas regards the Zionist programme as colonialism that should be resisted. Speaking at the Islamic University in Gaza on 22 October 1997, Sheikh Ahmad Yassin, who was the founder of Hamas in December 1987 and its leader until he was illegally assassinated by the Israelis on 22 March 2004, said, "I want to proclaim loudly to the world that we are not fighting Jews because they are Jews! We are fighting them because they have assaulted us, they killed us, they took our land and homes; they attacked our children and our women; they scattered us. All we want is our rights. We don't want more."

A two-state solution between Israel and the Palestinian people will be possible only when the Israelis end their occupation of the West Bank (although they withdrew settlers from Gaza, the Strip is now effectively a prison under Israeli control), all the settlers are withdrawn from the West Bank or a compromise is reached, 9-10,000 Palestinian political prisoners are released from Israeli gaols (the majority have not been charged with offences and are being held illegally, including children), East Jerusalem is recognised as the capital city of a Palestinian State and the right of return of Palestinian refugees (UNSCR194, 11 December 1948) is dealt with.

A further problem which will have to be dealt with is the barrier wall/fence that has been constructed, in some places 10 km from the Green Line of partition, which has prevented Palestinian farmers from farming their own land and resulted in the destruction of hundreds of thousands of olive trees. This wall is far more intimidating than the Berlin Wall was.

In my opinion, one of the barriers to reaching peace in the Middle East is the Israeli constitution, which requires election of Members of the Knesset through proportional representation. Invariably, this results in coalition Governments. If a determined Israeli Prime Minister takes a bold step towards a peaceful settlement, it is highly likely that one of the extremist parties will withdraw from the coalition, leading to the election of another Parliament.

SCIENCE AND POLITICS: AN UNLIKELY MIXTURE

Meeting with Yasser Arafat in Ramallah.

In 1896 Theodor Herzl founded the World Zionist Organisation, whose aim was to create a Jewish State. Zionist lobbying resulted in the Balfour Declaration of 1917 and, eventually, to the UN recommending partition of Palestine, on 29 November 1947. The State of Israel was declared on 14 May 1948. The violence that erupted as a result led to the slaughter of Palestinians and destruction of their villages (the Nakba or 'Palestinian Holocaust'), resulting in over 750,000 of them seeking refuge in the Egyptian-administered Gaza Strip, the Jordan-administered West Bank, Lebanon, Syria, and Jordan. After the 1967 war more Palestinians fled and, today, the UN Relief and Works Agency (UNRWA) provides aid in 59 refugee camps. 70% of Palestinians are refugees from their own land – about 4.5 million people today. They have not received, nor will they accept, compensation for their losses. Many of the refugee families still have the keys to their former homes or papers to prove their ownership and they want the right of return to their home.

After the Oslo Agreement was signed on the White House lawn on 13 September 1993 and President Arafat shook hands with Israeli Prime Minister Rabin, tensions between Hamas and the Fatah Party increased. Fatah was weakened considerably when President Arafat died in Paris on 11 November 2004 and President Mahmoud Abbas was elected 61 days later, on 9 January 2005.

Eventually, Hamas was persuaded to take part in an election process and, on 25 January 2006, they won 74 seats in the Palestinian Legislative Council, with Fatah winning only 45 seats. The Western powers were not prepared to accept this result and started to arm Fatah members in the Gaza Strip, the powerhouse of Hamas. This led to a bloody conflict between Hamas and Fatah supporters in June 2007, which resulted in Hamas taking effective political control in Gaza.

On Saturday 9 June 2007, I joined a march, 'Enough is Enough' to Trafalgar Square to mark the 40th anniversary of the occupation of Palestine (5 June 2007), where I spoke from the plinth of Nelson's Column. There were dozens of speakers that day and I decided in my speech to call for a minute's silence to remember all those who had lost their lives in this conflict; I also asked those who prayed to pray that no more lives would be lost. I couldn't believe the silence that descended on Trafalgar Square; it was a moving event. The conflict between Hamas and Fatah supporters began the next day. Until Hamas and Fatah can be persuaded to work together again for the common good of the Palestinian people, an acceptable two-state solution in the Middle East is not possible.[1]

The first debate in the parallel debating chamber of Westminster Hall, led by Phyllis Starkey (Member of Parliament for Milton Keynes South West) on 30 November 1999, was on 'Palestinian Refugees', and I was able to contribute. After that I spoke many times about Palestine, both in Westminster and elsewhere.

I attended an interesting debate at the Oxford Union on 30 April 2009 when five of the six people debating the motion 'That This House Would Negotiate with Hamas' were Jewish. Gabrielle Rifkind (cousin to Malcolm Rifkind) proposed the motion and David Aaronovitch and I supported her. In opposition to the motion were Professor Shai Felman, Ron Gidor (from the Israeli Embassy) and Malcolm Rifkind, a former Conservative Foreign Secretary. We persuaded our audience to carry the motion.

I have visited the region three times, in May 1998 with Eileen, in January 2005 as a UN Observer of the Presidential election, and in April 2008. After each visit I have grown even more determined to campaign against the human rights abuses that the Israelis are inflicting daily on the Palestinian people. There are strong feelings throughout the Muslim world on this issue, including amongst Muslims living in Britain. I cannot understand why the nations of the world allow this situation to continue. Peace between the Israelis and the Palestinians is the key to peace throughout the Middle East.

On my first visit to Israel and Palestine with Eileen in 1998 we entered Gaza at the Israeli-controlled Karni crossing point, which is mainly used to transport cargo. Our entry into Gaza was delayed for what seemed like an eternity and for no apparent reason, despite the fact that we were guests of the UN and travelling in UN vehicles. However, this gave us an opportunity to watch the queues of vehicles transporting goods in and out of Gaza; each vehicle was thoroughly inspected before it was allowed to proceed. Those leaving were deliberately delayed. A lot of the fresh fruit got spoiled during these long waits. Strawberries grow well in the Gaza Strip.

During this visit we spent most of the day with UNRWA looking at education, housing and health projects in the Jabalia refugee camp. I was struck by how close together the homes are built, so close in fact that coffins can only be brought out over the corrugated tin roofs until a wider road is reached. The houses are very primitive and most of them are cold and damp.

We stayed at a hotel in East Jerusalem and travelled to Hebron, Ramallah and Bethlehem. The Qualandia check point, near Ramallah, was not as well developed as it is today, and there was a stretch of road on the Ramallah side of the checkpoint which was in very bad condition; it was in much better shape when we used it on my two further visits.

In Ramallah our delegation met President Arafat in his compound (the Mukataa), which was mainly flattened by the tanks of the IDF, who bombarded the place for several months in 2002. I also met President Arafat at the Dorchester Hotel on Park Lane, London, when he visited Britain to discuss with British Gas the possibility of supplying Gaza with gas from the Mediterranean Sea.

On our first visit we were able to meet Palestinian leaders at Orient House in East Jerusalem, which was 'confiscated' by the Israelis shortly after our visit. A visit to Bir Zeit University enabled us to discuss with the students the difficulties that 'closures' (road blocks) had on allowing them to access the university on a daily basis. We also spent some time with the BBCs Middle East correspondent Jeremy Bowen, both in a restaurant and at the High Commissioner's Residence in East Jerusalem.

We met the Jewish women too who started Machsom Watch to record human rights abuses at the main check points, where Palestinian men, women and children are often treated badly. I have nothing but praise for the hundreds of Jewish woman who carried out this task on a daily basis, week in and week out. The American Colony Hotel was a good place to take refreshments in East Jerusalem after our visits.

I was very pleased when I was invited by our Foreign and Commonwealth Office to be one of the UKs UN observers of the Presidential elections in Palestine when Mahmoud Abbas (Abu Mazen) was elected as President of the Palestinian National Authority on 9 January 2005. We arrived several days before the election and attended several UN briefings in Ramallah. Our group visited polling stations in Qualqilya and in villages to the south east of Qualqilya. Although these places are close together on the ground, the presence of the barrier wall/fence and the positioning of the checkpoints made our journeys in our armoured UN Land Rover extremely difficult.

Our report-back on the Presidential election to the UN in Ramallah was very positive. Early on the day of the election we received a complaint that the dye used to dye the index finger after a person was recorded as attending a polling station washed off easily, and that this enabled people to vote more than once. I volunteered to have my index finger dyed and immediately tried to remove the black dye, but it wasn't possible. My finger stayed dyed for several weeks afterwards. Guns were not allowed inside polling stations but I saw one or two men carrying them in, which I recorded.

SCIENCE AND POLITICS: AN UNLIKELY MIXTURE

During this visit we were able to pay our respects to President Arafat by laying a wreath at his mausoleum in the compound at Ramallah, where he was buried on 12 November 2004.

We also visited Balata refugee camp, near Nablus, where we saw the effect of the regular incursions into the camp by the IDF. Whilst taking lunch in a restaurant in Nablus we saw bullet holes in the restaurant's windows. The Jewish settlers who live in the hills surrounding Nablus often fired down into the city and into Balata refugee camp.

Immediately outside the main gate of Balata camp – the people fled there from Tel Aviv during the Nakba – is the site of Jacob's Well, today housed inside a Greek Orthodox Church, which was being restored when we visited it. Occasionally, Jewish settlers from the hills surrounding Nablus try to capture this church to convert it into a synagogue but, when this happens, the Muslims come out of Balata camp and stop them!

On my second and third visits to Israel and the Occupied Palestinian Territories, and once in London and once in Manchester, I have been able to talk at length to former Israeli soldiers, who have served in the Israeli Defence Force (IDF), about their abuses of Palestinians of which they now feel so guilty and ashamed that they have started to reveal their feelings through an organisation called Breaking the Silence. I admire all those Jewish people and organisations that are prepared to criticise their own people for the policies their Government are pursuing. Perhaps peace in the Middle East will arise from such internal pressure?

From 13 to 18 April 2008, I was invited to lead a fact-finding delegation of Members of Parliament to Israel and the

Occupied Palestinian Territories, which was sponsored by the British Group of the International Parliamentary Union (IPU) and organised by Gillian Watt of the Council for the Advancement of Arab-British Understanding (CAABU). Tom Levitt (Member of Parliament for High Peak), Anne Snelgrove (Member of Parliament for Swindon), Sarah Teather (Member of Parliament for Brent East) and Gillian Watt and I were based in the Meridian Hotel in East Jerusalem.

We each wrote reports on what we saw and heard, and I compiled a report for the IPU magazine. This was a fact-finding mission at a crucial time in the long history of the Middle East Peace Process.

On our arrival in the region militant Palestinians were firing Kassam rockets into Israeli towns, particularly Sderot, on a daily basis, and the Israeli Defence Force was making regular incursions into the Gaza Strip to eliminate the militants, resulting in the death of hundreds of innocent civilians.

The situation in Gaza was bleak, with no public transport, few cars on the roads due to a severe fuel shortage and the few with jobs walking to work and often arriving late. Hardly any materials were going in or out of Gaza – no construction materials, not even wood for coffins, and no concrete. $93 million was available to replace homes in very poor condition, but work could not go ahead. Construction workers were unemployed and businesses that rely on imports and exports were destroyed.

The majority of people in Gaza relied on the UNRWA food distribution programme, which provided only 60% of nutritional requirements. We saw food distribution in the Beach Camp. Oxfam had declared the situation in Gaza as an emergency and ran a voucher scheme to feed 500 families in Gaza City, using supplies from local farmers.

Electricity supplies frequently broke down, and fuel supplies were limited to two to three days when we visited, even at Al-Shifa Hospital, the main trauma centre, where we saw some terrible injuries inflicted by the ongoing conflict.

We were informed that 80 patients would die if electricity failed for more than 30 minutes at Al-Shifa Hospital, where there were 16 intensive care beds, 12 coronary care beds, ten operating theatres and 30 cots for premature babies. The hospital treated 250 kidney dialysis patients, who would also die if electricity failed for more than one week. 26 dialysis machines were operating but ten were broken at the time of our visit. 80% of the 1.4 million Gazans suffered mental health problems.

Medicines and other consumables were in short supply, 50% of the ambulances were out of action, there was no transport for staff, and spare parts could not be obtained to repair broken equipment. Two day's supply remained of nitrous oxide, an anaesthesia gas. The laundry had been out of action for months, and patients were not getting adequate food supplies to help them recover.

Al-Shifa Hospital, one of seven hospitals on the Gaza Strip, appeared to be well equipped, and the 430 doctors and 480 nurses were extremely dedicated and well trained.

The Israelis were reluctant to allow patients to be transferred out of Gaza, especially those who had been badly injured as a result of an IDF attack. Very sick patients were unable to go across the Erez check point in Palestinian ambulances, and back-to-back transfer was difficult, so patients walked or were pushed on stretchers across the border.

60 tons of untreated sewage flowed into the sea off the Gazan coast, some of it landed on Israeli beaches. Ashkelon, where there is also a desalination plant, is extremely close to the border.

Dr Eyad El-Sarraj, a mental health specialist who led 'To End the Siege on Gaza', a non-partisan campaign, summed Gaza up with his five D's – deprivation, despair, dependency, disintegration and defiance – and claimed that the Israeli blockade of Gaza bred more militants. "The Peace Process is in formaldehyde", he told us.

UNRWA's then Commissioner General in Gaza, Karen Koning AbuZayd, was worried that rising prices in Gaza were causing a demand for higher wages and salaries, which was expected to reduce the amount of money available for their programmes at a time when food prices were increasing worldwide.

Sderot, the Israeli town closest to the border with Gaza was receiving, on average, 15 to 20 Kassam rockets a day, usually when the children were going to and from school and at about 8.00 p.m. and midnight. On 8 February 2008 it received 70 rockets between the hours of 7.00 p.m. and 10.00 p.m. 1,400 rockets arrived in 2007 and 900 in the first three months of 2008. 500 buildings had been damaged and ten people killed and many more injured by Kassam rockets since firing began in 2004.

Air raid sirens give Sderot's 20,000 citizens 15 to 17 seconds to seek cover. The bus shelters had been turned into bomb shelters, and the fronts of public buildings facing the border, schools included, were protected by reinforced concrete shields. Shalom Halevi, Sderot's public relations officer, feared that there was worse to come, with the arrival in Gaza of the longer-range Grad B rockets.

On leaving Gaza on 15 April 2008 prior to our visit to Sderot the following day a Kassam rocket fell yards from us at the Erez check point. We waited several hours at the Palestinian checkpoint, about a quarter of a mile away, until the Israeli checkpoint staff felt that it was safe for us to walk through their checkpoint. We took shelter in the toilets immediately inside the checkpoint, which had been made bomb proof. Two Kassam rockets fell before we arrived at the checkpoint; one remained unexploded in the vehicle crossing point. This was the first time I had walked through a tera-Hertz scanner, which effectively strips people of their clothes but reveals any objects they might be carrying in their clothing. I had seen one of these scanners being developed in a Home Department Research and Development laboratory near St Albans some months earlier.

Tom Levitt reported in our IUP article that the villagers of Azzun are "truly the victims of a 21st Century cultural and economic apartheid". Anne Snelgrove found that her time 15 years previously in Coalisland in Northern Ireland, teaching whilst Chinook helicopters whirred a few feet overhead and armed soldiers patrolled the streets in full combat gear, was "good preparation for a visit to Israel and the Occupied Palestinian Territories", whilst first-time visitor Sara Teather "found it very hard to settle to anything for some days on my return".

Collective punishment was being doled out to all of Gaza's 1.4 million citizens, children and adults alike, and whether they voted for the Fatah or Hamas party or neither party. The majority were suffering, ironically because the international community did not recognise Hamas's victory in one of the few democratic processes in the Middle East.

Can Israel ever be secure whilst it is alienating its close neighbours in this way? There is a rising recognition amongst Israeli citizens that peace must be made with the help of the international community otherwise Israeli citizens will be in a continuous state of alert.

Despite the Annapolis agreement there wasn't much evidence of progress towards peace in the occupied Fatah-controlled West Bank. The agreed reduction of road closures wasn't apparent on the ground, whilst work on building illegal settlements continued with a greater urgency.

Azzun is a small town of 10,000 to 11,000 people situated immediately adjacent to a main road. The main access to the town was sealed off by an earth mound and razor wire, allegedly because some children were caught throwing stones at illegal settlers' cars. A long detour, which heavy vehicles could negotiate only with difficulty, was the only access to Azzun. As a result businesses were collapsing.

The town was being 'punished' in other ways too. Loud music was played at night to keep the townsfolk awake. The evening before we visited Azzun Israeli soldiers shot out most of the town's street lights. Azzun remained sealed off for days and 30 times, both before and after the siege, 24-hour curfews were applied. This disrupted the education not only of the town's children but also those from adjacent neighbourhoods who attended a college in Azzun. 35 children were arrested and removed, contrary to the Geneva Convention, to the Negev Desert; 15 were still missing when we visited.

Matters were made worse when Israel launched 'Operation Cast Lead' in the Gaza Strip on 27 December 2008, and the

SCIENCE AND POLITICS: AN UNLIKELY MIXTURE

whole world watched in horror as the Israeli Defence Force (IDF) smashed its way through Palestinian towns and villages, leaving poisoned land and a trail of unbelievable destruction from which Gaza has not yet recovered. Pressure from the Western powers led to a ceasefire on 18 January 2009 and a subsequent withdrawal of the IDF from Gaza.

The wall built by the Government of Israel near Bethlehem.

Inspecting the remains of Kassam rockets in the Israeli town of Sderot.

I was pleased to see Vanessa and Corin Redgrave, Harold Pinter and Michael Mansfield QC at meetings on Palestine in the House of Commons. At one meeting in the House of Commons all of those attended as well as Martin Sheerman, a US playwright, the actress Dame Eileen Atkins and the concert pianist Katherine Wolfe. Alexie Sayle, actress Miriam Margoyles and Bruce Kent are also supporters of the Palestinian's bid for justice. When meetings are called on the Israeli-Palestinian conflict in the Houses of Parliament they are standing room only meetings.

As a Member of the All-Party Parliamentary Jordan Group I visited Jordan with Eileen from 14 to 21 February 2009. We were able to meet King Abdullah II and several Members of both Houses of Parliament. The main focus of conversation at all our meetings in Jordan was the conflict between Israel and the Palestinians. We were shown the sights in Amman, the capital city where we were based during our stay. Scenes for the film *Gladiator* were filmed in the coliseum in Amman. One of the finest Roman cities must be the old city of Jaresh to the north of Amman; it is stunning.

We also visited Mount Nebo, which overlooks the Jordan Valley and is the place where Moses showed the Israelites the 'Promised Land'. It is possible from this place to see the Dome on the Rock in Jerusalem, particularly when the sun is glinting off it in the evening sky. From there we travelled through the desert (I experienced my first desert sandstorm) to the Dead Sea, in which we tried to swim. But the finest tourist spot of all in Jordan is undoubtedly Petra, with its magnificent Treasury building, and the neighbouring Roman City. A tourist needs four days to investigate this area thoroughly.

Kashmir

In 2010, 20.6% of Bolton's 276,800 citizens were members of ethnic minority communities and the figure in the Bolton South East Constituency was considerably higher than that figure. Apart from sizeable Polish, Irish, Ukrainian and West Indian communities the largest groups were of South East Asian origin. Muslims outnumbered Hindus by approximately 2:1 and Indians outnumbered Pakistanis by approximately 2:1. A considerable number of the Indian community, Muslims and Hindus alike, had origins in the State of Gujarat.

Wars and famine in sub-Saharan Africa resulted in an increasing number of people from the African countries seeking refuge in Bolton. After the break-up of the former Yugoslavia and the conflicts that arose as a result, a significant number of people arrived in Bolton from the affected countries.

People from Kashmir have settled in Great Lever and Farnworth, and I soon became aware of their concerns after I was elected to Parliament. I joined the Kashmir, India, and Pakistan APPGs and, when I retired, I was vice-chairman of the Pakistan APPG. It seemed like there was a lobby every month in Parliament by one Kashmiri faction or another. Indeed, I often pointed out to my Kashmiri constituents that there were too many factions, all competing for attention from Parliamentarians, which made understanding the politics of Kashmir extremely difficult at times.

When the British left the Indian sub-continent there was a bloodbath between Hindus and Muslims, as Pakistan and India established their own countries (East Pakistan later became self-governing Bangladesh). One or two of the Indian

SCIENCE AND POLITICS: AN UNLIKELY MIXTURE

States did not immediately join the union and they were eventually taken over and their rulers forced to give up power. In Kashmir the ruler consented to India taking over, which resulted in conflict and division of the country along a disputed 'line of control'. Azad Kashmir is effectively controlled today by Pakistan, although it elects its own Government, which assembles in the capital, Muzaffarabad. The rest of Kashmir is Indian-occupied apart from a small portion of mountainous terrain that is occupied by China.

Militants invade Indian-occupied Jammu and Kashmir across the line of control, which has resulted in conflict between the armed forces of Pakistan and India. Bearing in mind that both these countries possess nuclear weapons, this is a very dangerous situation which urgently needs a peaceful resolution. The problem is that there are Kashmiris who would like to see their country reunited, with both Muslims and Hindus coexisting side-by-side, and there are others who would like to see Azad Kashmir united with Pakistan and Jammu and Kashmir remaining as part of India. In the Indian-occupied part of Kashmir there are regular human rights abuses that seldom come to the attention of those of us living in the West.

The problems of the Indian sub-continent often spill over into Britain. Such was the case with the murder of the 48-year-old Deputy High Commissioner of India in Birmingham, Mr Mhatre. On Friday 3 February 1984, Mohammed Bhatti and another man, both armed, kidnapped the diplomat as he was travelling from his office to his home and took him to Mr Bhatti's home, where he was guarded until Sunday 5 February by Mohammed Riaz and Abdul Quayyum Raja. The Jammu Kashmir Liberation Front demanded the release of their political prisoners in India and a ransom of £1 million to be paid for Mr Mhatre's release.

At 7.00 p.m. on the Sunday, Mr Mhatre was taken by car to a farm in Leicestershire by Mohammed Riaz, Quayyum Raja, Mussarat Iqbal and other unidentified people, where he was shot three times by Iqbal and died. Mr Mhatre was found by the farmer and his wife when they returned home at 10.00 p.m. Mohammed Riaz stayed in the car but Quayyum Raja helped Mr Iqbal to get Mr Mhatre out of the car. However, when he saw Iqbal draw a gun he protested strongly; Quayyum Raja believed that Mr Mhatre was going to be released in Leicestershire until that moment. Mussarat Iqbal and another ring-leader, Aslam Mirza, escaped and have never been arrested for this murder.

Quayyum Raja, who has relatives living in Bolton, was arrested and remanded in custody in March 1984. In February 1985, Quayyum Raja, then aged 27, Mohammed Bhatti and Mohammed Riaz were convicted of the kidnapping and murder of Mr Mhatre and given life sentences of 18, 20 and 12 years (recommended by the trial judge), respectively. The sentences of Quayyum Raja and Mohammed Bhatti were reduced to 15 and 18 years, respectively, on appeal; Mohammed Riaz did not appeal against his sentence.

In 1988 Leon Brittan, then Secretary of State for the Home Department, set a minimum tariff of 25 years for serious offences and applied this tariff retrospectively to Quayyum Raja. This resulted in a campaign on behalf of both Raja and Riaz. When I was invited by my Kashmiri constituents to consider the injustice that had been inflicted on Quayyum Raja by the Home Secretary setting tariffs retrospectively I decided to support their campaign. I joined demonstrations outside 10 Downing Street and at the Home Department, and wrote letters to successive Labour Home Secretaries asking them to look again at these tariffs. It was a touching occasion when Quayyum's very elderly mother travelled all the way from Azad Kashmir to see her son in prison. Lawyers acting on behalf of Raja and Riaz tried unsuccessfully to get the longer tariffs reduced.

In 2002, the Law Lords ruled that the setting of tariffs for individual prisoners by the Home Secretary breached the European Convention on Human Rights, and the Government handed back tariff-setting powers to judges under the Criminal Justice Act 2003. On 11 August 2004, Justice Stanley Burnton concluded that the correct tariff should be 21 years from the date of Quayyum Raja being remanded in custody and he was released after serving this tariff.

Mohammad Sarwar (Member of Parliament for Glasgow Govan), Ann Cryer (Keighley), Gordon Prentice (Pendle), Marsha Singh (Bradford West) and I were invited by the then Government of Azad Kashmir to visit Pakistan and Azad Kashmir from 8-13 September 1999. The Prime Minister of Azad (Jammu) Kashmir at the time was Barrister Sultan Mehmood Chaudhry, who was a regular visitor to Britain. Gordon and I insisted on paying for our own hotels and air travel because we had arranged with the High Commissioner in Delhi to visit India as well. In Islamabad we stayed in the Marriott Hotel, which was destroyed a few years later by a truck bomb that killed dozens of people and injured scores more.

Our visit coincided with the dying days of the Government of Nawaz Sharif. We spent a considerable amount of time in discussions with his Ministers, and Mohammad Sarwar was also granted an audience with the Prime Minister, all to no avail. Within days of us leaving Pakistan General Pervez Musharraf organised a bloodless military coup. He became President when President Rafiq Tarar, who we also met during our visit in the rather grand Presidential Palace, resigned in 2001, and Musharraf served as President of Pakistan until 2008, when democracy violently returned to the country (Mrs Benazir Bhutto was assassinated). Musharraf was also a regular visitor to Westminster.

In Pakistan, apart from our visits to the Ministries, we were taken to Rawalpindi to see a new eye hospital there, which was impressive. But the main reason for our visit was to visit Azad Kashmir and talk to its Ministers. The drive along the Jhelum valley in Land Rovers, accompanied by several armed soldiers, was spectacular. The road was heavily potholed and had collapsed in several places into the fast-flowing river below. We saw several HGVs, heavily decorated in Pakistan and usually heavily loaded too, being rescued from the river bed after they had slipped off the road. This isn't a road to travel on at night!

Our first stop was Muzaffarabad, where we were accommodated in an old hotel, largely built of wood. When I went out onto my balcony I discovered that I was immediately above the confluence of the fast-flowing Jhelum and Neelum rivers (this hotel was tipped into the rivers by the deadly earthquake in Kashmir on 9 October 2005). An elderly retainer with a very old rifle stood on guard at the end of the corridor down which I accessed my bedroom.

The President of Azad Jammu and Kashmir, Sardar Mohammad Ibrahim Khan, presented each of us with a handmade wooden box, with compartments which I now us to keep my cufflinks in.

Another long journey down the Jhelum Valley took us to

the village of Chakothi on the line of control, where we could see the Indian Army and their huge guns on the mountain tops. The Pakistan Army had laid out all the shell cases that had damaged buildings in the village and killed people, and the unexploded munitions that they had collected, on tables for us all to see. It was hard to imagine that, as we stood in a field amongst such spectacular scenery, we might be killed any minute. However, the Army Officer who lectured to us assured us that the sun was in the wrong place for the Indian troops to be able to set their sights on targets accurately, which was of some comfort to us.

Returning along the Jhelum Valley we called in at two camps for 'displaced persons', mainly farmers and their families who could no longer farm close to the line of control. They showed us the injuries that they had sustained before they had to flee. Many of them had lost legs and arms. Conditions in these camps were appalling.

After a rest back at our hotel in Islamabad our next outing was to Mirpur, where many British Kashmiri families have built villas, for their holidays and for their retirement. These villas were in various stages of completion. At the border between Pakistan and Azad Kashmir we were greeted by a huge crowd; garlands were hung round our necks. When, we arrived in Mirpur the reception was even more spectacular; flower petals were thrown at us as we were shown onto a stage in a marquee, decorated with flowers, and traditional hats were placed on our heads. A long round of speeches began. A reception was also held for us on the banks of the Mangla Dam Lake, which supplies water to the region.

SCIENCE AND POLITICS: AN UNLIKELY MIXTURE

Campaigning for the release of Kashmiri prisoner Quayyum Raja – opposite Downing Street on Whitehall; Bolton Cllr Mohammed Ayub is standing next to me with the poster and Cllr Mohammed Iqbal is on the extreme left of the picture.

(Left to right) Marsha Singh MP, Mohammad Sarwar MP, Gordon Prentice MP, Ann Cryer MP and me, with the President of Pakistan (in the centre) in Islamabad.

SCIENCE AND POLITICS: AN UNLIKELY MIXTURE

At Chakothi on the line of control in the Jhelum Valley, Azad Kashmir looking at spent and unexploded Indian ammunitions.

I knew my Bolton friend Mumtaz Chishty had promised to meet and greet us in Mirpur, where his family lives, and he did. Hanging on my wall at home is the plate that was given to me by the Administrator of Mirpur, Chaudhary Muhammad Ayub. How can I ever forget my visit to Pakistan and Kashmir?

The first Kashmiri family that I ever met in Bolton, in the early 1970s, visited Islamabad in the period running up to the 2010 General Election. Tragically, Jameel Ahmed and his wife were attacked by burglars in a house in Islamabad; Jamil died as a result of his injuries. On the day of the 2010 General Election I visited their Bolton home to give the family my condolences. As far as I am aware the police in Islamabad have not charged anyone with Jameel's murder.[2]

On 26 June 2008, the Chishty family suffered a tragedy too. A wheelie bin was pushed against the front door of their house in Great Lever and set alight. By the time the fire was discovered the door and its frame were well alight. As fireman Steve Morris tried to rescue Mrs Begum, Chishty's wife, the gas meter exploded. 71-Year-old Mrs Hameeda Begum died and Steve Morris was extremely badly burned. Mumtaz's granddaughter, Alana Mian, who was visiting from Australia with her mother, died at the age of four on 2 August 2008 as a result of smoke damage to her lungs. Both mother and daughter were rescued from the fire by firemen. I attended Alana's funeral at the Macca Mosque in Grecian Crescent, Bolton on 7 August 2008. Nobody has been brought to justice for these two murders.

From Islamabad Gordon Prentice and I flew on to Delhi *via* Lahore. We stayed in the very luxurious Hotel Imperial that had been booked for us by the British High Commission in Delhi, at a discount price thank goodness. Gordon immediately went down with a very bad stomach upset and was extremely ill for more than a day. However, he recovered and we were able to meet several important Government officials, although all the politicians were out in their constituencies fighting a General Election.

Nevertheless, we were able to have several straightforward discussions about Kashmir. Of course, the Indian Government has a completely different perspective on this problem. A request to visit Jammu and Kashmir was denied us. A visit to the beautiful city of Srinagar will have to wait for another day. Very few British politicians are ever allowed to visit this part of the world; I wonder why? The area is not freely accessible to NGOs or the British media either.

I enjoyed working with the different communities that make up the Bolton South East Parliamentary constituency, and I was very pleased to receive a Special Achievement Award in 2007 at the Bolton Diversity Awards evening. It was appropriately named after a friend and Labour Party colleague, Anne Gough, who worked with the minority communities in Bolton for several decades. Anne battled with breast cancer for a few years and, sadly, died in the summer of 2007. I attended her funeral on 6 July 2007.

NOTES

1. An agreement was reached between Hamas and Fatah in April 2011 but has not led so far to peace.

2. Four people were arrested and charged in May 2011. St Simon's and St Jude's C. of E. Primary School dedicated a new community room to Jameel; it was opened on Friday 17th June 2011 by my successor Yasmin Qureshi MP.

CHAPTER TWELVE

SCIENCE AND TECHNOLOGY SELECT COMMITTEE

After the 1997 General Election the Government Whips' Office circulated a list of Select Committees and asked us to choose three in preference order. My first choice was the Department of Environment, Transport and Rural Affairs (DETR) Select Committee because I had gone down to Parliament with a strong interest in local government and housing in particular.

However, I faced strong competition, and Louise Ellman (Member of Parliament for Liverpool Riverside and former leader of Lancashire County Council) and Graham Stringer (Member of Parliament for Manchester Blackley and former leader of Manchester City Council) were appointed to this committee from the North West. In making their appointments the Whips have to take into account a fair distribution of jobs between the regions, among other considerations.

Ann Taylor, Leader of the House, expressed her surprise to me over my choice of Select Committees. She thought I would have preferred to serve the Science and Technology Select Committee. Ann became our Chief Whip in 1998. When John Prescott, Deputy Prime Minister and Secretary of State at the DETR, set up the Environmental Audit Select Committee in November 1997, I applied to be a Member and was appointed. I served this committee until 31 March 2000, when a vacancy arose on the Science and Technology Select Committee for which I applied, encouraged to do so by its then chairman Dr Ian Gibson (Member of Parliament for Norwich North), who had been Dean of the School of Biological Sciences at the University of East Anglia before his election to Parliament, in 1997. I was appointed and served the committee (see later in this chapter) until my retirement in 2010.

After the General Election in 2005, when the Labour Party returned fewer Members of Parliament, Liberal Democrat Phil Willis (Member of Parliament for Harrogate and Knaresborough) became chairman of the Science and Technology Select Committee. Although Phil was not a scientist or an engineer, he was a good chairman of the committee and had a good understanding of all the issues that we dealt with. It is generally accepted that Members should be encouraged to serve the committee even though they may have little understanding of scientific principles, providing that they are enthusiastic about the work of the committee. Ian Gibson was upset by this change of chairmanship, but we persuaded him to remain on the committee.

Until the General Election of 2010 the membership and

chairmanships of Select Committees were in the hands of the Whips' Offices. After 2010, and after the allocation of the chairmanships of each Select Committee to a political party (based proportionately on the number of seats that each party wins), each major political party became responsible for election of the chairmen of Select Committees as well as their memberships. Today there are 11 Members on the committee compared with 14 between 1997 and 2010.

When the Government created the Department of Business, Innovation, and Skills (DBIS) in 2007, with Lord (Peter) Mandelson as its Secretary of State, the Science and Technology Select Committee was dissolved and the Innovation, Universities, Science and Skills Select Committee was set up, with an unwieldy remit. Its chairman was Phil Willis. In several debates in the House of Commons chamber Members who had served the Science and Technology Select Committee argued that it should be re-established, and it was on 1 October 2009.

Serving a Select Committee, whilst extremely worthwhile, is very time consuming. The Science and Technology Select Committee meetings were usually held on Wednesday mornings and quite frequently on Monday afternoons. When inquiries have been advertised and written evidence sought, piles of submitted evidence needs to be read, usually at the weekends, before the relevant committee meeting.

For each inquiry the Select Committee appoints advisers, who help the Clerks of the committee select appropriate witnesses to give evidence to the committee and write the reports. Each Select Committee has a Principal Clerk, a Second Clerk and several assistants, and also appoints specialists, who are the people most involved in writing reports. Amendments to reports are considered by Members of the committee before they are published. When reports are published there is usually a press conference at which journalists can question Members of the committee about their findings. Depending on the subject of the inquiry, sometimes these reports are launched outside the Palace of Westminster.

There are regular visits associated with each inquiry, either within Britain or abroad. When we travelled abroad (at least once a year in Europe and at least once a year further afield), we needed permission from the Whips' Office to be away for up to a week. Occasionally we were recalled to take part in a critical vote in the House of Commons.

The proceedings of all Select Committees – the Press Notices, the Minutes of Evidence and the full Reports – are available on the internet at http://www.parliament.uk/science or by 'Googling' House of Commons Science and Technology Select Committee.

I am often asked how Members of the Science and Technology Select Committee select the topics for the inquiries it pursues. The committee gathers a long list of suggestions from various sources. Most of its Members have contacts that propose inquiries or have inquiries that they want to pursue, and the chairman of the committee and its Principal Clerk and Second Clerk meet with a large number of outside organisations who propose inquiries to them. Once or twice a year Members meet in private to decide which inquiries to launch; usually several are launched at the same time. Some are long inquiries on a subject that Members want to investigate in depth; others are relatively short ones, often on topics of current public interest.

In addition, it is necessary to scrutinise the work of the Government, which requires Secretaries of State, Ministers and their senior civil servants, Chief Executive Officers of the Research Councils, Chief Executives of other Government Agencies, Vice-Chancellors of universities, Chief Executive Officers of the Higher Education Funding Councils and others, depending upon the title of the inquiry, to give evidence to the committee. When invited to give evidence to a Select Committee witnesses must attend, otherwise they can be legally ordered to do so. Only one witness in my time serving on the committee had to be summonsed to attend; he made a rotten witness. We wanted Prince Charles, Prince of Wales, to attend several times, particularly when we conducted inquiries on GM crops and homeopathy on which he was known to have strong views, but we were told that this was not possible.

For each report that a Select Committee publishes the Government is required to produce a report in response within a fixed timescale. It is often said that the most effective way to scrutinise the work of the Government's Executive is through the work of Select Committees and in my opinion that is true.

I am often asked whether the work of the Select Committee made any impact. Below I give selected examples to suggest that the work of the Science and Technology Select Committee did have considerable impact between 1997 and 2010.

I joined the Science and Technology Select Committee when it was finalising an inquiry on cancer research. The report, *Cancer Research – A Fresh Look*, which was published on 16 August 2000, recommended that the Government matched the funding that the charities were raising for cancer research, and that the two major charities that were carrying out research in this area, the Cancer Research Campaign and the Imperial Cancer Research Fund, should consider a merger.

After this inquiry Professor Mike Richards was appointed as the first 'Cancer Zsar'. The Government contributed funding that matched the funding given for cancer research by the charities and in 2002, the two major charities merged and became Cancer Research UK. However, it wasn't long before the committee realised that the extra Government funding was not being used by the NHS for cancer research and, on 25 April 2002, another report, *Cancer Research – A Follow-up*, recommended that the 'Cancer Zsar' should carefully audit this money and ensure that it is spent on cancer research. Under the 1997-2010 Labour Government considerable progress was made in cancer research, improvements were made in the translation of research into clinical practice and survival rates for the common cancers improved significantly.

Several Members sitting on the committee had an interest in energy policy. On 8 May 2001, the committee published *Wave and Tidal Energy*. We concluded that Britain could have been the front runner in the development of wind turbines but that we had lost out in this race to Denmark. We proposed, therefore, that we should lead the world in the development of wave and tidal power. As a result of our report, the Government decided to invest in research and development in the generation of electricity from wave and tidal power, and Britain is at present ahead of the rest of the world in developing this technology.

On 12 June 2003, the committee published *Towards a Non-Carbon Fuel Economy: Research, Development and Demonstration*, which reviewed Britain's progress in adopting a renewable energy strategy. On 9 February 2006 *Meeting UK Energy and Climate Needs*, a report on carbon-capture and storage (both pre- and post-combustion capture of carbon dioxide), was published, which helped the Government to formulate its carbon capture and storage policy a few years later.

In 1997 Sir David King, a chemist from Cambridge University, was Chief Scientific Adviser (CSA) to the Prime Minister. The committee always believed that his office should be in the Cabinet Office; it remained in the Department of Business, Enterprise and the Regions (DBER; previously in DTI, then in DBIS). We argued too that each State Department should have its own Chief Scientific Adviser (in the Department of Transport it makes sense to appoint an engineer to this post) and that their work should be co-ordinated by the CSA to advise the PM. Apart from the Treasury this recommendation has been accepted.[1]

In 1997 scientists and engineers were recruited into the civil service as 'generalists', whereas previously they had been recruited and used as scientists. We also proposed that Government departments should revert to the previous situation and that the CSA in each department should carry out an audit of the civil servants with scientific or engineering expertise. Increasingly, the policy decisions made today require this kind of expertise.

On 21 March 2001, the committee published *The Scientific Advisory System* and *The Scientific Advisory System: Scientific Advice on Climate Change*. These reports examined how Government used the advice available to formulate its policies. On 22 October 2002, a report was published on *Government Funding of the Scientific Learned Societies* which looked in particular at how the three 'Royal Academies' spent their

Government grants. This was the first time a Select Committee had looked in depth at the work of the Royal Society.

The committee is always concerned with the quantity and quality of science education in our primary and secondary schools, as well as in the universities and further education colleges. The report *Science Education from 14-19*, published on 11 July 2002, resulted in a rethink about the way science is taught in our secondary schools. Pupils remarked to us that even though they were not going to specialise in science, they wanted to be able to understand the science that is covered by the media. Therefore, the committee recommended that science should be a core subject for all pupils in secondary schools and, out of this proposal, new science syllabi were developed, including the various *21st Century Science* syllabi, which I highlighted in an Adjournment Debate on 15 January 2008. We were accused of 'dumbing down' science, but *21st Century Science* syllabi also allowed the three principal branches of science – physics, chemistry and biology – to be taught separately in schools for those who want to specialise in science.

The Science and Technology Select Committee discussed the impact of the Research Assessment Exercise on universities several times, and we also took up a campaign to investigate why so many science departments were closing in our universities.

After the terrorist attacks on the twin towers of the World Trade Centre in New York and on the Pentagon, Washington DC, on 11 September 2001 (9/11) the committee decided to carry out an inquiry into counter measures to a chemical, biological, radiological or nuclear (CBRN) attack in Britain.

We visited the Defence Science and Technology Laboratory (Dstl) and the Centre for Applied Microbiology and Research (CAMR) at Porton Down (both had a strong military focus at that time) in the UK, interviewed senior staff of the newly created Homeland Security Department (established on 25 November 2002) in the West Wing of the White House in Washington, and visited the Lawrence Livermore National Laboratory (where some of the work on the first atom bombs was carried out), near San Francisco, and the Centre for Disease Control in Atlanta in May 2003.

This was a very difficult inquiry to carry out because a lot of the material we needed to access was secret. Nevertheless, we saw enough material and took enough evidence, sometimes out of the public gaze, to be able to make important recommendations to the Government. Our report, *Scientific Response to Terrorism*, was published on 6 November 2003.

In San Francisco we stayed in the Fairmont Hotel on Nob Hill, where one of my predecessors, George Tomlinson (Member of Parliament for Farnworth) was present when the charter that created the United Nations was drafted and signed, in the Garden Room. George was the principal negotiator for the UK.

On 6 October 2003, the committee published *Light Pollution and Astronomy*, the result of a short inquiry that had been proposed by Tom Harris (Member of Parliament for Glasgow South). Members of the committee visited various groups of astronomers around the country to talk about this report; I visited the Godlee Observatory at the University of Manchester Institute of Science and Technology (UMIST), which I was unaware of before my visit. This inquiry turned out to be more interesting than I had anticipated when we embarked on it. It arose partly as a result of astronomers complaining that they were unable to investigate the night sky in Britain because of badly-designed street lights and other outdoor lighting equipment. The report led to new legislation that allows people affected by light pollution to get councils to take action against those who are unnecessarily causing it, and companies began to redesign outside lighting equipment, both to make it more efficient and to prevent light being spilled into the sky.

I persuaded the committee to carry out an inquiry into the EU REACH (Registration, Evaluation and Authorisation of Chemicals) Regulation, which resulted in the publication of *Within REACH: the EU's New Chemicals Strategy*, on 12 May 2004. This is a major piece of EU legislation which has had a huge impact on the UK chemical industry and which came into force fully in 2011. Its intention was to take off the market unsafe chemicals used in consumer products and replace them wherever possible by safer chemicals.

On 20 July 2004, the committee published *Scientific Publications; Free for All?* which weighed up the pros and cons of allowing 'open access' to all scientific publications on the internet, without cost to the user. The major income of most learned societies arises from their publication of scientific journals and magazines, so this inquiry proved to be very controversial. At least it propagated a healthy debate that was just starting up when we began our inquiry. The debate continues today.

The Use of Science in UK International Development Policy, published on 26 October 2004, was a report that had a significant impact on the Department of International Development (DfID) and its thinking at the time. DfID and

Science and Technology Select Committee visit to the Office of the Joint Program for Chemical and Biological Defense, USA.

its Secretary of State Hilary Benn were persuaded by this report to appoint a Chief Scientific Adviser. The report showed that a country could develop economically and socially by engaging with science and engineering and the innovation of its people.

In June 2004 we visited Malawi, one of the poorest countries in the world at the time, and looked at agricultural and health programmes that Britain was engaged in there. I was almost reduced to tears on a visit to a hospital in the country's principal city, Lilongwe, where patients were sharing beds, sleeping between the beds and in the corridors, and sleeping on the veranda, where the outside temperature dropped to below freezing point at night. Most HIV/Aids patients, and there were lots of them, died of preventable tuberculosis because of a shortage of drugs. Our visit coincided with the arrival in Malawi of the retro-antiviral drugs, so I expect matters have improved since our visit.

We also discovered that Malawi was training its fair share of nurses only to see them leave to work in other countries, including Britain, or to join international research programmes that were situated in Malawi. Following a recommendation to our Government, Britain helped to retain Malawi's nurses by increasing their pay through foreign aid, and we stopped recruiting them into our NHS.

Professor Colin Pillinger and his team at the Open University excited the nation just before Christmas in 2003 by the launch of Beagle 2, which unfortunately failed to 'phone home' after making a flawed landing on Mars. In light of criticism of this project our committee decided to investigate whether it had been value for money, and we decided that it was. Our report, *Government Support for Beagle 2* was published on 2 November 2004. The publication of *2007: A Space Policy* on 17 July 2007 gave a real boost to the UK space industry, which is one of the most important in the world. Our recommendation that a UK Space Agency be set up was accepted by the Government, and the 2010 Committee agreed to review the work of this new agency.

Advances in technology can sometimes outdate legislation. The Human Fertilisation and Embryology Act 1990, which arose out of the 1988 Warnock Report, was typical of an out-of-date Act, so we decided to carry out an extensive investigation into *Human Reproductive Technologies and the Law*. The report was published just before the 2005 General Election, on 24 March 2005. We travelled to various clinics within Britain and also to Sweden and Italy in November 2004 to take evidence. In Italy we took evidence from the Bioethics Committee in Vatican City, from the Minister in the Italian Government responsible for this policy area and from the

Italian Government's Bioethics Committee. I was most impressed by the grasp that the Catholic Bishops on the Vatican City's committee had of this subject.

At the final meeting to consider this report on 14 March 2005 we found over 70 amendments on our agenda, which were clearly designed to sink the report without trace. We met in the afternoon and, by 5.30 p.m., we had dealt with only a few of the amendments. A filibuster was clearly under way so, when we adjourned for refreshments, I told the chairman that I was going to try to guillotine the business. In all my 13 years in Westminster I never heard of another Select Committee at which this procedural measure was used.

When the committee returned to its business at 6.00 p.m., I moved that it conclude its business at 9.00 p.m. that evening. Chris Shaw, the Committee's Principal Clerk, asked the chairman to adjourn the meeting whilst he sought legal advice. To my relief, and I expect the relief of several other Members of the Committee, the Principal Committee Clerk told us that my motion was in order, and the chairman, Dr Ian Gibson, put it to the vote. Fortunately, it was carried (but only by the chairman's casting vote) and business was allowed to continue until 9.00 p.m., when the remaining amendments fell.

Tony McWalter (Member of Parliament for Hemel Hempstead) walked out when I succeeded with my motion, but I don't think he understood the gravity of the situation. We had travelled extensively to collect evidence, not to mention several sessions in Westminster also collecting evidence from witnesses, and we had spent many hours considering the contents of this seminal report. Because of the pending General Election we were about to lose it. In the end it was published.

This report became the platform for the Secretary of State for Health to publish a Draft Bill, which was considered by an *ad hoc* committee of both Houses of Parliament after the General Election of 2005. Phil Willis, who became chairman of the Science and Technology Select Committee after the election, was chairman of this committee, which met between 16 August and 25 November 2005.

In late 2007, the final Bill was published and considered by both Houses. It became the Human Fertilisation and Embryology Act 2008. This was one of the most controversial Bills ever considered during my 13 years in Parliament. A lot of work had to be done behind the scenes in order to convince Members that this piece of legislation was necessary, and I applauded the Minister of Public Health of the day, Dawn Primarolo, for grasping some very difficult arguments and steering the Bill through the House of Commons.

We published two further controversial reports that were taken into consideration when this Bill came before Parliament, *Government Proposals for the Regulation of Hybrid and Chimera Embryos*, published on 5 April 2007, and *Scientific Developments Relating to the Abortion Act 1967*, published on 31 October 2007.

The Government considered privatising the Forensic Science Service in 2004-2005, and our committee conducted an inquiry which recommended that it stay within the control of the Government in a report, *Forensic Science on Trial*, published on 29 March 2005. The Labour Government converted the service into an arms-length agency of Government; after 2010 the Coalition Government announced a complete sell-off of this service.

In 2006 our attention was drawn to the EU Physical Agents (Electromagnetic Fields) Directive, which had been supported by the UK's Health and Safety Executive. If our Government had accepted this Directive in its original form it would have meant the shutdown of all Magnetic Resonance Imaging (MRI) scanners in use throughout our NHS. Our committee conducted a short but significant inquiry, and the report (published on 29 June 2006) stopped this Directive from proceeding. It has been amended since.

On 31 July 2006, the committee published *Drug Classification; Making a Hash of It?* This report was extremely critical of the ABC Classification of Drugs which is an important part of the Misuse of Drugs Act 1971. We recommended its replacement by a system of classification of harmful drugs, including alcohol and tobacco, developed by Professors Colin Blakemore and David Nutt and their co-workers, which they published in a peer reviewed paper in *The Lancet*.

We also considered whether cannabis should be considered as a Class B or Class C Drug, as it then was (it was reclassified from Class B to Class C by Home Secretary David Blunkett in October 2001), and recommended that it remain a Class C Drug. Secretary of State for the Home Department, Jacqui Smith, reclassified it to Class B in 2008, also against the advice of the Advisory Council on the Misuse of Drugs, chaired by Professor David Nutt.

It was this reclassification of cannabis, as well as classification of ecstasy as a Class A drug, that led the chairman of the Advisory Council on the Misuse of Drugs, Professor David Nutt, to be dismissed by Secretary of State for the Home Department Alan Johnson. On 8 November 2006, the committee published a report entitled *Scientific*

Advice, Risk and Evidence Based Policy Making. We were critical of David Nutt's dismissal.

The Science and Technology Select Committee: former Conservative chairman Michael Clark MP is in the chair and I am standing with Lynne Jones MP and Ian Gibson MP, chairman.

Science and Technology Select Committee Members Phil Willis MP (chairman; extreme left), Desmond Turner MP (fourth from right), me, and Adam Afriyie MP (extreme right) with British-born astronaut Dr Piers Sellers[2] (second from left) and other astronauts from the NASA STS-121 mission.

On 28 November 2006 we were visited by five of the seven astronauts from the NASA STS-121 mission that had flown to the International Space Station in July 2006. One of them, Piers Sellers,[2] was a British-born astronaut who had become an American citizen in order to take part in NASAs missions. By 2010 he had completed three space shuttle missions and made six space walks.

Human Enhancement Technologies in Sport, published on 22 February 2007, was an interesting inquiry which took us to Australia in October 2006 to collect evidence. We began our inquiry by taking evidence from Linford Christie and Dr Roger Palfryman, who was the Medical Officer for the British Olympic Cycling Team. Apart from techniques such as training at high altitude, this inquiry was mainly about the illicit use of drugs in sport and the ease with which they can be detected. Erythropoietins (EPOs), for example, occur naturally and are manufactured for the treatment of cancer patients who suffer from anaemia; they help the production of red blood cells, which carry oxygen to our cells and are widely used (or misused) by athletes.

On 18 October 2007, the publication of *Investigating the Oceans* gave a boost to marine scientists. We discovered that they were not well funded and that the governance of research in this policy area lacked clout. With climate change very much on the agenda today, the study of the behaviour of our oceans and acidification of the sea by the carbon dioxide produced by burning fossil fuels is becoming ever more urgent.

This investigation took us to the USA, where between 20 and 25 May 2007 we visited Boston, Washington, the University of Rhode Island and New England. In Boston we were privileged to talk to the team at Harvard University which developed the open frame submarines that were able to examine the RMS *Titanic* and the MV *Derbyshire* on the beds of the Atlantic Ocean and South China Sea, respectively (see Chapter 14). In New England we visited the world-famous Woods Hole Oceanographic Institute which uses the open frame submarines in its investigations of the oceans of the world.

I persuaded the committee to carry out a short inquiry into *The Funding of Science and Discovery Centres* but the report, published on 22 October 2007, unfortunately had little impact. I expect more of these centres will close in future due to a lack of funding. The Bolton Technical Innovation Centre closed at the end of March 2011 (see next chapter).

In June 2007 the Government announced that the Science and Technology Select Committee would be replaced by the Innovation, Universities, Science and Skills Select Committee, with a much wider remit, and I volunteered to serve on it. It examined subjects such as the Leitch Report, Equivalent or Lower Level Qualifications (ELQs) and Science Budget Allocations, and was involved in prelegislative scrutiny of the Draft Apprentices Bill. Members that served on it had been either on the Education Select Committee or the Science and Technology Select Committee previously. However, in its first session it did manage to carry out important inquiries into *Biosecurity in UK Research Laboratories* (the report was published on 25 June 2008) and *Renewable Electricity-Generation Technologies* (report published on 19 June 2008).

The most significant reports of its second session (2008-2009) were *Sites of Special Scientific Interest*, published on 29 July 2009, and two reports on engineering – *Putting Science and Engineering at the Heart of Government*, published on 23

July 2009, and *Engineering: Turning Ideas into Reality*, published on 27 March 2009, which gave a boost to the engineering professions. We discovered that there were over 40 organisations representing the interests of engineers, including the Royal Academy of Engineers, far too many for each of them to be effective in determining Government policy, although the Royal Academy of Engineering is influential in that respect.

Under pressure from both within and without Parliament, the Government re-established the Science and Technology Select Committee for the 2009-2010 session of Parliament, my last session on the committee. The leaked emails from the Climatic Research Unit at the University of East Anglia, which some people used in an attempt to discredit the science of climate change, dominated this session, with publication of a report on 31 March 2010.

For me, the most rewarding inquiry in my final session on the committee was *Bioengineering* (a report published on 25 March 2010), which looked at research on stem cells and its translation into clinical practice, and the barriers in the UK to research and development on genetically modified crops and synthetic biology.

At University College, London, we saw evidence of success in using stem cells to treat macular degeneration of the eye in animal studies that was about to be translated into human studies at Moorfields Eye Hospital, and we saw short lengths of trachea being constructed *in vitro* from stem cells for implantation into patients. We also heard about the complexities of existing legislation that was slowing the research down.

At Imperial College, London, we held discussions with a

multidisciplinary team who were engaging in synthetic biology research. Their approach to a living being is to consider it as an engineer would consider a machine, built up of component parts each of which in turn can be reduced to its engineering components. Obviously, once a living machine has been deconstructed, the individual parts can be used to construct a new machine, preferably living and useful. This is another example of advances in technology outpacing existing legislation. Undoubtedly, Parliament will need to bring in Acts that define the ethical boundaries for this kind of research, otherwise it may go beyond the boundaries of what is currently acceptable.

The committee also looked at the various ways in which climate change could be tackled through geoengineering, for example through the use of trillions of reflective mirrors in the sky, by capturing carbon dioxide with 'artificial trees' or by stimulating the growth of carbon dioxide-capturing algae in the sea through their fertilisation with iron salts. The committee looked in particular at *The Regulation of Geoengineering* (in a report published on 18 March 2010), which will require the negotiation over a long period of time of some international treaties.

The committee also looked at *The Government's Review of the Principles Applying to the Treatment of Independent Scientific Advice Provided to Government* (report published on 14 December 2009) and *The Impact of Spending Cuts on Science and Scientific Research* (report published on 23 March 2010).

The Innovation, Universities, Science and Skills Select Committee introduced 'Evidence Checks', the first report on *Early Literacy Interventions*, published on 18 December 2009, and the second on *Homeopathy*, published on 22 February

2010. These short inquiries were designed to test whether the Government based its policies on evidence or not. The homeopathy inquiry, which Dr Evan Harris pressed for, stirred up a hornets' nest when we concluded that the NHS should stop funding it because the treatments were nothing more than examples of the placebo effect. I wasn't a keen supporter of this type of inquiry.

The Government also required Select Committees to carry out 'Pre-appointment Hearings' at which we questioned the suitability of eminent people, who came before the committee, for appointment to key Government posts, but after they had been selected for their jobs. I could see no point in these interviews.

After the 2010 General Election it was accepted that the substantial work of the House of Commons Science and Technology Select Committee, combined with substantial lobbying of Government by various outside organisations, resulted in the incoming Coalition Government ring-fencing science funding, although inflation was expected to result in a 10% erosion of the funding in the four years 2010-2014 (which became 2010-2015 after legislation was passed for fixed-term Parliaments).

NOTES

1. The Treasury appointed a CSA after the 2010 General Election.

2. On 16 January 2016 Dr Piers Sellars announced that he had been diagnosed with stage four pancreatic cancer.

CHAPTER THIRTEEN

OTHER WORK FOR THE STEM SUBJECTS

∽

I was a Fellow of the Royal Society of Chemistry (FRSC) when I was elected to Parliament. The RSC had two Parliamentary Advisers in 1997, Donald Anderson (Member of Parliament for Swansea East; now Lord Anderson) on the Labour benches and Michael Clark (Member of Parliament for Rayleigh, who retired in 2001) on the Conservative benches. They decided to retire from their positions in 1998 and the Royal Society of Chemistry appointed me in place of Donald Anderson.

Few Conservative Members took an interest in the STEM subjects and several RSC Parliamentary Advisers were appointed from the opposition benches. Mark Lancaster (Member of Parliament for Milton Keynes North) whose father (the Reverend Ronald Lancaster) created Kimbolton

Fireworks, took the most interest in the RSC. Mark was a bomb disposal officer in the Territorial Army and worked in Iraq. The RSCs Parliamentary Adviser in the House of Lords was Lord (Jack) Lewis of Cambridge University, a fellow chemist.[1]

Four times a year I attended the RSCs Parliamentary Affairs Committee (PAC), at which we discussed relationships between the learned societies and Parliament. Before my appointment, and despite my long membership of the RSC, I had never been inside the RSCs headquarters in Burlington House. I hosted a number of RSC functions in the Palace of Westminster, which were organised by Dr Stephen Benn, the RSCs Parliamentary Affairs Officer, whose father Tony Benn was the Member of Parliament for Chesterfield until he retired before the 2001 General Election.

I came to know the Benn family quite well during my stay in Parliament. Stephen's wife, Nita Clarke, worked in the Political Office at 10 Downing Street. Stephen's brother, Hilary was elected to Parliament in a by-election in 1999 for

With Michael Clark MP, Donald Anderson MP, and Dr Stephen Benn (RSC).

the Leeds Central Parliamentary constituency following the death of Derek Fatchett MP and was a Minister in the Labour Government.

I remember following Tony Benn out of New Palace Yard at the House of Commons after the Dissolution of Parliament in 2001. His car was loaded up with his belongings, with his favourite chair hanging out of the back and the boot lid up. He stopped at Carriage Gates to talk to the police on duty there, and I waited patiently. It must have been an emotional day for him. I followed him up Victoria Street, round Hyde Park Corner and up Park Lane and lost him at the north end of Park Lane as he headed for Notting Hill where he lived.[2]

Someone suggested that I add Tony Benn's name to an Early Day Motion that I put down immediately after the 2001 General Election, to see if the clerks in the Table Office would notice. His 'signature' had been deleted when the EDM was published the following day.

Tony Benn's American-born wife died in the autumn of 2000, aged 74. After the Memorial Service for Caroline Benn at St Margaret's Church, in March 2001, Cherie Blair and Mary Wilson were being escorted to the Speaker's House, when their escort heard Mary Wilson ask whether Cherie knew when the General Election was likely to be held, so she could plan a holiday. Their escort decided to drop back in case they overheard a State secret. Even so, Mary Wilson was heard to say to Cherie Blair, "Well! Harold never told me when the election would be held".

When I was elected to Parliament the RSCs 'Links Day' was well established. The RSC made attempts to link a chemist with the local Member of Parliament in every Parliamentary constituency. Once a year, in June, those chemists who participated in the scheme were invited down to a morning conference in Parliament, which was followed by a lunch in the House of Lords, hosted by Lord (Jack) Lewis[1] in my day, and a meeting for them in the afternoon. This event was one of the longest-established scientific events of the Parliamentary calendar and attracted some high-level speakers, from the political parties as well as from outside Parliament. The RSC involved many of the other learned societies in the STEM policy area to participate in 'Links Day'.[3]

Much to my surprise, Professor N. B. Chapman, who was one of the most influential people in my life (see Chapter 3 in Volume 1), came to the RSC's Links Day in 1997, when he was well into his retirement years, and I was extremely grateful to him for making the effort. The last I saw of NBC was when I attended a reunion of the 1961 chemistry graduands at the University of Hull, organised by Professor Ray Walker. About 12 of us attended and NBC and his wife joined us for lunch on Saturday 7 July 2007. He died at the age of 91 on 6 March 2008.

After my arrival in Parliament, Dr Stephen Benn decided to inaugurate an event at which scientists in the early stages of their careers could put questions to Members of the Science and Technology Select Committee, as well as receive presentations from Ministers and leading scientists. 'Voice of the Future' was followed by a lunch and also become a well-established and popular event.[3] The prizes for an essay competition, sponsored by the RSC, were presented annually in the House of Commons by Bill Bryson, and the RSC invited Members of Parliament and others to attend a Christmas Party in the Houses of Parliament.

The President of the American Chemical Society (ACS)

visits the RSC in July every year to attend its Annual Meeting at Burlington House. Stephen Benn decided that it would be a good idea if the ACS President and their accompanying officers and guests were entertained in one of the private dining rooms at the House of Commons by the President and President Elect of the RSC and other officers of the RSC and their guests. This event, which we called 'The Presidents' Dinner', renamed after 2010 as the 'Transatlantic Dinner', was always an enjoyable event, with impromptu speeches at the end. The first dinner was held on 18 July 2002.

At a dinner held on 14 July 2004 I presented the then President, Professor Sir Harry Kroto, a Nobel Prize Winner for Chemistry, with a brick mounted on a nice wooden plinth that I had had made in Bolton. Harry was educated at Wolfenden Primary School, where I had been chairman of the governing body, Bolton School and Sheffield University. When Wolfenden School was closed prior to its demolition, I promised Harry that I would give him a bit of his old school. I had forgotten that it was not built in the reign of Queen Victoria and was devoid of any elaborate decoration, such as bottle blue or green wall tiles or stained glass windows. One day, after I made my request to the Local Education Authority for a memorable piece of the school, I found a bag of bricks had been left at my home, which I cleaned up.

My 'brick speech' on 15 July 2004 about the history of five humble bricks which I heaved onto the table in a captain's case went down quite well (the table almost went down well too with the weight of the bricks), especially with our American guests. The brick I gave to Harry, mounted on a plinth, was highly decorative and came from Withnell Brick Works, which once operated near Chorley in Lancashire. Apparently, he kept

1961 Special Honours Degree Chemistry graduates at their reunion at the University of Hull (seated are Professor Roy Baldwin and Professor Norman Bellamy Chapman).

With my Westminster assistant Kathryn Sutcliffe and Nobel Laureate Professor Sir Harry Kroto[4] and Mrs Kroto at the RSCs Summer Soiree at the Royal Academy.

With Eileen and Nobel Laureate Professor Sir Harry Kroto[4] at Bolton Town Hall (24 February 2005).

the 'Last Brick from Wolfenden School' in memory of his primary school days.[4]

I also became involved with the Parliamentary and Scientific Committee, which was founded in 1939 to promote science and engineering in both Houses of Parliament. It organises regular presentations by leading scientists and engineers and occasional visits outside Parliament. An Annual Lunch is held with a very high level guest speaker (Nobel Prize winners Paul Nurse and James Watson, Chris Patten, Charles Clarke MP, Sir David King, Lord May and Princess Anne have all been guest speakers), always in the River Room at the Savoy Hotel until it closed for an expensive refurbishment in 2008. After that the lunches were held on the House of Lords terrace, but not everybody who wanted to attend could after that.

At one of the Savoy lunches I sat next to James Watson, one

of the scientists who realised that DNA had a double helix structure (his seminal paper with Francis Crick was published in *Nature* in 1953). Watson and Crick were awarded the Nobel Prize for Physiology or Medicine in 1962, along with Maurice Wilkins. It was an X-ray study of the DNA molecule obtained by Rosalind Franklin that led to their discovery, but only a maximum of three people can share a Nobel Prize.

At the end of his speech to the Parliamentary and Scientific Committee Watson said, "I am often asked why I play God. Well, someone has to play God", and he sat down. He was one of several Nobel Laureates whose autographs I collected during my Parliamentary career. The autographed menu card is in the 'diary' that I have deposited in the Bolton archives.

I held the positions of vice-president, deputy chairman, treasurer and vice-chairman of the Parliamentary and Scientific Committee, and I chaired the Editorial/Management Board of its quarterly journal *Science in Parliament* for five years.

In 1997, Dr Eric Wharton asked me whether I would help him to organise poster sessions for scientists in the early stages of their careers, in the Houses of Parliament. This had not happened before and it was proposed that they be run along the lines of the poster sessions held at scientific conferences. I first met Eric when he invited me to present The Magic of Chemistry at two venues in Oxfordshire during the first National Week of Science, Engineering and Technology ('SET7 – 7 days plus of SET'), 18-28 March 1994. He lived with his wife Sue at Chilton near Didcot and was very active in the Society of Chemical Industry (SCI).

The first of these sessions, under the brand name 'SET for Britain', was held in 1998 for physical scientists. Eric and his 'team' spread their wings and organised several sessions a year, involving not only physical scientists (mainly chemists and physicists) but also those engaged in research and development work in the life sciences and engineering. They raised enough money not only to mount the exhibitions of posters but also to provide refreshments and sizeable cash prizes, certificates of participation and medals, which were cast professionally in Birmingham.

These became very popular occasions, which were visited by many Members of Parliament, including Ministers. The trick was to have a photographer – Frank Dumbleton when I was involved – on hand to take a photograph of the student with their Member of Parliament, whom the student and organisers had invited upfront to attend the event. Eric's 'team' even organised several 'SET for Europe' events; the first of these was held in Heidelberg.

Sadly, Eric died in June 2007 (his funeral was on 14 June). When Sue Wharton suggested about 12 months later that we should try to continue to organise these events in Eric's memory, we got together a small organising committee under the umbrella of the Parliamentary and Scientific Committee, and 'SET for Britain' reappeared in March 2009, and has been repeated in March ever since. Each year the person presenting the best poster in the eyes of the judges now receives a special 'Wharton Medal'.

Dr Ian Gibson noted that, although 'think tanks' were popular with politicians, there wasn't even one acting in the STEM policy area. As a result Newton's Apple was launched on 16 October 2006 and I became a Trustee and Board Member (I retired in the summer of 2016). The main work today of Newton's Apple is to hold 'Newton's Heirs Science

Policy Seminars' around the country to which scientists are invited to listen to various presentations about the ever-increasing role that science plays in Parliament.

Paul Abbott, a teacher at Mount St Joseph's School in the Farnworth part of my constituency, had the bright idea of opening a Technical Innovation Centre (TIC), which was run rather like the Music Centre runs in Bolton. NESTA provided Paul with a grant of £100,000 to get the project off the ground and he managed to persuade the North West Regional Development Agency (NWRDA, abolished by the 2010 Coalition Government) to build a state-of-the-art building in Minerva Road, Farnworth, at a cost of £2.5 million; it was equipped with £500,000 worth of equipment. I was invited to be chairman of the Board and served in that capacity from 2004-2008. Schoolchildren came, designed or invented new products, and manufactured prototypes on some of the most advanced equipment available.

We decided to equip the building with an 'open' IT system, rather than become reliant on Microsoft or any other provider, and we bought expensive equipment such as one of the first 3D printers that built coloured objects. The building had a virtual planetarium, advanced workshop equipment, a flight simulator and various CAD packages available on computers in a computer suite. The two-storey TIC building had in its heart an engineering hall, with a heavy-lift crane fitted overhead. There was also an adaptable lecture theatre. Princess Anne formally opened the Technical Innovation Centre on 30 October 2006.

Paul's dream was that those using the TIC would be able to protect the intellectual property rights of their new designs or inventions which would, in the long term, start to provide

SCIENCE AND POLITICS: AN UNLIKELY MIXTURE

it with royalties to keep it running. For the first three years of its operation we managed to secure Government grants, and generated further income by making our facilities available for conferences and seminars. The Royal Bolton Hospital, next door to the TIC, used the building quite a lot. A small amount of money came in from industry and commerce too, but we were unable to persuade a major company to back this brave experiment, despite the fact that there was a lot of national and international interest in the idea. I started a series of lectures by distinguished scientists and engineers. The first presentation was given by Professor Colin Pillinger, mentioned above.

In 2008, it became almost impossible for the TIC Board to secure the £300,000 to £500,000 per annum necessary to sustain the project, and I persuaded the NWRDA to hand over their capital investment to Bolton Metropolitan Borough Council providing that they agreed to fund the project for a further three years. Bolton met that commitment but, sadly, cuts in local government funding under the 2010-2015 Coalition Government forced a change of use of the purpose-built TIC

With Paul Abbott.

building in 2011. Children still visit the centre to study science but not in the numbers originally planned.

With Mollie Temple, Vice-Chancellor of the University of Bolton, welcoming Science Minister Lord Sainsbury to the university to open the Innovation Zone in April 2003.

I became a Patron of the Catalyst Museum at Widnes, which is now an activity centre for children, the Catalyst Discovery Centre. Bryan Davies, chairman of its Board of Trustees, told me in March 2011 that Halton Borough Council had been forced to withdraw its support for Catalyst and a successful campaign was launched to keep it open.

I was a visiting Professor in the Department of Chemistry at the University of Liverpool from 2002 to 2007 and I joined the External Advisory Board in the School of Chemistry at the University of Manchester on 27 October 2006. On 26 April 2002, I opened the refurbished Robert Robinson Laboratories at the University of Liverpool.

While I was a Member of Parliament the Royal Society set up a 'pairing scheme', which links Members of Parliament with a Royal Society Fellow working in a university, either actually in their constituency or nearby. I was always linked with a Fellow working in a department at the University of Manchester. In addition, I supported a number of other organisations that promoted science education, such as STEMNET.

I was talking to Claire Curtis-Thomas (Member of Parliament for Crosby) at a SETPOINT event, held on 24 March 2006 in a hotel at Mellor, near Blackburn, when a man came over and stood with us. I half recognised him but I wasn't sure who he was, so I thought I had better introduce him to Claire. "Have you met Claire Curtis-Thomas MP?" I asked. "As a matter of fact I have", the man said, "I sleep with her most evenings". Claire was a chemical engineer before her election to Parliament in 1997 and used Parliament to promote the role of women in science and engineering. She didn't stand at the 2010 General Election.

NOTES

1. Baron (Jack) Lewis of Newnham died aged 86 on 17 July 2014.

2. Tony Benn died aged 89 on 14 March 2014.

3. Before I retired Dr Stephen Benn moved to the Society (now The Royal Society) of Biology Headquarters where he co-ordinates Parliamentary activity for them jointly with the RSC and the Institute of Physics (IoP).

4. Professor Sir Harry Kroto died aged 76 on 30 April 2016.

CHAPTER FOURTEEN

ALL-PARTY PARLIAMENTARY GROUPS (APPGS)

∽

I joined a number of the All-Party Parliamentary Groups (APPGs) when I was elected to Parliament and became an executive member of several of them. In my early days I was secretary to the University Group. From 1997 until 2009, I was treasurer to the Warm Homes Group, which campaigned on energy efficiency and fuel poverty. Sadly, there are probably almost as many people today, or maybe more, in fuel poverty than there were when the Labour Government came to power in 1997, although there was a period when the numbers were reduced substantially, mainly due to introduction of schemes such as the Warm Front Programme. The Warm Homes Group campaigned successfully for a reduction in VAT on energy-saving materials, such as cavity wall insulation and loft insulation. VAT on these materials was reduced from 17.5% to 5% by the Labour Government (the maximum reduction allowed under EU rules).

My interest in housing led me to accept the job of secretary to the All-Party Parliamentary Group on ALMOs (Arm's Length Management Organisations). These were created by the Labour Government to take over the management of council housing as an alternative to full stock transfer into a Housing Association (a policy created by the Tories). Bolton set up Bolton at Home and, when I retired from Parliament, several political colleagues tried to persuade me to apply to join the Board. However, the tenants voted in 2009 for Bolton at Home to become a registered social landlord in 2011. I have always opposed stock transfers of this kind.

Indeed, during my time in Parliament I was a supporter of the Defend Council Housing movement and I spoke at their meetings in the Houses of Parliament and at various conferences around the country. The main aim of this organisation was to prevent stock transfer of council housing.

I was also a member of the Moonlight Robbery Campaign, which campaigned for reform of the Housing Revenue Account (HRA) which local authorities used to manage council house stock. We were particularly concerned that those council house tenants who were paying rent were subsidising the Housing Benefit of those council house tenants who were in receipt of this benefit, both through payment of their rent and through the taxes they paid; in other words they suffered a 'double whammy', which we regarded as unfair. Just before the Labour Government lost power in 2010 the Housing Revenue Account structure was reformed.

My background in medicinal chemistry and my

involvement in the 'drugs debate' following the murder of Dillon Hull (see Chapter 3) left me in no doubt about joining the Drug Misuse Group. I was its chairman for ten years. One of the vice-chairmen was David Cameron, who became Prime Minister in 2010. He was genuinely concerned about the problems that people experience with addiction, and I hoped that his continued interest in this issue would lead to some new policies under the Tory Government, although I had my doubts because Parliament is part of an extremely conservative establishment in this country.

Very few politicians are prepared to express radical views in this policy area, but Paul Flynn (Member of Parliament for Newport East) is one of them. However, sadly, he was not taken seriously by our Ministers because his views came across as being rather aggressive to and critical of successive Labour Home Department Ministers who were responsible for this policy area.

In my first session in Parliament I decided that I would lobby Home Department Minister George Howarth (Member of Parliament for Knowsley North and Sefton East) with my views on the legalisation (preferably) or decriminalisation of cannabis. I was particularly concerned about the large number of young people who were receiving criminal records as a result of being caught with small amounts of cannabis on their person. In 1997 the cannabis on sale on the streets of Britain mainly came from Morocco through Spain, and its THC (tetrahydrocannabinol) content was quite low, in the region of 5%. George listened but nothing changed. I have never advocated the use of cannabis, but nor do I encourage people to smoke tobacco or drink excessive amounts of alcohol.

When Mo Mowlam was responsible for the Government's

With Howard Marks[1] at the Oxford Union (16 February 1998); *The Mail on Sunday* columnist Peter Hitchens is sat opposite).

drugs policy in the Cabinet Office she didn't hide the fact that her views on cannabis were similar to mine, and I wasn't surprised when Bob Ainsworth (Member of Parliament for Coventry North East), who had been responsible for the Government's drugs policy as a Home Department Minister, came out with his attack on the 'war on drugs' in a speech in the House of Commons on 16 December 2010.

When the Labour Government came to power in 1997 Keith Hellawell, a former Chief Constable in the West Riding of Yorkshire, was appointed as 'Drugs Zsar', with Mike Trace as his deputy. During the few years that Keith held this position he issued an Annual Report, which was debated in Parliament and allowed people like me to express our views.

In 1997, before the Labour Government set up the National Treatment Agency (NTA) for Substance Abuse, it was extremely difficult for an addict to get treatment in the

NHS for their addiction. Only 6% of heroin addicts were in treatment at that time. There were long waiting lists for treatment and many became long-term addicts or, in desperation, sought private treatment. A number of relatives of addicts and even addicts themselves pleaded with me in my early days as a Member of Parliament to get them onto a waiting list for treatment. Some died before they could get treatment. Street heroin is 'cut' with other substances to increase the profit of dealers. The buyer really doesn't have any idea of the strength of street heroin and overdosing is a common problem.

The most chaotic addicts were in and out of prison and committing a lot of crime to sustain their heroin habit. They lost their jobs, left their families and slept rough on the streets. In 1997, I met Dr Adrian Garfoot, who had set up the Laybourne Clinic in East London in 1990 to deal with the most chaotic heroin addicts. Between 1990 and 2000, this private clinic dealt with 1,200 patients. Adrian believed that it was necessary to treat his long-term addicts, many aged between 30 and 40, by injecting them with heroin or methadone. These addicts, who were all intravenous drug injectors, had developed a very high tolerance level to opiate drugs. His treatments were based, however, on harm reduction and he reduced the dose levels given to his patients. The recidivism rate at the Laybourne Clinic was 7%; elsewhere it was much higher. The majority of his patients were able to lead normal lives again and some of them became prominent members of society. Family life was restored and many of the addicts were able to work again.

Dr Garfoot's treatments were regarded as unconventional and he was reported to the Home Office who, in 1992, brought him before a drugs tribunal under the Misuse of Drugs Act 1971. He was charged with irresponsible prescribing. After hearing all the evidence his case was dismissed and he was allowed to continue practising.

After the Shipman murders the General Medical Council set up an Interim Orders Committee, and Dr Garfoot was brought before it on the same charge. I was one of the witnesses in his defence and was called before the GMC committee. In my opinion, the verdict was a foregone conclusion. It appeared to me that few if any of the doctors sitting around that table were aware of what was happening in the real world or had any experience of drug addiction. Adrian was referred to the Professional Conduct Committee of the GMC and struck off. He appealed to the Privy Council but lost his appeal. After Adrian was struck off at least three of his patients died because they could no longer get treatment from him.

The Laybourne Clinic struggled on for a few more months before it was forced to close. Because of Shipman's behaviour, about 20 doctors who had been treating long-term intravenous heroin users were also struck off. Probably a number of those deserved striking off, but that was not the case with Adrian, in my opinion. He returned to King's Lynn where his brother, the Reverend John Garfoot, was a Methodist preacher. John defended Adrian strongly throughout these difficult times. The Garfoots' Member of Parliament, Henry Bellingham (Member of Parliament for North West Norfolk), appealed to Ministers for help on the floor of the House on several occasions, and so did I, but we were unable to help reverse what we regarded as the unfair treatment of a caring doctor.

In the belief that bringing in more legislation to control the misuse of drugs merely displaces the problem, I opposed classification of khat as an illegal drug. Communities in Britain that originate from the Horn of Africa, such as the Somali community, chew the leaves of a tree that are flown in fresh on a daily basis from that region of the world and sold in shops that sell fruit and vegetables. The leaves of the tree that provide khat contain intoxicating chemicals called cathinones. Just as I retired, Parliament classified mephedrone, a cathinone which was sold on the internet, as a 'plant food'.[2]

In my capacity as chairman of the All-Party Parliamentary Drug Misuse Group I was invited to speak all over the country, at the Oxford and Durham Unions, at national and international conferences, as well as at individual events, such as a debate that the North West Rotarians held at Rivington Barn, near Bolton, on 4 October 2001. I wrote many articles on the subject, including one for the *Bolton Evening News*.

I remember speaking at the launch of a book, *Drugs and the Party Line* by Kevin Williamson, in the Jubilee Room in Parliament at which Irvine Welsh, author of *Trainspotting*, who wrote the foreword for the book, and Howard Marks ('Mr Nice') also spoke.[1] I came to know Howard quite well; we appeared on the same 'bill' several times at the Oxford and Durham Unions. On 12 February 1998 at the Oxford Union, he stood up next to me to lead the debate in favour of legalisation of cannabis, when a spliff dropped out of his pocket at my feet. Fortunately, I saw it drop to the floor, so I put my foot on it before Chief Superintendent Brian MacKenzie, President of the Chief Superintendents Association (now Lord MacKenzie), who was sitting opposite to us, could see it. Paul Betts, the father of Leah Betts, who was alleged to be the first death caused by ecstasy, was one of our opponents that evening. Our side won the debate by 293 votes to 198.

Howard was a very charismatic character who wrote about his colourful life at Oxford and as one of the world's leading smugglers of cannabis in his time in a book by the same name as the recent film, *Mr Nice* (released in 2009). Judy, his wife, has written a sequel, *Mr Nice and Mrs Marks,* published in 2006. Howard was a raconteur, a travel writer and a popular DJ in clubs. On my first appearance with him at the Oxford Union the debating hall was packed to capacity. The students mobbed him after our debate to get him to sign copies of his book which they were thrusting at him.

I was billed to appear with Howard at the Durham Union on 2 February 2007 (we had debated the legalisation of cannabis there before, on 6 October 2000, when *The Mail on Sunday* correspondent Peter Hitchens was one of our main opponents) but there had been some kind of misunderstanding and he didn't turn up, which left me to put the case for legalisation of cannabis against an opposition whose main speaker was Jan Berry, chair of the Police Federation.

In May 2001, *Mixmag* magazine gave me the number one spot, ahead of Oona King (then Member of Parliament for Bethnal Green and Bow; she was defeated by George Galloway), as the Member of Parliament who had the greatest interest in the misuse of drugs and related issues at that time.

The Proprietary Association of Great Britain (PAGB) is the trade association which represents all the companies that produce over-the-counter (OTC) medicines. About 100 products on sale on the shelves of chemist's shops contain the anti-congestant materials ephedrine and pseudoephedrine, and the PAGB brought to my attention that the Government were proposing to make them all Prescription Only Medicines (POMS). The Government received reports that there had been a small number of cases of conversion of these materials into the illicit street drug methamphetamine.

The PAGB suggested that the Drug Misuse and Primary Care and Public Health APPGs hold a one-day inquiry into this proposal. Dr Howard Stoate (Member of Parliament for Dartford), a General Practitioner and chairman of the Primary Care and Public Health APPG, and I questioned various key witnesses and produced a report that suggested that the proposal should not be proceeded with, and it wasn't, much to the relief of pharmacists.

I spoke to a person from the Medicines and Healthcare products Regulatory Agency (MHRA), which was responsible for the proposal to make ephedrine and pseudoephedrine POMS, who admitted that they unaware of all the evidence until we ran our inquiry and produced our report. I wasn't aware, for example, that the pilots and cabin crew of the world's passenger aircraft regularly use these medicines to prevent problems with congestion of their nasal passages in flight.

Although I was a Member of the Commonwealth Parliamentary Association (CPA) during all of my 13 years in Parliament and attended most of their annual meetings, I only joined one of their delegations to a Commonwealth country. In September 2005, I led a cross-party delegation to Jamaica, where we stayed in the Pegasus Hotel in Kingston. Although we were there to discuss agriculture, tourism and relations between Britain and Jamaica in general, I was very keen to discuss the illicit drug trade with Jamaica's officials and politicians.

Of course, the sugar and connected rum trade and the banana trade are important income earners for Jamaica. We were taken to see how bad coastal erosion had become in parts of the island and to coconut groves which 'yellow leaf' disease had wiped out across the island as well as to banana plantations. A trip to the Blue Mountains and the Mavis Bank Coffee Estate allowed us to see another important product of Jamaica being grown and processed.

At the time of our visit Kingston was the homicide capital of the world, with 50 deaths annually per 1,000 of population in a small island of only 2.5 million people. Corruption was endemic. Columbian cocaine was being shipped to the USA and Europe from Jamaica, and the UN and the UK Government were attempting to stop this trade. Drive-by shootings were a regular occurrence and people in the worst affected housing districts of Kingston dug trenches along their streets in an attempt to stop this violence.

At Schiphol Airport in Amsterdam I had seen evidence of the fact that there could be 20-30 'mules' on each flight coming in from Jamaica and the Caribbean rim countries. Several UK police officers were embedded in the Jamaican Constabulary Force at that time.

We held discussions with our High Commissioner in Jamaica and his staff, with the Governor General, with the President of the Senate, with the Speaker of the House of Representatives, with Bruce Golding MP and members of the then opposition Jamaican Labour Party (actually Conservatives), with the Prime Minister, the Rt. Hon. P. J. Patterson QC, who indicated that he would stand down at the next General Election, and with various Ministers of the Peoples National Party, including the Hon. Portia Simpson

MP, who became one of Jamaica's Prime Ministers. Both Houses of this bicameral Parliament share the same small chamber in the Parliament Building for their meetings.

One of the most interesting visits for me was to the headquarters of the Caribbean Regional Drug Enforcement Training Centre at Twickenham Park, St Catherine, which was UN and UK Government funded. Law Enforcement Officers from other Caribbean Islands were trained there, along with those from the Jamaican security forces, by people from Britain and elsewhere. However, I wondered whether all this effort would merely in the end displace Jamaica's problem to elsewhere in the world. Shortly after our visit I became aware that the Columbian drug barons were exporting their product to several West African countries for the European trade. Judging by the havoc created in Mexico in recent years, they diverted a lot of their trade to the USA overland through the Central American States too.

My interest in the misuse of drugs also persuaded me to join the Hepatology Group when it was launched in the presence of George Best, Alex, his wife, and Professor Roger Williams, the surgeon who had given George his new liver. George became our first Patron but, tragically, he died some months later, on 25 November 2005, after he had wrecked his second liver with alcohol as well.

I was vice-chairman of the Hepatology Group until I retired. My interest in the Group came partly from the fact that the Hepatitis C virus was killing a lot of intravenous drug users and that many people were carrying the virus without realising it. Our second Patron was Anita Roddick, the inspiration behind Body Shop, who came to a Hepatology Group meeting on 20 February 2007. She contracted

Hepatitis C through blood transfusions that she received during child birth in 1971 and, sadly, was diagnosed too late to be saved. She died aged 64 on 10 September 2007.

I also became interested in hepatology as a result of one of my Farnworth constituents, David Fielding, coming to one of my Advice Surgeries. I remember how yellow David looked on that day. I had seen that skin colour before when my best friend Derrick Pickervance had died with jaundice. Obviously, David's liver was ceasing to function. He explained that both he and his brother Brian, who were haemophiliacs, had contracted the Hepatitis C virus through NHS blood transfusions. Brian also contracted the HIV/Aids virus and died in 1990 as a result, aged 46. David contracted both Hepatitis B and C from contaminated blood in 1981.

With Lord (Alf) Morris and others presenting a 'carpet of lilies' to 10 Downing Street (each lily represented a person who died from a blood transfusion contaminated with the Hepatitis C virus)

SCIENCE AND POLITICS: AN UNLIKELY MIXTURE

With George Best, first Patron of the Hepatology APPG.

Just before Christmas in the year I saw David he was taken into Manchester Infirmary, where he was expected to die. He and his partner decided to get married in hospital before he passed away, then 'Jimmy's' Hospital in Leeds asked Manchester Infirmary to rush him over there for a liver transplant. What a Christmas present, a second life for David (and his wife and children).

A lot of the blood used by the NHS in the 1960s and 1970s was imported into the UK from the USA, where prisoners were paid to donate it. A lot of them were intravenous drug users spreading the virus in gaols through sharing syringes.

I became one of the main campaigners on the Labour benches, putting the case across that better compensation should be paid to people like David Fielding, or their relatives in case of death. I worked very closely with Lord (Alf) Morris in the House of Lords, who was responsible for setting up the Archer Inquiry, to which both David Fielding and I gave evidence (I gave my evidence in June 2007). I was a Member too of the Haemophilia APPG and became its secretary on 10 December 2009; I remained so until I retired in 2010.

In 2010, Lord Morris got a Private Member's Bill through in the House of Lords, which he wanted me to adopt in the House of Commons. Effectively, it implemented the recommendations of Lord Archer,[3] the most controversial of which was on the question of compensation. I was drawn number one in the Private Members' Bills Ballot in 2009, so I consulted the Public Health Minister, Gillian Merron (Member of Parliament for Lincoln), before deciding what action to take. She was clearly going to object to Alf's Bill, if I decided to take it forward. In any case, it was a very short Parliamentary session and I wanted to adopt a Bill which was likely to be successful. Instead, I decided to steer through the Mortgage Repossessions (Tenants Protection etc.) Bill (see Chapter 7) which received Royal Assent on 8 April 2010.

Until 2011, those who contracted the HIV/Aids virus received better compensation than those who contracted the Hepatitis C virus from contaminated blood. On 21 December 2009, Paul Goggins (Member of Parliament for Wythenshawe and Sale East) and I went along with a group of haemophiliacs and their relatives to see Health Secretary Andy Burnham at his Leigh constituency office. I believe we convinced Andy to take a serious interest in this issue but, a few months later, Labour lost the 2010 General Election.

The main point that we got across was that, at the very least, all victims of contaminated blood should be treated on a level playing field; there should not be differentiation between those who contracted only the Hepatitis C virus and those who contracted either the HIV/Aids virus or both. As a result of our meeting, Gillian Merron made an announcement that the Government would bring forward a review of the Skipton Fund from 2014 to 2010.

Thirty-six-year-old Andrew Marsh of London sought a judicial review in the High Court after the Government refused to implement most of the recommendations of the Archer Report. The Government refused to pay compensation on the same basis as in Ireland on the basis that the Irish blood transfusion service was found to be at fault, which was not the case in the UK. Mr Justice Holman ruled in April 2010 that the Government's approach "has been, and remains, infected by error".

Backbenchers persuaded the 2010 Conservative Government to allow them to choose some business that is taken in Government time. One of the first substantive debates was on the issue of contaminated blood. Whilst the substantive motion over the question of compensation was voted down on 14 October 2010, the Minister of Health, Anne Milton (Member of Parliament for Guildford, formerly a nurse), promised to take the issue away, consider it and report back to the House before the end of 2010. A substantial number of Conservative Members spoke in favour of the substantive motion. Successive Governments have refused to accept liability for the contaminated blood but, as in the Irish Republic, compensation can be paid by Government without an acceptance of liability.

The Secretary of State for Health, Andrew Lansley, in a statement to the House of Commons on 10 January 2011 announced that the sum of £25,000 paid from the Skipton Fund to those who had contracted the Hepatitis C virus in England would be doubled and that this would apply retrospectively to those who had reached Stage 2 (serious damage to the liver or requiring a liver transplant).

The annual payment for those with the Hepatitis C virus will be £12,800 in future and those who contracted both viruses from contaminated blood will receive twice this amount. He also announced that a charitable trust would be set up to help victims of contaminated blood or their families to receive financial help when they get into difficulties, and that £300,000 would be set aside for three years for the counselling of victims should they require it. Free prescriptions were also announced, along with posthumous payments to the families of those who had died before 29 August 2003 of up to £70,000 (£20,000 for 'Stage 1 victims' and a further £50,000 for 'Stage 2 victims'). In total it was estimated that this would increase payments by £100-130 million for the Hepatitis C victims of contaminated blood.

Whilst David Fielding welcomed most of these proposals (see *Bolton News* dated 12 January 2011) he felt that the lump sums were still inadequate to provide for families in case of death, for example to provide a home for a surviving wife and children.

I joined the Chemical Industry APPG, which is supported mainly by Members of Parliament with substantial chemical plants or research laboratories in their constituencies, and became its chairman. Later, another chairman, Dr Ashok Kumar (Member of Parliament for Middlesbrough South and East Cleveland), became Parliamentary Private Secretary to Hilary Benn, and he persuaded me to become chairman again in his place. At that stage the Group was not meeting as often as it should have been. It has always been supported by the Chemical Industries Association (CIA), so I decided to approach their new Chief Executive, Steve Elliot, with a view to reinvigorating the Group. I suggested that we also try to involve representatives of the RSC, the Society of Chemical Industry (SCI), the Institution of Chemical Engineers (IChemE) and other organisations associated with the industry, and we did. We relaunched the APPG on 7 December 2006. My last Adjournment Debate in Parliament was on 'The UK Chemical Industry', on 30 March 2010.

Tragically, Dr Ashok Kumar, who was a chemical engineer, died just weeks away from the 2010 General Election, on 15 March. I discovered that he had been having treatment for cardiovascular disease for some time. Ashok worked hard to retain his Middlesbrough and East Cleveland seat, which he won in 1997. Prior to that he had won the Langbaurgh by-election in 1991, but lost the seat to a Conservative at the 1992 General Election.

My other executive positions in APPGs were as secretary to the Britain-Palestine Group, vice-chairman of the Group on Pakistan and secretary to the Fairs and Show Grounds Group. In Parliament there is an All-Party Parliamentary Group for nearly every country on earth. I joined the India, Pakistan and Kashmir Groups, as well as several other APPGs that represented the interests of other countries in the Middle East, such as Jordan, Qatar and Bahrain. I was active too in the APPGs on the MV *Derbyshire*, Vaccine Damaged Children, Fireworks, the Market Industry, Non-Profit-Making Members' Clubs, Pharmaceutical Industry, NW Pharmaceutical Industry, Pharmacy, Trade Unions, and Dying Well Naturally, and I attended a lot of other APPG meetings as and when I thought fit.

For the Special Interest Group of Municipal Authorities (Outside London) (SIGOMA), I was the Executive Member for Greater Manchester, and I was the NW Executive Member for Neil Turner's (Member of Parliament for Wigan) 'PCT Below Target Group of Labour MPs'. This Group lobbied successive Secretaries of State for Health to speed up the redistribution of resources within the NHS, so that the needs of areas where people had the poorest health were met. Between Farnworth in my constituency and the more affluent area of Heaton/Lostock in the Bolton West constituency there was a 10-15 year gap in life expectancy which, in my opinion, was unacceptable. Dr John Reid, when he was Secretary of State for Health, made the most progress for us in narrowing the gap between the richest and poorest parts of England. SIGOMA campaigned similarly for the Government to aim its local authority grants to areas of greatest need.

When a Conservative Government is elected it is ruthless at shifting grants to local authorities who regularly return Conservative Members of Parliament; the Westminsters and Wandsworths were well looked after, as well as the shire counties, under the previous Conservative Government. Labour Governments have been far too slow in meeting the needs of our poorest communities.

Because I was interested in anything to do with the sea I joined the MV *Derbyshire* APPG, which had been campaigning on behalf of the MV *Derbyshire* Family Association to open a full public inquiry into the sinking of this merchant vessel. The most active of its Members were Liverpool Members, such as Maria Eagle (Member of Parliament for Garston and Halewood), who chaired this APPG until she became a Minister, and Eddie O'Hara (Member of Parliament for Knowsley South) who also chaired this APPG.

The MV *Derbyshire* sank in the South China Sea during Typhoon Orchid on the evening of 9/10 September 1980, with the loss of 44 lives, including the wives of two officers, before it could send out a distress call. It was registered in Liverpool, where many of its crew and their relatives lived. The *Derbyshire* was a single screw ore-bulk-oil (an OBO) combination carrier, carrying iron ore from Canada to Japan, and was built on the River Tees by Swan Hunter, one of six sister ships, and handed over to Bibby Tankers on 10 June 1976 (originally named the *Liverpool Bridge* but renamed by Bibbys in 1978). The ship was twice the weight of RMS *Titanic*.

Between the loss of the *Derbyshire* in the autumn of 1980 and August 1998, 1,632 seafarers lost their lives in bulk carrier incidents alone. Initially, the focus had been on the structure of the MV *Derbyshire* and it sister ships and the possible cracking of 'frame 65'. A formal investigation under Mr Gerald Darling QC reported in March 1988 that the cause of the disaster was not clear, but the report was critical of the ship's crew. The MV *Derbyshire* Family Association, with Paul Lambert as its chairman (he lost his 19-year-old brother Peter in the disaster), pressed the Government for a full inquiry.

Six weeks after the MV *Derbyshire* sank a Japanese tanker spotted an empty lifeboat belonging to the ship and an upwelling of oil was also discovered. In March 1994, the International Transport Workers Federation raised money for the wreck to be located on 8 June 1994 by Oceaneering Technologies. This was followed by a groundbreaking survey of the ship, which lay two and a half miles down on the bed of the South China Sea.

Marine engineers at the University of Harvard developed the open frame submarine technology that allowed the first photographs of RMS *Titanic* to be obtained after Robert Ballard's team located the wreck in September 1985. They used the same submersible to obtain 135,774 photographs of the *Derbyshire* wreck which allowed the MV *Derbyshire* Family Association and the MV *Derbyshire* APPG to persuade the then Secretary of State for Environment, Transport and Rural Affairs (DETR) and Deputy Prime Minister, John Prescott (Member of Parliament for Hull East), to open a full public inquiry under Mr Justice Colman to consider the new evidence.

The ship's crew were exonerated of blame; it was found that 'green water' had crashed down onto the forward of the nine hatch covers and smashed it, leading to rapid ingress of seawater throughout the ship, which essentially exploded into an estimated 2,500 separate pieces. Prior to the main incident there had been water entry into forward spaces through pipe fittings and unprotected ventilators on deck, which had lowered the bow of the ship in the water.

(Left to right) Reverend Peter McGrath, Paul Lambert MBE and Captain Dave Ramwell, all officers of the MV *Derbyshire* Family Association, at the opening of the MV *Derbyshire* exhibition, Maritime Museum, Liverpool on 7 September 2012.

MV *Liverpool Bridge*, which was renamed MV *Derbyshire*.

I highlighted the facts about the sinking of the MV *Derbyshire* in an Adjournment Debate on 25 June 2002 and suggested that the hold covers of these bulk carriers were below strength. They have been strengthened since.

Paul Lambert was awarded an MBE by the Queen for his efforts; he now lives in Huyton, Liverpool and I am still in touch with him and Captain Dave Ramwell, who also played a key role in this story. Their efforts and the efforts of many others who took an interest in the sinking of the MV *Derbyshire* and its sister ships led to major improvements in the safety of ships, and I am proud that I played a minor role in this story.[4]

Competition in the shipping industry has driven costs downwards. Many ships sailing the high seas today are rust buckets, their crews are poorly trained and they are badly paid. It has been common practice in recent decades for British-owned ships to 'flag out' in foreign ports to keep costs down. John Prescott, when he was Secretary of State at the DETR, was successful in bringing in measures that made 'flagging in' ships in Britain more attractive again.

For centuries General Lighthouse Authorities (GLAs; Trinity House is by far the most important) have been protecting seafarers from danger around the 20,000 miles of British and Irish coastlines. They provide all the lighthouses and buoys that warn ship's crews of the dangers they face and maintain these facilities all year round in all kinds of weather. In order to carry out this work they collect 'light dues' from the shipping that enters British and Irish ports. Whenever there is a proposal to increase these light dues, the ships' owners protest strongly. Since the advent of navigation through the use of global positioning systems (GPS) these protests have grown stronger. However, shipping has been relying on one satellite until recently. Until GPS has proved itself and back-up satellites have been made available it makes sense to maintain the traditional navigational aids.

Trinity House has reduced its costs considerably. It has sold off assets and automated lighthouses and buoys, mainly through solarisation. I defended the continuing collection of light dues by the GLAs on more than one occasion in Parliament. When I spoke in an Adjournment Debate on 2 June 2009 there had been no increase in light dues since 1993 and, in the ten years preceding this debate, Trinity House had reduced its cost by 50% in ten years.

As a Member of the Market Industry APPG I constantly heard complaints about so-called pedlars, actually illegal street traders, stealing the trade of market and street traders and small and medium sized businesses, and I decided to see if I could change the Pedlars Acts of 1871 and 1881, which were clearly being abused.

I highlighted the problem by presenting a Private Member's Bill under the Ten Minute Rule on 21 February 2007. I also used Early Day Motions and written and oral Parliamentary Questions to bring the seriousness of this problem to the attention of successive Ministers, and I wrote to them and sought meetings with them. There was a lot of support for what I was attempting to achieve across the House.

I worked very closely with Graham Wilson, Chief Executive of the National Association of British Market Authorities, and the National Market Traders Federation, but I also had the support of the Institute of Licensing, the Local Government Association, the Association of Town Centre Managers (I was a Member of the Town Centre Management APPG), and the Association of Chief Police Officers (ACPO).

A pedlar, who is expected to trade goods whilst on the move, is granted permission to trade in any local authority area across England or Wales by the local police force which issues a pedlar's certificate at a cost of only £12.50. One of the problems is that there is no consistency in the appearance of these certificates, and they are easy to forge. I gathered that police forces were keen to lose this function to local authorities, but this is a move opposed by legal pedlars.

When a person is caught trading as a pedlar without one of these certificates, or is not conforming to the Victorian Acts of Parliament, and they are taken to court, the fines are so paltry that those prosecuted regard them as a business expense, and they carry on trading illegally. Genuine pedlars believe that the cost of these certificates should rise significantly and that the courts should issue higher fines for illegal trading.

Illegal pedlars stand still in areas where there is a high footfall of potential buyers of their goods, but the police and trading standards officers find it extremely time consuming and difficult to provide the evidence in court that a person has been caught illegally trading. Many of these illegal street traders have barrows and stands that are extremely difficult to move and in some areas they obstruct the free passage of shoppers. To avoid being prosecuted they move a few yards one way, then back again. This is particularly the case in popular tourist spots such as in the Shambles in the City of York.

In Section 2 and Schedule 4 of the Local Government (Miscellaneous Provisions) Act 1982 provision is made for local authorities to designate streets in the centre of towns and cities where street traders can sell goods from fixed pitches, providing that they have procured a street trading licence, which can cost several hundreds of pounds. It is those street traders who are not prepared to pay the high cost of these licences that illegally trade as pedlars and at which my Pedlars (Street Trading Regulation) Bill was aimed. One of the main provisions of my Bill allowed those enforcing the legislation to confiscate the illegal street trader's goods, which is not the case with the present legislation.

A rising number of local authorities have successfully sought Private Acts of Parliament to deal with illegal street traders, but most of these Acts ban pedlars from working in their areas, even legally, and are vigorously opposed by legal pedlars. When a large town or city enforces one of these Acts of Parliament the illegal street traders are merely displaced to other local authority areas, often to smaller authorities who cannot afford the £100,000-£200,000 that it costs to employ a Parliamentary Agent to steer a Private Act of Parliament through both Houses of Parliament.

After I presented my Pedlars (Street Trading Regulations) Bill to the House of Commons on 21 February 2007, Christopher Chope (Member of Parliament for Christchurch) rose to speak in opposition to it. I tried on several of the following sitting Fridays to get a Second Reading for my Bill at the end of the day's business, but he was always there to shout 'object!' when the clerk read out the title of my Bill and I had formally moved that it be given a Second Reading. Consequently, despite widespread support for my Bill across the chamber of the House of Commons, it failed to reach its Committee Stage. Ironically, the Member of Parliament for Bournemouth, next door to Christchurch, was in favour of my Bill. Bournemouth later applied for a Private Act of Parliament, along with a number of other local authorities, including Manchester, which now enforce their Private Acts of Parliament against illegal street traders but not against pedlars trading legally.

In the 2007-2008 session of Parliament I tried to get my Bill through the House of Commons as a Presentation Bill, but Christopher Chope again prevented it from proceeding into its Committee Stage. However, I had not wasted my time. I persuaded the Parliamentary Under-Secretary of State at the Department of Business, Enterprise, and Regulatory Reform (DBERR), Gareth Thomas (Member of Parliament for Harrow), that the existing law was being abused, and he authorised a research project, which was conducted by researchers from the University of Durham. Their report was very informative. This measure brought many pedlars together to form a body representing their views, and I had the pleasure of attending one of the Durham consultation meetings with them in London. They were an interesting group of people.

Following publication of the Durham report I expected the Government to bring in legislation, primary or secondary, to deal with the existing abuse and do away with the need for so many local authorities to waste taxpayers' money, but a General Election prevented that from happening. In my opinion, not all local authorities need legislation but those that do should be able to adopt legislation by resolution of their Council.

For my efforts NABMA presented me with their Award for Outstanding Achievement on 12 December 2007 (actually awarded in September). I had moved the debate on considerably.

Under the chairmanship of Ian Stewart (Member of Parliament for Eccles) the Vaccine Damaged People APPG, of which I was a member, campaigned successfully for improvements in the compensation paid to this group of people. My interest in this APPG arose from the mother of a vaccine damaged child, who lived in Great Lever, approaching me for help.

I have already dealt with my work as secretary to the Britain-Palestine APPG and as a Member of the APPG on Kashmir in Chapter 11.

NOTES

1. Howard Marks died on 10 April 2016.

2. Against the advice of its Advisory Council on the Misuse of Drugs (ACMD) Parliament announced the classification of khat as a Class C drug on 3 July 2013; it is now an illegal substance.

3. Lord Archer of Sandwell died on 14 June 2012 and Lord Morris of Manchester died on 12 August 2012.

4. I was present at the Maritime Museum in Liverpool on Friday 7 September 2012 when it opened its exhibition on the MV *Derbyshire* story.

CHAPTER FIFTEEN

OPENINGS, VISITS, RECEPTIONS AND LOBBIES

⇁

Members of Parliament are occasionally invited to open new or refurbished buildings. One of my first engagements was to open the refurbished Pack Horse Hotel in Nelson Square for Gordon Macdonald (Macdonald Hotels also acquired the Last Drop Village and the Egerton House Hotel; they sold all three hotels on within a few years) on 25 September 1997. I thought how nice it would be to see the plaque on the wall in the foyer on each of my future visits to the hotel, but when I visited the hotel again just a few weeks after this event an oil painting was hanging where the plaque had been.

I opened Hawthorne House on the site of the Royal Bolton Hospital on Monday 6 October 1997 as a place of rehabilitation for people who had suffered serious mental illness. When Cllr Frank White was Mayor of Bolton in 2006 he reopened Hawthorne House as a home for older women with dementia. The Royal Bolton Hospital also invited me to open their new CAMHS (Children and Adolescent Mental Health Service) building on 12 December 2001.

On 25 November 1997 I presented an Investor in People Award to Danisco Pack at their headquarters in Plodder Lane, Farnworth.

In late November 1998 I reopened Alderbank in Kearsley, which had undergone a £300,000 transformation to rehabilitate elderly people in a pioneering scheme. On 12 June 1999 I opened the Willows Community Centre and, on 16 July 1999, I cut the first sod on Derby Street for commencement of work on the first bus corridor in Bolton, the Leigh/Atherton/Bolton bus corridor, with a 'silver' engraved spade.

Age Concern gave me the privilege of opening their new Farnworth Learning and Resources Centre at the corner of Queen Street and Cross Street on 6 September 2000 and, on 26 October 2000 I presented British Turntable Co. Ltd. with an ISO9001 award.

On 17 November 2000 I opened the Pikes Lane Health Centre on Wigan Road accompanied by one of its patients, a very shy little boy whose name is unforgettable – Jack Daniels.

The Labour Government completely transformed the infrastructure of most of our universities. Therefore, I was very pleased when the University of Liverpool invited me to open some new laboratories for my former Salford University colleague, Professor Stanley M. Roberts, in their Robert Robinson Laboratory on 26 April 2002.

I felt privileged to be invited on 5 August 2002 to present

Cutting the first sod for the first bus lane in Bolton on Derby Street on 16 July 1999 with chairman of the Greater Manchester Passenger Transport Committee Cllr Guy Harkin.

the badminton medals for the Manchester Commonwealth Games at the Bolton Arena.

When I was elected to Parliament Mytham Road Primary School in Little Lever village had two demountable classrooms at the back of the school which were in a lamentable condition. It was one of my manifesto commitments to have them replaced. After the election of the Labour Government they were replaced with a brick-built extension to the school. In 1997 there were few computers in either primary or secondary schools. In 2010 our schools were very well equipped with IT equipment. Mytham Road Primary School kindly invited me to open their new computer suite on 30 April 2004. On 24 November 2006 I opened another extension, which provided a reception area for the school.

The New Bury Residents' Association invited me to attend the opening of their new Community Centre in St James's Street on 23 May 2001. They tried to get a celebrity to open the building, such as steeplejack Fred Dibnah or comedian Peter Kay. The following is an extract from the *Bolton Evening News* article which appeared on 4 May 2001:

"John McDermott, the Association's publicity officer, said: "We have already asked Peter Kay and Fred Dibnah but they are both very busy. We have got Dr Brian Iddon, MP for Bolton South East, coming down but we want a local celebrity to attend to give it a bit more glamour.""

In the end I opened the building. I opened an Urban Care Centre at 84 Campbell Street, Farnworth on 30 April 2002.

The three Bolton Members of Parliament opened a new dialysis unit on the site of the Royal Bolton Hospital on 23 May 2003. Although managed by the Royal Bolton Hospital, the unit is an outpost of the main unit at the Royal Salford Hospital (formerly Hope Hospital). It saves some of our dialysis patients from travelling the longer distances they had to travel before these local facilities were provided.

We attended several openings at the Royal Bolton Hospital over the 13 years of the Labour Government and I spent quite a lot of time lobbying for improvements there, especially for the conversion of all the old Nightingale wards into modern wards (completed by 2010) and for a new maternity and children's services unit, which opened in 2011.

I opened a centre at 61B Bradford Street for The Haulgh Community Partnership on 12 October 2003. Bolton Wanderers FC mascot Lofty the Lion and I opened a new kitchen that had been provided for Greenfold Special School by Asda, Farnworth and their Parent Teachers Association on 6 October 2004.

I opened the refurbished Job Centre in Farnworth on 10 June 2005 and on 1 July 2006 I opened the Summer Fair and a new extension at St Simon's and St Jude's Primary School in Great Lever.

I cut the first sod for the construction of a Children's Assessment and Observation Unit (adjacent to the Accident and Emergency Department) at the Royal Bolton Hospital on 5 January 2007 and Health Minister Beverley Hughes opened the unit on 3 December 2007. On the occasion of their 7th anniversary in Bolton, Labour Ready (Manchester Road) invited me to open their Construction Industry Skills Certification Scheme (a Construction Industry Training Board – CITB – qualification) Test Centre on 22 June 2007.

In a visit to hear about the work of the Bolton Substance Misuse Group at Bentley House on 23 May 2008 I opened an office for the Bolton Users Group (BUG).

I opened a Bakers, Food and Allied Trade Union Learning Centre at Park Cakes in Hulton Park Ward on 30 January 2009, an Evans Business Centre on Manchester Road on 8 May 2009 and 33 Victoria Square, Bolton, the first drop-in centre in Greater Manchester for those suffering from mental illness and their carers, on 9 October 2009.

My penultimate 'opening' engagement was to open a community centre at Prestolee C. of E. Primary School in Kearsley Ward on 25 July 2009. The residents of Stoneclough, Prestolee and Ringley villages campaigned for a very long time for the Council to provide community facilities to serve their villages. Bolton at Home provided Stoneclough Action 2000 and Beyond (SATAB) with temporary facilities in Crompton Street, Prestolee, which were well used by the older people and youth of this area. Several housing developments occurred in the area, the largest of which was on the site of the former Fletcher's paper mill on the A667 Bolton to Bury road. The Section 106 money from these developments was set aside for the building of a community hall.

Initially, the plan was to build the hall on a plot of land which the builder reserved on the former Fletcher's paper mill site fronting the A667 Bolton to Bury road. It was the size of a pair of semi-detached houses. However, council officials persuaded the residents to agree to build a dual use hall attached to Prestolee School instead. During the school day this hall is a gymnasium for the school and the hall is available for use by the community when it is not needed by the school. At least that is the theory. Sadly this agreement proved difficult to operate, at least in the beginning.

Like other Members of Parliament, I opened a number of events, presented prizes and certificates, both at school and college award evenings and in industry, I toured a lot of shop floors in industry, gave a lot of speeches at all kinds of constituency events, supported many charities both in the constituency and in the Palace of Westminster, and I met thousands of people to listen to their views.

I was invited to be a Patron of the Bury and Bolton Kid's Club Network and the Catalyst interactive science centre at Widnes.

The first weeks of a new session of Parliament are extremely busy ones, especially for new Members. It is impossible to accept all the invitations that arrive to attend meetings, lobbies, lunches or dinners and receptions. Within days I had been to receptions at the Speaker's House, at 10 Downing Street, at the Royal Society, to meet with representatives of the Royal College of Nursing, and to meet the press including a meeting with Sky Broadcasting staff in the Banqueting House, the only remaining part of Whitehall Palace, adjacent to the Ministry of Defence on Whitehall, which is a very impressive building.

Hull University held a reception too for all Members of Parliament who had graduated there. Labour colleagues John Prescott, Chris Mullin, Roy Hattersley, Tom Watson, David Hanson (whose birthday falls on the same day as mine – 5th July) and Kevin McNamara graduated at Hull.

Some lunches and dinners that Members of Parliament attend are annual events, such as the Showmen's Guild Annual Lunch, usually held in a venue close to the Houses of Parliament, and the Annual Pharmacy Dinner which is attended by around 1,000 people. The showmen or pharmacists from Bolton and the surrounding area invited us to sit on their tables. These were very pleasant occasions providing we were not disturbed by the division bells. I remember one Annual Pharmacy Dinner, held in the Queen Elizabeth II Conference Hall which lies on Victoria Street between the Methodist Hall and the Supreme Court, at which I got almost nothing to eat along with about 70 other Members of Parliament.

I managed to consume the cold starter, consisting of goat's cheese on a bed of rocket (or grass, as I call it) before the division bells rang. In our lobby I discovered our guest speaker for the evening, Minister for Public Health Hazel Blears. I was rather hoping that she would be speaking while we were voting. No such luck. As we arrived back she spoke, then the main course (guinea fowl) was laid on the table just as the division bells rang again. As we arrived back the sweet course was laid on the table just as the division bells went yet again. After that I suggested that the pharmacists move their dinner to a night when the House was not sitting (it changed to Wednesdays at 8.00 p.m.), which also allowed them to change their venue to the Lancaster Gate Hotel.

I always enjoyed my visits to schools. Shortly after my election to Parliament the UNICEF 'Put It to Your MP' campaign prompted me to write to every primary and secondary school in my constituency with a request for them to invite me in for a Question and Answer session, and many did, so I repeated this exercise in the late summer of every year after that. Some primary schools never invited me to visit them in all of the 13 years that I served as a Member of Parliament, and I often wondered why. All the secondary schools were keen for me to engage with them in their citizenship agenda.

One of the departments that the Labour Government expanded in the Houses of Parliament was the Education Unit. They can supply booklets to Members for visits to primary or secondary schools and they run interesting visits to the Houses of Parliament for schoolchildren.

Each year students studying politics or economics at Bolton Sixth Form College came down to Westminster for a guided tour on the Line of Route, a Question and Answer session with Bolton's three Members of Parliament and/or a visit to the Strangers Gallery in the House of Commons.

In the early days of the 1997 Labour Government I was invited to borrow three books from our Library Service, choose a good story and go to as many primary schools as possible to read it, to launch the Government's Literacy

Scheme. I read my story before the whole assembly of pupils at St John's C. of E. School in Church Road, on the Farnworth/Kearsley border. When I finished the Headmaster asked the school whether they had any questions to pose to their Member of Parliament. They had obviously been prepared for this. An older girl at the back of the hall immediately put her hand up and posed the question, "How many political parties are there, sir?" An excellent question I thought. Did she mean in Parliament (Independent Martin Bell – Member of Parliament for Tatton who replaced Neil Hamilton at the 1997 General Election – was in the House at that time) or altogether; and there are so many minority political parties – should I name as many as I could?

While I was churning the answer around in my brain a young boy sitting on the floor at the front was waving his hands round like a windmill, so hard that I thought he was going to bust his gut. So, I begged the Headmaster to take his question next. Innocently, he asked "In your line of business sir, do you go to a lot of parties?"

One of the many visits in my constituency was to the Asda store in Farnworth, where a group of children from Queen Street Primary School was invited to take part in the 2001 Stand Up for Kids campaign. The children were given an attractive questionnaire about the nutritional value of different foodstuffs and they were invited to tour the store with a teacher and look at the products on the shelves, in order to answer the questions. Billy the Banana was available for photographs, as indeed I was, with, or preferably without, Billy. Afterwards, we retired to the briefing room for pop and crisps (very nutritional) and I was invited to talk to the children. I thought that first I had better ask if they understood who I

SCIENCE AND POLITICS: AN UNLIKELY MIXTURE

was. So, I popped the question "Does anybody know what a Member of Parliament does for a living?" Straight away lots of arms went up. The first answer completely floored me. A nine-year-old boy said "I think you polish the Queen's jewels, sir." My mind boggled at the thought of 659 MPs all polishing the Queen's Jewels. The nearest I ever got to the Queen's Jewels was talking to the doormen and messengers in the House of Commons. They all wear a gold badge of office, which is one of the Queen's Jewels. The older ones are priceless.

Backbenchers are invited by the Queen to a reception in Buckingham Palace once in every Parliament. Eileen and I attended these gatherings on 12 July 1999, 4 November 2002, and 20 March 2007. Prince Philip and other members of the Royal Family are usually in attendance at these receptions. The hospitality was always very good, with particularly large gin and tonics.

At the 2002 reception, Parmjit Danda, the newly elected Member of Parliament for Gloucester, was asked by Prince Philip what he had done before he was elected. "I was a trade union officer" replied Parmjit, to which Prince Philip responded "Not much of a job that, is it?" Without thinking, Parmjit asked "And what were you doing before you became Prince Philip?" That story leaked into the national newspapers.

On our last visit to a Buckingham Palace reception Eileen and I thought that we were not going to be engaged in conversation with any member of the Royal Family when, suddenly, we were gathered into a group of people and I saw the Queen approaching. I was standing next to a rather tall and elegantly-dressed lady who had a double-barrelled name. As the Queen joined our group this lady asked "And did you

SCIENCE AND POLITICS: AN UNLIKELY MIXTURE

enjoy the film, ma'am?" (*The Queen*, which starred Helen Mirren and Michael Sheen). "I haven't seen it" the Queen responded, "It's all fiction and no fact", and she pretended to stick two fingers down her throat as if to say it made her sick to think about it. I was amazed.

Then she turned to me and, after a pause and without anything better to say, I asked the Queen "Do you think they will make Queen II, ma'am?" "No, no, I've already said that it's all fiction and no fact" she said, and she pretended again to stick two fingers down her throat. "But ma'am", I said with a wry smile on my face, "Just think of the royalties", and off she went. The elegant lady had wanted her to stay longer, and I think she was annoyed at the tone of my conversation, but then she had introduced the topic.

Members of Parliament are offered two tickets every year for the Buckingham Palace July Garden Parties and I offered these to our Party members. A number of them enjoyed a trip to London with an opportunity to visit the Palace. Because my youngest daughter Sheena could not attend the Garden Party I had been invited to as a councillor, I decided that two of these tickets should be obtained

At Buckingham Palace
on 12 July 1999.

SCIENCE AND POLITICS: AN UNLIKELY MIXTURE

Cllr Noel Spencer with his wife Alice on the day that the Queen presented him with his MBE.

to allow her to go before I retired and, on 22 July 2008, she was able to attend along with Eileen.

Cllr Noel Spencer was awarded an MBE for services to housing at Buckingham Palace on 8 May 2007, and Eileen and I were pleased to be able to celebrate with him and his wife Alice at a lunch in the Churchill Restaurant at the House of Commons. Cllr Spencer and I attended a lot of functions together; for example, on 27 March 2009 we celebrated the centenary of Farnworth Town Hall (opened 30 March 1909). In 2011-2012 Noel and Alice served as Mayor and Mayoress of Bolton.

Only the Grand Hall of Westminster is large enough to hold Members from both Houses of Parliament when they need to come together for special occasions. It is a rather barren place normally, but a red carpet is laid on the floor on which gold-coloured chairs with red seats are assembled, and bright lighting is provided, as well as heating for these special occasions.

Eileen and I were present in Westminster Hall on 30 April 2002 when the Queen and Prince Philip received addresses from both Houses of Parliament on the occasion of their Golden Jubilee.

Parliament receives many other important people, for example Heads of State and Prime Ministers, who address both Houses of Parliament. I was disappointed when Shimon Peres, who won the Nobel Peace Prize, addressed both Houses in the Queen's Robing Room in the House of Lords. His

Celebrating the centenary of Farnworth Town Hall with (left to right) John Pye, Shelley Williams and Cllr Noel Spence.

speech had a very Zionist content and it didn't sound to me like a speech that would bring peace between the Israelis and Palestinians. On 25 May 2011, an historic day, President Barack Obama addressed both Houses of Parliament in Westminster Hall.

We visited 10 Downing Street for receptions in the evenings, usually with our wives and on certain occasions with people from our constituency or town who were invited. When Ruth Kelly was Secretary of State for Education and Skills and Tony Blair was Prime Minister, I was invited to listen to the presentations of headteachers who were considered to be ahead of their field. One of the headteachers presenting on the 9 February 2006 was John Baumber of Rivington and Blackrod High School, who had been given the job of turning other schools round as an Executive Principal; in his case Ladybridge School was one of them. This led to the idea of schools working in clusters so that no school was isolated from others in the neighbourhood and best practice was spread in the cluster.

Cherie Blair invited three children and their teachers from schools in my constituency to join her in Downing Street on 25 April 2002 and, on 16 January 2008 I accompanied the Head Boy of St James's C. of E. Secondary School, Farnworth, to Number 10 to meet the Prime Minister at a special reception.

I visited 10 Downing Street too with two or three other colleagues after returning from my first two visits to Israel and the Occupied Palestinian Territories. These meetings with Tony Blair lasted about 30 minutes each. I came away from each of them with the impression that Tony was not very sympathetic about the situation that the Palestinians were facing at the time.

Members of the regional groups of Members of Parliament were invited from time to time to visit 10 Downing Street for a question and answer session with the Prime Minister. Between 12 and 15 Members attended on each of these visits, which were held around the Cabinet table. I attended my first meeting on 24 June 1998.

In July 2007, Gordon Brown met a group of NW Members of Parliament in the Cabinet Room at 10 Downing Street to gather our main concerns. George Howarth kicked off the meeting by suggesting that the Labour Party was losing credibility across the country and suggested Gordon was the cause of the problem. George asked him what he was going to do to improve the Labour Party's standing. The other Members round the Cabinet table were stunned. This confrontation leaked into the newspapers the following day.

I asked Gordon why people were encouraged to borrow money when they clearly couldn't afford to pay it back. I had been worried for some time about people receiving mortgages from building societies at rates of 100%, and over in some cases, and about people in debt being sent credit card application forms through the post, to encourage them to top up their already existing debts on other credit cards. Mine was the only question he didn't answer at the end of the meeting.

On 15 January 2008, Gordon Brown invited me to attend a breakfast meeting with him at 10 Downing Street, just before he set off on a tour of China and India. It was considered essential to form good diplomatic relationships with the rapidly-developing BRIC (Brazil, Russia, India and China) countries at that time. About six Labour Members were present. We gave Gordon a briefing in each of what was considered to be our specialist areas; I was invited as a

Member with a specialist interest in science and technology.

One of my visitors in the House of Commons asked me what kinds of things I got up to as a Member of Parliament. I told her: "I'm with Registration Officers in Wales today [10 May 2006]. Tomorrow [11 May] I'm doing drugs, and on Friday [12 May] it's euthanasia". She looked a bit alarmed and said "I hope one thing is not leading to the other?"

I was very pleased when Pat Entwisle (chair of Bolton South East CLP and my Election Agent in 1997) and her friend Edith Holden were able to visit Westminster on 30 November 1999. It was an effort on that day for Pat to walk the whole Line of Route; we had to stop several times. After that Pat was diagnosed with breast cancer; she died on 27 July 2003 and I attended her funeral on 4 August 2003. Pat did a tremendous amount of work for the Labour Party. In a Service and Bravery series of posters Bolton MB Council published one on the Entwisle family. Pat's family had a history of service with the Farnworth Fire Service and she became the Borough Librarian at Farnworth Library when few women held senior posts.

My offices arranged for our constituents as well as Party members to visit the Houses of Parliament and I led a number of delegations to see Ministers on various issues.

Humour is in short supply in the chamber of the House of Commons, but Stephen Pound (Member of Parliament for Ealing), formerly a bus conductor, was considered to be one of the most humorous of the Labour backbenchers between 1997 and 2010; in 2010 he became a Government Whip. One day I saw him walking up and down the Members' Tea Room with one arm in a sling, and I was foolish enough to ask him what he had been doing. "Wanking" he quickly responded. I pressed him for the truth. Early in the life of the Parliament and before the Belfast Agreement he was on the Northern Ireland Select Committee, which was paying one of its many visits to that part of the UK. Stephen travelled separately to Belfast Airport and, on arrival, sought a taxi to take him to the hotel where the Select Committee was staying. The first taxi refused to take him, then the second, then the third in the rank, and so on. At this stage, extremely frustrated, Stephen went back into the airport arrivals lounge and hit a vending machine, which broke his wrist. The vending machine survived. Stephen hadn't realised that there were two taxi ranks, one to take travellers to Catholic areas of the City and one to take them to Protestant areas.

On another occasion Stephen visited a high security prison in the West Country. As they were being shown round, they entered the gymnasium, where several inmates were being put through their paces by a rather burly trainer. Stephen was daft enough to ask the trainer how he handled inmates who caused trouble, so the burly trainer told Stephen that he would demonstrate the technique, whereby he grasped Stephen round the chest and lifted him off the floor.

Travelling back on the train to London, Stephen started to get a growing pain in his chest. By the time he had reached London he was feeling an intense pain in his chest and decided to go for treatment to St Thomas's Hospital. The triage nurse asked him where he had been when the 'accident' occurred. "In gaol" responded Stephen. "How did you get out?" asked the nurse. "I'm a Member of Parliament" replied Stephen.

On the 14 June 2004, Stephen Pound asked Home Department Minister Hazel Blears a question on binge drinking during which he said "In that Las Vegas of drinking that is central Ealing, night after night people move from being verbose to jocose to bellicose to lachrymose, and end up comatose".

Another colourful Member of Parliament was Bob Marshall-Andrews QC (Member of Parliament for Medway). He wasn't expected to survive the General Election of 2005 but won his seat by just 213 votes. He was elected in 1997 and retired in 2010.

All Labour Members of Parliament were issued with pagers in 1997 so that we could be contacted by the Whips' Office, with announcements on votes in the House of Commons and other matters. At the first Annual Conference after the 1997 General Election the press mocked pagers after we were all seen to be reaching for them at the same time during the conference when the Party managers contacted us on various issues. The joke in the media was that we were being advised as to when our hands should go up for votes, but most of us were *ex officio* delegates, with no voting rights.

Most male Members clipped their pagers to their belts or trousers. They had a habit of falling off, and some ended up in toilets. Bob Marshall-Andrews and members of the Old Testament Prophet's Dining Club, which he set up, decided that they would hold an event at our annual conferences at which a Golden Pager Award would be presented to the most boring speaker on the Labour benches. One of these broken pagers was sprayed with gold paint and attached with Blu-Tack to one of those wires that waiters stick their orders on in some restaurants, a practice that has almost died out today. I attended only one Old Testament Prophet's Lunch, in 1997 in a Mexican restaurant on Horseferry Road at which several members of the Press Lobby addressed us. I think my bill came to £43, which astonished me when I received it, because

Bob had given me a figure of about half that amount. That day I had left well before 2.30 p.m. because I had a Parliamentary Question to pose to the Foreign Secretary. The bill that I received was for my share of all the drinks; my colleagues had carried on drinking well into the afternoon of that day, partly at my expense, as I discovered.

Preparing for the Rehab UK pancake race.

The House of Commons team in the Rehab UK pancake race.

Bob Marshall-Andrews was travelling to Heathrow Airport in a taxi one day when the cabby turned round and said "Give us a clue guv." Bob had noticed that the cabby had been looking at him in the mirror.

"Well", said Bob, "I'm a Member of Parliament but you've

probably seen me on the telly. I've appeared on the *Kilroy Show*, *Have I Got News for You* and various other political programmes, not to mention on several debate shows with people like John Humphreys".

"Na" replied the cabby, "Terminal 3 or Terminal 4?"

The brain injury charity Rehab UK has organised an Annual Parliamentary Pancake race since 1996, usually on College Green, and I joined the House of Commons team of five for several years until my retirement in 2010. A House of Commons team races against a team from the House of Lords and another team of journalists. These events attract a lot of media attention, which helps to raise the profile of Rehab UK. A famous person usually referees the race, chef Gary Rhodes for example. Pancakes are tossed as runners run round the course and, if one is dropped, the runner is supposed to return to the beginning of the course and run again. Needless to say, the rules are not always completely obeyed. The runners wear a chef's tall hat and apron.

Unfortunately, only four Members of Parliament turned up for the 9 February 2010 race, and I stupidly volunteered to complete two laps of the course in the Embankment Gardens. I ran the first and last laps. As I ran the first lap I saw a television camera at the end of the first straight, so I tossed the pancake almost immediately in front of it. Fortunately, as I discovered later, it was the Granada TV camera.

The second straight was along a tarmac path parallel with the River Thames, and it had a lot of tree roots breaking through the tarmac. As I approached a second television camera (unfortunately a Sky News TV camera), I twisted my ankle on one of the tree roots, tossed the pancake and it landed on my left hip, at which I slid it back into the pan without touching it. Despite my injury, I managed to win the final lap for our team and we won the cup and 'medals'.

Before the start of the race, I noticed a young woman, dressed in Lycra and wearing trainers, in the media team. She looked very competitive. As I discovered later she was a Sky News reporter. Their team lost. When the 'clip' appeared a few hours later on Sky News they showed my mistake and the Lycra woman's coverage suggested that Members of Parliament don't only cheat with their expenses, they cheat in pancake races too. She also featured her 'clip' on her blog, which my researcher Gemma discovered. Clearly, she hadn't entered into the spirit of the race; she was far too serious for my liking.

One of the most informative periods of my Parliamentary career came in the 2002-2003 Parliamentary session when I joined up for the Police Service Parliamentary Scheme. This scheme is one of several that are organised from outside Parliament, this one by Sir Neil Thorne and his administrator Elizabeth Hunt. Quite a few Members choose to serve in a branch of the armed forces while other Members work with a charity or with a major company.

I volunteered to spend 30 days with the Greater Manchester Police looking at all aspects of their work. Induction day at Chester House was 24 May 2002, when I was introduced to Chief Constable David Wilmot and Deputy Chief Constable David McCrone. Then I was placed in the capable hands of the Chief Constable's Staff Officer, Stewart Hindley, who was responsible for putting my programme together.

In Phase I of the programme I toured the different departments in Chester House, visited the police training school at Sedgley Park, Prestwich, and called on the Forensic Science Service at Bradford Park. This I found very interesting because the scientists use a lot of applied science in their work.

Preparing to board the Greater Manchester Police helicopter at Barton Airport.

At the Reunion Dinner of the Police Service Parliamentary Scheme with (left to right) Stuart Hindley, Michael Todd and Brian Wroe.

For Phase II of the scheme I was posted to work with F Division of Greater Manchester Police (GMP) at Salford Divisional Headquarters (then on The Crescent, opposite the university) and at Swinton Police Station. After an induction session with Chief Superintendent Brian Wroe and his management team I completed two early day shifts (7.00 a.m.-3.00 p.m.), two evening shifts (3.00 p.m.-1.00 a.m.) and two night shifts (9.00 p.m.-7.00 a.m.), mainly spent patrolling in cars and vans during the summer of 2002.

I met Brian Wroe again several years later, on 9 June 2011, when Eileen and I attended a Labour Party Gala Dinner in Leigh, where he was the Toastmaster and Master of Ceremonies, a career that he embarked upon following his retirement from the police force.

Phase III of the scheme involved all the participants on the scheme looking at the work of police in The Netherlands, between 23 and 26 September 2002. We were based in Amsterdam and The Hague. This trip was interesting for me because we learned a lot about illicit drugs and prostitution. During the week several Members decided to return to Westminster for a debate on Iraq but I volunteered to stay in The Hague.

Phase IV was the busiest phase, when I visited an operations room, which received incoming calls from the public, saw the work of the Air Support Unit at Manchester Airport, where a fixed wing aircraft is kept, and Barton Airport, where the helicopter is kept (there was a call-out while I was there and I was invited to join the crew for a trip over moors near Bury, where a woman had been reported missing), visited the Traffic Network Section, the Mounted and Dog Training Unit, the Tactical Aid Unit, the Major Crime

Investigation Unit, the Firearms Training Branch and the Discipline and Complaints Branch.

I also saw the other work of the police at Manchester Airport, visited the Transport Police, spent a day with an Armed Response Unit and visited the identification suite at Longsight Police Station. I was the first civilian to be allowed by GMP to go out with an Armed Response Unit for a whole shift.

Neil Gerrard (Member of Parliament for Walthamstow), who was born in Prestolee in my constituency, was on the Police Service Parliamentary Scheme when he was invited to observe an identity parade. All the young men lined up and the police officer in charge asked all those on the parade if they were happy to go ahead when suddenly the accused said he was unhappy. When asked why, he blurted out "Well I'm not wearing a hat and I had one on at the time." His solicitor dragged him out of the parade as quickly as he could and took him to one side to give him a lecture. By the time I joined the scheme ID parades were conducted digitally, without the need for all the people to be present at the same time.

I attended a football game between Manchester United FC and Aston Villa FC at MUFC's ground at Old Trafford. I say I attended the game; actually I spent the morning at Stretford Police Station, where the briefing for the day took place, and the rest of the day was spent observing what goes on behind the scenes at a football match including in the observation room in the ground. I didn't see very much of the game but I saw an awful lot of the people who attended that day.

I learned so much from my experiences with the police that I wrote quite a long report, which I presented to Chief

Constable Michael Todd at a debriefing session with him and his management team, held on 7 March 2003. Michael Todd arrived in Manchester while I was on the scheme. My biggest criticism of what I had seen was that the IT systems the police were using at that time were out of date. Indeed I felt that the police needed to engage more with the advances in technology of the day to keep one step ahead of their rivals, the serious criminals. If a vehicle is stopped by the police today they can receive details of the driver and the vehicle at the scene within minutes, which is how it should be.

It was a sad day when I attended Mike Todd's funeral service in Manchester Cathedral on 11 April 2008 after he had been found dead in Snowdonia in mid-March. The presence of so many people there on that day, including most of the Greater Manchester Members of Parliament and others besides, was indicative of the respect that we all had for Mike – a sad ending for such a talented man.

CHAPTER SIXTEEN

MORE ABOUT LIFE IN BOLTON

⸎

Eileen and I still live in Avoncliff Close, although we have added an extension to the property. We shop in the local shops, can access Bolton town centre in less than 20 minutes and we have the West Pennine Moors on our doorstep. We live in the shadow of Falcon Mill in Halliwell (Holy Well) on the edge of the Hill Top conservation area, which is quite close to one of the ancient routes from north to south and *vice versa* in Smithills, where the Holy Well was situated. Falcon Mill is a Grade 2 Listed Building and was the first mill in the world to be built with a concrete floor, although it appears to have wooden floors to a visitor.

It wasn't unusual for cotton (and wool) mills to catch fire. The machinery dripped oil onto the wooden floors, and it only took a few sparks from the machinery to set these places ablaze. The wooden floors absorbed the oil and deadened some of the noise of the clattering machines. When the mills caught fire, however, the heavy machinery fell through the floor to the next floor and a domino effect could occur, with machinery ending piled up on the ground floor or in a basement.

Calvin and Cameron at Avoncliff Close.

Eileen's parents Ivy and Jim Barker.

When we moved to Avoncliff Close in 1989, Falcon Mill was still working as a cotton spinning mill, working three shifts. But, it wasn't long before the remaining cotton spinning and weaving mills in Bolton all closed. The machinery was shipped off to India or Egypt or scrapped. Today, like many of the remaining mills in Bolton, Falcon Mill houses several different companies trading in different ways. Many of Bolton's other mills have been converted into blocks of apartments.

Bolton Council's engineers designed a traffic management scheme for Halliwell Road several years ago. The idea was to slow the traffic down, thus reducing the number of accidents on the road, and provide parking bays. In my opinion, this scheme made matters worse. A Lloyds bank, quite close to where we live, is one of the danger spots. People park on double yellow lines on a corner, where the road narrows as it approaches a Pelican crossing, so that they can jump out of their car to withdraw money from an ATM. If a driver negligently opens an offside door at this point the door will collide with any passing traffic. Eileen's small Suzuki Swift car was scratched along its full length on 2 November 2006 by a driver getting into his car without looking, immediately before Eileen passed it. There was no argument with our insurance company; they paid out immediately in the knowledge that the other driver was clearly the cause of the accident. I took photographs of the damage from every angle.

We thought that was the end of the matter but, well over two years later, Eileen received a summons to attend court. The other driver had met a 'clipboard solicitor' in Victoria Square, Bolton, who had encouraged him to take his case to court. We attended court on two separate days, on 17 February and 19 March 2010. There wasn't time to hear the case on the

SCIENCE AND POLITICS: AN UNLIKELY MIXTURE

first day, so we had to return. The other driver lost the case, not surprisingly in view of the evidence available. When Eileen's barrister, who was acting for Eileen's insurance company, told us of the cost on 'our' side of the case, we were astonished. In my opinion this racket should be stopped; these solicitors are one of the causes of the rapid increase in car insurance that we have witnessed in recent years.

Bolton is one of the places where the 'cash for crash' scam has been used extensively. Two cars 'sandwich' an innocent driver's car and the car in front stops suddenly, causing the innocent driver to collide with it; the second car then runs into the back of the car driven by the innocent driver. Most of the cash comes not from the physical damage to the cars but from alleged personal injuries to the passengers in the two other cars.[1]

Eileen's parents lived in a council house at St Marks Walk off Nelson Street in Great Lever, and we visited Jim and Ivy Barker on a regular basis. Jim served in the army in North Africa; he didn't have a good word for 'Monty' (Field Marshal Viscount Montgomery). Like most servicemen that served in World War II and saw some horrific sights, Jim was reluctant to talk about his war experience. He worked on the railway before he retired. Eileen's mum was crippled with rheumatoid arthritis.

On Sunday 15 November 1998, before we were due to return to London, we called on Jim and Ivy at their home to find that Ivy had had a stroke earlier in the day, and we found her lying on the landing at the top of their stairs with Jim holding her hand. After spending three months in hospital, very reluctantly Eileen and her sister Jean sought admission for her to a nearby care home called Millview, which was built ten years earlier on the site of a forge at the corner of Fletcher Street and Bridgeman Street in Bolton. Tay Care Homes built Millview and we were very pleased with the care given to Ivy when she was admitted to Millview on 15 February 1999. Later, BUPA took Millview over and the care given to its residents wasn't as good in our opinion.

Ivy lived in Millview until she died in the Royal Bolton Hospital on 12 April 2006, aged 85. Her funeral was on 21 April 2006. Jim died in the Royal Bolton Hospital on 13 July 1999, his 81st birthday.

Eileen and I try not to return to a place on holiday that we have visited before, although we have been to Sorrento twice. After working at the University of Potenza in June 1993 we treated ourselves to a holiday in the Capo di Monte Grand Hotel there, which is situated on a cliff with water flowing down between several swimming pools. One of the highlights of the holiday was a tour of the Amalfi coast, visiting places such as Amalfi, Positano and Ravello. We also spent two days looking at Herculaneum and Pompeii. It's a small world. Staying in the Capo di Monte Grand Hotel were two teachers from the Withins School in Bolton (Pauline and Mike Doyle) who I knew quite well.

As we queued to check in our baggage at Manchester Airport for our second visit to Sorrento we met Barry Montgomery, a GMB trade union official, and his wife who, we discovered, were heading for the Capo di Monte Grand Hotel in Sorrento. When we had gone along to the travel agent one of the best deals that we came across was a package holiday to the hotel we had stayed in many years earlier, the Capo di Monte Grand.

We particularly like the Canary Islands and have visited

SCIENCE AND POLITICS: AN UNLIKELY MIXTURE

Lanzarote, Tenerife and Fuerteventura. Now Eileen's son Lee is living in Gran Canaria we visit that island at least once a year. We were there twice in 2010 together, and Eileen returned again towards the end of 2010. We have also holidayed in Cyprus, Majorca, Lido di Jesolo (near Venice), Puerto Banus on the Costa del Sol, Malta, Bulgaria (the Black Sea coast), Cuba, Barcelona, Madeira, Barbados and Crete, and we have cruised out of Palma round the Mediterranean and visited our twin town of Paderborn on more than one occasion.

We had an interesting experience in August 1998 when we visited Corfu, where we stayed in an old hotel, Hotel Kissimi, on the harbour side in Kassiopi. There were good views of Albania and its mountains across a short stretch of sea, with wonderful sunsets, and we visited that country during our visit, which was an interesting experience. We had booked our holiday at the last minute and, during our two-week stay, we realised that three other Members of Parliament had booked the same holiday destination – Jim Dobbin (Member of Parliament for Heywood and Middleton),[2] Elliot Morley (Member of Parliament for Scunthorpe) and John Battle, then Minister responsible for Science in the Labour Government (Member of Parliament for Leeds West). We all ended up in the same small village with our partners for a two-week holiday, although we were not all staying in the same hotel. Evenings were rather like evenings in the Strangers Bar in the House of Commons.

The last wedding of a member of the Iddon family was that of my nephew John Iddon, who is a policeman. He married Charlotte Corris at the Gibbon Bridge Hotel, near Chipping in the Trough of Bowland, on 7 June 2009. Their first child,

Lucy Jayne, was born on the morning of 1 September 2010, just a few hours before Noah, son of Eileen's eldest son Lee and his Spanish partner Lilian, was born in Gran Canaria on 2 September.

Altogether, Eileen and I have five grandchildren – Abigail and Matthew (the children of my daughter Sheena and her husband Darren), Noah, the son of Eileen's eldest son Lee, and Calvin (born 30 July 1994) and Cameron (born 29 March 2004), the sons of Eileen's youngest son Ian.

Charlotte's mum and dad (the Corris family) were keen Harley Davidson bikers and, over the 2010 summer bank holiday weekend, attended a Harley Davidson rally in Scotland. Tragically, a car driven by a French male driver on the wrong side of the road hit them on a bend near Stirling while they were returning from the rally on Monday 30 August 2010, and killed them both.

At the wedding of nephew John Iddon to Charlotte Corris (left to right) Andrew Chambers, Eileen, Pam Iddon, John and Charlotte and brother Graham and me.

Eileen with Lee and Lilian, Calvin and his dad Ian (Eileen's youngest son).

Anybody involved in voluntary activities makes a lot of contacts which has enormous benefits. However, it also means attendance at a lot of funerals. On 22 September 2006, I attended the funeral of my friend Vince Simpson. The family asked if I would pay a tribute to Vince on the day, and I did, but it was difficult. Later, on 20 October 2007, I was privileged to be able to give the Simpson family a posthumous Lifetime Achievement Award at the New Unity Centre in Johnson Street, which recognised all the contributions that he made to civic society in Bolton.

I was also invited by another dear friend's family, the family of Derek Patel who was well-known in Bolton's Hindu society, to pay a tribute to him at his funeral on 5 January 2007; he died on 28 December 2006. Derek campaigned to acquire land from Bolton Council in Hacken Lane and was the driving force in acquiring grants and raising money in his community to establish the Indian Sports Club there. A few years before he died the club was successful in receiving grants to extend it by building a sports hall. I provided a plaque for the club to mark all his hard work.

When I met Eileen she had three very close friends, Joyce Monks, Karen Tomlinson and Pat Entwistle; they seemed inseparable and had some good nights out together. On 26 December 2001 Joyce was admitted to the Royal Bolton Hospital with cancer of the throat and died on 19 January 2002 (the funeral was on 28 January). Karen was diagnosed with breast cancer and suffered with cancer for several years. She was admitted to Bolton Hospice for the final time on 9 March 2003 and died there on 13 March (her funeral was on 19 March). These were losses that Eileen found difficult to come to terms with.

2003 was a bad year for us. Pat Entwistle's brother Michael was found dead in his home on 22 March, Eileen's cousin Graham Hughes, a fireman died of a heart attack while attending a fire on 25 March, and her Aunt Joyce died on 13 August.

When we lived in London, Eileen wanted to visit two places in particular, the Ritz on Piccadilly and the Ivy Restaurant in the West End. We managed to visit the Ivy on 15 October 2008. Eileen was disappointed because there were no celebrities to be seen anywhere in the place, at least none that we recognised. I was disappointed by the menu; there was a poor choice, although I have to admit that it wasn't as expensive as I thought it might be. The main problem with the Ivy is that a booking has to be made quite a few weeks in advance of the visit. There are better restaurants in London than the Ivy in my opinion.

SCIENCE AND POLITICS: AN UNLIKELY MIXTURE

Presenting a posthumous award for Vince Simpson to Sylvia Simpson and (left to right) Vince Simpson Jnr, Maria (Vince's children), and Dolores (Vince's partner).

When I was elected to Parliament we tried to reserve one weekend each month to stay in London and relax, or see the sights. That proved impossible but, over the years, Eileen and I were able to see together *Miss Saigon*, *Cats*, *Starlight Express*, *Chicago*, *Buddy*, *Just Like That* (a play about Tommy Cooper), *Billy Elliot*, and *Whipping it Up* (a play about the Labour Whips' Office, starring Richard Wilson). We holidayed in London several times with our grandson Calvin, and Eileen and he saw together *The Lion King* and *Starlight Express*. I joined them one evening to see *Blood Brothers*, Calvin's enlightened choice. Since I left London I have caught up with *Phantom of the Opera*, which Eileen had already seen with Joyce Monks, *The Lion King*, and *Les Miserable's*.

When I was a Member of Parliament Eileen and I received invitations to the main civic functions, although mostly we were unable to attend the installation of new Mayors, which is an event held on a Wednesday in May, because of my duties in Parliament. However, we tried to attend the Mayor's Charity Ball each year as well as the Civic Dinner, when the Mayor and Mayoress of Bolton entertain the 'chain gang', the Mayors and Mayoresses of the nine other Greater Manchester towns or cities.

Each Remembrance Sunday I laid a wreath at the Farnworth War Memorial and dashed off to attend the second half of the ceremony in Victoria Square, Bolton, when the armed forces and veterans march through the square. Eileen and I also attended the Remembrance Concert in the Albert Hall in Bolton Town Hall as well as the Bolton United Veterans Association Annual Remembrance Dinner, today held in the Round House club in Halliwell. Our dear friend Cllr Frank White was their President and Cllr John Walsh their Vice-President until 2012.

A Member of Parliament receives invitations to attend a lot of events in their home town, although I didn't attend as many as our Mayors attend, but I did get a good impression of the amount of good work done by Bolton's citizens. I helped a number of organisations apply for grants to keep them going. One of these was Diversity in Barrier Breaking Communication (DBBC) run by Dorothy and Alan Martland. Alan, I discovered, was born in Rufford.

After realising that I came from Tarleton, Alan produced a photograph of some scouts and asked me if I knew any of the boys. I could name them all, much to the surprise of Alan, who was our patrol leader. We had known each other in Bolton for several years before we realised that we had also known each other in our youth.

In the 1990s Dorothy Martland, Cllr Frank White and other leading townspeople worked with Bolton Wanderers FC in an attempt to bring community radio to Bolton. This team operated with several trial licences and Bolton's Housing Direct Labour Organisation's apprentices built a soundproof broadcasting unit for them in the Market Hall on Ashburner Street, where DBBC operated from until 2016. In the competition they failed to be awarded the main licence. This was won by Tower FM, which was launched in a mill on Brownlow Way, Bolton, on 22 March 1999.

In my opinion, and in the opinion of others, Tower FM has not lived up to its promise to be a community radio station; its main output is music, interrupted by advertisements. The Bolton group has now obtained a permanent licence to broadcast Bolton FM radio, which does cover local events, and is run by local people for the benefit of local people.

NOTES

1. The insurance companies appear to be trying to control these 'scams' and car insurance premiums appear to be stable or going down.

2. Jim Dobbin died aged 73 during a Council of Europe visit to Poland on 6 September 2014.

CHAPTER SEVENTEEN

LAST DAYS AS A MEMBER OF PARLIAMENT

I was one of the first Members of Parliament to announce my retirement – to my Constituency Labour Party (CLP) Management Committee on 2 October 2006. The selection process for my successor was under way the following summer. Whilst an early announcement takes the focus off the sitting Member, it allows their constituency party to take its time over finding the best possible replacement. I was very keen for the constituency to select from an open shortlist and not to be bound by an all-women shortlist.

Some Members of Parliament, especially those representing safe seats, hang onto power until the last possible moment in the belief that they will hold a bargaining chip for entry into the House of Lords. In cases like that there is a greater chance of the National Executive Committee of the Party parachuting in a Prospective Parliamentary Candidate, which can upset local members of the party.

The Bolton South East CLP General Management Committee received 53 applications, and 18 hopefuls turned up for an informal hustings meeting on 1 July 2007 at Dixon Green Labour Club in Farnworth. Out of those the Executive shortlisted Kevin Meagher, chairman of the CLP, Julie Hilling, who became the Member of Parliament for Bolton West, Nargis Khan, a barrister from London with local connections, Phil Collins, speechwriter (2005-2007) to Tony Blair, Richard Jackson, a veterinary surgeon, Akhtar Zaman, a local councillor, and Yasmin Qureshi, also a barrister with local connections, who won the selection process.

The shortlist was drawn up on 6 August 2007 and the successful applicant was selected on 26 August. The front-runners were Kevin and Yasmin; she moved into a flat in the constituency and, helped by a popular party member, visited as many other party members as she could contact, more than once in some cases. She impressed the members by handwriting letters to them as well. Yasmin Qureshi launched her election campaign at Dixon Green Labour Club on the evening of 5 October 2009, with Ken Livingstone as the guest speaker.

Yasmin Qureshi MP

Before Tony Blair retired as Prime Minister he made a series of policy speeches around the country. One on science and technology was presented to Royal Society Fellows at the University of Oxford. I decided not to interfere in any way with the selection of my successor, but I got a call from Phil Collins inviting me over to 10 Downing Street on 18 October 2006 to discuss with him the proposed content of this speech. What Phil had in mind seemed perfectly sensible to me and I agreed to read his draft speech. Good job I did too. In it Phil mentioned the *two* important textile inventions of the Industrial Revolution, Kay's flying shuttle and Arkwright's water frame.

"What Parliamentary seat have you applied to be shortlisted for?" I asked Phil. "Yours" he replied. "Well", I said, "You had better mention Samuel Crompton's invention of the spinning mule then". As a result Tony Blair referred to the *three* important textile inventions of the Industrial Revolution at Oxford. They were, of course, James Hargreaves's spinning jenny, invented in 1764, Richard Arkwright's water frame, invented in 1769, and Samuel Crompton's spinning mule, invented between 1775 and 1779.

Phil asked me what kind of members belonged to the Bolton South East CLP and his face fell when I told him that, in my opinion, the majority of its members could be labelled as 'old Labour'. In the end the Bolton South East CLP did not shortlist him to succeed me (I did not influence their decision).

After a short spell as the speechwriter for Secretary of State for Work and Pensions James Purnell (Member of Parliament for Stalybridge and Hyde) and another brief interlude at the London School of Economics, Phil Collins became a journalist with *The Times* newspaper. My last direct contact with him was when he chaired a fringe meeting for Dignity in Dying (the rebranded Voluntary Euthanasia Society) in Manchester's Midland Hotel at the Labour Party's 2010 Annual Conference. Today, he frequently appears on television news programmes such as *Newsnight*, *Sunday Politics* and the *Andrew Marr Show*.

I attended my last Bolton South East CLP General Management Committee meeting to say my farewells and to thank the members for their loyal support over more than 13 years on 1 March 2010.

The English Defence League held a rally in Victoria Square, Bolton on Saturday 20 March 2010, which cost Greater Manchester Police a small fortune to provide cover. Quite a number of shops closed for the day because they knew people would stay away from the town centre.

I was extremely busy right up to the last day of Parliamentary business before the 2010 General Election. A Budget was presented by Alistair Darling on Wednesday 24 March, was debated on 25, 29 and 30 March, and the House rose for a very short Easter recess on 31 March. We were back, unusually, on the day after Easter Monday, on Tuesday 7 April, and Gordon Brown went to Buckingham Palace at 10.00 a.m. on that Tuesday. It was announced that Parliament would be dissolved on Monday 12 April. That is the last day that Members of Parliament can use their title or enjoy the privileges of Parliament before returning to Westminster, if they are returning. I was not.

Gemma and I had spent months clearing my Westminster office. Two years previously I had transferred all the Westminster casework files to my Bolton office and started to sort my papers into subject boxes, with a view to depositing a lot of the material in archives. I spent the remaining months thinning this material out and arranging most of the papers in chronological order within the boxes.

Five full file boxes went to the Wellcome Trust Library archives, on Euston Road in London, three on the misuse of drugs and two on euthanasia. I discovered that the Voluntary Euthanasia Society's papers were deposited there, so it seemed appropriate to add to the Wellcome Trust's archives and counterbalance their arguments. Later, I persuaded Elspeth Choudhary-Best of ALERT to arrange for the Wellcome Trust to pick up her papers to add to what must be the largest archive on euthanasia in this country, at a time when the subject was hotly debated.

Twenty-five boxes of my papers, which cover every subject discussed in this book, are deposited in the Bolton archives along with my unusual diary, which is a series of arch files containing plastic wallets filled with material that tracked my Parliamentary career.

On the very last day of official business in both Houses of Parliament, Thursday 8 April, Lord Best managed to get the Mortgage Repossessions (Tenants Protection etc) Bill through its final stages in the House of Lords, and it received Royal Assent that afternoon. Parliament was prorogued the same evening. We had cause for celebration. Lord Best and I were awarded jointly Parliamentarian of the Year Award 2010 by Citizens Advice, which we collected on the afternoon of 7 July. The guest speaker at the ceremony was Vince Cable, Secretary of State at the Department of Business, Innovation, and Skills (DBIS). I wished him well in his new job. As it turned out, he needed it.

I took Eileen, Gemma and Dr Stephen Benn out for lunch

the following day at the Millbank Pizza Express restaurant, and we returned to my office, where Gemma produced a magnificent celebration cake which she had baked. On our way back to the office I decided to visit the main Vote Office in the House of Commons to collect some copies of my Act of Parliament. I was told politely that they could not give me any copies because I was not a Member of Parliament any more. When I visited my office the following morning to collect my emails, all the furniture was piled up in the middle of the room and the computers were disconnected. I handed in my key to the office at the desk on the way out and left.

On 26 March 2010 I attended a party at the Holiday Inn in Bolton to celebrate George Caswell's retirement (which he announced on 13 November 2009), and in the evening I attended my last Civic Dinner as a Member of Parliament. Sadly, my former Council colleague Jack Foster died in the Royal Bolton Hospital on 17 April, and I attended his funeral on 23 April.

With Eileen and Dr Stephen Benn at the Pizza Express Restaurant, Millbank.

The Members of Parliament who retired in 2010 at a reception given by the Speaker, John Bercow.

In the meantime, the election campaign was being conducted around me whilst I was making way for my successor in the Bolton office. I was negotiating a smooth transfer of the office and its equipment with Yasmin Qureshi along with a transfer of all my casework files to her in the definite knowledge that she would win the election in Bolton South East. I was hoping too that she would re-employ my staff and, with the exception of Gemma, who worked in Westminster, she did.

For the first time in British history the three main party leaders, Gordon Brown, David Cameron and Nick Clegg entered into three 90-minute-long televised debates, which were held at 8.30 p.m. on Thursdays 15 (ITV), 22 (Sky News Channel) and 29 April (BBC 1). These had a huge impact on the outcome of the General Election. After the first debate 'Cleggmania' erupted across the media. In my opinion, we were well and truly into US Presidential-style politics.

SCIENCE AND POLITICS: AN UNLIKELY MIXTURE

One of the defining moments of the 2010 General Election campaign was Gordon Brown's encounter with 65-year-old Labour supporter Gillian Duffy in Rochdale on 28 April 2010. She raised an issue of great concern to herself and others during the campaign – immigration. After a pleasant roadside chat with her, Gordon was transported off in his Jaguar only to discuss this engagement without realising that the Sky TV microphone was still recording his voice. He was heard by reporters to say "She was just a sort of bigoted woman". When he arrived at his next engagement, the *Jeremy Vine Show* on BBC Radio 2, they had received the 'clip' and Jeremy Vine played it back to him whilst he was being recorded by a television camera. Gordon looked devastated in the news bulletins on TV. The rest is history.

The Labour Party lost 91 of its Members of Parliament on 7 May 2010, including former Home Secretaries Jacqui Smith and Charles Clarke. The Tories won 306 seats, Labour 258 and the Liberal Democrats 57. It was clear that the numbers were stacked against Labour.

No single party won the General Election of 7 May 2010; after several days of political horse trading, the first Coalition Government since World War II was established in Britain, with the Liberal Democrats propping up the Tories. I was born under a Coalition Government and, almost 70 years later, retired under one too.

On Friday 30 April, I drove a hired van to London, and Eileen and I emptied our flat in Dolphin Square in the pouring rain over the weekend. Gordon Brown announced his resignation as Prime Minister on Tuesday 10 May, visited Buckingham Palace on 11 May, and that was the end of another era of British politics. Parliament resumed its business on Tuesday 18 May, with the Queen's Speech on 25 May, and the Budget on 22 June. We were all condemned to another period of austerity under another Tory Government.

I received a handwritten letter, dated 20 April, from the Leader of the House, Harriet Harman, which read:

Dear Brian

Just a note to thank you for all you've done while you've been in Parliament. Your values and deep progressive roots were always there – but added to that you brought a distinctive voice on science and the environment. I don't know of any other backbencher who got 2 laws enacted.[1]
So you made a huge difference through your own commitment and determination. Thank you – and best wishes for the future.

Harriet.

I don't know how busy people find the time to write these letters but they are greatly appreciated.

For the first time in years, Eileen and I were able to attend the installation of the new Mayor and Mayoress, Cllr John and Cllr Lynda Byrne, in Bolton on 26 May. On the 26 June, we attended a memorial service at the Alma Lodge Hotel in Stockport to celebrate the life and work of Jim Siddelley, who had withdrawn from my selection conference in 1994. Jim managed to visit me in Westminster on 23 June 2009.

SCIENCE AND POLITICS: AN UNLIKELY MIXTURE

Receiving Honorary Membership of the Society of Chemical Industry from David Green, chairman of the Board of Trustees.

I received Honorary Membership of the Society of Chemical Industry on 9 July 2003. On the evening of the 26 May 2010, I collected an Honorary Fellowship at the Annual Meeting of the Institution of Chemical Engineers and, on the evening of 7 July 2010, I received an Honorary Fellowship from the Royal Society of Chemistry (RSC) (both awards were agreed on 10 December 2009). My dream in my youth had always been to be a chemist but, never in my wildest dreams, had I dreamed of joining some of the most famous chemists worldwide in this form of recognition. On each occasion I thought about the suffering that my parents had been through to put me there.

At my final 'thank you' party, which I held at Farnworth and Kearsley Labour Club on 24th September 2010, I received a Special Achievement Award from the Bolton Labour Party, signed by its chairman Len Thomas, and by the leader of

Bolton MB Council, Cllr Cliff Morris, which I greatly value. I continued to work in the Bolton office until 5 July 2010, when Karen completed her time with me, which was also the day of my 70th birthday.

I can confirm that there is life after national politics. After my retirement I started to get involved again in local politics in the constituency where I cut my political teeth, the Bolton North East (previously Bolton East) Parliamentary constituency. I am often asked whether I regretted making the decision to retire from Parliament, if I miss it, and if I am enjoying my retirement. On my visits to schools the most common questions were "What is the best part of the job?" and "What is the worst part of the job?" Together with my staff, we were able to help so many people for whom we did some incredible things; that was the best part of the job, helping people. A Member of Parliament can open doors that others cannot open.

Somebody once told me that I will know when to retire – "Your body will tell you", that person said. And it has. So I made the right decision at the right time. I did miss being involved in national politics for a few months but, at this distance in time, I am amazed that I kept the pace up for so long.

The worst part of the job, especially in the winter months, was travelling to and from London. Now, when the BBCs *Antiques Road Show* starts on television on a Sunday evening, I can stay and watch the whole programme, at least as long as they are broadcast! I am catching up on the programmes that I missed on the Yesterday channel.

My three score years and ten are over. Now, every day is a bonus, and I intend to live them to the full. That's 'My Story'.

I hope you enjoyed reading it (assuming you made it to the very end!).

NOTES

1. Effectively it was three Acts of Parliament, two Private Members' Bills and the Government's Statistics and Registration Service Act 2007 (see Chapter 7).

APPENDIX 1

LIST OF PARLIAMENTARY SPEECHES★

LIST OF ADJOURNMENT DEBATES WHICH I INITIATED

1997-1998 SESSION
- Mediation Services (17 December 1997)

1998-1999 SESSION
- Procedures in the Case of Sudden Death: the Case of David Cunliffe (23 July 1998)

1999-2000 SESSION
- Methadone and Other Heroin Substitutes (7 December 1999) (WH)
- Down's Syndrome (4 July 2000) (WH)

2000-2001 SESSION
- Secured Lending to Non-Status Borrowers and IGroup plc (25 April 2001) (WH)

2001-2002 SESSION
- Hepatitis C (14 November 2001) (WH)
- Futile Care Policies and Euthanasia (22 May 2002) (WH)
- Safety of Ships and Seafarers at Sea (25 June 2002) (WH)

2002-2003 SESSION
- Employment Rights for Registration Officers (3 June 2003) (WH)

2003-2004 SESSION
- Workplace and Roadside Drug Testing (14 January 2004) (WH)
- People with Down's Syndrome (Education) (14 September 2004) (WH)

2005-2006 SESSION
- The Right-to-Buy Scheme (11 January 2006)
- The Driving Standards of Older Drivers (15 March 2006)

2006-2007 SESSION
- Affordable Housing in the North and Midlands (17 January 2007) (WH)
- Organic Food or Organic Fraud? (16 October 2007) (WH)

2007-2008 SESSION
- 21st Century Science Teaching (15 January 2008) (WH)
- Biosimilar Medicines (2 April 2008)
- Liver Disease (21 May 2008) (WH)

2008-2009 SESSION
- Mountain Rescue Teams (21 January 2009) (WH)
- Private James Smith and World War I (3 March 2009)
- Impact of Unregulated Importation of Health Food Products from the Channel Islands (5 May 2009) (WH)
- Food Safety and the Public Analysts Service (2 June 2009) (WH)
- Addiction to Prescription and Over-the-Counter Medicines (16 June 2009) (WH)

2009-2010 SESSION
- Peripheral Arterial Disease (2 March 2010) (WH)
- The UK Chemical Industry (30 March 2010) (WH)

LIST OF SPEECHES GIVEN IN OTHER ADJOURNMENT DEBATES

1997-1998 SESSION
- Illegal Drugs (19 November 1997)

1998-1999 SESSION
- Dietary Supplements (10 March 1999)

1999-2000 SESSION
- Palestinian Refugees (30 November 1999) (WH)
- GMOs and Biotechnology (13 January 2000) (WH)
- National Strategy for the UK Textile and Clothing Industry (14 March 2000) (WH)

2000-2001 SESSION
- The Government's Policy on Illegal Drugs (21 March 2001) (WH)

2001-2002 SESSION
- Electoral Law (4 July 2001) (WH)
- Housing (15 November 2001) (WH)
- Empty Homes (16 May 2002) (WH
- Fireworks (30 October 2002) (WH)

2002-2003 SESSION
- Heroin Addicts (26 November 2002) (WH)
- Middle East Peace Process (10 December 2002) (WH)
- Marine Pollution (8 January 2003) (WH)
- Gulf War Illness (5 February 2003) (WH)
- Animal Experiments (19 March 2003) (WH)
- Dr Adrian Garfoot (25 June 2003) (WH)
- Housing (13 November 2003) (WH)

2003-2004 SESSION
- The Sustainable Energy Act (30 March 2004) (WH)

2005-2006 SESSION
- Council Housing Finance (29 June 2005) (WH)
- Forensic Sciences (18 October 2005) (WH)

2006-2007 SESSION
- Drugs Policy in Prisons (14 March 2007) (WH)
- Remploy Factory Closures (13 June 2007) (WH)
- The Impact of Health Funding on Health Inequalities (9 October 2007)

2007-2008 SESSION
- Global Security (Middle East) (24 January 2008) (WH)
- Assisted Dying (11 November 2008) (WH)

2008-2009 SESSION
- Economic Aid to Palestinian Territories (27 January 2009) (WH)
- Dr Adrian Garfoot (16 March 2009)
- Light Dues (2 June 2009) (WH)
- Spending on Railways in the North of England (1 July 2009) (WH)

LIST OF SPEECHES RELATED TO MY BILLS/ACTS OF PARLIAMENT

2002-2003 SESSION
- First Reading of the Marine Safety Bill (11 December 2002)
- Second Reading of the Marine Safety Bill (28 February 2003)
- Report Stage and Third Reading of the Marine Safety Bill (16 May 2003)

2005-2006 SESSION

- Presentation of the Registration Service Bill (a Ten Minute Rule Bill) (23 November 2005) (later adopted by the Government and incorporated into The Statistics and Registration Service Act 2010)

2006-2007 SESSION

- Presentation of the Pedlars (Street Trading Regulation) Bill (a Ten Minute Rule Bill) (21 February 2007) (also a Presentation Bill in the 2007-2008 session of Parliament)

2007-2008 SESSION

- Presentation of the Road Traffic (Accident Compensation) Bill (a Ten Minute Rule Bill) (19 November 2008)

2009-2010 SESSION

- First Reading of the Mortgage Repossessions (Protection of Tenants Etc) Bill (16 December 2009)
- Second Reading of the Mortgage Repossessions (Protection of Tenants Etc) Bill (29 January 2010)
- Third Reading of the Mortgage Repossessions (Protection of Tenants Etc) Bill (26 February 2010)

LIST OF SPEECHES RELATED TO SELECT COMMITTEE REPORTS

2000-2001 SESSION

- Cancer Research – A Fresh Look (11 January 2001)

2001-2002 SESSION

- Genetics and Insurance (25 October 2001) (WH)
- Wave and Tidal Energy (10 January 2002) (WH)
- The Research Assessment Exercise (27 June 2002) (WH)

2002-2003 SESSION

- Science Education from 14 to 19 (3 April 2003) (WH)

2003-2004 SESSION

- Light Pollution and Astronomy (12 February 2004) (WH)
- The Scientific Response to Terrorism (18 March 2004) (WH)
- Nanotechnology (24 June 2004) (WH)
- REACH (9 September 2004) (WH)

2004-2005 SESSION

- The Use of Science in International Development (17 March 2005) (WH)

2005-2006 SESSION

- Scientific Publications: A Free for All? (15 December 2005) (WH)
- Forensic Science on Trial (20 April 2006) (WH)

2006-2007 SESSION

- Innovation Policy (24 January 2007) (WH)
- Drug Classification: Making a Hash of It (14 June 2007) (WH)

2007-2008 SESSION
- The Funding of Science and Discovery Centres (15 May 2008) (WH)

2008-2009 SESSION
- Investigating the Oceans (2 April 2009) (WH)

OTHER PARLIAMENTARY SPEECHES

1997-1998 SESSION
- Maiden speech (21 May 1997)
- Oxford and Cambridge College Fees (19 November 1997)
- Second Reading of the Cold Weather Payments (Wind Chill Factor) Bill (23 January 1998)
- Child Support Agency (9 February 1998)
- Second Reading of the Teaching and Higher Education Bill [Lords] (16 March 1998)
- Vitamin B_6 (24 June 1998)
- University Research (14 July 1998)

1998-1999 SESSSION
- Second Reading of the Protection of Children Bill (26 February 1999)
- Drugs (2 July 1999)

1999-2000 SESSION
- Second Reading of the Medical Treatment (Prevention of Euthanasia) Bill (28 January 2000)
- Second Reading of the Warm Homes and Energy Conservation Bill (10 March 2000)

2000-2001 SESSION
- Embryology (15 December 2000)

2001-2002 SESSION
- Second Reading of the Homelessness Bill (2 July 2001)
- Drugs Strategy (9 November 2001)
- Second Reading of the Home Energy Conservation Bill (30 November 2001)
- Second Reading of the Commonhold and Leasehold Reform Bill [Lords](8 January 2002)
- Report Stage of the Commonhold and Leasehold Reform Bill [Lords](13 March 2002)
- Third Reading of the Commonhold and Leasehold Reform Bill [Lords](13 March 2002)
- Report Stage of the Home Energy Conservation Bill (10 May 2002)
- Energy Towards 2050 (20 June 2002)

2002-2003 SESSION
- The Government's Drugs Policy (an Estimates Day Debate) (5 December 2002)
- Drugs Policy (13 Jan 2002)
- The EU Food Supplements Directive (20 January 2003)
- Report Stage of the Local Government Bill (10 March 2003)
- The Water Bill [Lords](10 November 2003)

2003-2004 SESSION
- Second Reading of the Housing Bill (12 January 2004)
- Second Reading of the Energy Bill [Lords](10 May 2004)
- Summer Recess Adjournment – on the 'Bolton Prostitution Forum' (22 July 2004)
- Second Reading of the Mental Capacity Bill (11 October 2004)
- Consideration of Lords Amendments to the Housing Bill (8 November 2004)

2004-2005 SESSION
- Report Stage of the Mental Capacity Bill (14 December 2004)
- Second Reading of the Drugs Bill (18 January 2005)
- The EU Food Supplements Directive (25 January 2001) (Opposition Day Debate)

2005-2006 SESSION
- The Influence of the Pharmaceutical Industry (8 December 2005) (an Estimates Day Debate based on a report by the Health Select Committee)
- Second Reading of the Road Safety Bill (8 March 2006)
- Human Reproductive Technologies and the Law (an Estimates Day Debate based on a report of the Science and Technology Select Committee) (3 July 2006)

2006-2007 SESSION
- Second Reading of the Statistics and Registration Service Bill (8 January 2007)

- Report Stage and Third Reading of the Statistics and Registration Service Bill (13 March 2007)
- Second Reading of the Vehicle Registration Marks Bill (23 March 2007)
- The Marine Environment (19 April 2007)
- Opposition speech to the Drugs (Reclassification and Roadside Testing) Bill (a Ten Minute Rule Bill presented by Christopher Chope MP) (25 April 2007)
- Third Reading of the Mental Health Bill (9 July 2007)
- Scientific Advice, Risk and Evidence-Based Policy Making (an Estimates Day Debate) (9 July 2007)
- Machinery of Government (a debate on the future of the Science and Technology Select Committee) (24 July 2007)

2007-2008 SESSION
- Second Reading of the Housing and Regeneration Bill (27 November 2007)
- Topical Debate on the Government's Drugs Policy (3 April 2008)
- Report Stage of the Energy Bill (30 April 2008)
- Second Reading of the Human Fertilisation and Embryology Bill (12 May 2008)
- The Science Budget (an Estimates Day Debate) (7 July 2008)

2008-2009 SESSION
- Debate on the Royal Address (8 December 2008)
- Second Reading of the Coroners and Justice Bill (26 January 2009)

2009-2010 SESSION

- Students and Universities (an Estimates Day Debate based on a report from the Science and Technology Select Committee) (10 December 2009)
- Access to Higher Education (15 March 2010)

*Speeches given in main chamber unless indicated by WH = Westminster Hall debating chamber. These speeches can be accessed by searching Google for House of Commons *Hansard*.

APPENDIX 2

PHOTOGRAPHS AND OTHER ILLUSTRATIONS

I thank the people or organisations listed below for their kind permission to publish photographs. Every attempt has been made to contact copyright holders but this was not always possible. The author is happy to be contacted by copyright holders who feel that their photographs have not been acknowledged and apologises for any unintended omissions in this respect. Many of the photographs are from the author's own archives or from family collections.

The photograph of the author in the introductory pages appears with permission of the Parliamentary Labour Party.

CHAPTER 1
P. 44.   Cllr Kevin Jones.
P. 48.   Cllr Kevin Jones.

CHAPTER 2
P. 66	top. *Bolton Chronicle*.
P. 66	bottom. *Bolton Evening News*.
P. 70.	*Bolton Evening News*.
P. 76.	Bolton Metropolitan Borough Council.
P. 97	top. Bolton Metropolitan Borough Council.
P. 97	bottom. Bolton Metropolitan Borough Council.
P. 99	top. Bolton Metropolitan Borough Council.
P. 99	bottom. Bolton Metropolitan Borough Council.
P. 108	top. Bolton Metropolitan Borough Council.
P. 108	bottom. Bolton Metropolitan Borough Council.
P. 115.	Photographer Harry McGuire.

CHAPTER 3
P. 155. With the permission of Paul Routledge.

CHAPTER 4
P. 176. Parliamentary copyright, House of Commons Photographer 1997 Deryc Sands.

CHAPTER 5
P. 199. Cancer Research UK.

CHAPTER 6
P. 224.	The Labour Party.
P. 239.	Bolton NHS Foundation Trust.
P. 253.	The Labour Party.

CHAPTER 7
P. 260. Royal Society for the Prevention of Cruelty to Animals.

SCIENCE AND POLITICS: AN UNLIKELY MIXTURE

CHAPTER 9
P. 291   top. University of Bolton.
P. 291   bottom. University of Bolton.
P. 295.   Bolton Wanderers FC.
P. 296.   Bolton Wanderers FC.
P. 310.   Shree Swaminarayan Mandir Art and Culture Centre.

CHAPTER 10
P. 322.   Consumers for Health Choice.
P. 331.   Photograph taken by Andreas Wiesner.

CHAPTER 11
P. 336.   Photograph taken by Yasser Arafat's staff.

CHAPTER 12
P. 369.   Photograph taken by staff of the Joint Program for Chemical and Biological Defense, USA.
P. 374   top. Dr Stephen Benn.
P. 374   bottom. Science and Technology Select Committee.

CHAPTER 13
P. 381.   Dr Stephen Benn.
P. 385   bottom. The Royal Society of Chemistry.
P. 386.   University of Bolton.
P. 391.   University of Bolton.

CHAPTER 14
P. 397.   The Oxford Union.
P. 405.   The Haemophilia Society.
P. 406.   Photograph taken at the launch of the All-Party Parliamentary Hepatology Group; used by kind permission of David Amess MP, chairman.

CHAPTER 15
P. 423.	Transport for Greater Manchester.
P. 431.	Austin Mitchell MP.
P. 433.	Photograph taken by Chris Woolley on behalf of Bolton Metropolitan Borough Council.
P. 439	top. Rehab Group.
P. 439	bottom. Rehab Group.
P. 442	top. Greater Manchester Police.
P. 442	bottom. Published with the approval of Sir Neil Thorne.

CHAPTER 16
P. 455.   Bolton Metropolitan Council.

CHAPTER 17
P. 464.	Parliamentary copyright, House of Commons 2010 Photographer Terry Moore.
P. 467.	Society of Chemical Industry – SCI.

SCIENCE AND POLITICS: AN UNLIKELY MIXTURE

INDEX

Note: Terms in Appendix I are not covered.

Aaronovitch, David, 338
Abbas, President Mahmoud (aka Abu Mazan), 337, 340
Abbott, Paul, 389, 390
Abbottabad, 218
ABC classification of drugs, 215, 373
Abdulla II, King of Jordan, 348
Abortion, 258, 331, 372
Abortion Act 1967, 372
Abu Ghraib Prison, 211
AbuZayd, Karen Koning, 344
Academy schools, 198, 254
Adams, Gerry, 211
Adelaide Street, 79-81
Adjournment debates, 147, 164, 168, 172, 202, 266, 272-288 (CHAPTER 8; see also Appendix I), 306, 320, 326, 327, 366, 410, 415, 416
Adonis, Lord Andrew, 220, 226
Adoption, 197, 223
Adoption meetings, 110, 121
Advance decisions, 216
Advice surgeries, 101-102, 129, 130, 137, 158, 405
Advisory Council on the Misuse of Drugs (ACMD), 373, 420
Affordable housing, 210, 285
Afghanistan (invasion) 196, 197, 234, 246
African National Congress (ANC), 69, 235
Age Concern, 74, 422 (Farnworth)
Agency workers, 251
Ahmadinejad, President Mahmoud, 226
Ahmed, Jameel, 356, 358
Aid to developing countries, 188-189, 212, 222, 235, 251, 336, 368-370
Ainsworth Arms public house, 79
Ainsworth, Bob, 207, 397
Airedale NHS Trust, 328
Albert Hall, Bolton, 30, 31-32, 62-63 (fire), 290, 456
Albert Hall, London, 36
Alcohol sales, 188, 205
Aldermen (including Hon. Aldermen), 29, 39, 106, 108
ALERT, 330, 462
Alexander, Douglas, 191
Alker, Jim, 84, 108
Allanson, Brian, 84
Allotments, 44-45
All-Party Parliamentary Groups (APPGs), 394-420 (CHAPTER 14)
All-women shortlists, 126, 458
ALMOs APPG, 395
American Chemical Society, 383-384
American Colony Hotel, Jerusalem, 340
Amputations, 286-287
Amsterdam, 403, 443
Anderson, Donald, 199, 380, 381
Anderson, Janet, 132
Andrew Marr Show, 233, 461
Animal welfare, 169, 222
Annapolis Agreement, 346
Annual Policy Meeting (Labour Party), 63, 75, 84
Anti-Fascist (Anti-Nazi) League, 37, 61
Antiques Road Show, 468
Anti-Social Behaviour Orders (ASBOs), 180, 188, 205

SCIENCE AND POLITICS: AN UNLIKELY MIXTURE

Apprentices, 76, 78, 82, 235, 243, 376, 457
Arafat, Yasser, 336, 337, 339, 341
Archer Inquiry, 407, 408 (Report)
Archer, Lord, 407, 420 (death of)
Armed Forces Day, 285
Arterial disease, 286
Arts and Humanities Research Council, 208
Arts Committee, 46, 57
Asda Stores, 295 (Burnden), 425 and 429 (Farnworth)
Ashcroft, Lord, 231, 241
Ashdown Drive, 15-16, 20-21
Ashdown, Paddy, 164, 181
Ashton, Joe, 179, 190, 326-327
Assisted Area Status, 59
Assisted dying/physician assisted suicide, 326, 327, 328, 329, 331, 332 (Bill)
Assisted Places Scheme, 173, 174
Association of British Insurers, 308
Association of Chief Police Officers (ACPO), 416
Association of Town Centre Managers, 416
Astley Bridge Branch Annual BBQ, 107
Astronomy, 367
Atkinson, Morrell, 40, 55, 59
Attacks on MPs and their staff, 130
Attorney General, 165, 301
Austin, Ian, 192
Avoncliff Close, 117, 300, 446, 447, 448
Ayub, Chaudhary Muhammed, 356
Ayub, Cllr Mohammed, 355
Azad Kasmir, 350, 352-354, 356
Azzun (West Bank), 345-346

Bagley, Dave, 278
Bahrain, 333-334, 411
Bain, Willie, 250
Bakers, Food and Allied Trades Trade Union, 425
Balata refugee camp (West Bank), 341
Balfour Declaration, 336
Balkans, 234
Ballard, Robert, 413

Ballot Bills, 257, 259, 258, 407
Balls, Ed, 191
Bankers' bonuses, 245, 251
Bank of England, 177, 232, 242
Banks, Tony 138, 169-170
Bar (of the HoC), 160, 200, 271
Barker, Ivy and Jim (Eileen's parents), 447, 449, 450 (deaths of)
Barnes, Arnold, 18, 20
Barnes, Gladys, 18
Barrett, John, 150
Barton Aerodrome, 56-67, 442, 443
Barton, Oliver, 265
Bassam, Lord (Steve), 270
Bate, Carla, 304
Bateman, Carly, 277
Bates, John, 166-167
Battle, John, 451
Battle of Passchendaele, 284
Battle of the Somme, 284
Baumber, John, 434
Beach refugee camp, Gaza, 342
Beagle 2, Mars lander, 370
Beckett, Margaret, 129, 254
Bed blocking in the NHS, 188, 204
Bees Knees nightclub, 23
Belfast (or Good Friday) Agreement, 175, 176, 184, 204 (monitoring), 211, 319, 437
Belfast Airport, 437
Bell, Martin, 162, 429
Bellingham, Henry, 399
Ben-Gurion, David, 334
Benjamin, Campbell, 72, 97, 106, 108
Benn, Caroline, 382
Benn, Hilary, 369, 381, 410
Benn, Dr Stephen,[1] 381, 383, 384, 393, 462, 463
Benn, Tony, 193, 381, 382, 392
Ben-Tovim, Atarah, 33
Benzodiazepine tranquillizers, 275
Bercow, John, 240, 464
Bercow, Sally, 240

Bermingham, Gerry, 102
Berry, Doris, 39
Berry, Jan, 401
Berry, Roger, 183
Berry, Tony, 82
Best, George, 404, 406
Best, Lord (Richard), 270, 462
Beswick, Alan, 89
Betts, Leah and Paul, 400
Bhattacharya, Rishi, 306-307
Bhatti, Mohammed, 350, 351
Bhutto, Benazir, 353
Bibby Tankers (ship owners), 412
Bichard, Michael, 128
Big Ben, 152
Big Brother, 227, 240, 280
Biggles, 65-66, 119
Binge drinking, 234, 437
Bingo, 26
bin Laden, Osama, 197, 218 (death of)
Bioengineering, 377
Biosecurity, 376
Biosimilar medicines, 286
Birch, Peter, 109
Birtenshaw Hall Special School, 53
Bir Zeit University (West Bank), 339
Bitterberg, Gunter, 52, 73
Blackburn Road, 43, 44, 49, 57, 83
Blackburn Road by-pass, 43
Black Friday, 242
Blackrod, 39, 434
Blackstone, Tessa, 289
Blair, Cherie, 157, 212, 382, 434
Blair, Tony, 111, 121, 125, 126, 127, 128, 129, 156, 157, 171, 172, 175, 179, 181-182, 187, 191-193, 203, 207, 208, 211, 213, 217, 220, 222, 226, 227, 228, 231, 232, 254, 315, 434, 459, 460
Blakemore, Prof. Colin, 373
Bland, Tony, 328
Blears, Hazel, 170-172, 232, 246, 247, 427, 437
Blundell, Private Richard, 285
Blunkett, David, 128, 166, 206, 217-218 (resignation), 220, 224 (2nd resignation), 373

Blunt, Crispin, 327
Boardman, Robert, 165
Bolton Accommodation Project (BAP), 87-88
Bolton Affiliation of Tenants' Associations (BATA), 85
Bolton Affiliation of Tenants' and Residents' Associations (BATRA), 85
Bolton and District Civic Trust, 21
Bolton at Home, 95, 395, 425
Bolton Bond Board, 88
Bolton Castle public house, 18
Bolton Community Homes, 90
Bolton Council for Community Relations (BCCR), 47, 69-72
Bolton [County] Borough Council, 19, 55, 73
Bolton Crown Court, 293, 313
Bolton District Labour Party (Local Government Committee), 24, 25, 26, 27, 29, 34, 40, 47, 50-51, 52, 55, 63, 65, 73, 82, 96, 103, 467
Bolton Diversity Awards, 358
Bolton East constituency, 27, 28, 37, 51, 68, 101, 468
Bolton East CLP, 38, 40, 101, 107
Bolton Family Court, 313
Bolton Festival, 57-58
Bolton FM, 457
Bolton General Hospital, 8, 69, 82, 101, 284
Bolton Institute of Higher Education, 61, 169, 208, 289-291
Bolton-le-Moors Round Table, 15
Bolton Magistrates' Court, 292-293 (petition against closure), 313
Bolton Market Hall, 50
Bolton [Metropolitan Borough or MB] Council: see Chapters 1 (pp. 1-59) and 2 (pp. 60-106)
Bolton MB Council Labour Group, 47, 48, 51, 74, 77, 85, 286
Bolton Mountain Rescue Team, 280
Bolton Neighbour Dispute Service, 91, 92, 144
Bolton North East constituency, 28, 73, 122, 143, 144, 148, 285, 468
Bolton North East CLP, 25, 59, 83, 107
Bolton Primary Care Trust, 139
Bolton Racial Equality Council (BREC) 36, 72
Bolton Register Office (see also Mere Hall), 265

Bolton Riding Club, 21

Bolton's archives, 387, 462

Bolton School, 28, 38, 69, 384

Bolton's ethnic minority communities, 36, 43, 48, 102, 349

Bolton Sixth Form College, 428

Bolton South East constituency, 28, 68 (first PPC selection for this seat), 100-106, 121, 143, 277, 300, 349, 357, 424, 464

Bolton South East CLP, 101-105 (PPC selection for 2010 General Election), 137-138, 145, 148, 436, 458, 459 (PPC selection for 2010 General Election), 460, 461

Bolton's red light areas, 277

Bolton's Roll of Honour, 283, 285

Bolton Substance Misuse Group, 425

Bolton Technical Innovation Centre (TIC), 376, 389-391

Bolton Town Hall, 26-27, 44, 46, 47, 48, 58, 62, 115, 122, 125, 129, 137, 185, 233, 265, 279, 283, 285, 290, 297, 386, 456

Bolton Trades Council, 225

Bolton United Veterans' Association, 181, 283, 456

Bolton Wanderers FC, 294-296, 424 (Lofty the Lion mascot), 457

Bolton West constituency, 27-28, 37, 51, 68, 83, 122, 137, 143, 158, 293, 411, 459

Bolton Youth Orchestra, 32, 36

Booth, Geoffrey, 37

Boothroyd, Betty, 131, 160-161, 185

Bounds, Peter, 77

Bourguiba, President Habib, 7

Bowen, Jeremy, 339-340

Bowes, David, 165

Bowling Green public house, 83

Boxing Day tsunami (2004), 212

Boys, Carol, 280

Bradford and Bingley Building Society, 241

Bradford Ward Labour Club, 103, 104, 110, 146, 148

Bradshaw, Ben, 171

Brake, 309 (Campaign of the Month Award)

Brand, Jo, 307

Branson, Richard, 319

Breaking the Silence, 341

Breighttrust Colliery, 2

Bretton Hall College, 36, 112

Brexit, 59

Bribery law reform, 243, 251

BRIC countries (Brazil, Russia, India and China), 435

Briggs, William, 14-15

Britain-Bahrain APPG, 333-334, 411

Britain-India APPG, 349, 411

Britain-Jordan APPG, 348, 411

Britain-Kashmir APPG, 349, 411, 420

Britain-Pakistan APPG, 349, 411

Britain-Palestine APPG, 334, 411, 420

Britain-Quatar APPG, 411

Britain's Secret Shame, 302

British Broadcasting Corporation (BBC), 73, 162, 168, 172, 208, 232, 233, 276, 278-279, 297 and 300 (Fred Dibnah), 302, 307, 339, 464, 465, 468

British National Party (BNP), 61, 237

British Rail, 61, 512

Brittan, Leon, 351

Broadbent, Hugh, 95-96

Bromley Cross, 39, 53

Brooke, Peter, 133

Brothels, 57, 277

Brown, Gordon, 127-128, 177, 179, 191, 192 and 205 (euro decision), 211, 220, 231, 232, 233, 238, 242, 244, 245, 246, 247, 249, 251, 252, 253, 254, 435 (meetings with NW Group of MPs), 461, 464, 465

Brown, Ian, 78

Browning, Angela, 320

Bryant, Chris, 231

Bryson, Bill, 383

BSE ('mad cow disease'), 178

Buckingham Palace, 83, 191, 430-431 (receptions), 431 (Garden Parties), 432, 461, 465

Budd, Sir Alan, 218

Budgets, 127-128, 160, 177, 191, 231, 238, 246, 461, 466

Building Schools for the Future Programme, 250

Building Services Manager, 76, 78, 79

Buprenorphine, 274

Burlington House, 220, 221, 268, 381, 384

Burnham, Andy, 253, 408

Burnside, David, 318

Burnton, Justice Stanley, 352
Burt, Alistair, 25
Bury and Bolton Kid's Club Network, 426
Bury North constituency, 25, 73, 102, 225, 249
Bury South constituency, 86
Bush, President George, 241
Business of the House motions, 200, 201, 227, 256
Bus Lane, Leigh-Atherton-Bolton, 422, 423
Butler Inquiry, 208
Butler-Sloss, Dame, 329
Buy-to-Let, 269
Byers, Stephen, 163, 196, 202, 217 (resignation), 247, 249
Byrne, John and Lynda, 108, 466

Cabinet government (LAs), 174
Cabinet Office, 294, 316, 365, 397
Cabinet Room, 435
Cable, Vince, 462
Callaghan, Jim, 58
Cameron, David, 164, 232, 253, 396, 464
Campaign for Nuclear Disarmament, (CND), 204
Campbell, Alistair, 191, 208
Campbell, Ian, 32-36
Canavan, Dennis, 162, 182
Cancer research, 363, 364
Cancer Research Campaign, 364
Cancer Research UK, 199, 364
Cancer Zsar, 364
Cannabis, 167, 373, 396, 397, 400, 401
Cannon Street health centre, 148
Cannon Street Hindu Temple, 310
Canon Row Pass Office, 133
Canon Slade CE School, 53
Canvin, Marion, 89
Capital punishment, 58
Capo di Monte Grand Hotel, Sorrento, 450
Caravan Club, 6
Carbon (dioxide) capture and storage, 236, 365, 378
Carbon-free energy generation, 364
Carbon monoxide poisoning, 92-93
Careline, 89

Care Not Killing (CNK) Alliance, 330, 331, 332
Caribbean Regional Drug Enforcement Training Centre, Jamaica, 404
Carlisle, Mark, 62
Car manufacturing, 189-190
Carmody, Paul, 29
Carpet of Lilies, 405
Carr, Roland, 51
Carr-Gomm, Richard, 88
Carter, Paul, 122
Cash, Bill, 172
Cash for crash insurance pay-outs, 449
'Cash for peerages', 227
Casino nightclub, 18, 22
Castle, Barbara, 83
Castle Hill Primary School, 5, 13, 31-32
Castle Hill Youth Club, 53
Castle Street, 51-52 (gas explosion)
Castle Street Housing Action Area, 51
Castle Street Methodist Chapel, 44
Caswell, George, 77-78, 79, 82, 84-85, 89, 90, 91, 95, 463 (retirement)
Catalyst Museum, 391, 426
Cathinones, 400
Catholic Children's Rescue Society, 88
Cattle Market public house, 79
Causing death by careless driving, 305
Cecilia Street, 52 (gas explosion)
Central Lobby, 152, 161
Central Ward, 48, 49, 50, 54, 56, 61, 82, 94, 106, 143
Centre for Applied Microbiology and Research (CAMR), 367
Centre for Disease Control, Atlanta, 367
Chadwick Street Teachers Training College, 17
Chairman's Panel, 175
Chakothi, 354, 356
Chalfont Street Primary School, 43-44, 53
Chambers, Andrew, 113, 121, 125, 452
Chambers (nee Iddon), Sally, 113, 121, 125
Channel Islands, 325-326
Channel Tunnel, 217
Chapman, Prof. N B, 383, 385
Charities reform, 223

Charles House, 45

Charlton, Simon, 296

Chartered Borough Status, 84 (150th anniversary)

Chartered Institute of Housing, 269

Chastelain, General John de, 175

Chaudhry, Barrister Sultan Mehmood, 352

Chaytor, David, 162, 225, 249

Chemical, Biological, Radiobiological and Nuclear (CBRN) Warfare, 366

Chemical Industries Association (CIA), 410

Chemical Industry APPG, 410

Chief Scientific Advisers (CSAs), 190, 365, 369 (DfID), 379

Chilcot Inquiry/Report, 203, 218

Child poverty, 243

Children's Centres, 234, 251

Children's Commissioners, 187 (Wales), 209 (England)

Child Support Agency (CSA), 145, 173, 201, 229

Child Trust Funds, 209

Chishty family, 356, 357 (and house fire)

Chope, Christopher, 418, 419

Choudhary-Best, Elspeth, 462

Choudhry, Sadia, 137, 138

Christie, Linford, 375

Church, East and North Ward, 36, 41, 42, 48, 56

Church House, 126

Churchill Restaurant, Palace of Westminster, 432

Churchill, Sir Winston, 162, 163-164

Citizens Advice, 269

Citizens Advice Parliamentarian of the Year Award, 270, 462

City Challenge Board, 93-94 (members), 265

City Challenge Scheme, 93, 94

Civic functions, 455-456, 463, 466

Civil contingency planning, 209, 236

Civil partnerships, 210

Clare Court, 93, 95

Clarence Street Women's College, 16-17

Clark, Dr David, 185-186

Clark, Michael, 374, 380, 381

Clarke, Alan, 50

Clarke, Charles, 206, 207, 208, 247, 248, 290, 386, 465

Clarke, Donald, 48, 49, 50

Clarke, Kenneth, 293

Clarke, Nita, 381

Clay Cross, 13

Clegg, Nick, 164, 464

Clerks of the House, 161

Cliffs of Moher, 7

Climate change 178, 226, 228, 229, 236, 365, 375, 377, 378

Climate Change Levy, 180

Climatic Research Unit, UEA, leak of emails, 377

Clipboard solicitors, 448

Clock Tower (housing Big Ben), 152

Coalition Government, 164, 215, 254, 372, 379, 389, 390, 465

Coats Crafts, 14

Coats, J and P, UK Ltd, 14, 60

Cocaine, 167, 215, 403

Codeine, 275, 276

Cohen, Sam, 39

Collins, Phil, 220, 459-461

Colman, Mr Justice, 413

Commission for Africa, 217

Commission for Equality and Human Rights, 223

Committee of Selection, 263

Committee of Toxicity of Chemicals in Food, Consumer Products and the Environment (COT), 320

Committee Room 14, 126

Commonhold and leasehold reform, 197, 317, 318 (Act of Parliament 2002)

Common land management, 223

Commonwealth Games, Manchester, 202, 423 (presentation of medals)

Commonwealth Parliamentary Association, 402

Communications Allowance, 227, 231

Communication Workers Union (CWU), 109, 247

Community Charge (see Poll Tax)

Community Health Councils, 100, 184

Community Infrastructure Levy, 236

Community radio, 457

Community Relations Officer, 37, 40

Compensation schemes (see also contaminated blood):
　For mesothelioma, 228
　For miners, 181
　For Japanese PoWs, 181
　For vaccine-damaged people, 184, 420
Competition Bill, 174
Comprehensive education, 43, 54, 61-62, 101
Comprehensive Spending Review, 177
Compton Group, 316
Compulsory Competitive Tendering (CCT), 72, 74, 77, 86
Compulsory Treatment orders, 229
Concessionary fares, 197, 229
Congestion charges, 206
Connell, Anthony, 97, 108
Connelly, Shaun, 303
Consensus Business Group, 319
Constituency office, 118, 137, 138, 142, 225, 273, 461, 464, 468
Constituency weeks, 150
Constitutional reform, 175, 181, 210, 236, 251
Construction Industry Training Board (CITB), 425
Consumers for Health Choice, 321, 322 and 324 (petition), 325
Contaminated blood, 268, 405, 407-409 (HoC debate on), 410
Cook, Robin, 151, 192, 203 (resignation), 222 (death of)
Copperfields nightclub, 18, 22-23
Corner, June, 100
Coroners' courts, 243-244, 305
Corporate manslaughter, 228
Corris family, 451, 452
Corston, Jean, 112, 127
Council for the Advancement of Arab-British Understanding (CAABU), 342
Council house R&M, 72, 75, 80, 86, 234-235
Council of Churches, 147
Council of Europe, 19, 457
Countryside access, 184, 190, 243 (coast)
Courts management, 205
Coventry Cathedral, 315
Coward, Ken, 79
Cox, Jo, 158

Crausby, David, 83, 97, 122, 142, 143-144, 148, 291, 296, 312
Credit crunch, 241, 243, 319
Credit unions, 89
Crewe and Nantwich by-election, 237
Crick, Francis, 387
Crime levels, 94, 111, 191, 234, 250
Criminal Justice Act 2003, 302, 352
Criminal Justice and Police Bill, 188
Crisis, 269
Crompton, Samuel, 4, 17, 19, 38, 57, 460
Crompton Way, 18, 20, 23, 37, 61
Cromwell Green and Visitor's Entrance, 152, 213
Crook, Ernie, 37, 71
Crook, Lilian, 24, 26
Crossing the floor, 162, 163
Crossrail, 228
Crown Courts, 166, 205, 293, 313
Crown Dependencies, 325 (Guernsey and Jersey)
Crown Prosecution Service (CPS), 165, 228, 304
Crown (Queen's) Jewels, 430
Cruck cottages, 14, 16
Crudas, John, 232
Cryer, Ann, 352, 355
Crystal Mark Award, 94
Cullen Report, 204
Cunliffe, David, 273, 274
Cunliffe, Lawrence, 47
Cunningham, Dr Jack, 136
Curtis-Thomas, Claire, 200, 392
Customer care, 82-83
Customs and Excise, 215, 217

Dalyell, Tam, 110-112, 178, 195, 202, 214
Danda, Parmjit, 430
Daresbury, 187
Darfur, 235
Darling, Alistair, 238, 246, 461
Darling, Gerald, QC, 413
Dart Radio Service Co., 51
Darzi, Lord (Ara), 238, 254
Data Protection Act, 139

Davies, Keith, 293
Davies, Quentin, 162
Davies, Ron, 179
Dean, Billy Joe, 157, 301-302
Dearden, Joan, 140-141, 158
Decent Homes Standard, 235
Defence Science and Technology Laboratory (Dstl), 367
Defend Council Housing, 395
Deferred Divisions, 189
Delhi, 352, 357
Denham, John, 203 (resignation)
Department for Education and Employment, 128
Department of Justice, 230, 292
Deputy Speaker, 164, 175, 276
Derbyshire, MV, 376, 411-413 (APPG), 412-415, 420 (exhibition)
Derby Street School, 35
Derby Ward Labour Club, 103, 109, 140
Devenish, Harry, 39
Devine, Jim, 162, 249
Devlin, Bernadette, 27
Devolution, 173, 175, 212, 228
Diabetes, 287
Diamond Synchrotron, 186-187
Diana, Princess of Wales, 128-129
Dibnah, Fred, 45, 297-300, 424
Digital broadcasting, 228
Digital economy, 251
Dignitas, 328
Dignity in Dying (DiD), 327-330, 461
Dingle Peninsula, 6-7
Dingwall, David, 20, 27, 33, 34, 39, 40, 43, 47, 50, 52, 53-56, 62, 65, 82, 106, 143
Dingwall, Vera, 55, 106 (marriage to David Young)
Direct Grant Grammar School, 69
Direct Labour Organisations (DLOs), 72
Disability rights, 180 and 197 (Commission), 209
Disasters Emergency Committee, 212
Diversity in Barrier Breaking Communications (DBBC), 456, 457
Divisions, 161
Dixon Green Labour Club, 103, 119, 459

DNA, 188 (retention of samples), 224, 387 (structure)
Dobbin, Jim, 216, 451, 457
Dobson, Ellis, 51
Dobson, Frank, 182, 186
Dogs, 56 (dangerous), 67, 174, 187, 204 and 259 (hunting with)
Dolphin Square, 134-136, 155-156, 248, 465
Domestic violence, 38, 209, 296
Donaghy, Martin, 30, 67, 97
Donaldson, Lord, 250, 264
Door Keepers, 131 161-162, 325
Dorries, Nadine, 154
Dors, Diana, 15
Dossier of Shame, 99
'Double effect', 326
Double jeopardy rule, 205
10 Downing Street, 127, 220, 245, 247, 252, 253, 352, 381, 405, 427, 434-435, 460
Down's Syndrome, 280, 281, 281
Down's Syndrome Association, 280
Draft Bills, 150, 173, 200, 227, 237, 372, 376
Draft legislative programme, 228, 229
Drayson, Lord Paul, 192
Driving Me Crazy, 307
Dromey, Jack, 227
Drug addiction, 88, 275, 276, 399
Drug misuse, 158, 173, 276, 279, 443, 462
Drug Misuse APPG, 168, 275, 276, 396, 400, 402
Drugs and the Party Line, 400
Drugs Act 2005, 215
DrugScope, 276
Drugs Zsar, 397
Drug testing 275 (workplace and roadside), 279 (workplace)
Duffy, Gillian, 465
Dummy Bills, 271
Dunblane shootings, 93
Dunleavy, Deborah, 148
Dunwoody, Gwyneth, 199
Durham, 8 419
Durham Union, 400, 401
DVLA, 305, 306

Dying Well Naturally APPG, 411

Dziubas, Dorothy, 13

Eagle, Maria, 412

Eagley Mills, 14, 60

Early Day Motions, 150-151 (House of Commons Cat), 169-170, 207, 296 (domestic violence), 314, 317-318 (Estates and Management Ltd), 325, 326, 382, 416

Early One Morning, 283

East coast main railway line, 249 (nationalisation)

Eastham, Hilary, 90, 95

Eastwood, Don, 24, 65, 82

Eccles constituency, 73, 131, 419

Ecclestone, Bernie, 187, 192

Ecstasy, 373, 400

Education Committee, 34, 53, 62, 82

Education Maintenance Allowances, 215, 250

Edwards, Wally, 29

Eldon Street Residents' Association, 24

Elected Mayors, 174

Election agents, 29, 106, 146, 147, 148, 152, 436

Election manifestos, 30, 41-42, 68-69, 123-124 (1997 General Election), 131, 206

Election promises (mine in 1997), 145-146

Electoral Commission, 188, 240, 244

Electoral fraud, 223

Electoral reform, 181, 183 [City of London (Ward Elections) Act], 187-188, 223

Electricity generating technologies, 376

Elizabeth Tower (formerly the Clock Tower), 158

Elliot, Steve, 410

Ellman, Louise, 359

El-Sarraj, Dr Eyad, 344

Embryos, legislation for research on, 186, 189, 236, 245, 370-372, 377

Emergency Towing Vehicles (ETVs), 260, 261, 264

Employment protection, 173, 198, 209, 251, 267

Employment Select Committee, 101

Employment Tribunals, 266

Energy Act, 236

Energy conservation, 394

Energy needs (UK), 365

Energy review, 226

Energywatch, 228

Engineering, 60, 61, 192, 365, 369, 376, 377, 387, 388, 392

English Defence League, 461

Entwisle, Pat, 106, 152, 436 (visit to Palace of Westminster with Edith Holden)

Entwistle, Barrie, 117

Entwistle, Harry, 55

Entwistle, Laura, 304

Entwistle, Pat, 116, 454

Environmental Audit Select Committee, 360

Ephedrine, 401, 402

Equal pay, 243

Equivalent or Lower Level Qualifications (ELQs), 376

Erez crossing point (Israel-Gaza), 343, 345

Erythropoietins (EPOs), 286, 375

Estate agents, 228

Estates and Management Ltd, 316, 317, 318

Estates Gazette, 319

Europa Industrial Estate, 303, 319

European Architectural Heritage Year, 19

European Constitution, 212, 227, 249

European Convention on Human Rights, 352

European Directives, 205, 306, 309, 321, 323-325, 373

European Economic Community (EEC), 13, 31

European Elections, 83, 183, 214-215 (2004), 247

EU enlargement, 204

European Regulations, 321, 322, 368 (REACH)

European Scientific Committee on the Safety of Food, 323

European Social Chapter, 173

Euthanasia, 258, 326-332, 436, 461, 462

Evans, Bob, 146, 147

Evans, Gareth, 74

Evans, John, 68

Evidence-based policy, 374, 379

Excel Centre, G20 Summit, 245

Exhumation, 273

SCIENCE AND POLITICS: AN UNLIKELY MIXTURE

Expert Group on Vitamins and Minerals, 320

Explanatory Notes (to Bills), 150

Expulsions (PLP), 162, 182, 186

Extradition legislation, 204

Extraordinary rendition, 211, 235

Failing schools, 198

Fairmont Hotel, San Francisco, 367

Fairs and Showgrounds APPG, 411

Falconer, Lord (Charles), 230, 331, 332

Falcon Mill, 446, 448

Falcon public house, 83

Falkland Islands, 101

Farmer, John, 46, 48

Farnworth, 8, 16, 22, 39-61, 68, 82, 88, 93, 95, 103, 104, 122, 137, 146, 147, 165, 198, 304-308, 314, 349, 367, 389, 405, 411, 422, 424, 425, 429, 434, 436, 459, 467

Farnworth and Kearsley Labour Club, 103, 104, 109, 146, 467

Farnworth Town Hall, 88, 93, 137, 432-433 (centenary)

Farnworth War Memorial, 456

Fatah, 337, 345, 346, 358

Father of the House, 193, 195

Fathers4Justice, 213

Fawkes, Guy, 130

Federal Reserve (USA), 241

Fees Office, 135, 155, 239, 249

Felman, Prof. Shai, 338

Festival Committee, 57

Festival Hall, 63

Fidler, Michael, 24

Field General Court Martials, 284

Fielding, David, 405, 407, 410

Financial Institutions, collapse of, 241-242

Financial Services Act, 281

Financial Services Authority (FSA), 184, 232, 245

Firefighters, 12 (retained), 205

Fireworks, 173, 259 (and APPG), 262 (Bill), 411 (APPG)

First past the post voting system, 183, 251

Firwood Fold, 3-4, 14-15, 16-17, 18, 19-22 (see also 'Old School House')

Firwood Fold stables, 18, 20, 21

Firwood Hall, 1-3, 5

Firwood Special School, 20

Fiscal incentives, 242

Fitzhenry, Gerry, 94

Fitzpatrick, Jim, 263

Flint, Caroline, 215, 247

Flooding, 236, 251

Fluoridation of water, 312

Flynn, Paul, 105, 172, 194, 396

Foley, Maurice, 71

Food Advisory Committee, 320

Food and Diet Co. 319

Food safety, 173, 287-288

Food Standards Agency (FSA), 180, 286, 287, 324

Foot and mouth disease, 190, 232

Football hooliganism 184

Foot, Michael, 68 250, 253 (photograph)

Forensic science, 372, 442

Forfeiture, 316, 317

Fortalice, 88

Forth, Eric, 267

Fort Sterling, Horwich, 293-294

Foster, Derek, 105

Foster, Ian, 93

Foster, John (Jack), 39, 65, 93, 96, 98, 463 (death)

Foster, Joyce, 93

Foster, Michael, 67, 174, 259, 260

Foundation Hospital Trusts, 204

Four Ps of Politics, 157

Fox hunting, 67, 174, 187, 198, 204, 206, 214, 259

Franklin, Rosalind, 387

Fraud trials, 228, 229

Fred Dibnah, Steeplejack, 297

Freedom of Information, 145, 173, 184

Freedom of Information Commissioner, 239

Freeholds, 317

Freemen of Bolton, 110

Friends of Palestine (VIPs), 348

Fuel poverty, 394

495

Funding of political parties, 184, 187-188, 192, 201, 223, 227, 231, 236, 240-241
Fund raising, 106-107, 109-110, 116, 142, 146, 148
Future Jobs Fund, 250, 251

Gallipoli, 283
Galloway, George, 162, 227, 401
Gambling reform, 215, 233-234
Gapes, Mike, 147
Garfoot, Dr Adrian, 398, 399
Garfoot, Revd. John, 399
Gawthorpe Hall, 33
Gaza, 335, 336, 337, 338-339, 342-347
General Elections (1974), 20, 27, 28, 31, 37, 336, 337, 338-339
General Election (1979), 37, 46, 54, 58
General Election (1987), 69, 73
General Election (1997), 87, 97, 102, 121-125, 128, 142, 145, 146, 152, 164, 264, 265, 273, 289, 314, 320, 359, 429, 438
General Election (2001), 122, 128, 145, 146, 158, 190, 193, 201, 265, 271, 381, 382
General Election (2005), 122, 145, 148, 162, 163, 215, 219, 227, 231, 265, 296, 325, 360, 370, 371, 372, 438
General Election (2010), 122, 138, 143, 145, 148-149, 163, 172, 177, 231, 240, 248, 249, 253, 259, 269, 356, 360, 379, 392, 408, 410, 438, 461, 464, 465
General Election Fund, 106, 109, 146, 148
General Lighthouse Authorities (GLAs), 415, 416
General Medical Council (GMC), 329, 399 (Interim Orders Committee)
Generic drugs, 274, 286
Genetically Modified (GM) crops, 186, 363, 377
Geoengineering, 378
Gerrard, Neil, 444
Gibraltar, 101
Gibson, Dr Ian, 163, 186, 248 and 256 (resignation), 360, 371, 374, 388
Gidor, Ron, 338
Gill, Henry Arthur, 225
Glasgow Airport attack, 232
Glasgow East by-election, 237
Glasgow North by-election, 250
Gleneagles G8 Summit, 222

Glenrothes by-election, 238
Global Positioning Satellites (GPS), 415, 416
GMB Union, 79, 103, 450
Godlee Observatory, UMIST, 367
Goggins, Paul, 408
Golden Pager Award, 438
Golding, Bruce, 403
Golding, Baroness Llin, 213
Gold reserves, 177
Goldsmith, Walter, 318
Goldsmith Street Housing Action Area, 51
Goodwin, Fred (Fred the Shred), 242, 245
Gore, Ellese Ruth, 304
Gough, Anne and Graham, 52, 358
Gould, Philip, 191
Government Communications HQ (GCHQ), 145
Government Literacy Scheme, 180, 428-429
Government Numeracy Scheme, 180
Government Of All The Talents (GOATS), 255
Government Stationery Office, 164
Government Whips' Office, 25, 153, 206-208, 263, 359, 360, 362, 438 (see also Whips' offices)
Graham, Tommy, 162
Granada TV, 306-307, 440
Grandchildren, 452
Grand Committee Room, 272
Greater London Assembly/Authority, 180, 182, 212, 237
Greater Manchester County Council (GMC), 20, 39, 43, 53, 57
Greater Manchester Courts Committee, 292
Greater Manchester Fire and Rescue Service, 72
Greater Manchester Passenger Transport Committee, 423
Greater Manchester Police (GMP), 273-274, 279 (Committee), 441, 442 (Forensic Science Service and helicopter), 443, 445 (IT equipment), 461
Great Hall of Westminster (see Westminster Hall)
Great Lever Labour Club, 103, 109
Great Lever Ward, 5, 55, 278, 309, 349, 357, 420, 425, 449
Greaves, Andrew, 144
'Green Armband Brigade', 27
Green cards, 160

SCIENCE AND POLITICS: AN UNLIKELY MIXTURE

Green Goddess, 12
Greenspan, Alan, 241
'Green water', 413
Gretna Green, 117-118
Grieve, David, 275
Grime, Donald, 79, 108
Grimes, Andrew, 24, 58
Ground rents, 316 ('grazing'), 318
Guantanamo Bay, 197, 211
Guernsey and Cornwall Fire and Rescue Service, 261
Gujarat, 349
Gulf War syndrome, 312
Gurkhas, 246

Haemophilia APPG, 407
Hague, William, 136, 164, 182, 193
Hain, Peter, 176
Haiti earthquake, 251
Halevi, Shalom, 344
Halifax Bank of Scotland (HBOS), 241, 242
Hall, David, 300
Hallam University, 112
Halle Orchestra, 32
Halligan, Lisa, 303
Hall-i'th-Wood, 38
Halliwell Industrial Estate, 14
Halliwell, Raymond, 36, 37, 40, 46
Hall Lane travellers' site, 95
Hamas, 334, 337, 338, 345, 346, 358
Hamilton, John, 37, 43
Hamilton, Neil, 162, 429
Handguns, 93, 131, 167, 173, 223, 238
Hansard, 172, 173, 200, 327
Hanscomb, John, 22, 39, 51, 67, 85
Harasiwka, Frank, 122, 146, 148
Hardcastle, Frank and Thomas, 1-2
Hare and Hounds public house, 157, 302
Harkin, Guy, 39, 40, 96, 423
Harman, Harriet, 178-179, 227, 232 (elected deputy leader), 466
Harris, Captain Bill, 181

Harris, Dr Evan, 186, 244, 379
Harris, Joanne, 280
Harris, Tom, 154, 367
Harrison family, 116-118, 447 (Calvin and Cameron), 451 and 452 (Calvin, Lee and Noah), 453 (Calvin, Ian and Lee), 455 (Calvin)
Harrison-Machin, Noah, 452
Harrison, Steven, 301-302
Harrison, Susannah, 18, 46
Hart, Gladys, 48
Hartshorne, Elaine and John, 63, 82, 100
Hatch covers (ships), 413, 415
Haulgh Community Partnership, 277-278, 424
Have I Got News For You, 440
Haworth, Don, 297
Haworth, Sue, 59
Hayman, Baroness, 226
Healey, John, 254, 267, 268, 270
Health and Diet Co., 319
Health and Safety Executive, 373
Health Food Manufacturers Association (HFMA), 321, 322, 324 (petition)
Health foods (herbal substances, vitamins and minerals), 319-326; European Directives and Regulations on, 321-325
Health Reform Act, 238
Health Scrutiny Committees, 188
Heath, Ted, 13, 31, 193
Heathrow Airport, 147, 192, 222, 231, 439-440
Heavy Goods Vehicles (HGVs), 308-309 (safety), 353 (Pakistan)
Hellawell, Keith, 397
Henley by-election, 237
Henoch-Schoenlein purpura, 8
Hepatitis B virus, 405
Hepatitis C Virus (HCV), 275, 404, 405, 408-410
Hepatology APPG, 404, 406
Heppell, John, 171
Hereditary peers, 174, 180, 198-199, 205-206
Heroin, 166, 167, 215, 273, 274, 275, 276, 326, 327, 398, 399
Herzl, Theodore, 336
Heseltine, Michael, 99

Hesketh Lane (nos. 74-78), 12
Hewitt, Patricia, 162-163, 223, 249
Heyes, Richard, 44
High Court of Session, Admiralty Jurisdiction, 262
Higher Education Bill, 206, 208
Highly indebted countries, 197, 222, 235
High Speed 2 (HS2), 250, 251
Hill, David, 208
Hill, Keith, 170-171, 172
Hillsborough football disaster, 328
Hindley, Stewart, Chief Constable's Staff Officer at GMP, 441, 442
Hinduja brothers, 192
Hindus, 36, 61, 310, 349, 350, 452, 453
Hippocrates, 332
Hitchens, Peter, 397, 401
HIV/Aids, 217, 369, 405, 408
Holdsworth, Dean, 296
Holidays, 6-7, 450-451
Holman, Justice, 408
Holmes, Paul, 285
Holmeswood with Rufford St Mary the Virgin Church, 10-11
Holt, Eddie and May, 46
Home Front Memorials, 315, 316
Homeland Security USA, 367
Homelessness, 76, 87-89, 95, 98, 181, 187, 269
Homeopathy, 363, 378-379
Homes and Communities Agency, 235
Hoon, Geoff, 163, 208, 247, 249
Hoot (credit union), 89
Hornby, Kevan, 51, 76
Horsa Street, 25
Horwich, 39, 51, 61, 142, 293, 294
Houghton Weavers, 82
House of Commons Library, 132, 133, 149, 164
House of Commons reform, 149-151, 173, 199, 206
House of Commons security, 130, 131, 152, 212-214
House of Commons souvenirs, 157
House of Lords, 152, 191, 210, 226, 254, 270, 329, 440, 458
House of Lords appointments, 184, 209

House of Lords Committee on Medical Ethics, 328-329
House of Lords Private Members' Bills, 258, 407
House of Lords reform, 145, 146, 180, 197, 198-199, 204, 205-206, 210, 230
Housing Act 1988, 84, 87 (see also 209)
Housing Action Areas, 51, 91, 100
Housing Area Forums, 85
Housing Associations, 87, 88, 90-91, 395
Housing Benefit, 98, 228 (reform), 310-311 (reform), 395
Housing clearance, 98-99
Housing Committee, 46, 50, 51, 53, 63-64, 72, 74-75, 76, 79, 80, 82, 84, 85, 90, 91, 92, 94-96, 100, 106, 108, 135, 143
Housing Committee, chair's briefing, 84
Housing Direct Labour Organisation (HDLO), 45, 72, 74-75, 76-80, 79 (Management Committee), 81, 82, 86, 95, 97, 116, 297, 457
Housing Finance Act, 13
Housing Investment Programme (HIP), 58, 98
Housing regeneration, 75, 91, 94, 98-100
Housing Revenue Account (HRA), 254, 395
Housing Waiting List, 90-91
Housing Working Party, 63, 75
Howard family, 114
Howard, Michael, 86, 164, 219
Howarth, George, 396, 435
Howarth, Harry, 25-26
Howarth, Robert Lever, 48, 49, 51, 56, 77, 93, 108, 110, 265
Howcroft public house, 79
Howells, Kim, 291
Hughes, Beverley, 247, 425
Hull, 6, 8, 55, 210, 327, 413, 427
Hull, Bill, 11
Hull, Dillon, 158, 166-168, 396
Hull, Jane, 166-167
Hulton Lane Hospital, 8, 145
Human enhancement technologies, 375 (in sport)
Human Fertilisation and Embryology Acts, 189, 236, 245, 370 (1990), 372 (2008)
Human Reproductive Technologies and the Law, 370
Human rights, 184, 187, 223, 329 (Act), 333, 338, 340, 350, 352 (European Convention on)

Human tissue legislation, 210
Human trafficking, 244, 278
Humphreys, John, 440
Hunt, Nicky, 296
Hunter, Anji, 191
Hurst, Barbara, 53, 54, 65
Hussain, Quadir, 168
Hussein, Saddam, 312
Hutton, John, 239, 247
Hutton Report, 207, 208
Hybrid embryos, 372
Hyde, Wynn, 22

Iceland bank collapses, 242, 319 (Kaupthing)
Iddon, Eileen (second wife), 50, 73, 89 104, 108, 110, 113, 115, 117-118 (marriage), 121, 125, 134, 136, 147, 156, 185, 190, 221, 300, 337, 338, 348, 386, 430-433, 443, 446, 447, 448-449 (RTA), 450-453, 454 (her close friends), 455, 456, 462, 463, 465, 466
Iddon family (deaths of previous generation), 8-10, 9 (father)[2]
Iddon, Frank, 11
Iddon, Graham (brother) and Pam, 9, 10-13, 113, 452
Iddon, Charlotte, John and Lucy Jane, 451, 452
Iddon, Merrilyn Ann (first wife),[3] 1, 3, 4, 6, 7, 8, 9, 13-15, 16-18, 25, 31, 51, 56, 63, 73, 83, 115-116, 117 (divorce), 185
Iddon, Sally (d), 1, 4-8, 31-32, 33, 56, 62, 83, 112-114, 121, 125, 265 (wedding)
Iddon, Sheena (d), 1, 4-7, 13, 31-32, 36, 62, 112-114 (wedding), 431, 452
Identity cards, 223
Identity parades, 444
Igroup plc, 282
Illsley, Eric, 249
Iqbal, Cllr Mohammed, 355
Iqbal, Mussarat, 351
Immigration, 180-181, 197, 217 (Sangatte), 224, 234, 236, 243, 246, 465
Imperial Cancer Research Fund, 364
Imperial College, London 377
Incapacity Benefit, 183, 228
Income tax, 58, 180 (10p rate), 231, 233 and 238 (10p rate)

Independence Party, 148
Independent MPs, 162 163, 203, 429
Independent Parliamentary Standards Authority (IPSA), 135, 155, 243, 249
Indian Sports Club, 453, 454
Information Tribunals, 239
Inheritance tax, 233
Inland Revenue, 215
Innovation, Universities, Science and Skills Select Committee, 361, 376, 378
Institute of Fiscal Studies, 246
Institute of Licensing, 416
Institute of Physics (IoP), 393
Institution of Chemical Engineers, 410, 467 (award of Honorary Fellowship)
International Criminal Court, 188
International Development Bill, 188
International Monetary Fund (IMF), 235
International Parliamentary Union, 342
International Space Station, 375
International Transport Workers Federation, 413
Iran, 130, 226, 235, 319
Iraq and Iraq War, 122, 148, 178, 202-204, 208, 211, 215, 219, 234, 238, 319, 381, 443
Irish Blood Transfusion Service, 408, 409
Irish Republic, 6-7, 176, 226, 242 (bank collapses), 249 (European Constitution), 349, 415
Irish Republican Army (IRA), 136, 177, 211 (Northern Bank robbery), 222
Isherwood, James Lawrence, 10, 59
Islamabad, 218, 352, 354, 355, 356, 357
Islamic University, Gaza, 334
Israel (see Palestine and the Middle East)
Israeli Defence Force (IDF), 339, 341, 342, 343, 346-347
Ivy Restaurant, 454

Jabalia refugee camp, Gaza, 339
Jackson, Robert, 162
Jacobs, Bill, 209
Jacob's Well (West Bank), 341
Jamaica, 402-404 (and Labour Party)
Jamieson, David, 260
Jammu and Kashmir, 350, 357
Jammu and Kashmir Liberation Front, 350

Japanese Gardens, 39
Jeffries, Michael, 303
Jenkin, Patrick, 59
Jenkins, Katherine, 156
Jenkins, Roy, 182
Jeremy Vine Show, 465
Jerusalem, 335, 339, 340, 342, 348 (Dome on the Rock)
Jinks, S, 13
Job Centre Plus, 216
Jobseeker's Allowance 244
Joffe, Lord, 329, 330
John Lewis List, 239
Johnson, Alan, 207, 208, 220, 230, 232, 290, 373
Johnson, Boris, 182, 237
Johnson, Colin, 57-58
Johnson, Ellen, 9
Johnson Fold Credit Union, 89
Johnson Fold Primary School, 28
Johnson, Melanie, 325
Johnston, Eric, 65
Johnston, Peter, 51, 52, 63-64, 65, 74-76, 119
Joint Intelligence Committee, 202
Jones, Digby, 254, 255
Jones, Helen, 86
Jones, Jack, 250, 253
Jones, Lynne, 244, 374
Jones, Nigel, 130
Jordan, 336, 348, 411
Jowell, Tessa, 207
Juan-Thomas, Athena and Richard, 15-16
Justices of the Peace (JPs), 57, 72, 73

Karni crossing point (Israel-Gaza), 338-339
Kashmir, 349-357 (tension between India and Pakistan)
Kassam rockets, 342, 344, 345, 347
Kassiopi, Corfu, 451
Kaufman, Gerald, 68
Kay, Rosa, 140, 158
Kearsley, 39, 50, 54, 61, 65, 103, 146, 178, 312, 319, 422, 425, 429
Kelly, Christopher, 249

Kelly, Dr David, 207, 208
Kelly, Ruth, 97, 122, 142, 143, 158, 189, 196, 220, 225, 226, 244-245 (resignation), 266, 289, 296, 312, 434
Kennedy, Jane, 179, 247
Kennedy, Ludovic, 327
Kent Fire and Rescue Service, 261
Kenyon, Frank, 53
Kershaw, Mary, 42
Key, Robert, 93
Khan, President Sardar Mohammed Ibrahim, 353
Khat, 400, 420
Killarney, 6
Killeen, Peter, 29
Kilroy Show, 439-440
Kimbolton Fireworks, 380-381
King, Prof. David (Government CSA), 190, 365, 386
King, Oona, 401
Kingston, Jamaica, 402, 403, 404 (Parliament)
Kinnock, Neil, 250, 253 (photograph)
Knapton, Karen, 264, 265
Knight, Jack, 26
Knowles, Kevin, 18, 23, 46
Kosovan Albanians, 184
Kroto, Prof. Sir Harry, 384, 385 (and Mrs Kroto), 386, 393 (death of)
Kumar, Dr Ashok, 410-411
Kyoto, 177
Kyoto Protocol, 198

Labour clubs (Bolton), 103
Labour Friends of Palestine and the Middle East, 334
Labour Middle East Council 334
Labour Party Annual Conference, 102 (1987), 156, 232 (2007), 244-245 (2008), 438 (1997), 461 (2010)
Labour Party General Secretaries, 127
Labour Party leader (TB to GB), 232
Labour Party Special Conference (Manchester), 232
Lambert, Paul, 413, 414, 415
Lamplighter Restaurant, 50, 143
Lancashire County Council, 53, 359
Lancashire County Fire Brigade, 12

Lancashire County Police Force, 309
Lancashire Fusiliers, 283, 284
Lancaster, Mark, 380, 381
Landfill Tax, 197 (see also 205)
Land Registry, 316
Lansley, Andrew, 409
Lantor, 79-80
Last Drop Village, 255, 421
Lawrence Livermore National Laboratory, 367
Lawrinson, Karen, 129, 137, 139, 141-142, 153, 273, 468
Laybourne Clinic, 398, 399
Leader of the House, 151, 164, 203, 231, 360, 466
Leaders of the Conservative Party, 164
Leaders of the Liberal Democrat Party, 164
League Against Cruel Sports, 67
Learning and Skills Council, 184, 228
Leaseholds, 197, 316-318
Legg, Thomas, 249
Leicester, 55-56, 265, 268
Leitch Report, 376
Le Mans, 50
Lestor, Joan, 73
Letts, Quentin, 170-171
Letwin, Oliver, 193
Lever, William Hesketh (later Lord Leverhulme), 37, 38
Leverhulme, Lord, 37, 38, 57-58
Leverhulme Park, 38
Leverhulme Trust, 38, 69
Levitt, Tom, 342, 345
Levy, Lord (Michael), 227, 228
Lewis, Ivan, 86
Lewis, Lord Jack, 381, 383, 392
Lewis, Steven John, 304
Lewis, Terry, 65-66, 68, 131, 176
Licensing legislation, 204-205
Light dues, 415, 416
Light pollution, 367-368
Lilford family, 12
Lilley, Peter, 178
Line of Route, 151, 216, 272, 428, 436
Lisbon Treaty, 227, 249

Literacy interventions 378
Litherland, Neil, 95, 135
Little Lever, 13, 39, 95, 103, 281, 283, 423
Little Lever Labour Club, 13, 103
Little Lever School, 70-71
Liver disease, 275, 404, 405, 407, 409
Liverpool Bridge, MV (renamed the *MV Derbyshire*), 412, 414
Liverpool Maritime Museum, 414, 420 (MV *Derbyshire* exhibition)
Liverpool Pals, 284
Liverpool Philharmonic Orchestra, 33
Livingstone, Ken, 162, 182, 186, 194, 201, 212, 237, 459
Living wills, 216
Lloyds TSB Bank, 241, 242
Local authorities, 174, 184, 188, 205, 223, 235, 253, 267, 273, 287, 395, 412, 417, 418, 419
Local Care Trusts, 188
Local Economic Partnerships (LEPs), 177
Local Government Association (LGA), 416
Local Government Conference, 55
Local Government (Miscellaneous Provisions) Act, 417
Lofthouse, Nat, 18, 294, 295
London Assembly (see Greater London Assembly)
London bombs, 136, 221, 232
London Underground, 132, 184, 220-221 (7/7), 222
Lord Speaker, 210, 226
Low Value Consignment Relief, 326
Lumley, Joanne, 246

Macclesfield Labour Group, 286
Macdonald, Gordon, 421
MacDonald, Gus, 192
Machin, Lilian, 452, 453
Machsom Watch (Israel), 340
MacIvor, Ken, 79
MacKenzie, Chief Super. Brian, 400
MacKinley, Andrew, 283
MacNeil, Angus, 227
Macular degeneration, 377
Made in Britain, 300

Magic mushrooms, 215, 216
Magic of Chemistry, 104, 109, 115, 131, 387
Magistrates' Courts, 205, 292
Magnetic Resonance Imaging (MRI), 243, 373
Maiden speeches, 163-164
Mair, Thomas, 158
Major, John, 175
Make Poverty History, 217, 222
Malaria, 217
Malawi, 369-370
Malloch-Brown, Sir Mark, 254
Management and Finance (M&F) Committee, 46, 53, 79
Manchester United FC, 444
Mancroft Avenue CCTV, 94
Mandela, Nelson, 69-71 (and cricket trophy)
Mandelson, Peter, 175-176, 191, 192 (his two resignations), 247, 248, 361
Mangera, Mo, 97
Mangla Lake and Dam, Azad Kashmir, 354
Marine legislation, 243
Marine Safety Act, 259-264
Marine science, 375
Maritime and Coastguard Agency, 260
Market Hall, 50 (Knowsley St), 457 (Ashburner St)
Market Industry APPG, 411, 416
Marks, Howard ('Mr Nice'), 397, 400, 401, 420
Marks, Judy ('Mrs Nice'), 401
Marriner, Ronald, 309 (conviction for murder)
Marris, Rob, 332
Mars, 370
Marsden, Paul, 163
Marsh, Andrew, 408
Marsh, Joyce, 26
Marshall-Andrews QC, Bob, 438, 439
Marsland, Shirley, 107
Martin, Michael, 186 (election as Speaker), 195, 239, 240 (resignation), 250
Martland, 456 (Alan and Dorothy), 457 (Dorothy)
Mason, Roy, 136
Mason, Ryan, 309 (murder)
Maternity/Paternity pay, 197, 223
May, Lord, 386

McBride, Damian, 192
McBrien, Flo, 280
McCartney, Ian, 196, 227
McCartney, Robert, 211 (murder)
McCracken, Betty, 84, 108
McDonnell, John, 183, 185
McGrath, Revd. Peter, 414
McGuinness, Martin, 226
McKechnie, Sheila, 285
McKillop, Tom, 242
McNamara, Kevin, 327, 427
McWalter, Tony, 371
Meagher, Kevin, 148, 459
Mediation, 91-92, 273
Medicines Act 1968, 324
Medicines and Healthcare Products Regulatory Agency (MHRA), 286, 402
Medicines Control Agency, 321
Mellor, David, 132
Meltdown Monday, 242
Members' Cloak Room, 133
Members' Entrance, 134
Members' Lobby, 131, 162
Members of Parliament, accommodation, 132-133, 151
MPs, allowances and expenses, 135, 144, 154-155, 239, 243, 249
MPs, communication methods and devices, 152-154, 255-256
MPs, financial commitments, 156
MPs, salaries, 134, 135
MPs, second home allowances, 155-156
Members' Tea Room, 133, 149, 150, 436
Menezes, Jean Charles de, 222
Mental capacity Act, 215, 216, 328
Mental disorders, 229
Mental illness, 129-130
Men Who Made Labour: The PLP of 1906, 225, 256
Mephedrone, 400
Mere Hall, 113, 144, 265 (Register Office)
Merron, Gillian, 207, 407, 408
Merseytravel, 200
Mersey Tunnels Bill, 200, 201

Mesothelioma, 228
Methadone, 274, 398
Methamphetamine, 402
Mhatre, Ravindra, 350-351
Michael, Aelish, 300
Michael, Alun, 180
Middle East Peace Process, 173, 203, 235, 342
Middleton, Robin, 260, 261
Milburn, Alan, 217 (resignation)
Milford Haven Sound, 261
Miliband, Ed, 191-192
Militant Tendency, 58
Millennium Dome, 173, 174-175
Miller, Gary, 65, 67
Milner, Frank, 32
Milner, Martin, 32
Milosevic, Slobodan, 184
Milton, Anne, 409
Minelli, Dr Ludwig, 328
Miners' Hall, 30, 73
Miners' strikes, 13, 72-73
Minimum wage, 173, 180, 250
Ministry of Defence, 141-142, 188 427
Mintoff, Dom, 214 (daughter)
Mirpur, Azad Kashmir, 354, 356
Mirza, Aslam, 351
Misuse of Drugs Act 1971, 215, 373, 399
Mitchell, Senator George, 175
Mixmag magazine, 401
MLX249, 321, 323
Modernisation Committee, 148-150, 151, 200, 201, 216, 272
Molyneaux, Alf, 300
Monetary Policy Committee, 177
Monks, Joyce, 454, 455
Montserrat, 193
Moon, Tony, 40
Moonlight Robbery Campaign, 395
Moor, Dr David, 327
Moorcroft, Danielle, 277
Moore, Jo, 196
Moore, Nicole, 165

Moorfields Eye Hospital, 377
Moor Lane Fire Station, 72
Moran, Margaret, 162, 249
Morgan, Rhodri, 180
Morley, Dolores, 117, 455
Morley, Elliot, 162, 249, 315, 451
Morphine, 275, 326
Morris, Cliff, 143, 293, 468
Morris, Estelle, 217 (resignation)
Morris, Lord (Alf), 268, 405, 407, 420 (death of)
Morris, Steve, 357
Morris, Baroness Trish, 290
Morris, Judge William, 290, 303
Mort family, 15
Mortgage default, 241, 243, 269, 270
Mortgage Interest Rates, 59, 98, 234, 269, 281-282 (sub-prime lending)
Mortgage Repossessions (Protection of Tenant etc) Act, 270, 408, 462
Motoring, 101 (HoC Club), 170-171 (Motorcycling APPG)
Moule, Nick, 97
Mowlam, Mo, 125, 175, 222 (death of), 396, 397
Mugabe, Robert 235
Mulley, Fred, 101
Mullin, Chris, 179, 427
Muncaster, Cyril and Evelyn, 6
Murphy, Paul, 176
Musharraf, General Pervez, 353
Music Centre, 32-35, 35 (first committee members), 36
Muslims, 36, 43-44, 244, 334, 338, 341, 349, 350
Muzaffarabad, 350, 353

Nablus, 341
Nakba (Palestinian Holocaust), 336, 341
Napoleonic Law, 323
NASA, 374, 375
National Air Traffic Services (NATS), 177, 184
National Association of British Markets Authorities (NABMA), 416, 419 (award)
National Asylum Seekers Support Scheme (NASS), 181
National Care Service, 251, 253

National Consumer Council, 228
National debt, 174, 251
National Executive Committee (Labour Party), 105, 186, 201, 212, 248, 459
National Front, 37, 43, 46, 47, 61
NGOs, 357
NHS Direct, 180
National Health Service (NHS), 122, 125, 139, 173, 180 (internal market), 188 (Local Care Trusts), 191, 197, 234, 238 (60th anniversary), 243 (constitution), 250, 254 (Foundation Trusts; see also 204), 280, 281, 287, 326 (palliative care), 328, 364, 370, 373 (MRI scanners), 379 (homeopathy), 398 (drug addiction), 405 and 407 (blood transfusions), 411
NHS, Next Stage Review, 238
NHS reform, 198, 204 (Wales), 234, 238
National Housing Week, 89
National Institute of Clinical Excellence (NICE), 180, 286
National Insurance Contributions (NICS), 183, 234, 246
Nationalisation, 145, 249-250
National Lottery, 173, 262
National Market Traders Federation, 416
National Offenders Management Service (NOMS), 209, 229
National Police Improvement Agency, 313
National Treatment Agency (NTA), for substance abuse, 288, 397
National Week of Science, Engineering and Technology, 387
Natural England, 223
Natural Law Party, 122
Neighbour Dispute Service, 91-92, 144
NESTA, 173, 389
New Deal Programmes, 173, 177, 216, 250
New Labour, 111, 121, 254
Newman, Ellen, 303
New Palace Yard, 134, 381
New Scientist, 195
Newsnight, 172, 461
Newton's Apple, 388-389
New variant CJD, 178
New Year's Eve Dances, 27
Nicholls, Albert 85

Noble, John, 106
No-fault compensation, 308
Nolden, Karl, 52
Nominated insurance companies, 317
Non-Profit-Making Members' Clubs APPG, 223, 411
Norman Shaw Buildings, 133, 134, 182
North Atlantic Treaty Organisation (NATO), 184
Northern Ireland (NI), 27, 136, 165, 173, 175-176, 184, 192, 206, 211, 228, 234, 345
NI, Assembly, 176, 211 and 226 (elections), 318
NI, First Minister, 226
NI, IRA arms decommissioning, 177, 197, 211, 222
NI, Judicial Appointments Commission, 209
NI, Peace Process, 175-176, 221, 226, 234
NI, political parties, 211, 226
Northern Ireland Select Committee, 437
Northern Rock Building Society, 232, 241
Northern Way 210
Northey, Brian, 107
North Ward, 26, 43
North West (NW) Group of Labour MPs, 186
NW Pharmaceutical Industry APPG, 411
NW Regional Development Agency (NWRDA), 187, 389, 390
NW Regional Government, 145 (see also 237)
Norwich North by-election, 248
Nuclear Decommissioning Authority, 209
Nuclear Non-Proliferation Treaty, 230
NUPE, 68
Nurse, Sir Paul, 386
Nursery vouchers, 173, 174
Nursing care, 188
Nutt, Prof. David, 373, 374
Nutter family, 96
Nwokeochar, Amicie Onyema, 305, 306
Nye, Sue, 191

Obama, President Barack, 246, 434
Obesity, 234
Observer newspaper, 21, 246
Oceaneering Technologies, 413
Octagon Theatre, 283, 288, 300 (The Demolition Man)

Ofcom, 198, 204
Office for Fair Access (to universities), 208
Office of National Statistics (ONS), 228, 266
Office [US] of the Joint Programme of Chemical and Biological Defense, 369
Ogden, Robert, 20, 22
O'Hara, Brian, 96
O'Hara, Eddie, 412
Oil prices, 186, 238
Oil tanker disasters, 260-261
Older drivers, 305-306, 307
Oldhams Lane Primary School, 53
'Old school house', Firwood Fold, 3, 17, 19
Old Scotland Yard, 133
Old Testament Prophets, 438 (dining club)
Olympic cycling team, 375
Olympic Games, 220, 222, 223
Omagh bomb, 176, 179
OMOV (one member, one vote), 102, 105
O'Neill, Albert (Bert), 37, 71
Open access publishing, 368
Open frame submarines, 376, 413
Openings (of buildings etc) 421-426
Open University, 138, 370
Operation Cast Lead, 346
Opiate drugs (see also codeine, heroin and morphine), 168, 275, 326, 398
Opus Dei, 189, 245
Organic food, 286
Osborne, George, 233
Oslo Agreement, 337
OverCount, 275
Overseas aid, 188-189, 212, 222, 251, 336, 370
Oxfam, 342-343
Oxford Union, 96, 330, 338, 357, 400, 401
Oyston, Owen, 142-143
Oxtoby, Bob, 289, 291

Pack Horse Hotel, 15, 421
Paderborn, 35, 50, 51, 52, 73, 451
Paderborn House, 64, 265
Pagers (for MPs), 153, 438
Painters, 79, 81, 86

Paisley, Ian, 211, 226
Pakistan, 102, 197, 218, 349, 350, 352-356
Pakistan APPG, 349, 411
Palestine and the Middle East, 38, 101, 173, 185, 208, 235, 333-348 (CHAPTER 11), 336 and 338 (refugees), 338 (Presidential Election), 339 (road closures), 433-434, 434 (meetings with Tony Blair)
Palestinian Legislative Council (PLC), 337
Palestinian National Authority (PNA), 340
Palestinian VIP supporters, 348
Palfryman, Dr Roger, 375
Palliative care, 326, 330
Parchment, 169
Parliament Act, 198, 206
Parliamentary and Scientific Committee, 386, 387, 388
Parliamentary Education Unit, 428
Parliamentary Labour Party (PLP), 105, 149, 158, 224-225 (centenary), 247, 256 (centenary)
PLP chairs, 127
PLP meetings, 112, 125-127, 198, 246, 250, 253
PLP secretaries, 127
Parliamentary Questions, 164, 200, 266, 311, 314, 325, 326, 416, 439
Parry, Sue, 91-92
Partington, Keith and Helene, 83
Patel, Derek, 453
Pathfinder Projects, 210, 216
Patten, Chris, 386
Patterson, Rt. Hon. P J, 403
Payment Protection Insurance, 281
Peacock, Chris, 138-139
Peacock, Ella and Norman, 15
Pedlars, 416-419, 417 (licences)
Pedlars Acts, 271, 416, 418
Pedlars (Street Trading Regulation) Bill, 418
Peel Commission, 334
Peet, Michael, 319
Pennington Andrew, 130
Pension claw-back rule (reform of), 310-311
Pensions, 183, 184, 185, 197, 209, 228, 229, 235, 267, 316
Pentagon, 196, 366
Peoples National Party, Jamaica, 403
Percivals, 50

Peres, Shimon, 433
Peripheral Neuropathy, 320
Perry, Gordon, 96
Perry, John, 40
Perry, Norma, 31
Perry, Paul, 24
Persia, Shah of, 319
Peterloo Housing Association, 87
Petra, 348
Pharmaceutical Industry APPG, 411
Phillips, Haydn, 240
Phillips, Tony, 107
Pickup, Syd, 309 (see ViSOR)
Pike, Peter, 266-267
Pillinger, Dr Colin, 370, 390
Pizza Express, Millbank, 463
Planning permission, 22, 23, 298, 317
Planning reform, 204, 236
Pledge cards, 125
Points of Order, 161
Police Community Support Officers (PCSOs), 234
Police Federation, 401
Police Information Technical Organisation (PITO), 309
Police Service of Northern Ireland, 211
Police Service Parliamentary Scheme, 202, 441-445
Policy Review Sub-committee, 46
Poll Tax (Community Charge), 83, 98
Portcullis House, 132, 133, 152, 161
Porton Down, 367
Port Sunlight, 37, 38
Post mortems, 244
Post Office, 30, 131, 184 (plc), 238 (Card Accounts)
Post office closures, 231, 238
Postwatch, 228
Pound, Stephen, 436-438
Powell, Jonathan, 175, 191
Power, Jean and Gordon, 24, 26
Prayers, 160
Pre-Budget Report, 177
Prentice, Bridget, 293
Prentice, Gordon, 198, 352, 355, 357

Prescott, John, 55, 125, 169, 177, 193, 203, 210, 228, 254, 294, 298, 360, 413, 415, 427
Prescription drugs/Over the Counter Medicines (OTCs), 275-276 (addiction to), 401
Prescription Only Medicines (POMS), 402
Presentation Bills, 258
Presentations (of awards, medals, etc), 422-423, 426
Prestolee CE Primary School and Community Centre, 425
Pretty, Diane, 330
Price, Dave and Margaret, 15
Priestley, Dennis, 57
Primarolo, Dawn, 276, 372
Primary Care and Public Health APPG, 402
PCT Below Target Group, 411
Primary Care Trusts (PCTs), 180, 223
Prime Minister's Questions, 149, 153, 169, 176, 213, 232 (last for TB), 251-252, 253
Prince Charles, Prince of Wales, 363
Prince Philip, 430, 433
Prince's Chamber, 152
Princess Anne, Princes Royal, 136, 386, 389
Private Acts of Parliament, 183, 200, 418, 419
Private Eye, 193
Private Finance Initiatives, 177
Private Members' Bills, 174, 257-271 (CHAPTER 7), 329, 332, 407, 416, 418, 469
Private Members' Clubs APPG, 223
Private Security Industry, 187
Privy Council, 399
Privy Counsellors, 159
Programme Motions, 149-150, 189
Proportional representation (PR), 181-182, 251, 335
Proprietary Association of Great Britain (PAGB), 401, 402
Prorogation (prior to Dissolution), 191, 206, 264, 382, 461, 462
Prostitution, 244, 276, 277, 278 (including the Ipswich murders), 279, 443
Prostitution Forum (Bolton), 278
Pseudoephedrine, 401, 402
Public Analyst Service, 287, 288
Public Health, 177, 276, 325, 372, 402, 407, 427
Public Private Partnerships, 177, 184

SCIENCE AND POLITICS: AN UNLIKELY MIXTURE

Purchase, Ken, 333
Purdy, Debbie, 330, 331, 332
Purnell, James, 247, 460
Purple powder incident, 213

Al-Qaeda, 195-196, 197
Qualqilya (West Bank), 340
Quangos, 145, 288 (abolition of)
Quantitative easing, 242
Quayle, Tom, 79
Queen Elizabeth II, 182, 210, 300, 315, 415, 430-431 (discussing the film starring Helen Mirren and Michael Sheen), 432, 433 (Golden Jubilee)
Queen Elizabeth II Conference Centre, 427
Queen Mother, 201 (death of)
Queen's Addresses to Parliament (State Opening of Parliament), 127, 129, 150, 180, 184, 210, 215, 228, 229, 267, 304, 466
Queen's Honours Lists, 294, 300, 415, 432
Queen's Robing Room, 151, 433
Queen Street Primary School, 429
Quereshi, Yasmin, 139, 238, 358, 459, 464
Question times (see also Prime Minister's Questions), 164, 165, 168, 170, 206, 231, 244, 273
Quin, Joyce, 264, 265

Rabin, Yitzhak, 337
Race relations, 184-185
Rail Accident Investigating Body, 204
Railway bridges, 312 (repairs)
Raja, Abdul Quayyum, 350-352, 355
Ramallah, 336, 339, 340, 341
Ramsbottom, 54
Ramwell, Captain Dave, 414, 415
Rantzen, Esther, 275
Rashid, Haroon, 146-148
Rawnsley, Andrew, 127-128, 173
Raynsford, Nick, 97
Reagan, Tommy, 40
Reay, Gemma, 139, 140, 220, 233, 268, 276, 441, 461, 462, 463, 464
Rebellions (Labour), 178-179, 201, 203, 207, 215-216, 226, 230, 255-256
Receptions (lunches, dinners etc), 426-428, 430-431, 434

Red Lion public house, 133
Redmond, Robert, 28
Red Rose Tendency, 65
Redundancies at Bolton firms, 60-61
Reebok Stadium, 294
Reed, Laurence, 28
Referendum Party, 122
Regional Assemblies, 204, 212, 237
Regional Development Agencies (RDAs), 177, 187, 250, 389, 390
Regional government, 145, 237
Regional Labour Party Office, 29, 156
Regional Select Committees, 231, 237
Registered social landlords, 95, 136, 235, 395
Registrar General (Registration Service), 266
Registrar of Trades Unions, 268
Registration, Evaluation and Authorisation of Chemicals (REACH), 368
Registration of electors, 223
Registration Officers, 264, 265, 266, 267, 436
Registration Service, 265, 266-267 (reform)
Regulatory Reform Committee, 266
Regulatory Reform Orders, 266
Rehab UK Annual Parliamentary Pancake Race, 439, 440
Reid, Dr John, 176, 217, 230, 283, 411
Religious hatred, 223
Remembrance Day/Sunday, 456
Remploy, 238, 256
Rent Officers, 87, 266
Rents and rent arrears, rent collectors, etc, 13, 59, 64, 74, 75, 80, 87, 89-90, 98, 311, 395
Research Assessment Exercise (RAE), 366
Residential-Turned-Let properties, 269, 270
Resigning the Whip (PLP), 163
Respect Party, 162
Retirement (announcement), 458
Returning Officer, 147
Revascularisation, 287
Rhodes, Gary, 136, 440
Riaz, Mohammed, 350-352, 355
Richards, Prof. Mike, 364 (Cancer Zsar)
Riddings, Keith, 165

Rifkind, Gabrielle, 338
Rifkind, Malcolm, 338
Rigby, James, 18, 20, 22
Right of return, 335, 337
Right-to-Buy, 87, 90, 209, 269, 285
Right to die, 330, 331-332
Right to life, 329
Riley, Gerry, 89
River Jhelum, 353, 354, 356
River Neelum, 353
Rivington, 39, 400, 434
Road Peace, 304
Road safety, 222, 300-309
Road Safety Act, 304, 308
Road Traffic (Accident Compensation) Bill, 308
Robert Fletcher's Paper Mill, 61, 426
Roberts, Prof. S M, 422
Robertson, George, 178
Robinson, Geoffrey, 192
Robinson, George and Lavina, 14, 15, 16
Roddick, Anita (founder of Body Shop), 404-405
Roe, John, 75-76, 77, 79, 84, 119
Rooker, Jeff, 320
Roper, John, 68
Rotch, 319
Routledge, Paul, 155
Royal Academy, 220, 385
Royal Academy of Engineering, 377
Royal Assents, 180, 187, 189, 191, 208, 226, 236, 237, 258, 264, 268, 270, 305, 408, 462
Royal Bank of Scotland (RBS), 241, 242, 245, 282
Royal Bolton Hospital, 101, 110, 111, 239, 390, 421 and 422 (Hawthorne House), 422 (Children and Adolescent Mental Health Service – CAMHS), 424 (Dialysis Unit and Nightingale wards), 425 (Children's Assessment and Observation Unit), 450, 454, 463
Royal Commissions, 168, 198-199
Royal Gallery, 152
Royal Institution of Chartered Surveyors, 22
Royal Mail, 231, 247, 248
Royal Society, 366, 392 (MPs Pairing Scheme), 427 (reception), 460
Royal Society of Biology, 393

Royal Society of Chemistry, 220, 221, 268, 287, 380 (Fellowship and Parliamentary Advisers), 381 (Advisers and Parliamentary Affairs Committee), 382-383 (Links Day), 383 (Christmas Party and Voice of the Future), 384 (AGM, President and Presidents' Dinner, HoC), 385, 393, 410, 467 (award of Honorary Fellowship)
Royal Ulster Constabulary (RUC), 179, 211
Rufford, 10, 456
Rule of 78, 282
Rumworth Labour Club, 70, 103, 104, 107, 109
Rumworth Lodge, 23
Rutherford Appleton Laboratories, 187
Rutter, Dave, 59, 107
Ryder, Rt. Hon. Lord Justice, 313

Sackville, Tom, 77, 83
Safeguarding children, 311-312 (use of computers)
Sainsbury, Lord David, 192, 391
Saint Andrews Agreement, 226
St George's Church, 34
St George's Road, 34, 48, 118, 138, 142, 225
St Helens constituencies, 68, 102
St James's CE Secondary School, 165 (coach disaster), 434 (at 10 Downing Street)
St John's CE Primary School, 429
St Pauls Parochial Hall, 32, 34
Saint Peter's Way (A666), 16, 43, 57, 83, 168, 277
St Simon's and St Jude's CE Primary School, 358, 425 (extension opening)
St Stephen's Hall, 152
St Thomas's Hospital, 437
Salford Magistrates' Court, 292, 293
Salford Pals, 284
Salisbury-Addison Convention, 199
Salmen, Rudi, 50, 52
Salmond, Alex, 183, 231
Salvation Army hostel, 87
Sandbach, Charles, 283
Sandline International, 193
Sangatte, 217
Sarwar, Mohammad, 352, 355
Sauter, Professor Fritz, 7
Saving Gateway Accounts, 243

SCIENCE AND POLITICS: AN UNLIKELY MIXTURE

Savoy Hotel, 386

Scapa Flow, 141-142

Scheinmann, Dr Feodore, 274

Schiphol Airport, 403

School meals, 226

Schools Concert Band, 35

Science, Government advisory system 365, 373-374, 378

Science and international development, 368

Science and Technology Select Committee, 186, 215, 236, 359-379 (CHAPTER 12), 361-363 (administration), 371 (guillotine of a meeting)

Science discovery centres, 376 (funding of)

Science education, 366, 392

Science funding, 376, 378, 379

Science, funding of learned societies, 365

Science in Parliament, 387

Science, open access publishing, 363

Scottish National Party (SNP), 183, 214, 227, 231 (Independence), 237

Scottish Parliament, 175, 182, 231

Scull, Cliff, 40, 47, 56, 96, 102

Sderot, 342, 344, 345, 347

SDP, 68

Seabridge, Inspector Ian, 279

Seatbelts on coaches, 165-166

Secretary of State's Representative (SOSREP), 260, 261, 264, 271

Section 28 repeal, 205

Section 106 money, 426

Security, 243 (airports)

Security industry, 93, 187

Security (Palace of Westminster), 130-131, 152, 212, 213, 214

Seddon, Paul William, 166-167

Sedgemore, Brian, 163

Sefton, Alice, 314, 315

Select Committees, 199 (reform), 361 (election of chairs)

Selection (at 11-plus), 5, 54, 62, 225

Selection (of PPCs), 67, 68, 102-105, 145, 155, 458-459

Sellers, Dr Piers, astronaut, 374, 375, 379

Sellers Packs (Homes Bill), 187

September sittings, 200, 201, 227

Serious Organised Crime Unit (SOCA), 215

Serjeant-at-Arms, 132, 151

SET For Britain, 387-388

SET For Europe, 388

SETPOINT, 392

Sex offenders, 204, 309-310

Sharif, Nawaz, 352

Sharpe Street hostel, Walkden, 87

Sharples High School, 53, 116

Shaw, Chris, 371

Shaw, Jim, 165

Shaw, Hugh, 271

Sheerman, Barry, 418

Shelter, 269, 285, 296 (Strip for Shelter)

Sherrington, Elaine, 116

Sherrington, Jim, 73, 82

al-Shifa Hospital, Gaza, 343

Shipman, Dr Harold, 187, 243, 326, 399

Shore, Peter, 22

Short, Clare, 162, 192-193, 203 (resignation)

Showmen's Guild, 427 (Annual Lunch)

Shree Swaminarayan Gadi, 310

Siddelley, Jim, 103, 104, 466 (celebration of his life)

Sierra Leone, 173, 193, 234

Simon, Frank, 299, 300

Simon, Sion, 231

Simpkins, Alice, 22, 23

Simpson, Alan, 186

Simpson family, 72, 453, 455

Simpson, Keith, 262

Simpson, Mark, 278-279

Simpson, Hon. Portia, 403, 404

Simpson, Sylvia, 72, 455

Simpson, Vincent, 24, 47, 70-71, 117, 453, 455

Simpson, Vincent Jnr, 72, 455

Singh, Marsha, 147, 158, 352, 355

Sites of Special Scientific Interest, 376

Sitting Fridays, 258, 262, 267, 268, 271, 418

Sitting hours, 149, 200, 216

Skagen Court, 89

Skinner, Dennis, 107, 109, 160, 176, 212, 255

Skipton Fund, 408-410

Sky Broadcasting, 427 (reception), 440-441, 464, 465

Smallman, Richard, 85

Smart meters, 237

Smith, Chloe, 248

Smith, Chris, 202, 203

Smith, Geraldine, 247

Smith, Iain Duncan, 164, 216

Smith, Private James, 283-285

Smith, Dame Janet, 243

Smith, Jaqui, 247, 373, 465

Smith, Les, 283

Smithills Hall, 16

Smithills Moor Grammar School, 5

Smoking ban, 223 (see also 271)

Snelgrove, Anne, 251, 252, 342, 345

Snuff, 161-162

Social care, 188, 204, 252-253

Social Services Committee, 40, 46, 89

Socialist Labour Party, 146

Socialist Workers Party, 61

Society of Chemical Industry, 387, 410, 467 (award of Honorary Membership)

Society of Registration Officers (SoRO), 264, 265 (annual conference venues), 266-267, 268 (2007 annual conference)

Solar power, 236, 416

Soley Days, 127

Somali communities, 400

Sorrento, 450

Soulby, Tom, 307

Sousse, Tunisia, 7

South Africa, 69, 235

South China Sea, 376, 412, 413

Southport, 9, 10, 13, 16, 265, 285

Southworth, Helen, 131

Sovereign's Entrance, 151, 306

Space research, 370 (policy), 375

SPD, 50, 52, 73

Speaker, election of, 185-186, 190, 195, 240

Speaker's House, 160-161, 382, 427 (reception), 464 (reception for MPs leaving Parliament in 2010)

Speaker's powers, 227

Speaker's procession, 161

Special Advisers (SPADS), 191

Special Educational Needs (SEN), 187, 281

Special Galleries, 160, 213

Special Interest Group of Municipal Authorities (Outside London)(SIGOMA), 411-412

Spellar, John 312

Spencer, Noel, 97, 106, 107, 108, 137, 432 (collecting MBE award), 433

Spin doctors, 191

Spinners' Hall, 48, 225

Sport England, 239

Sports Council, 21

Spread Eagle public house, 83

Staithes Youth Camp, 33

Stand Up For Kids campaign, 429

Starkey, Phyllis, 185, 338

Starkie family, 1, 5

Starmer, Keir, 330 (DPP)

Statistics and Registration Service Act, 268, 469

Statistics Bill, 267

Statutory Instruments, 255, 325

Statutory Officers, 266

Stazicker, Margaret (Aunt Maggie), 10-11

Stem cells, 186, 189, 377,

STEMNET, 392

Stern Report, 226, 228

Stewart, Ian, 131, 419

Stoate, Dr Howard, 402

Stock transfer, 84-85, 285-286, 395

Stone family, 15, 131

Stoneclough, 157, 301, 302, 425

Stoneclough Action 2000 and Beyond (SATAB), 425-426

Stones, Ray, 108

Stop the War Coalition, 204

Story, John, 79

Strangers, 161

Strangers' Bar, 161, 451

Strangers' Dining Room, 161

Strangers' Gallery, 161, 212-213 and 214 (security screen), 428

Strategic Defence Review, 178

Strategic Rail Authority, 184
Straw, Jack, 210, 293
Street surgeries, 198
Street trading, 416-419 (see also Pedlars)
Stringer, Graham, 359
Sub-prime lending, 241, 281-283
Sudan Red I food dye, 287
Suicide Act 1961, 328
Sunday Politics, 461
Supreme Court, 210, 427
Sure Start Schemes, 197, 234, 251
Suspensions (PLP), 163, 249
Sutcliffe, Kathryn, 138, 140, 385
Swan Hunter, 412
Swimming, 136, 238-239
Sydall, Joe, 85
Synthetic biology, 377, 378

Taking the Oath in the HoC, 129, 195
Taliban, 196
Tapsell, Peter, 177
Tarar, President Rafiq, 353
Target seats, 148
Tarleton, 11, 12 (High School and Melling's corn mill), 12-13 (Fire Station), 456
Tattersall, Robert, 138
Tavistock Square, 221 (7/7)
Tax credits, 180, 197
Tax-free savings (ISASs, PEPs and TESSAs), 173
Tax legislation, 58, 180, 187 (businesses), 193, 231, 233, 238, 246 (see also Poll Tax)
Taylor, Ann, 28, 51, 58, 68, 69, 70, 73, 164, 360
Taylor, Dari, 132
Taylor, David, 171-172, 194, 271
Taylor, Matthew, 191
Taylor, Nigel, 35, 36
Tchenguiz family, 318, 319
Teather, Sarah, 342, 345
Telford, Frank, 40
Temple, Mollie, 289, 290, 291, 391
Temple-Morris, Peter, 162
Tenancy Agreement (revised), 94
Tenant Liaison Officers, 85

Tenants' Associations, 80-81, 85
Tenant Services Authority, 235-236
Ten Minute Rule Bills, 186, 258, 267, 268, 271, 308, 326, 416
Terrorism, 179, 184, 196-197, 204, 220-222 (7/7), 224, 234, 366, 367
Terrorists (detention) 224, 238,
Tetrahydrocannabinol (THC), 396
Textile industry, 60, 102, 460
Thatcher, Margaret, 46, 53, 58, 83, 87, 90, 135, 247
That's Life, 275
The Hague, 443
The Haulgh, 277, 278, 424
The Netherlands, 11, 202, 217, 324, 443
Thomas, Gareth, 419
Thomas, Len and Linda, 108, 467
Thomas, Richard, 239
Thomas, Sir Robert, 39
Thone, Hans, 52
Thorne, Sir Neil, 441
Thurnham, Peter, 73, 77, 285
Thynne Street HDLO Depot, 78, 79, 80
Tighnabruaich, 110
Timms Stephen, 130
Titanic, RMS, 376, 412, 413
Titley, Gary, 83, 152, 209
Tobacco advertising, 187
Toby (a parrot), 140-141
Todd, Chief Constable Michael, 442, 445 (funeral)
Tomlinson, George, 367
Tomlinson, Karen, 116, 454
Tonge and the Haulgh Branch, Labour Party, 25
Tonge Branch, Labour Party, 24 (members), 25, 26, 27, 38, 58, 71, 116
Tonge Cricket Club, 44
Tonge Moor Residents' Association, 18, 22-23
Tonge Ward, 18, 26, 39, 46, 73
Tonge Ward Conservative Club, 46
Tonge Ward Labour Club, 25, 26, 27, 71, 116
Tootell, Tom, 37
Topical Debates and Questions, 231
Topp, Benjamin, 57
Topp Way, 57

Tottington Primary School, 36
Tower FM, 457
Town Centre Management APPG, 416
Townleys, 8, 69, 82, 101, 284
Toxic debt, 242
Trace, Mike, 397
Trade Unions APPG, 411
Trafalgar Square, 172, 220, 323, 337
Trainor, Bert, 24, 25
Trainor, Tommy, 25
Trainspotting, 400
Train to Gain Scheme, 235
Tranquillizer Addiction APG, 275
Transfer of Undertakings Protection of Employment (TUPE), 267
Travelodge, 288
Treasury Bench, 164
Treaty of Brussels, 13
Tredinnick, David, 323
Tribunal system reform, 228
Tribune, 250
Trident, 230, 235
Trigger ballots, 145
Trimble, David, 211, 319
Trinity House, 415, 416
Trust schools, 225
Turner, Desmond, 374
Turner, Neil, 411
Turner Report, 229
Turton, 39, 53 (UDC)
Tutankhamun, 15
Twenty First Century Science, 366
Twigg, Stephen, 163
Twin towns, 35, 50, 451
Twist, G, 13
Tynan, Bill, 259, 262
Typhoon Orchid, 412
Underground Garage, Palace of Westminster, 134
Unemployed Workers' Advice Centre, 104
Unemployment, 60-61, 101, 189-190, 211, 216, 217, 243, 245, 250, 251 (NEETS)
Unilever, 38
UNISON, 103, 268

United Kingdom Independence Party, 148
United Kingdom Space Agency, 370
United Nations (UN), 255, 276, 336, 338-339, 340, 367, 403, 404
UN Children's Fund (UNICEF), 428 (Put It To Your MP campaign)
UN Relief and Works Agency (UNRWA), 336, 339, 342, 344
UN Security Council (UNSC), 202, 203, 204 (resolutions)
United Utilities, 311
Unity Centre, 61, 453
University APPG, 394
University College, London, 377
University of Bolton, 289- 290 (inauguration ceremony), 290 (first Chancellor), 291, 391 (opening of Innovation Zone)
University of Cambridge, 365, 381
University of Durham, 136, 419
University of East Anglia, 360, 377
University of Glasgow, 29
University of Harvard, 375, 413
University of Hull, 383 and 385 (reunion), 427 (reception for MP graduands)
University of Leeds, 112
University of Liverpool, 391, 392 and 422 (opening of new laboratories)
University of Manchester, 18, 138, 367, 391-392 (External Advisory Board)
University of Oxford, 168, 400-401, 460 (see also Oxford Union)
University of Potenza, 450
University of Salford, 83, 91, 105, 116, 118-119, 168, 185, 274, 422
University of Sheffield, 384
University students' tuition fees, 168, 173, 206, 207-208
Unsworth, Frank, 5
uPVC window frames, 80, 81, 92, 297
Urban Outreach, 278
Urban regeneration, 210, 293
USDAW, 109, 146

Vaccine-damaged People APPG, 184, 411, 419, 420
VAT, 173, 242, 280, 326, 394-395

Vatican Bioethics Committee, 370-371

Veritas Party, 148

Veterans Day, 285

Victoria Crosses, 284

Victoria Hall, 33, 82, 290

Victoria Square, 30, 46, 58, 66, 448, 456, 461

33 Victoria Square – drop-in centre for mentally ill people, 425

Victoria Tower, 151, 152, 169

Vienna, 7

Vienna Woods, 7

Vincent, Sid, 73

Vine, Jeremy, *Jeremy Vine Show*, 465

Violent and Sex Offender Register (ViSOR), 309-310, 313

Vishwad Hindu Parishad Temple and Community Centre, 61

Visitors' Centre, Palace of Westminster, 152, 213

Visits (to schools etc), 426, 428

Vitamin B_6, 319, 320, 321, 323

Vocational diplomas, 225

Voluntary Euthanasia Society (VES), 327, 328, 461, 462

Vote Office, 463

Voting record, 255

Waddington, Philip, 34

Walker, Prof. Ray, 383

Wallace, Tim, 118

Walsh, John, 85, 96, 456

Walsh, Walter, 39

Wareing, Bob, 163 (deselection)

Warm Front Programme, 394

Warm Homes APPG, 394

Warnock Report 1988, 370

War on Drugs, 38, 167-168, 397

Warwick Agreement, 212

'Wash up' (for Bills), 270

Water conservation, 169, 205

Water rates, 311

Watson, James, 386-387

Watson, Tom, 191-192, 231, 247, 427

Watt, Gillian, 342

Watt, Margaret, 70-71

Watton, Gary, 35

Watton, Ted, 34, 35

Wave and tidal energy, 364

Weapons of Mass Destruction (WMD), 202, 203, 208

Webb, Billy, 166

Websites, 154, 172, 255-256, 312

Weddings, of family members, 113, 114, 265, 451-452

Welfare reform, 173, 178, 183, 230

Wellcome Trust archives, 462

Welsh Assembly, 175, 180, 182

Welsh, Irvine, 400

West, Sir Alan, 254

West Bank, 335, 336, 346

West coast main railway line, 134, 206, 227

West End shows, 455

Westhoughton, 1, 39, 61, 82, 225

Westminster Hall (Great Hall of Westminster), 152, 201, 272, 432, 433, 434

Westminster Hall chamber, 172, 185, 206, 237, 272, 273, 327, 338

Westminster Underground Station, 132

Whalebone, Terry, 29

Wharton, Dr Eric, 387, 388

Wharton Medal, 388

Wharton, Sue, 387, 388

Whelan, Charlie, 191

Whips' Offices, 105, 200, 270, 361, 455 (see also Government Whips' Office)

White, Eileen, 15, 24, 26, 74, 116

White, Frank, 15, 19, 24-25, 39, 72, 73-74, 86, 102-103, 107, 116, 279, 283, 290, 293, 422, 456, 457

White House, 337, 367

White Papers, 166, 199, 226

Whittle, Sue, 59

Widdecombe, Ann, 220, 330-331

Wiles, Dr John, 330, 332

Wilkins, Maurice, 387

Williams, Inspector David, 279

Williams, Lord, 301 (Attorney General)

Williamson, Kevin, 400

Williamson, Laurie, 75

Willis, Gareth, 301
Willis, Phil, 360, 361, 372, 374
Wilmot, Chief Constable David, 441
Wilmslow Financial Services, 281
Wilson, Graham, 416
Wilson, Harold, 28, 30, 31, 58, 136, 382
Wilson, Maria, 455
Wilson, Mary, 382
Wilson, Tyson, 225
Windfall tax, 177
Windle, S, 13
Wind power, 236, 364
Wingates Temperance Band, 33
Winter Fuel Allowance, 198
Winter of Discontent, 58
Winterton, Ann, 216, 329
Winterton, Nicholas, 285
Winterton, Rosie, 172
Withins School, 18, 450
Withnell Brick Works, 384
Woburn Avenue, 1-4, 7, 15, 17, 44, 131
Wolfe, Tom, 57
Wolfenden Street Primary School, 53, 384, 386
Women's Land Army, 314-316
Woods Hole Oceanographic Institute, 376
Wood Street Socialist Club, 37, 38, 104
Woodward, Shaun, 162
Woolas, Phil, 246
World Bank, 235
World Trade Centre (Twin Towers), 196, 366
World Trade Organisation (WTO), 235
Worsley constituency, 68, 131, 176
Wrigley, Caroline and Mark, 107
Written Statements, 200
Wroe, Brian, 442, 443
Wynne, Anthony, 301

Yassin, Sheikh Ahmad, 334
Yates, John, 227-228
Young, David, 20, 28-31, 40, 58, 68-69, 94, 101-106 (deselection), 106 (marriage to Vera Dingwall), 110-112 (obituaries), 119, 139

Young, Sir George, 99
Young, Grace (nee McCowat), 29, 69, 102, 110
Young (previously Dingwall), Vera, 106, 110
Youth Concert Band, 35, 36
Youth Training Scheme, 82
Yugoslavia, 173, 349

Zimbabwe, 235
Zionism, 334, 336, 434

NOTES

1. In 2014 Dr Stephen Michael Wedgwood Benn became the 3rd Viscount Stansgate when his father Tony Wedgwood Benn died.

2. My mother died on 22 July 1959 (see Volume 1).

3. Following divorce (Decree Nisi granted 17 May 1988) Merrilyn was married again, to John Guest.